THE CAMBRIDGE GUIDE TO THE ARTS IN BRITAIN

VOLUME 1   PREHISTORIC, ROMAN AND
EARLY MEDIEVAL

The Cambridge Guide to the Arts in Britain

The Cambridge Guide to the Arts in Britain

edited by
BORIS FORD

VOLUME 1

PREHISTORIC, ROMAN AND EARLY MEDIEVAL

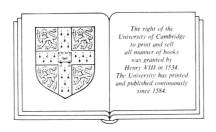

The right of the
University of Cambridge
to print and sell
all manner of books
was granted by
Henry VIII in 1534.
The University has printed
and published continuously
since 1584.

CAMBRIDGE UNIVERSITY PRESS

CAMBRIDGE
NEW YORK   NEW ROCHELLE   MELBOURNE   SYDNEY

Published by the Press Syndicate of the University of Cambridge
The Pitt Building, Trumpington Street, Cambridge CB2 1RP
32 East 57th Street, New York, NY 10022, USA
10 Stamford Road, Oakleigh, Melbourne 3166, Australia

First published 1988

Printed in Great Britain at the University Press, Cambridge

British Library cataloguing in publication data

The Cambridge guide to the arts in Britain.
  Vol. 1 : Prehistoric, Roman and Early
  Medieval
  1. Arts – Great Britain
  I. Ford, Boris
700′.941   NX543

Library of Congress cataloguing in publication data

The Cambridge guide to the arts in Britain.
  Includes bibliographies and indexes.
  Contents: v.   1. Prehistoric, Roman, and Early
  Medieval – v.   2. The Middle Ages, 1100–1500.
  1. Arts, British.   2. Arts–Great Britain.   I. Ford, Boris.

NX543.C36   700′942   87–11671

ISBN 0 521 30971 9

Contents

Notes on Contributors

Michael Alexander is Berry Professor of English Literature at the University of St Andrews. He is the author of the verse translations of *Beowulf* and *The Earliest English Poems* in Penguin Classics; and he is himself a poet.

Richard N. Bailey is Professor of Anglo-Saxon Civilisation at the University of Newcastle upon Tyne. He has written widely on Anglo-Saxon art and on ecclesiastical archaeology. His main interests are in pre-Norman sculpture.

Martin Biddle is Director of the Winchester Research Unit. His principal work has been in the archaeology and history of the early medieval town and of the church, and in the art and architecture of Early Renaissance palaces. His publications include *Winchester in the Early Middle Ages* and *The Future of London's Past*.

R. Allen Brown is Professor of History at the University of London, King's College, and Director of the annual, international Battle Conference in Anglo-Norman Studies. His publications include *English Castles*, *The Tower of London*, *The Normans*, and *The Normans and the Norman Conquest*.

Mildred Budny is a Senior Research Associate at the Parker Library, Corpus Christi College, Cambridge, specialising in Anglo-Saxon manuscripts, embroideries, and other arts. Her publications include *The Anglo-Saxon Embroideries at Maaseik* and *St Dunstan: Poet, Artist, Craftsman, and Patron*.

Barry Cunliffe is Professor of European Archaeology at the University of Oxford. He has been involved in several field work projects in Britain and Spain. His publications include *Rome and Her Empire*, *The Celtic World*, *Roman Bath Discovered*, and *Fishbourne: Roman Palace and its Gardens*.

Sheppard Frere is Emeritus Professor of the Archaeology of the Roman Empire at the University of Oxford. He is the author of *Brittania, a History of Roman Britain*, *Verulamium Excavations* (in three volumes), and joint author of *Roman Britain from the Air*. He edited the periodical *Britannia* 1970–9.

Richard Gem has worked for the Inspectorate of Ancient Monuments and now works for the Cathedrals Advisory Commission for England. He is President of the British Archaeological Association. He is currently writing books on *The Architecture of Anglo-Saxon England* and *Architecture in Europe 500 to 1000*.

Jacquetta Hawkes OBE (Mrs J.B. Priestley) is an author and archaeologist. She was one-time UK secretary for UNESCO and archaeological correspondent for the *The Observer* and *The Sunday Times*. Her books include *Prehistoric Britain* (with C.F.C. Hawkes), *Unesco Cultural History of Mankind* Vol. I Part I: *First Great Civilisations*, and *Shell Guide to British Archaeology*.

Isabel Henderson is a Fellow and Tutor of Newnham College, Cambridge, and a Director of Studies in the History of Art for a number of Cambridge colleges. She is the author of *The Picts*.

Janet Huskinson is a Fellow and Tutor of Newnham College, Cambridge. Her chief area of interest is the art of the later Roman Empire. She is working on a volume on Romano-British sculpture in Eastern England for the *Corpus Signorum Imperii Romani*.

Cherry Lavell has edited *British Archaeological Abstracts* since 1966 and co-edited, with Eric Wood, the Collins Archaeology series.

Roger Ling is Reader in Classical Art and Archaeology in the University of Manchester. He has been Field Director of the British Research Project at Pompeii since 1978. His publications include *The Greek World*, *The Hellenistic World to the Coming of the Romans*, and a revised and annotated edition of Donald Strong's *Roman Art*.

Christopher Page is Senior Research Fellow in Music at Sidney Sussex College, Cambridge. He directs the ensemble 'Gothic Voices', making recordings and giving concerts in Britain and abroad. He is the author of *Voices and Instruments of the Middle Ages*.

Peter Salway is Honorary Professor at the Open University, where he was formerly Regional Director and Professor of Archaeology and History. He is author of Volume 1a, *Roman Britain* in the *Oxford History of England*, and *Frontier People of Roman Britain*.

General Introduction

BORIS FORD

If English literature is, by common consent, pre-eminent in the world, the same would not often be claimed for Britain's arts as a whole. Indeed, the British people sometimes strike foreigners, and even themselves, as rather more philistine than artistic. And yet, viewed historically, Britain's achievements in the visual and applied arts and in architecture and music, as well as in drama and literature, must be at least the equal, as a whole, of any other country.

The Cambridge Guide to the Arts in Britain is not devoted, volume by volume, to the separate arts, but to all the arts in each successive age. Histories of the independent arts are legion. But being of their natue self-centred, they provide a very poor impression of the cultural richness and vitality of an age. Moreover, these separate histories obscure the ebb and flow of artistic creation from one age to the next.

When the arts in Britain are viewed collectively, it can be seen how often they reinforce each other, treating similar themes and speaking in a similar tone of voice. Also it is striking how one age may find its major cultural expression in music and drama, and the next in architecture or the applied arts: while in a later age there may be an almost total absence of important composers compared with a proliferation of major novelists. Or an age may provide scope for a great range of anonymous craftsmen. These contrasts in the degree to which the individual arts have flourished are not fortuitous, but are bound up with the social aspirations and characteristics of the age, with its beliefs and preoccupations and manners, which may favour expression in one art rather than another.

The Cambridge Guide is planned to reveal these changes and the resulting character of the arts and the balance between them. Thus these volumes do not consist of a sequence of mini-surveys of the separate arts. Rather, they are designed to help readers find their bearings in relation to the culture of an age: identifying major landmarks and lines of strength, analysing changes of taste and fashion and critical assumptions. And these are necessarily related to the demands of patrons and the tastes of the various overlapping publics.

These volumes are addressed to readers of all kinds: to general readers as well as to specialists. But virtually every reader is bound to be a non-specialist in relation to many of the arts under discussion, and so the chapters on the individual arts do not presuppose specialist knowledge nor do their authors use specialist language. On the other hand, these volumes are not elementary nor naive; they assume a measure of familiarity with the arts in Britain, and above all a wish to understand and appreciate the artistic achievements of successive ages in Britain.

Volume 1 is not typical of the series as a whole. In the first place it covers an enormous span, from prehistoric times to the aftermath of the Conquest. Therefore it has been divided into three parts: a comprehensive Prehistoric part; and Roman and Anglo-Saxon parts, each with their cultural and social surveys and their individual studies in the arts. Moreover, very few artists are known by name, and the role of the artist-craftsman was unlike that of the individual artist in later ages.

Each of the nine volumes in this series contains five kinds of material:

The Cultural and Social Setting

This major introductory survey provides a map of the cultural landscape, and an examination of the historical and social developments which affected the arts (both the 'high' and popular arts):
(a) The shape and pattern of society; its organisation, beliefs, ideals, scepticisms.
(b) How the concerns of society were embodied or reflected in the individual arts, and in the practical arts and crafts; the notion and 'function' of art at that time.
(c) The character and preoccupations of the separate arts, and of patrons and audiences. Why particular arts tended to flourish and others to decline in this age.
(d) The organisation and economic situation of the arts.

Studies in the Individual Arts

These studies of individual artists and themes do not aim to provide an all-inclusive survey of each art, but a guide to distinctive achievements and developments. Thus the amount of space devoted to the individual arts differs considerably from volume to volume, though it is interesting that literature is very strong in almost every volume.

In this section, one chapter will focus on a single town and one on a particular house or group of houses, as microcosms of the period.

Appendix

Bibliographies for further reading and reference.

Illustrations

The volumes are generously illustrated, though it has been decided not to include pictures of individual artists.

Index

This is the key to making good use of each volume. Many chapters naturally refer to the same historical developments and works of art. These have not been cross-referenced in the texts, because material common to various chapters has been fully noted in the Index. So the Index is the place from which to explore and take full advantage of the inter-disciplinary character of the volume: which is its distinctive strength.

Where the contributors to these volumes have been obliged to use specialist terms, they have for the most part explained these in the text. The following are among the most useful dictionaries for readers: *The Oxford Illustrated Dictionary*, *The Penguin Dictionary of Architecture*, *The Penguin Dictionary of Art & Artists*, and *The Penguin Dictionary of Music*.

In conclusion, I am greatly indebted to Professor Donald Mitchell and Dr Joseph Rykwert for their generous and detailed advice during the preliminary stages of this project; and to the staff of the Cambridge University Press for their sympathetic collaboration and unfailing patience, especially Sarah Stanton and Ann Stonehouse.

PREHISTORIC BRITAIN

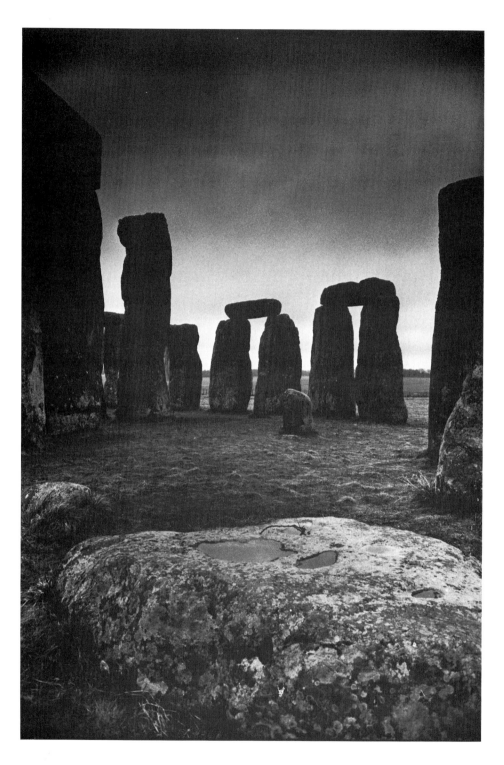

The megalithic sanctuary of Stonehenge on Salisbury Plain, Wiltshire. From a simple 'henge' of the late third millennium it had been brought to its magnificence by c.1600 BC.

Stone Age to Iron Age

JACQUETTA HAWKES

Introduction

How to begin at the beginning? It has been very positively stated that 'the oldest art is the work of men directly ancestral to modern humanity and has nothing to do with "fossil" species . . .'. In short that art began with *Homo sapiens* at the end of the Old Stone Age. Yet is this altogether true? The nine volumes which comprise this series are filled with the fruits of man's image-making capacity as it was exercised in that minute part of the earth's crust that has come to be known as Britain. It is true that it was only beneath the nobly arched cranium of our own later species that this capacity was developed to the height of producing what we now distinguish as the imaginative and decorative arts. Yet here at the beginning it must be right to give a thought to those aeons when such powers of the human psyche were slowly evolving in lower and sometimes thicker skulls.

If we do, then we are confronted hundreds of thousands of years earlier with that element of art that can be called pure form. It is manifest most clearly in an implement that has come to be known as the handaxe which was being shaped, probably by quite a variety of human types, over an astonishingly wide range of the Old World – in Africa, India, south-west Asia and Europe. Its makers, who must have carried its shape in their minds not as an instinct but a powerful tradition, needed simply a point, probably for digging roots, and an edge, say for hacking meat, yet as time went by they brought them together in a form that strikes us today as 'right' in harmony and balance. Not only did their shapers imbue their handaxes with rightness of form, but seem in their finest products to have finished them with a perfection of fine flaking quite beyond what was demanded for purely practical use. It looks, in fact, as though they were already giving their handiwork some psychic value, some emotional significance on the road to the superb ceremonial objects of long distant future generations.

This emergence of an aesthetic sense in the early hunters of the Old Stone Age, mysterious since it cannot be derived from the necessities of their way of life, and which we recognise and indeed find in ourselves, makes a

perfectly appropriate beginning for a history of British art since, as it
happens, southern and eastern England lay within the territory of the
handaxe makers and has yielded some of their finest artefacts. Their very first
specimens to be recognised, among them an elegant, finely pointed example,
were found in a brick-pit at Hoxne in Norfolk in 1797. The finder, John
Frere, showed extraordinary perspicacity for that time in suggesting that his
implements came from 'a very remote period indeed, even beyond that of the
present world' – by which he probably meant that they were 'antediluvian'.

Many other handaxes, as shapely a group as any in their vast range, lay in
the Thames river gravels at Swanscombe in Kent. Among them were found
some fossil remains of one of the men who had made them some quarter of a
million years ago – fragments of the thick skull that had housed the mental
templet of this earliest manifestation of pure form.

Swanscombe Man still had some primitive features which disqualify him as
a full member of our modern species. He hunted the Thames valley during a
warm phase of the Ice Age when game was plentiful and Britain still a part
of a western peninsula of Europe. Two more glaciations were to follow
before, late in the Old Stone Age, men of our own species made their way
into western Europe and there, astonishingly, some 26,000 years ago, began
to produce the carvings, modellings, paintings and engravings that can be
universally accepted as the first flowering of a fully imaginative art. The fact
that all these techniques were employed by hunting groups in France and
Spain is remarkable, but their use for the portrayal of their game animals in a
style of heightened realism is truly marvellous.

In addition to this animal art based on intense observation, highly
conventionalised sculptures and models of human beings were made from an
early phase and over a much wider area. Most of them were female figurines
often showing an opulent exaggeration of breast, thighs and belly. These
figures, so expressive of fecundity and maternity, could only be projections
from the inner world of the psyche to serve as magico-religious icons; so
whether there was an unbroken tradition linking them with the immensely
popular and widespread 'Mother Goddess' figurines of the early cultivators is
hardly significant. It was to prove an archetypal image liable to emerge in
art forms for the rest of our human history.

When the late Old Stone Age hunters of western Europe had brought their
animal art to its peak in late glacial times, they could still reach Britain over
land, and what was to be south-west England was only a few hundred miles
from the Dordogne centres of their cave art. They did in fact make their way
into Britain in small numbers, yet produced virtually no art either on cave
walls or to ornament their possessions. All that we have are two crude
engravings on bone, one of an apparently masked man and one of a horse's
head, found in the Pinhole Cave or Creswell Crags, Derbyshire, probably
some 12,000 years old. These deserve mention here not so much because,
however poor, they are the oldest examples of representational art in the
country, but rather because their very rarity and poverty illustrates a
phenomenon of lasting importance for any history of British art. This is the
powerful influence of its physical setting. Through all the volumes until men
took to the high seas we shall be dealing with the visual arts as they waxed

and occasionally waned in the exceptional conditions of offshore islands, and islands, moreover, with climatic conditions that could enhance that isolation. The influence on their inhabitants might be called the Thule Effect (as in any place, like Ultima Thule, very remote from civilisation, on the edge of the known world).

This can have several coherent yet distinct manifestations. First, as already suggested, there is the difficulty of access, the remoteness from continental growing points, that attenuated and modified migrations and the spread of cultural influences through trade and social contact. Thus the few Old Stone Age hunters who penetrated England and Wales may not have included anyone with the skills and knowledge required for painting and sculpture; and indeed would not have been able to support the specialised artists who, if one may judge from the Bushmen of Africa, were probably responsible for the masterpieces of France and Spain.

The second manifestation of the Thule Effect, conspicuous in post-glacial times when Britain became an island, was the 'sea change' that appears to have overtaken all immigrant settlers or cultural influences on arrival. Archaeologists have often commented on the fact that virtually all British artefacts can immediately be distinguished from their original continental counterparts. How this came to pass can only be imagined – a break in social structure, strange materials, the influence of native women; but that, given time, islanders would develop local pecularities is obvious enough – good examples being found in the shape and ornament of the later British Beakers (see p. 14), in stone circles and the architectural oddities of some of the megalithic (or huge stone) architecture of the remoter Scottish Highlands and islands.

This leads directly on to a third Thule Effect: the development of one cultural trait to fantastic lengths, often in the direction of gigantism. The extreme example is provided by the little population of Easter Islanders who laboured appallingly to hew out their colossal stone statues to haul and raise them to stand, fantastically hatted, gazing out to sea from ceremonial platforms. Another was the obsessive and long nurtured cult of fertility in Malta with its unique temple architecture and splendid sculptures of its female divinity.

Britain, though so much larger and more culturally diverse, was not without this insular inflation. We shall see how the island farmers and herders of the New Stone Age and earlier Bronze Ages, accustomed to handling enormous stones (megaliths) for the greater glory of their tombs, went on to develop the idea of ceremonial standing stone circles in Britain with their architectural climax in the unparallelled magnitude of Avebury and Stonehenge, Wiltshire. Silbury Hill, too, little though we know of its purpose, is recognised as the largest artificial mound in Europe. While after many centuries of quiescence the Thule Effect can surely be seen again when the tradition of the Celtic Britons' tribal hillforts culminated in the unrivalled mountainous earthworks of Maiden Castle, Dorset. Perhaps we can even look as far ahead as *Volume 2* and see it still at work when the European tradition of Gothic architecture led on to the extraordinary architectural feats of the English Perpendicular.

Farmers and artists of the New Stone Age (4000–1400 BC)

Britain remained very much a poorish fringe culture during immediately
post-glacial times when melting ice brought very watery conditions and the
last food gathering groups, though game was hunted, depended largely on
fishing and fowling or living off the seashore. They evidently remained
unable to produce either the simple little animal carvings or the equally
simple decorative designs of Scandinavian peoples whose material culture
they shared, nor, so far as we know, did they develop any figurative art to set
beside the lively rock paintings of eastern Spain. Theirs seems to have been a
life with little beyond bare subsistence.

Then early in the fourth millennium BC, when the post-glacial climate was
at its best – relatively warm and dry – and deciduous forests had spread in
the wake of pine, farming settlers began to cross into Britain with their
livestock, seed and skills, their traditions derived from western Europe in
general and France most nearly. To the history of British art their main
contribution lay in ceramics and in their stone-built tombs which certainly
qualify as architecture within the dictionary definition of 'the art or science of
constructing edifices for human use' (OED).

The invention of pottery had given early farming peoples mastery of a
plastic substance, with its offer of all manner of original opportunites to
satisfy the universal human urge to decorate even the most practical of
possessions. It cannot be said that the British potters (and they must often
have been women) were greatly gifted in their use of the medium, being far
outshone by some of their Scandinavian contemporaries. Working within a
general west European tradition of plain or lightly decorated wares, from the
first they produced good shapes in a great variety of regional styles. Rounded
bottoms were almost universal and if at first the potters favoured rather
heavy, baggy shapes, probably derived from leather prototypes, the
proportions were always satisfying; and from the first, that is to say from
about 3700 BC, in some regions they were building up subtler shapes. The
best were shallow bowls with gracefully out-turned lips above a shoulder
(carination), this upper zone often decorated with simple incised or impressed
designs, the whole producing a simple elegance of form. Moreover, the
ceramic artists devoted knowledge and effort to the technical aspect of their
craft, mixing the clay with carefully chosen grits (crushed flint, shell,
limestone and other rocks) to produce a paste that fires well, allowing thin
walls and fine burnishing of the surface. At this point it is perhaps worth
reflecting on the fact that hand-made pottery, both good and bad, was to
prevail in Britain throughout prehistoric times, the true wheel coming into
use only a little before the Roman conquest.

Before turning to the art and architecture of the megalith builders that has
left us our greatest inheritance from the New Stone Age, we should spare a
thought for a humbler one: the stone implements and weapons showing the
same mastery of 'pure form' that had first emerged from the depths of time
in the handaxes. The principal implement concerned is the polished stone axe
(or its variants the hoe and adze) of the utmost social importance both for
land clearance and the actual cultivation of the soil. Axes can be divided

between those made of the igneous rocks left by the volcanic upheavals in the west of Britain, and those of flint, often the good quality flint laboriously mined from the chalk. These tools were well proportioned and finely finished by grinding and polishing – it is overwhelming to contemplate the hours of labour that must have been spent at the grindstone. No wonder that the best, such as those from Cornwall, Wales and Cumbria, were widely traded, probably by the professional axemakers themselves.

As with the handaxes, through their supreme importance for the farmer's way of life, they acquired a sacred value expressed in ceremonial forms, the equivalent of our mayoral and parliamentary maces. A fine example is the long, slender specimen from Lincolnshire, the holy value of which must have been enhanced by the fossil belemnite showing on both faces. While British artist-craftsmen made such non-functional forms from local stones even finer axes, evidently never intended to be applied to a tree trunk, were imported in small numbers, probably by way of Brittany. These were of a lovely 'jadeite', thought to originate from the Alpine regions. With all this it is not surprising to find axes as sacred objects carved among the symbols of certain megalithic tomb-builders, notably in Brittany. Surely the god Thor can be heard thundering in the distance?

During the length of my own archaeological lifetime – half a century – disputes about the origins, history, religious and social meaning of megalithic tombs have been waged, often in circular motion. For a history of art many of the disagreements are of little importance: the monuments in all their variety and with their occasional rich ornamentation survive for us to see and to stir our wonder. That is what matters most, but there are now a number of facts about their background that are generally accepted.

Most megalithic tombs are to be found near our western coasts from Cornwall on both sides of the Bristol Channel and Irish Sea and along the Scottish seaboards from Galloway to Caithness. Many are on the remotest islands of the Outer Hebrides, the Orkneys and Shetlands. There can be no doubt, then, that the original groups of settlers spread by sea, hugging the Atlantic coast and occupying fertile land wherever it could be won. Towards the end of the fourth millennium their communities were settled and prosperous enough to build megalithic tombs demanding the name of architecture. Inevitably regional groups evolved, such as, for a good example, the chambered long barrows built on both shores of the Bristol Channel, the best on the Cotswolds and in South Wales. These regional differences, however, are outweighed by a shared tradition, sometimes still boldly referred to as a megalithic religion. All were communal tombs where men, women and children, presumably though not certainly members of leading tribal families, were buried, sometimes over long periods, in one instance known to have extended to a thousand years. Although primarily burial places, their plans and building sequences dictated by funerary rites, they also became sacred centres for their peoples. Little though we can learn of the rituals involved, these certainly included the sinking of pits perhaps for libations, fires and funeral feasts, often held in courtyards built at the chamber entrance, usually an important architectural feature. Bowls of food and drink might be provided for the dead, but there appears to have been no inclination to bury individuals with the best of their worldly possessions – this in striking contrast with the more autocratic and martial rulers of the following age.

New Grange and the Boyne passage graves

Among the varieties of funerary architecture formed from huge stones or megaliths one seems pre-eminent and more lastingly coherent and standardised than the others. This is the passage grave in which a relatively narrow entranceway leads into a chamber, with or without side cells, the whole covered by a circular mound (or cairn), often contained within a kerb and wall, rarely with an outer ring of standing stones. Although many such graves are small and unornamented, they include the grandest of all megalithic structures and have a monopoly of 'megalithic art'. This sculptural association gives strong support to the cultural coherence of the passage graves. It is found along the Atlantic routes in Brittany, in Ireland, in the small Anglesey group (Barclodiad-y-Gawres and Bryn Celli Ddu) and more feebly in the neighbourhood of what is architecturally the finest of all passage graves: Maeshowe in the Orkney islands.

In all these areas of passage grave settlement, sculptors worked to enhance the magico-religious power of their houses of the dead, but their attainment as artists was most uneven. There were bold and skilled carvers at work in Brittany, most notably at Gavrinis in the Gulf of Morbihan, but of all passage grave art the finest and most varied works are to be found in the great cemetery along the lower reaches of the Irish river Boyne, where many small graves are dominated by the carved mausolea of Dowth, Knowth and of New Grange. The three monuments share virtually all their art motifs in common, but each shows a distinctive preference among the symbols, perhaps determined by the artist or his employers, or possibly by differences of date. Radio carbon analysis at New Grange has, with an unusual consistency, dated it to about 2500 BC (3200 BC by the emended system).

In the past it has been claimed that the New Grange sculptures were primarily decorative – added as ornamental embellishments of the architecture. However, the recent excavation, with its record of all engravings however poor, confounds this always dubious judgement. It has revealed that by far the greatest number of the motifs, virtually all of which recur again and again, are roughly pecked on the stones in a crude and disordered manner, many of them hidden from sight, and so clearly without aesthetic intent. This realisation, together with the fact that although the Boyne motifs themselves are geometric and non-representational, they can be derived from features found on idols and other cult objects, or from formalised but still partially representational designs, is proof enough that they were symbolic in origin and still magico-religious in purpose. Yet it can be gratefully recognised that from rough and haphazard symbols New Grange art rises to the fine and essentially decorative enrichment achieved by more gifted and experienced sculptors and so to the truly monumental quality of the famous entry stone and its counterpart on the opposite side of the great cairn.

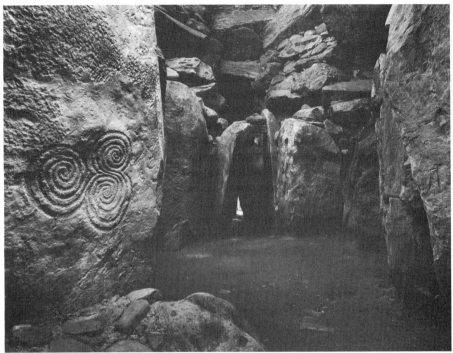

New Grange, the finest of the group of New Stone Age passage grave art, including a great range of spirals (2500 BC). (The dating of the prehistoric works of art is based on uncalibrated radio carbon figures.)

It is worth trying to picture the scenes of activity as New Grange was being built, more particularly the sculptor's part in it. There seems no doubt that those who built and those who carved worked together, probably under the guidance of priestly individuals well versed in ritual. Superior authority may have rested with heads of the family whose mausoleum it was to be and who were responsible for the provision of workers and materials.

At its height the activity would have approached that of building a church during the early Middle Ages. There would have been gangs dragging the hundreds of greywacke megaliths up the north side of the low hill from where they had lain, exposed and weathered. Others, the unskilled, were bringing water-worn stones from the river terrace to the south, perhaps using leather bags to shift the 200,000 tonnes needed for the cairn, while turves were cut to layer and secure the stones. Meanwhile other parties might be returning loaded with glittering white quartz blocks from the Wicklow mountain needed for the outer retaining wall of the cairn. (This showy wall, resting on the huge kerbstones, many of which were carved, must have served aesthetic as well as more mystical ends.)

There must also have been timber workers on site making planks, rollers, scaffolding, all needed for handling the megalithic blocks and particularly for the raising the vault of the massive corbelled roof to its height of six metres above the chamber floor.

Throughout the periods of high activity one can be sure that there would have been that distinctive sound of masons and sculptors at work, the steady taptapping as they drove their flint or quartzite gravers through the stone, cutting the sacred symbols or dressing surface irregularities from the megaliths of chamber and passage.

The most interesting problems for this history concern the relationship between the relatively unskilled carvers of rough symbols and the master carvers, and between the latter and the social and religious leaders of an enterprise that produced the earliest great decorative and monumental art in the British Isles.

The excavators became convinced that the actual cutting of sacred motifs and their presence, visible or invisible, within the mausoleum were of prime importance – rather as the celebration of Masses is of supreme importance in Roman Catholic communities. Nevertheless they recognised that the best carvings were designed for significant positions within the total architectural design. They believed the artists to have formed their own 'gang' and recorded:

> *Some of their work was done while the slabs were still lying about the site; they selected the most suitable surface and applied the various motifs. When the time came for the slabs to be utilized it sometimes happened that in the building the decorated surface was covered over by other stones, or if it was a kerbstone, had to be turned back-to-front as this was the way it fitted best. This fate did not befall the work of the master carvers. They applied the ornament when the stones were* in situ *and when and where it would show to best advantage . . . The apprentices were at work also, as witness a good deal of inferior ornament . . .*

(Michael J. O'Kelly, *New Grange*, 1982)

This privileged collaboration of the master carvers and the 'management' is most clearly shown in the entrance stone which proved to have been carved when it had already been set firmly in its position as the kerbstone in front of

The entrance stone to the New Grange passage grave, carved where it stands in the kerb before the entry passage. A sculptor's masterwork (2500 BC).

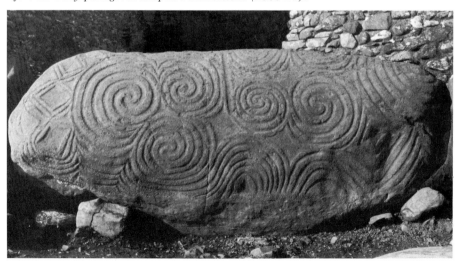

the passage opening – and even before the adjacent kerbstones had been put in place. The nearest rival to the entrance stone as a masterwork, set exactly opposite on the other side of the mound, had also received its ornament when already in its final position. These two kerbstones alone would be enough to prove the reality of close collaboration, but there are a number of other instances: corbel stones in the chamber roof had been carved before being built in but must have been already designed for their positions since the decorations were largely along the exposed edges; in some ways the most interesting example of all is the formal pattern cut along the narrow edge of the roof box capstone to be described below.

What in fact were the sacred symbols employed by the less skilled and master carvers alike, though it was only true artists who combined them into powerfully effective compositions? All, with the partial exception of the end cell capstone, were purely geometric. They have been assigned to ten groups of which half are curvilinear (spirals, concentric circles, arcs and meanders dominating) and half rectilinear – with zigzags, lozenges and radiating, sun or star-like patterns outstanding.

Nearly all these motifs, from the finest to the poorest, were pecked into the surface, though the separate peck marks might be rubbed smooth. Lozenges might be wholly pecked out or half pecked to give a chequered effect. Simple incisions occur and here and there can be seen to have been used as guidelines for pecking; this method may have been widely followed. The work of the master carvers was distinguished not only by their ability to form bold compositions but also by a most remarkable development of their technique, used mainly for spirals and zigzags. This was so to pick away the background to the motifs that they were reserved in strong relief, the design appearing in a positive instead of the usual negative form with far more striking effect. This most difficult technique, at New Grange seen at its best on the entrance stone, was practised also at nearby Dowth, but is hardly known outside the Boyne valley. It is another proof of the master carvers as individual artists, innovators striving to heighten the aesthetic effectiveness of their work rather than mere scribes of religious symbolism.

The question of individual merit between the master carvers is posed by the two finest kerbstones. Both have been executed in the relief technique, but while the spirals of the entrance stone are clean in line and emanate a vital sense of movement, those on its opposite number are fumblingly weak in line and almost static in effect. Were both the work of the same man who had developed his skill, as the similarity of technique led the excavators to believe, or were two artists of unequal gifts responsible? To me such a speedy heightening of powers would seem improbable, and the products of two artists of unequal gifts therefore to be preferred.

Religious ideas: fertility cults and their symbolism

If there is no doubt that here by the Boyne, and among some passage grave builders elsewhere we are witnessing artists working with the spiritual leaders of the community in buildings of magico-religious use, should anything be said about the beliefs and practices that were being served? If the meaning of the geometricised motifs were not enough one most extraordinary, and indeed unique, discovery at New Grange justifies it, hazardous though such speculation must be. The excavators found that just behind the passage entrance and set within the quartz retaining wall was a carefully constructed stone box resting on the first two roof slabs and with the front edge of its own roof slab carved with an eye-catching, formalised pattern of lozenges. It was assumed that this box was intended to take offerings for the dead, but local tradition that told of sunbeams entering the chamber led to a watch being kept over the period of the mid-winter solstice. It proved that for a few days on either side of the solstice the first rays of the rising sun did indeed strike through a deliberately constructed slit at the back of the box to penetrate the chamber and its terminal cell. The whole orientation and heights of the tomb must have been predetermined to secure this magical effect.

The idea of a ray penetrating the dark womb of the chamber evokes the idea of the fertility cult with its presiding female deity, well known to have prevailed among the pioneer farming communities of this New Stone Age. Spirals possibly derived from the 'eye goddess' aspects of this cult were widely associated with it, most strikingly in Malta and in a civilised context in Minoan Crete; so too were zigzags and arcs, conceivably the product of the hair and necklaces shown on many female idols. It can, then, reasonably be claimed that our first British sculptors were conspicuously working within one tradition (or perhaps sect?) of this ancient, widespread and psychologically deeply rooted fertility religion. The three stone basins in the side chambers and little marble-like balls may well have had some minor part in the cult.

It is surprising that the practice of carving more or less realistic idols of the goddess so prevalent in Mediterranean lands and the Iberian peninsula spread only feebly and erratically north of the Pyrenees. In Britain, though fragments have been found at other sites of the New Stone Age, only one figurine has come to light and that not in a megalithic context but at the bottom of a shaft in the Grimes Graves (Norfolk) flint mines. It is of no great artistic merit, roughly carved from a rounded lump of chalk to suggest, not unsuccessfully, the huge thighs and breasts of the 'mother goddess'. She was found presiding over a unique and dramatic specimen of a fertility shrine: a pile of deer antlers, chalk balls (reminiscent of the New Grange 'marbles') and a most deftly carved chalk phallus.

This little figurine probably dates from about the time when the Irish artists were working on the Boyne tombs. However, three other idols from England – quite different in type but undoubtedly belonging to a survival of the same tradition – have been dated to the Bronze Age round about 1700 BC. These are the so-called Folkton Drums, found in the secondary burial of a child at a round barrow at Folkton, Yorkshire. They deserve mention here for the excellence of their design and execution and because, since some of the patterns on them suggest wood-carving techniques, they serve to remind us that in tree-clad Britain there may well have been schools of wood-carvers whose handiwork is lost to us.

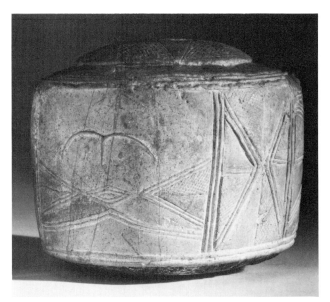

One of the three Folkton Drums delicately carved on squat cylinders of chalk. From a child's grave on Folkton Wold, Yorkshire (c.1700 BC). The 'owl faces' and eye symbols suggest that these drums are idols from a cult of the Mother Goddess (diameters 10–12 cm).

The Folkton Drums are squat cylinders, a few inches tall and in diameter, beautifully hewn from solid chalk and with raised discs on their tops. These idols appear to relate to the 'eye goddess' variety of the cult for each bears on the side opposite the geometric patterns a face of a well-known variety with eyes, raised brows and nose, while on the discs are well cut *oculos* or eye motifs, some rayed some in paired concentric circles.

Finally the eye motif introduces another most curious example of the carvers art, the little decorative balls that turn up as stray finds in north-east Scotland. They are of hardstones, so that their neat and regular yet oddly powerful ornamentation in a variety of nobs and lobes required far more labour and skill than working in chalk. At least one of them bears on each lobe an unmistakable rendering of the *oculos* motif. They appear to date from late in the New Stone Age. Whatever their use, it was certainly not practical.

Thin, scattered and uneven though the surviving physical evidences are, they are enough to convince us that through the centuries from the late fourth millennium BC, when the farming communities were increasing in numbers and social power and gradually clearing the lighter forests for cultivation and pasture, the creations of artists and architects (who are unlikely to have been distinguished by any such terms) were working almost entirely for religious and magical ends. Among them the builders of megalithic communal tombs, and the passage grave builders in particular, are of outstanding significance. Although the tombs may have been raised for leading chiefly families, the fact that men, women and children were interred in them over long periods and without any special honouring of individuals suggests that the land was farmed by simple tribal societies, free from any martial aristocracy of all-powerful overlords.

Warrior aristocrats and craftsmen

Round about 2000 BC this tentative picture of relatively easy and (dare one say it?) peaceful farming communities was to be quite rapidly changed by the arrival, mainly from the Low Countries, of groups of people still often known by the quaint, antiquarian name of Beaker Folk. Their influence spread rapidly throughout the British Isles, presumably by various forms of conquest, drastically changing the social and cultural scene.

Most strikingly, the influence of the Beaker Folk ended the building of communal tombs, introducing in its place the individual burial of both men and women in graves below round barrows. In these single graves the dead were furnished with their personal possessions, including occasionally the gold trinkets, such as the elegant basket earrings from a youth's grave at Radley, Berkshire, but more conspicuously with their weapons. Some groups had shafthole stone axes demanding laborious skill and sound design, while many had little bronze daggers and the tanged flint arrowheads and the wrist guards that prove them to have been above all archers equipped with powerful bows. Here, quite plainly, were the chiefs of a warrior elite with some beginnings of a fondness for treasured possessions and display. Even their pottery vessels tell of this way of life, for it can be assumed that their beakers were used for quaffing beer, and some of the best of the types developed by British potters (including handled mugs remarkably like those to be seen in pubs today) were quite strikingly ornamented and of fine hard wares.

This transformation to a more martial, possibly male-dominated and nomadic, society by the Beaker invaders reached its climax in a region centred on the rich pasturelands of Wessex in central southern England. It appears to have been brought about through the fertilisation of local culture

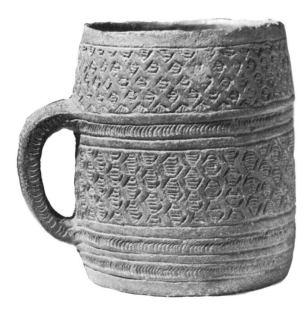

Mugs such as this one from Fordham, Cambridgeshire, are relatively rare in Beaker pottery (c.1700 BC).

already prospering from trade in gold and bronze and wealth in cattle, by influences from Brittany – very probably by the arrival after about 1700 BC of powerful chieftains. This ruling aristocracy brought Wessex for a time well to the fore of western Europe in its patronage of fine craftsmen, particularly of goldsmiths and workers in bronze and amber. The chieftains' graves, and more rarely those of their wives, far outdid those of the Beaker Folk in their display of personal aggrandisement and authority. Thus the greatest interest in the history of art focuses particularly on exquisite craftsmanship and design. If New Grange is the finest examplar of the communal arts of its time, the Bush Barrow at Normanton close to Stonehenge is the best examplar of the attainments of the Early Bronze Age craftsmen and the pride of their princely masters.

The great man, whose grave it was, tall and strongly built, had been laid on his back fully dressed and wearing his arms and ornaments. The skill and taste of his goldsmith was manifest in a large, lozenge-shaped pectoral of sheet gold, finely chased, and a comparable belthook, and in the wooden pommel of a flat copper dagger inlaid with a pattern in thousands of tiny (1 mm) gold pins – a feat of craftsmanship never surpassed in any age and undoubtedly the creation of a goldsmith as original as he was ingenious. A second much larger dagger was of polished bronze, a real fighting weapon with a stout midrib. It can be taken as representing a first step in that improvement of tools and weapons, both for practical use and in elegance of design, that was to be maintained during the next thousand years of the Bronze Age.

Gold pectoral and belt hook from among the rich grave goods, presumably of a prince, below the Bush Barrow on Normanton Down overlooking Stonehenge (seventeenth century BC).

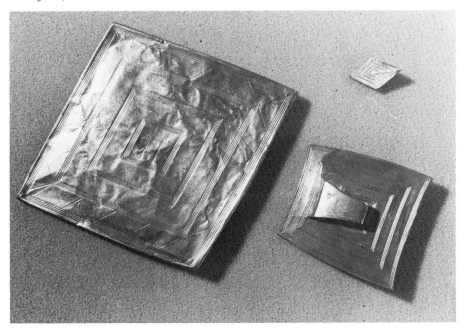

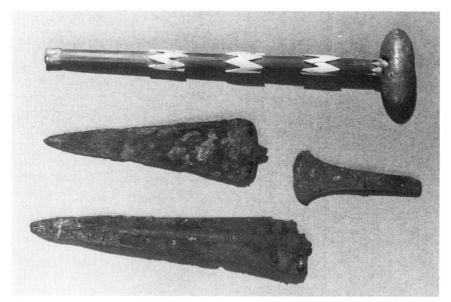

Bronze and copper implements from among the grave goods found below the Bush Barrow on Normanton Down (seventeenth century BC).

From the point of view of establishing the exalted status of the dead man, no other object in his grave is of as great significance as the sceptre that lay not far from his right hand. Its polished stone head was made from a fossil, probably of magical meaning, and the wooden shaft had been inlaid with carefully cut cylindrical bone mounts of zigzag form. Already, it seems, Britain was a sceptred isle, presumably with supreme rulers of god-like power.

Personal ornaments being made at much the same period as that of the Wessex chieftains are necklaces of amber or (in Scotland) of jet. The excellence of their design and execution is best seen in the jet specimen from Poltalloch in Scotland – a piece which any woman would be proud to wear today. Some judges see in them the origin of the sheet gold *lunulae* that were made in Ireland, some to be exported along the Atlantic coasts, including a few to south-west England. Others, however, believe that the geometric patterns engraved on these gorgets were derived from Beaker ornament. Whichever it may be (if either), they must have given the wearers a heightened sense of their own wealth and grandeur.

Another kind of possession found in graves of Wessex, and Wessex influenced, chieftains also belongs with one's imaginative picture of the heroic-aristocratic lifestyle. These are handled drinking cups of gold, amber or shale (from Kimmeridge, Dorset). The famous Rillaton gold cup from Cornwall, with its horizontal ribbing and ingeniously attached handle, had been hammered up from the lump with great technical skill. The amber and shale specimens seem to have been partially lathe-turned in a dexterous manner that allowed the handles to be carved in one piece. While these precious vessels are too small to suggest the hearty quaffing associated with Beakers, they do evoke proud wives waiting on their lords with gold cups familiar from heroic literature. Perhaps some drink more potent than beer was being made?

Throughout the rest of the British Bronze Age objects for personal adornment prove the continuing but ever-changing skills of the goldsmiths in the service of an elite. The aim was now for the glitter of broken surfaces rather than the sheen of sheet gold. Outstanding were the gold torques worn round neck or arms, twisted from square or flanged bars and, when the technique had been mastered, soldered strips. The variety of design and of method used to secure the glitter of torques and the ingenuity of their fasteners suggests the presence of a craft league of goldsmiths always ready to devise or adopt new ideas. One exceptional item of personal display comes from Mold, Flintshire. This amazing object in thick sheet gold was shaped to fit over some great man's shoulders, an armour of high fashion, the glitter secured by hundreds of *repoussé*-work (hammered into relief) ribs and bosses, finely milled for perfection of finish.

Over the same centuries bronzesmiths were busy perfecting the design and efficiency of tools and weapons, soon to include shapely rapiers and swords, and, at the end of the Bronze Age, fine ceremonial shields. Also, they made 'torques' for those who could not afford gold that were not in truth twisted, but cast in solid metal.

Jet necklace, c.1340 BC, from Poltalloch, Argyll. Amber was more commonly used in England.

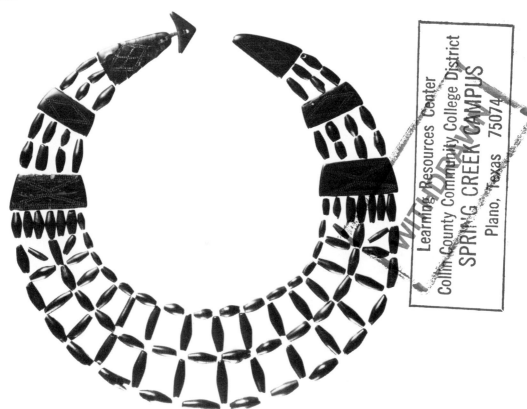

Avebury and Stonehenge

While it seems right in thinking of the arts of the British Bronze Age to lay the emphasis on all these minor creations of the artist-craftsman who held an important position in aristocratic societies, it is essential in a history that covers the art of architecture to give some account, however compressed, of the achievement of contemporary builders working, as their predecessors had done, to set the stage for religious ideas and rituals, but they cannot compare with the truly amazing achievements of the succeeding period.

The great examplar here is, of course, Stonehenge, the greatest of ceremonial buildings, which was brought to its magnificent climax early in the Bronze Age of southern England but which was rooted in the later phases of the Stone Age. During this period the Stone Age peoples in many parts of Britain were developing a form of sacred enclosure dubbed by archaeologists as a 'henge'. They are numerous in Britain and would appear to be a British creation, though a few seemingly henge-like monuments are now being recognised on the continent. In their simplest form they had a bank normally outside a ditch (the reverse of defensive earthworks) with one, or later two, entrances. They range widely in size and in internal features, of which circles of standing stones are the most striking. These stone circles may often have been part of the original construction, but as we know from the history of Stonehenge, they could be late additions.

It is one of the more surprising facts of the period that while the Beaker invaders and the Wessex chieftains seem to have subjected the old farming communities and changed the entire social structure, they took an energetic part in the development of henges. Presumably their religious ideas, which may well have been more sky-orientated, must have dominated, but merged with, the ancient fertility cults of the goddess.

Unhappily the history and chronology of the later henges and of Stonehenge itself have been plunged into uncertainty by the complexities of radio-carbon dating. Here such arguments must be avoided as far as possible and admiring attention given instead to the architectural refinements practised at Stonehenge. First, however, something must be said about Avebury, the runner-up in the order of magnificence of our henges. It does not deserve more attention here, since although it covers a far larger area than its rival, and is boldly planned, it has no true architecture, its great sarsen stones standing singly and quite unworked. It is, in fact, a relatively primitive circle-henge on an unprecedented scale.

Avebury's builders, enriched by good Wessex pasture, must have commanded a large labour force but not the service of a sophisticated, ambitious and innovating architect. This is not surprising, since all except the avenue of standing stones added in Beaker times was raised before the end of the Stone Age. Yet, what demands wonder in this place is its size and the labour it involved. The great bank, well over four hundred metres across, encloses a sacred area of over eleven hectares; it is about five metres high with a steep-sided internal quarry ditch originally nine metres in depth. Inside the ditch and bank the great circle was formed by up to one hundred huge, rugged sarsen boulders, the tallest standing 4.4 m above the ground. Within it the two smaller rings, irregular though they are, must have given the nearest approach to an architectural effect, one centred on a tall pillar stone, the other on a triangular structure of three sarsens, to be known as the Cove. The whole sanctuary, when bank and ditch were of gleaming white chalk, must have been an impressive sight, enhanced when the Avenue was added on its sinuous course up to Overton Hill. This was formed by one hundred pairs of sarsens about fifteen metres apart, each pair consisting of one tall and narrow stone facing a broader, squatter one. It is thought likely that these contrasting shapes are male and female symbols – and the same symbolism may also be present in the pillar and Cove. If this guess is a sound one, Avebury would seem to be linked with the fertility cult of the New Stone Age.

The Avenue ended on Overton Hill in the Sanctuary, and this now destroyed monument is of concern here since it suggests the possibility that the henges were sometimes supplied with wooden buildings on a large scale. Before the stone rings of Beaker times there had been a structure at the Sanctuary with no less than six concentric circles of holes that had held upright posts. Were they free-standing, simply a wooden version of the stone circles (as at Arminghall, Norfolk) or was there a building here with posts supporting a conical roof? There are comparable evidences in the enormous Durrington Walls henge (also in Wiltshire) and at the so-called Woodhenge nearby. Though this is a primitive plan for domestic architecture the size would make it impressive. On balance it would seem less likely than open rings, but the possibility cannot be ignored.

The long history of Stonehenge is widely known or, if not known, can easily be looked up. Here it is right, and more enjoyable, to concentrate on the power combined with refinement of its unique architecture as it was to be seen in its final grandeur.

Before that time there had been the simple embanked henge and Heel Stone of the third millennium, to be followed by the elaboration of Beaker times when the volcanic 'bluestones' were brought from the far west of Wales. These bluestones were to be moved and reshaped more than once before being set up in their present positions reflecting the circle and horseshoe of the enormous sarsens which now dwarf them. The chief interest of this second phase in the present context is that it proves that already in Wales the bluestones were embued with sacred or magical forces, while the ground to which they were to be brought with so much labour, the existing simple sanctuary of Salisbury Plain, must have had some vast numinous significance for the builders.

Coming now to the third main stage distinguished by the excavators, when the sanctuary was brought to the form that we inherit in its noble ruin, we have to think first of those individuals who conceived, organised and devised the many quite original architectural ideas and structural methods that went into the building. There must have been some paramount ruler able to command the work force required for so colossal an undertaking. It has seemed good sense to seek such a man from among the Wessex chieftains, even to identify him with the great man of the Bush Barrow, at Normanton, close by, though now opinion has shifted to a rather earlier date for

Stonehenge III. However this may, some day, prove to be, it seems unlikely that the ambitious overlord determined to provide his people and their beliefs with the grandest setting imaginable would also himself have been directly responsible for its design and erection. At New Grange it has been confidently claimed that gifted sculptors were a group apart who embellished the work of the tomb builders. At Stonehenge with its remarkable unity of design and construction there must have been an inspired architect in command of the work force, from the selection and roughing out of the sarsen boulders ('grey wethers') where they lay on the distant downs to their final precise shaping, raising and bonding. Surely this whole scheme was conceived within one man's mind?

What would have been the principal aims of this creative mind? One can try to appreciate them under the headings of size, strength, dramatic effect, good finish in the stone work and aesthetic refinements of detail.

The goal of awe-inspiring size and particularly of height is very evident. Some visitors today are apt to complain 'Stonehenge is so small'. One must try to imagine the human world of its time when few people had seen anything larger than simple huts – unless it was Avebury or an occasional ancient tomb already diminished in effect by the passage of centuries. The outer circle of thirty standing stones together with the thickness of the lintels rose five metres above the ground, while the central trilithon of the inner horseshoe rose to over seven metres. As has been observed, the tallest sarsen of the Avebury circle is 4.4 m.

When it comes to solidity of construction the effort involved was at least equally remarkable. The uprights weighing about 26 tons apiece in the circle, and considerably more in the horseshoe, were sunk into the ground to over one and a half metres and well wedged in their holes. With tremendous labour stone tenons were battered out on the top of the upright to fit into mortices sunk into the lintel stones, while the ends of the lintels were interlocked with tongue-and-groove joints. Through these devices the building was given a stability which, if it had not been for human onslaughts, would largely have endured for 3,500 years or more.

The architectural refinement of all-pervading importance was the thorough dressing of all the sarsen boulders (except the ancient Heel Stone) to form monolithic pillars of roughly rectangular section with their tenon and morticed lintels, the work being done with heavy stone mauls. The number of man hours demanded by this shaping, rough though it was for the uprights, was immense. Great skill and more labour were required so to shape and set up the pillars that their tops were of even height and the continuous ring of the lintels exactly level. The lintels themselves show the most subtle refinement, for not only were they gently curved to fit the diameter of the circle but were made slightly wider at the top to counter the effect of foreshortening when viewed from the ground. This highly sophisticated device is found nowhere else before Greek building.

Above all it is the force, concentration and unity of design that makes this temple such an extraordinary achievement for its time and place. It is not only the height of the stones towering up toward the numinous heavens, but their closeness together, including the narrow slits of the free standing trilithons, that gave wonderful effects of light and shade and a sense of silent power. It was a tremendous feat of the imagination that still draws the crowds and the worshippers today.

Did the possessor of this creative imagination find any of his inspiration in continental sources? This has become one of the main subjects of dispute in recent days. Professor R.J.C. Atkinson's brave hazard that he might indeed have been a Mycenean in the service of a Wessex chieftain appears to have been discredited by the combination of the earlier dating given by the adjusted radio-carbon analysis with the fashion (for fashion it is) wherever possible to see cultural change as being home grown rather than helped along by foreigners. To me this seems perverse in the light of what went before Stonehenge – cattle, grain crops with mixed farming, pottery, axes, megalithic tombs, and what followed in historic times – Belgic invasions, Roman conquest, Anglo-Saxon, Danish and Norse settlement, Norman conquest. These and all the other foreign contacts were at least as influential in arts and fine crafts as in other cultural changes to be chronicled in this and all succeeding volumes. The 'autochthonous' fashion feeds, perhaps, on the notion that because travel in ancient times was slow and unorganised, individuals or small groups did not move about, or become inspired by others who did. Stonehenge is unique in so many ways that it must, as a whole, be largely indigenous, yet it is hard not to believe that its architect must have held within his mind some awareness of monumental building, or temples and masonry and construction for visual effect. The British can certainly take pride in this work of unparalleled nobility in their prehistoric heritage, but surely it would not have been created if the country had been, not only an island, but also in total isolation.

Before and after the high days of Stonehenge most social effort involving manual labour went into raising free-standing circles that often remain impressive and even beautiful in their natural settings. They, too, must have been sacred tribal meeting places, but they were not architecture.

It has already been mentioned that throughout the later British Bronze Age the skills and talents of artist-craftsmen went mainly into goldwork and other objects of personal finery and into the specialisation and improved design of bronze weapons and tools. Although these things must have been made for a privileged upper class there is less evidence of the presence of supreme chiefs such as the great man of the Bush Barrow or he who ordered the raising of Stonehenge. In this later Bronze Age after about 1200 BC Britain was perhaps something of a backwater. The bronze smiths were not able to compete with those of now booming Denmark, its wealth largely based on the amber trade. Then from about the seventh century BC the British Isles began to be influenced by an iron-using culture from the continent known as the Hallstatt.

This was the product of direct contact and trade between the Celtic speaking 'barbarians' of central Europe and Gaul and the Greeks and Etruscans of the Mediterranean world. Contacts came first from the Greek colony of Massilia (Marseilles), but later Greco-Etruscan trade spread by the Alpine passes, the Etruscan element showing many oriental borrowings, particularly of animal art, that were to be of importance for the Celts. The

Celts may also have had some direct relationship with the Scyths or other near Eastern peoples.

The Celtic Iron Age and La Tène art

The Celtic aristocracy developed an understandable passion for wine and imported it from the south with elegant classical vessels for containing and serving it. It was these acquisitions above all that the Celtic artists were to seize upon for their own purposes.

The resulting Hallstatt culture, still deeply rooted in the Bronze Age ways, spread widely, making itself felt, as we have seen, as far west as Britain. It was the beginning of the age of Celtic expansion which reached its height when the tribesmen led by their wine-bibbing, horse-loving chieftains crossed the Alps, crushed the Etruscans and occupied Rome (390 BC).

Already, however, by the fifth century BC the artists among the Celts had begun to see that they could transform the Greek, Etruscan and perhaps Scythian art which they had regarded simply as foreign goods to their own ends. This they did, taking the rational, representational and decorative classical tradition and totally transforming it through their own passionate, intuitive imaginations. Articles which had been mere civilised adjuncts for feasting or fighting or dressing, pretty patterns such as the Greek palmette, became works of art charged with life, movement and symbolism. So there sprang from hybrid Hallstatt sources what has been described as 'the first true art style north of the Alps since the end of the Ice Age'. It is known to us as La Tène from a site on Lake Neuchâtel (Switzerland), and there seems no doubt that it was indeed a fully conscious anti-classical movement developed in a subtle understanding between wealthy barbarian tribal chieftains and artists who themselves, among the Celts, had a good social standing. Some people see in this great creation of a barbarian people, despite its frequent felicity and grace, something 'dark and uncanny'. In so far as this is true, it can perhaps be linked with the lingering barbarity of Celtic head-hunting and skull cults which was given rough artistic expression in sculpture in the south of Gaul (Entremont and Roquepertuse) and had at least faint manifestations in Britain. The same contrast of light and darkness is also, of course, apparent in the Celtic priesthood of the druids.

By the mid-fifth century BC La Tène art was carried by the rapid expansion of the Celtic peoples from its cradle lands round the Middle Rhine over central and western Europe over the Alps and Pyrenees. By the mid-third century BC its inspiration reached Britain, where among the already Celtic speaking peoples with their Bronze Age and Hallstatt traditions it was to have a late flowering, being brought to its purest perfection before being swamped by the spreading dullness and mediocrity of much provincial Romanisation. It is astonishing how few modern Britons are aware of this supreme achievement of their Celtic forebears.

By this time Britain was again a land ruled by wealthy tribal leaders, having left behind the somewhat more egalitarian society of her later Bronze Age. This aristocracy was inevitably one of heroic, martial ideals much given to intertribal wars and struggles for hegemony. In picturing the setting in which the artists worked it cannot be over-stressed that whereas from the New Stone Age of the megaliths almost all laborious social endeavour had gone into constructions for religious and cultic purposes, it was now, throughout mainland Britain, transferred to military ends: to the building of tribal hill-forts, culminating in such powerful strongholds as Maiden Castle or the stone-built counterparts in Scotland and Wales. It can surely be called an age of the secularisation of social goals, even though the Celtic imagination was alive with magical and spiritual ideas and symbols often made obscurely visible in art.

In the employ of such a war-like aristocracy it is a matter of course to find artists giving their genius to the splendid yet subtle enrichment of arms and armour, horse trappings, personal adornment for men and women – especially the ancient tradition for torques and armlets, drinking vessels and, a very special category, hand mirrors for the aristocratic ladies. Although gold might be used extravagantly for torques and other ornaments, and surfaces were sometimes gilded, bronze was overwhelmingly the material of La Tène art. No doubt wood was often employed, indeed wooden vessels with Celtic decoration have been preserved – as at Glastonbury. Nevertheless it is not only the chances of preservation that have led to an overwhelming preponderance of works of art in bronze and gold, for these metals were best suited to the spirit of the flowing La Tène style from its vital plastic forms surging like waves to the most delicate tendrils. Indeed, the indwelling influence of bronze and gold can be seen in the contrast provided by the famous wrought iron ox-headed firedogs, probably used to support logs or spits for princely feastings, which manifest a stark masculine rigidity all their own. They may have been the work of simple toolmaking blacksmiths, yet it is doubtful, for the best of the oxheads are works of art. It seems more likely that they were made by the smith who would have wrought not spades or coulters but his lord's long iron sword.

From the third century BC when La Tène art was first introduced to Britain, it soon developed its own distinctive qualities – an instance of the Thule effect in its positive aspect. That it was brought to its finest and purest by insular artists working for two centuries in misty lands undisturbed by Greek or Roman distractions would appear to be self explanatory. The powerful Celtic imagination could reach its highest flights free from all rational, prosaic restraints. If it is possible to generalise (for regional schools can be hazily recognised), the British artists created works that are wholly graceful, delightful to our eyes, a wonderful blend of delicate subtlety and restless vigour, without either classical formality or its psychological opposite, survivals of that dark, uncanny element of earlier times. The anti-classical feeling of British artists is evident in the fact that from the first they were more given to daringly assymetrical designs than their continental contemporaries; while freedom from the more barbaric spirit is simply apparent in the absence, until the Belgic invasions, of the human masks and animal monsters in which it had largely been manifest.

The simplest classification of all the treasures inherited from our early Celtic past is between the plastic (much of it repoussé work) and the linear.

Asymmetrical and symmetrical designs appear in both forms and so, too, does that La Tène characteristic of double, interlocking patterns in which what can be called the primary pattern interlocks with a background pattern, the eye selecting one or the other. This is perhaps most easily recognised in the linear forms where the 'background' pattern is hatched, sometimes in a basketry style, while the other is smooth, the predominance of one over the other depending largely on the fall of the light. Though essentially different, this device of the Celtic designer can be compared with that of the master carvers of New Grange in whose hands what had been the incised motif was left in relief with the excised background assuming significant forms of its own (see p. 9).

In an attempt to typify British La Tène art it has been said that it was based on 'swirling, rhythmic, circular patterns, often in triple'. Again, although human and animal forms are rare, 'faces that are not faces obtrude'. The truth is that this art that was so much more than decorative cannot be evoked in words but must slowly be absorbed and appreciated through the eyes and the imagination. Unfortunately reliable dating is difficult for various reasons, particularly because many of the best pieces have been found not in graves but as presumed votive offerings in rivers and bogs and because family treasures were liable to survive as heirlooms. However, this slight intellectual frustration does not spoil the aesthetic delight to be found even in some of the smallest pieces.

Perhaps war and martial values have never found a better justification than in the shields, helmets, sword scabbards and horse trappings the British artists made for their warrior lords.

One of the earliest La Tène works from Britain (third century BC) is a circular terminal, probably from a horse yoke, found in the Thames at Brentford. Though the design flows, it still shows its origins in the Greek palmette. A much more notable, but not altogether likeable, river find is from the Witham in Lincolnshire. This is a bronze-covered shield of the long, narrow shape, to be seen in classical sculpture beside the figure of The Dying Gaul. It was originally charged with a fantasticated boar, now preserved only in silhouette. Highly conventionalised horses heads, too can be seen on the mid-rib, but the design on the boss (umbo) is wholly abstract. Though organically powerful, it is an unusually static, even constipated work to come from a Celtic hand.

A second riverine shield, taken from the Thames at Battersea, is surely the most famous and written-about of all our masterpieces. Now believed to be as early as the second century BC, it is a symmetrical composition, wonderfully rich and harmonious, full of restrained movement.

All the studs on the Battersea shield are inset with red, vitreous enamel; studs of this have been used also on the Witham shield. It was in fact now displacing the coral which in early days had satisfied the Celtic taste for colour. In time the British artists were to show outstanding skill in developing the *champlevé* technique whereby designs were cut into the metal surface and filled by fusion with red, blue, yellow enamels.

Among other specimens of defensive armour (all of which may have been worn for parade rather than on the battlefield) is the horned helmet from the

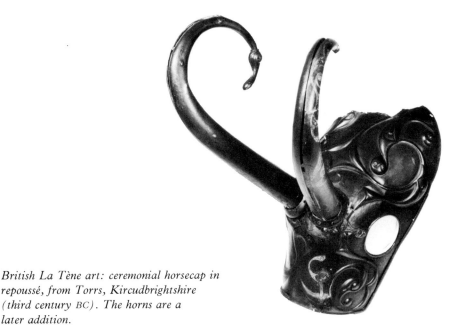

British La Tène art: ceremonial horsecap in repoussé, from Torrs, Kircudbrightshire (third century BC). The horns are a later addition.

Thames at Waterloo Bridge, a remarkable object which in its very shape seems to show more of the aggressive spirit that is otherwise curiously lacking in the Celtic armoury. The ornamentation of this helmet is, however, rather too tenuous with its wandering tendrils and leaflets, a style not uncommon in Britain during this first century BC. A far finer and probably rather older headpiece was for the protection not of a warrior but of his mount: this is the well-known frontal from Torrs in Scotland with its marvellous design absolutely at one with the odd-shaped object itself. Anyone wanting to enter into the spirit of the British artists of these last centuries BC could not do better than linger over the Torrs horse-cap, the exquisite shield boss from Wandsworth and the electrically live little bronze plaque from the bog finds at Llyn Cerrig in Anglesey. The Llyn Cerrig objects, which include a piece of a battle trumpet such as are known in Ireland, may have been connected with the Druids of Mona (Anglesey). There is an iron slave chain with neck rings for five that could have served for the victim of druidic sacrifice – a reminder of the dark under currents of Celtic life.

We turn now from armour to fighting weapons. Spear blades might occasionally carry linear ornament, but the main vehicle for art was the sword scabbard. Here the long narrow sheath demanded more formal linear engraving, brought to life, however, by the contrasting plasticity of the bronze shape. Almost as much a part of the heroic life as the warrior's armoury were his vessels for lordly drinking – already observed in the Bronze Age. Among several examples of tankards, one of the best is the shapely waisted example with its strongly moulded La Tène handle from Trawsfynydd on the western fringes of Wales – whether it held wine or some local brew is a question for guesswork.

Celtic artists served the aristocracy not only to embellish war but for peaceful display. For personal ornaments they could often work in that most plastic of metals: gold. This was particularly true of the traditional neck rings or torques that remained typical of Celtic dress – or undress, for warriors wore them when fighting naked. Of the many that survive a few are very splendid indeed. One penannular ring, from among the number found near Snettisham in Norfolk, has many twisted strands themselves twisted together and ending in massive rings with repoussé ornament of great finesse, the whole a splendid object (colour plate 3). Some believe that the Snettisham treasure may have belonged to the royal house of the Iceni.

Of all the possessions that graced the social life of the Celtic aristocracy the mirrors, whose design was at its height during the first century BC, are without question the most delightful and satisfying. Their form, and perhaps the idea of highborn and wealthy women being enabled to regard themselves in this manner, owed much to Rome, but the design chased on the mirror backs show the Celtic hand and eye at their truest and also appropriately at their most feminine. Moreover they prove the mastery of artists working in two dimensions and in the dual style already described. Of the two recognised masterpieces, one has the added interest of coming from the grave of some great lady, at Birdlip on the edge of the Cotswolds. The design on this mirror and on that of its rival from Desborough, Northamptonshire, appear to be symmetrical but in fact possess the slight, beautifying irregularities coming from a freehand lay-out (colour pl. 5). Other mirrors are wholly assymmetrical both in detail and in overall design. A good example is the 'Mayer' perhaps from the Thames, with its three roundels filled with versions of three-armed triskele patterns, a very common motif.

One historic event that strongly affected the development of British art should be chronicled here. This was the penetration of southern, eastern and much of central England by Belgic tribes of mixed Celtic and Germanic stock coming from the Low Countries. They were to conquer or dominate the native princes and their territories and to weld together larger kingdoms until, by the time of the Claudian conquest (from AD 43), Cunobelin of the Catuvellauni was ruling over the entire south-east. One result of the presence of these wealthy and militarily ambitious Belgic rulers was an increase in the use of human and animal forms which had been common in the continental La Tène but, as we have seen, had been rarely used in Britain. It appears in realistic or slightly caricatured animals and birds in the round (Milber Down), but occasionally in monster grotesques (the ramsheads from Harpenden, Hertfordshire) and much more typically in repoussé work and masks such as those on the bucket from a rich Belgic cremation burial at Aylesford, Kent. Here the bronze-bound bucket presents not only stern human masks with the typically Celtic staring eyes, wedge nose and slit mouth, but also fantastic horses with beaked mouths and bodies turning into scrolls. Although the dating has been questioned from time to time, I cannot doubt that the same Celtic spirit shows itself in the largest monument of all, the chalk-cut White Horse of Uffington that stretches its attenuated body along the downs (formerly, and properly, in Berkshire, now in Oxfordshire).

Belgic princes with their Roman connections were largely responsible for introducing coinage to Britain. Many of the coins, like those of Gaul, are based on the head (obverse) and chariot and horses (reverse) of King Philip of Macedon, by now almost unrecognisable in their disintegration. Strange that the Greek art which had played so considerable a part in the birth of La Tène should reappear at this time, so near its death.

During the decades after AD 43 when the first rush of Roman conquest was checked and delayed by the Britons of the highland zone, works of Celtic art could be produced for the still independent rulers. We can take as typifying their work the sumptuous gilt-bronze brooch found at Aesica on Hadrian's Wall (colour pl. 1). Despite its Roman context it is truly Celtic, full of swirling energy. Beside it can be put the massive bronze and enamel armlets found in Scotland and cast in the first or second centuries AD. They are of evidently Celtic design yet too heavy, aggressive even, as though made to meet and counter the implacable might of Rome.

It was, of course, in those parts of the British Isles never subject to Rome, in Scotland and Ireland, that the Celtic inheritance survived. The language defied conquest (even in Cornwall and Wales), while something of the feeling for the visual arts, like seed corn in a desert, could be regenerated to flourish again with the inspiration of the Christian Church.

Long-eyed Celtic mask from the handle of a bronze-bound wooden bucket from Aylesford, Kent. Stylised horses suggest Belgic influence dating from the time of Christ.

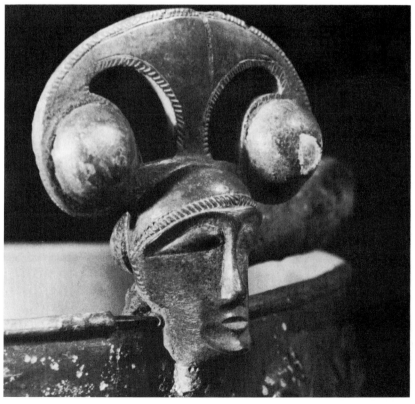

ROMAN BRITAIN

Part I
The Cultural and Social Setting

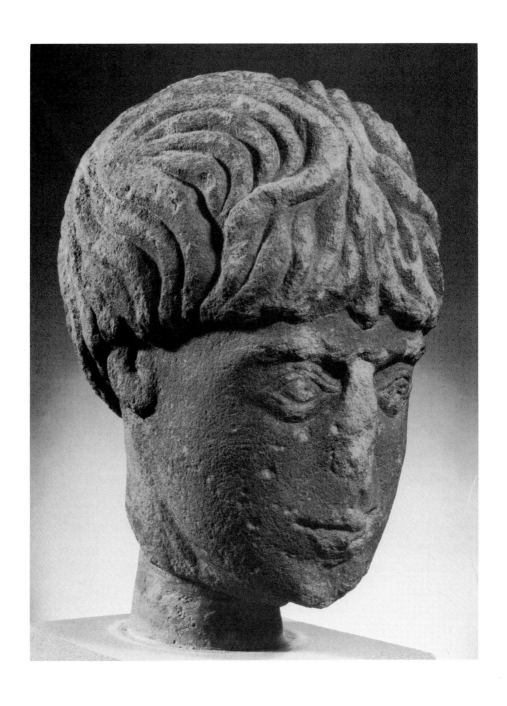

Head of the Romano-Celtic god Antenociticus; found at his temple outside the Hadrian's Wall fort of Benwell, Newcastle upon Tyne (probably second century AD).

The Cultural and Social Setting

PETER SALWAY

Introduction

Julius Caesar's expeditions serve to mark a new phase in the history and culture of Britain. Although the invasions of 55 and 54 BC did not result in immediate Roman occupation, extensive changes in society occurred on both sides of the English Channel in the period of nearly a hundred years that were to elapse before the Conquest under the Emperor Claudius (AD 41–54). Change was not restricted to the native Celtic peoples of Britain and Gaul. Rome herself went through the traumatic experience of the fall of the old aristocratic Republic, torn apart by the unbridled conflict of its leaders, and its replacement by the rule of the Emperor Augustus (27 BC–AD 14) and his successors.

Two interacting factors were critically influential in determining the way Roman society worked. One was the importance of the family. In Roman terms this had a very wide meaning, incorporating not only relatives but the whole household and dependants. This complex network of relationships was extended further by the 'client' system, by which large numbers of lesser people relied on the favours of individual great men and great families, and for whom the great themselves, in exchange for the prestige bestowed by an abundance of clients, accepted a traditional responsibility. At its most extreme, whole cities, regions, and even provinces of the empire could rely upon magnates near the centre of power to represent their interests. The emperors became the greatest patrons of all. The other factor was the supreme importance attached in the classical world to public recognition of success. Since traditional Roman religion centred around the family, the highest honour the living members could pay the dead was to emulate or outstrip the achievements of their forbears in the principal fields of public life: politics, public administration, the law and the army.

The replacement of Republic by Empire* did not do away with these driving

---

* In this chapter 'Empire' refers to the political system of the period; and 'empire' to the geographical territory under Roman rule.

forces at the centre of Roman life. Its ancient institutions, too, tended to be adapted to new roles rather than disappear. That the awesomely-prestigious Senate survived from the Republic throughout the Empire in the West – and beyond – is one, if perhaps the most striking, example of a trait that went deep in the character of Rome. Many of the old senatorial families were replaced by new, but it is an outstanding characteristic of Roman society that those elevated within it took on the traditional attitudes of their new stations in life, while those recruited into it from outside, from the non-Roman peoples within the imperial frontiers and from without, regularly adopted Roman tastes, values and ways of behaviour. This highly competitive world provided an environment in which the arts flourished. Indeed, Augustus himself, realising that the tradition of aristocratic patronage of the arts could be pressed into service to assist in casting the mantle of respectability and tradition over the new regime and in shaping the public image of the emperor, set a pattern for his imperial successors. The greatest acclaim in Roman society was bestowed for success in war and the extension of Roman power over new lands, as ordained by the gods. Themes of victory (see illustrations of distance slabs on pp. 81–2) and divine approval thus play a major part in official art under the Empire.

Caesar's own spectacular conquest of Gaul, in itself part of the final struggles between the magnates of the Republic, brought Rome to the English Channel. A copious flow of trade had for the best part of a century carried British exports to the Mediterranean, via Brittany and the Atlantic coast of France, and brought wine and other luxury products of the Roman world, enriching in the process the tribes of south-west Britain. This traffic was diverted after Caesar's destruction of the fleet of the Breton Veneti, who had dominated carriage across the northern sea. The focus shifted to routes that ran from north-east Brittany and the Cherbourg peninsula to the south coast of Britain, and subsequently moved again, with the heaviest traffic now coming from the lands that lay between the Seine to the mouths of the Rhine. In this, the permanent establishment of the Roman army on the latter river from 12 BC, with its massive need for supplies, must have played a critical part.

In Britain the archaeological record shows that in this final pre-Roman phase Kent and Essex received the bulk of the traffic. But much more than trade alone was involved. There were already close personal links between the Celtic tribes of north-eastern Gaul and both central southern Britain (notably Hampshire and Sussex) and Kent. Those Gauls are generally referred to as 'Belgic', a term whose exact significance has caused much scholarly dispute but which is convenient in indicating a culture that in the Late Iron Age was broadly similar throughout that region. The outstanding characteristic of these tribes was a society that centred round groups of warrior nobles, whose wealth and success seem essentially to have depended on war. The respect they paid to war was something, of course, which they shared with the Romans, but it was within the context of an immensely less complex society.

In some of the Gallic tribes further south which Rome encountered – and in due course absorbed – the internal political structure had evolved from chieftainship to an elective aristocratic magistracy. But in these northern tribes monarchy, often highly unstable, was usual. Roman authors confirm the frequent conflicts between tribes, within tribes, and within families, often around outstanding individuals. It is therefore not surprising that their most striking form of artistic expression was their output of superb pieces intended for the adornment of the great, particularly the trappings of war.

A rapid development of Belgic characteristics in southern Britain in the period between Caesar and Claudius is almost certainly to be attributed to the movement of individual nobles from Gaul to positions of influence and power across the Channel. Literary references in the Roman authors also show refugees from dynastic quarrels in Britain fleeing in the opposite direction and welcomed at Rome. Britain was being drawn more and more into the political and cultural orbit of the great power that was her neighbour. Sharper tribal identities now detected in Britain were accompanied by a powerful taste for the prestigious luxury objects manufactured in the empire, such as the magnificent Augustan silver cups found at Hockwold, in Norfolk, which could be acquired by rulers in eastern Britain. It was they who now controlled the principal flow of trade with other parts of the island and generated substantial exports themselves in slaves and other booty acquired in aggressive wars against their neighbours. In some cases their fine gold and silver coinage demonstrates that they were employing Roman moneyers; and the presence of Roman merchants at sites like Braughing in Hertfordshire is extremely likely. Perhaps they settled, as elsewhere outside the imperial frontiers, in semi-permanent expatriate communities.

What the presence (or absence) of such products of the empire can never by itself prove is political sympathy. Taste in art in the ancient world could as often as not be common on both sides of a political divide, and it was not unusual for trade to continue even during hostilities. Nor should our modern feelings on war make us overlook that an explicit and highly respected objective of warfare was booty, an attitude shared by Briton and Roman alike. The presence of works of art in particular archaeological contexts has to be interpreted according to contemporary values, not ours.

The Roman conquest

The military conquest of Britain started with the Claudian invasion in AD 43. By the end of the century the whole of England and Wales had been conclusively incorporated into the empire, and remained so for the next three hundred years. From time to time, in line with the twists and turns of policy and the fortunes of frontier warfare, parts of Scotland also came under direct Roman rule: the Lowlands at least felt the continuous proximity of Rome. Moreover, for reasons of state and the prestige of emperors, Roman Britain did not cease after the initial wars of conquest to attract more imperial interest than its position on the extreme periphery of the empire would at first sight seem to justify.

The Conquest not only changed the contexts in which art was produced or

imported: it also introduced new forms of art to Britain. The arrival of
Roman army and administration – and the unofficial retinue that
accompanied them – opened up the country to the full force of the
kaleidoscopic culture that was developing as the classical world of the
Mediterranean merged with those of the peoples Rome absorbed. In time it
produced profound changes in society, as Britons were gradually drawn into
the system and became Romans. It is true that these changes were more
marked in town than in country, and in the south and east of Britain than in
the north and west (except where there was immediate contact with the
garrisons of the Roman army), but even in the most remote rural settlements
the apparently small amount of visible alteration should not delude us into
thinking that the Britons' world remained unaltered.

The accidents of survival mean that what we now have of art in Roman
Britain falls almost entirely within the visual arts. Of literature produced in
Britain or by Britons we know practically nothing, though occasional
quotations from the classics in inscriptions – and an immense number of
representations of classical themes in the visual arts – make it clear that
classical literature was widely read. This was the first time Britain had had a
literate society, even if a vast proportion of those who could read doubtless
used their skill almost exclusively for the practical purposes of everyday life.
Music, too, must have been present. We cannot reasonably suppose that the
owner of the property at Keynsham, near Bristol, whose mosaic depicted
mythological figures playing pipes and tambourine, had no idea what music
was, any more than we can believe that the proprietor of the fine villa
(country house) at Low Ham, in Somerset, chose to have his grand reception
room floored with pictures of the story of Dido and Aeneas without having
read any of Virgil's *Aeneid* and without any expectation that his guests would
recognise and be impressed by them.

It is architecture which provides us with our most striking memorials of
Roman Britain. The full range of Roman expertise in design and
construction, according to the precepts of classical architecture developed in
the Mediterranean and adapted as the empire spread, was required to meet
the civil and military needs of the new province. Roman rule introduced to
Britain new materials, the design skills to work with them, the technologies to
exploit them, and the logistics to make construction in them achievable. In its
train architecture brought the other arts that were closely associated with it
in the classical world: sculpture in stone and bronze, mosaic, fresco,
decorative masonry, and plasterwork (see pp. 79–85). Sculpture was in itself a
major innovation for Britain, whether incorporated in structures or free-
standing. But perhaps most significant was the introduction of portraiture
and of narrative, in sculpture itself and in other visual arts. A complementary
arrival, with a similar function in the context of Roman society, was what we
might call monumental calligraphy: the art of carving and painting
inscriptions that were intended to be seen by the public and formed an
integral part of the structures they marked and adorned. Whether these
inscriptions recorded the donor of a building, a dedication to a deity or an
emperor, a victory, or the name, family details and career of an individual on
his tomb, they all stemmed from that overwhelming need for public
recognition and remembrance.

In the first two centuries AD, the age in which the province of Britain was born and grew to maturity, the classical tradition of munificence, of largely private patronage of public works, was at its height. Mirroring on a local scale the actions of emperors and great aristocrats, local worthies competed for membership of their local councils and enhanced their reputations and influence by expending personal wealth on civic amenities such as public baths for both sexes (the social centres of the Roman world), aqueducts, temples, markets, theatres, amphitheatres, statuary, and fountains. Sometimes greater men, who had ties of property or patronage with a particular locality, joined in these activities, and occasionally the emperor himself undertook such projects when there were personal or state reasons for doing so.

Further stimuli to the practice of public display were provided by religion and by attitudes to death. Public observation of the gods of the official Roman pantheon and of the cult of the Imperial Family were acts of duty and loyalty carried out by institutions and individuals alike. Office-holding in these cults was an important route to social status and advancement, particularly for new provincials and for freedmen. A large number of other cults, however, were imported into Britain from different parts of the empire. Many of these were in origin neither Graeco-Roman nor Celtic. We find, for example, Isis (Egyptian), Baudihillia (Germanic), and Jupiter Dolichenus (Syrian). At the same time, since Romans and Celts shared a powerful sense of fear of the supernatural beings they believed dwelt in every place and every feature of the landscape, there were also a vast number of dedications to very local deities. There was often an attempt to identify Roman and Celtic gods with one another, producing such deities as Mars Cocidius or Sulis Minerva, and this process of 'conflation' is frequently reflected in art. Attitudes to death and burial varied according to religion and local custom, but broadly speaking the welfare of the soul was felt to be vitally affected by whether the deceased was individually remembered by the living. Hence much effort went into funerary monuments and other means of preserving name and reputation. In time, however, all these cults were overshadowed by the religions offering personal revelation and in some cases salvation, which are often referred to collectively as the 'mystery religions'.

Art and society in Roman Britain

Art in Iron Age Britain had largely served an elite. The provincial Roman society of the Early Empire was very different. It is true that those members of the native aristocracy who saw their future in falling in with Rome had a good chance of retaining prominence and prosperity, but great opportunites opened up further down the ranks of society, with very considerable social mobility. Much – but not all – of the art that is found in Roman Britain reflects the tastes and needs of people of moderate means and position. The population, moreover, became ethnically more varied. At the top of the social pyramid were the senior officers and administrators who were posted in for relatively short tours of duty in careers that could take them all over the empire. Some were Italian, but increasingly they were drawn from the Roman citizen communities, or 'colonies', that had been deliberately founded

in the provinces. These colonies were established in the first place primarily
to provide for soldiers retired from the legions (in Britain: Colchester,
Lincoln and Gloucester). They were set up on lines mirroring the traditional
form of the Roman Republic itself, and possessed considerable local
autonomy, becoming potent centres for the spread of Roman culture.

This was not, however, the only way in which the soldiery had a major
cultural effect in the development of a province. Besides the all-citizen
legions, the garrison of Britain contained a roughly equal number of men in
the 'auxiliary' forces. These units had mostly originated in the conscription of
men from defeated or absorbed tribes, who were given Roman officers and
permanently posted to other parts of the empire where they were less likely
to make common cause with hostile elements. These soldiers brought with
them significant characteristics of their native cultures, particularly in the
religions they often continued to follow. But it was equally important that the
army daily immersed them throughout their long years of service in Roman
traditions, and trained them in a wide variety of skills. They were required to
learn to read and write, they were unceasingly exposed to Latin as the
language of command and communication, and they acquired the art of living
within a world ordered by law and the workings of a sophisticated
bureaucracy. That experience explains the importance for Roman provincial
culture of the fact that on discharge the auxiliaries received Roman
citizenship, the wives they had unofficially acquired during service were
recognised, and their children became legitimate. Even as serving soldiers
they were a privileged category, possessing the advantage rare in the ancient
world of a regular money wage in a secure job. Many of them probably never
saw fighting throughout their careers, but if they did could hope to be well
rewarded. On retirement they frequently assumed positions of importance in
local communities. Some veterans returned to their provinces of origin, but
many settled where they had formed ties. Local recruiting to legions as well
as to auxiliary regiments, as it developed, further strengthened connections
between units and the civilian populations in the towns and villages that grew
up around their permanent stations.

By far the largest element in the population of Roman Britain were those
native British who lived and worked in the countryside. Yet small numbers of
people can have a significant effect on culture. A pair of tombstones from the
settlement outside the fort at South Shields, at the mouth of the Tyne, are
immensely evocative. One records a freed Moorish slave, servant of a trooper
of the First Asturian Auxiliary Cavalry, who buried him in style. The other
is a memorial to another former slave, this time a woman of British birth
from the south of England, who had been freed and then married by one
Barates. The latter came from Palmyra, on the frontier of Syria, apparently a
merchant in business in the region of Hadrian's Wall. Both deceased are
depicted in sculptured relief as entirely Roman. The young man reclines on
an elegant couch, drinking wine served by a small boy. The lady is a
dignified matron, seated in a high-backed chair. Her work-basket is on one
side, her jewel box on the other, and in her lap a piece of material, a needle,
and a ball of wool. The identity of the sculptor of these two stones is, as
almost always, unknown. His style, however, adds another piece to our

appreciation of how this culture worked: under the Roman form there are strong hints that he, too, came from Palmyra.

The status of the arts

The status and functioning of artists and craftsmen in the ancient world varied considerably, due to large differences in the way the individual arts were regarded. Literature was at the top of the social scale. Roman education concentrated on the Greek and Latin literary classics, and on the practice of oratory. The latter was regarded as a practical training for public life, in government and the law. Though the political contexts for the making of speeches changed when Empire replaced Republic, its critical importance did not. Style was much admired, and leading Romans sometimes collected and edited editions of their own orations. Letters, too, were often consciously composed with subsequent publication in mind. Serious historical and philosophical writing was largely written by and for the same class of person, who also produced most of the prose treatises that have survived on subjects such as agriculture, estate management, architecture, and civil engineering. Verse was regarded as a polite accomplishment at which even emperors might try their hands, though a substantial portion of the major works that have survived are by professional poets who were patronised by the great and admitted into their social circles.

Of the visual arts, architecture was something in which a gentleman might take an active interest, both in respect of his own properties and in the public field. The Emperor Hadrian (AD 117–138), for example, considered himself competent to design on the grandest scale. Many of the best practising architects, however, were Greeks; and it is certain that for specific major works in the provinces skilled professionals were often brought in on a project basis, particularly in the more remote areas of the West where locals capable of handling such work were less readily available. There were, of course, highly competent architects, planners, engineers, and craftsmen in the Roman army, and their employment on public works outside the purely military is often suspected. Sculpture and painting were closely related to architecture. The leading practitioners were employed to decorate buildings, while their portable works were collected by the great. On the other hand, unlike architecture itself, these were not arts which members of the Roman upper class chose to practise themselves, and had more in common with the purely decorative arts such as mosaic and plasterwork or the design and manufacture of plate and jewellery.

The Claudian triumph

For political reasons the Emperor Claudius needed a conquest – and at the time opportunity, pretext, and potential for maximum prestige all pointed to Britain. It is not surprising, therefore, that in the first two decades of its incorporation into the empire the mood of the new rulers of Britain was one of triumph. This is typified by the establishment at a very early stage of the citizen colony at Colchester. This had not only been the royal centre of the most powerful of the British kingdoms that opposed Rome, ruled by the sons of the great Cunobelinus (Shakespeare's Cymbeline), but also had witnessed Claudius arriving in person to mark the triumphant end of the campaign. Colchester became the initial capital of the new province: the victory of the emperor was given massive architectural expression in the temple and precinct erected there as the setting for the provincial observance of the cult of Rome and the Imperial Family, subsequently after his death to become specifically the temple of the Deified Claudius himself.

Normal Roman practice was as far as possible to delegate the manning and expense of everyday administration to locals. In these early years only part of the area of Britain under Roman control was administered by regular local councils run by local notabilities, though where these were thought to be reliable friends of Rome the rewards in the form of power and comfort are reflected archaeologically in cities such as Verulamium (see chapter 2), near St Albans, which strongly resemble the citizen colonies. Much of the rest was left in the hands of British princely rulers, under Roman supervision. The latter was the system of 'client kingdoms' – or satellite native states – which Rome, particularly at this period, often found convenient both within and beyond the actual area of military occupation. One likely cultural result of such a policy was a wide divergence of cultural Romanisation according to the extent client kings and their peoples desired or had the means to adopt a Roman way of life.

In the first two decades after the Claudian invasion, the mood of the conquerors continued to feed on the imperial triumph, which itself was reflected in continuing military success. Confident that the original friends of Rome in Britain remained satisfied with the outcome of their adherence, the Roman provincial administration demonstrated its sense of security by considerably reducing its military presence in the regions initially taken, in order to move major units forward into contact with Britons not yet conquered. Indeed, had it not been for extreme maladministration, the terrible uprising led by Boudicca would not have taken place.

What is particularly significant in the present context is that the rebellion contained two very different elements. Boudicca and her client kingdom, the Iceni of Norfolk, had remained exceptionally un-Romanised. Whether this was by choice or not we do not for certain know. The amazing Late Iron Age treasures from Snettisham do not suggest her tribe had been poor, but it is startling to compare what looks like her royal residence (a group of Iron Age round houses inside Roman defences at Thetford) with even the early stages of the probable palace at Fishbourne of King Cogidubnus, her south-coast contemporary (see pp. 54–5 on Fishbourne). Alongside her in leading the rebellion were the Trinovantes of Essex. Their leading nobles had been drawn into a ruinous lifestyle that went with involvement in public affairs at the provincial capital. Having had the first seat of government of the new province planted in their midst at Colchester, social and political pressures to take part must have been irresistible. It is hardly surprising that the Temple of the deified late Emperor Claudius became the symbol of their grievances.

Participation in the ceremonial of the Imperial Cult and contribution to the adornment of its physical setting were expected of anyone who was anyone, and, while no Celtic noblemen will have found alien the idea of maintaining personal prestige through conspicuous consumption, the ultimate cause of their despair is likely to have lain in difficulties in converting the old-style wealth of tribal economy into the never-ending flow of ready cash each would now require. The leaders of both the Iceni and the Trinovantes had been particular friends of Rome: the violent rejection of Roman rule which the uprising represented is thus all the more significant. It is unclear whether a majority of the rebels would in the end have abandoned permanently all taste for Roman culture. That, because of the lack of correlation between art and politics already noted, is improbable, but there is no doubt about their extreme disillusion with life in a Roman province, as they experienced it.

After a cliff-hanging period in which the savagery of Roman vengeance looked like destroying what little of Romano-British society the rebels had left, triumph over Boudicca was finally superseded by a phase of very low-key reassertion of Roman predominance. Renewed campaigning, however, was in the end to push the permanent frontiers of the province far into highland Britain. By the end of the first century AD, Wales and the South-West had been conclusively incorporated, and the northern frontier lay much where it was still to be at the end of Roman rule. These advances were accompanied by the dismantling of the remaining client kingdoms. The way was now open for a relatively uniform development of society in Britain on Roman provincial lines. Successive governors seem to have applied a combination of the carrot and the stick to help this process along. It is true that under the emperors of the Flavian dynasty in the latter part of the century the triumphal mood reappeared, but the victories were increasingly far away from the settled provincials of southern and central Britain. The cultural atmosphere inside the province is caught by the historian Tacitus' account of how his own father-in-law, as the best known Flavian governor of Britain, pursued a linked policy of urban development and education.

In order to encourage uncultivated Britons who dwelt in scattered settlements – and were thus only too ready to fall to fighting – to live in a peaceful and inactive manner by offering them the pleasures of civilisation, Agricola urged them privately and helped them officially to build temples, public squares with public buildings (forums), and town houses. He praised those who responded quickly, and severely critized the laggards. In this way competition for public recognition took the place of compulsion. Moreover he had the children of the leading Britons educated in the civilised arts, and openly placed the natural ability of the Britons above that of the Gauls, however well trained. Little by little there was a slide towards the allurements of degeneracy: assembly rooms, bathing establishments and smart dinner parties.

(Agricola, 21)

The Imperial peace

Signs do exist in the archaeology that this Flavian initiative ran out of steam. However, it is also true that by the middle of the second century Roman

Britain had reached that stage of development by which it is perhaps best known today. It was a settled land, with a population size and density as great as at the height of the Middle Ages, before the Black Death. The landscape was dominated by agriculture and dotted with innumerable small farms, which were mostly still Iron Age in appearance. Almost all displayed some degree of access to Roman consumer products, and this was sometimes quite large, if not at the level found in the urban settlements. Except where it had been acquired as crown land, the countryside of lowland Britain seems to have been largely in the hands of a landowning gentry of moderate wealth, possessing modest Roman country houses (villas), and providing the members for the councils who met in and ran the day to day business of the district from the equivalent of county towns. Those towns were in the main equipped with the principal amenities of Roman urban life, but, in line with the middling wealth of the councillors who must largely have paid for them, these did not match the grandeur or extravagance met in equivalent towns in some other provinces.

Although industry was largely located in the countryside, the towns were the main commercial as well as social and administrative centres for their districts, and were complemented by a network of smaller towns and villages. The use of money as the everyday basis of life had by now spread through society. Long-distance, large-scale trade throughout the empire was enormously facilitated by excellent roads and shipping and by the establishment of peace and good order. Public and private taste were in continuous exposure to material objects and cosmopolitan ideas from afar.

At this stage in the history of the province, the still exceptionally large army of Britain was mostly stationed in the frontier region, and there were fairly sharp differences between the upland parts of the country and the lowlands. North of York there were very few towns of the southern sort and hardly any villas, but the same period saw the beginnings of a large number of settlements of urban type and heterogeneous population that developed alongside the numerous garrisons in the border distric itself and the hill country behind.

Though these civil settlements were fairly basic, the army of the Early Empire itself was equipped to a high standard, and in many respects in standards of architecture, civil engineering and the provision of amenities for its men outstripped the cities of the south. The legions were still regularly commanded by men of senatorial rank, and these, like a substantial number of other officers in both legions and auxiliary units, served in each post for a relatively short time as part of careers in public life that normally took in civil as well as military appointments, at Rome as well as in the provinces. In addition, there were many career officers, through direct entry from the middle classes or working up from the ranks. Most could be accompanied by their families, and often were. It is not just due to the accidents of survival that so much of artistic note from this period is found in the regions dominated by the presence of the army.

In both North and South, a feature of the countryside which is of considerable importance in the search for the context of Romano-British art is the multitude of holy places and religious monuments. These ranged from tiny wayside shrines ('To the Genius of this Place'; 'To the Nymphs'), from mausolea, cemeteries, and isolated temples, to great, sprawling agglomerations (as at Springhead in Kent) and the pilgrimage centres of the healing cults, like Bath (see chapter 1 on Architecture). In certain cases we can suspect continuity with pre-Roman worship (for example the circular temple on Hayling Island), and sometimes that the sanctuaries preserved the sacred groves of Celtic religion. In Gaul it is not uncommon to find complexes of big buildings out in the countryside which are more usually associated with towns: theatres, enclosed piazzas (forums), public baths, and large temples. With their locations perhaps originally determined by pre-existing centres of religious importance – and perhaps also reflecting well-attested Gallic customs of tribal and inter-tribal gatherings – these seem to have provided meeting places (*conciliabula*) where no towns existed, and where religious, political, commercial, and social activities could intermingle. No such complexes have yet been certainly named in Britain, but it is not impossible that this is the original context for Roman Bath, and a number of more rustic versions could tentatively be identified in southern Britain.

The cities and towns of the mid-second century themselves did not achieve their developed state without a fresh impetus which seems to coincide with the arrival of the Emperor Hadrian in person in AD 122, in the course of a vast tour of inspection through the empire. Hadrian in Britain is not solely Hadrian's Wall. He was a person of huge imagination and determination, and while the Wall itself was an extraordinary piece of military and architectural design, there were other projects, some at local level, probably urged on by the emperor, others perhaps directly ordered and financed by himself or his principal officers. The radical recasting and finishing of the part-completed Flavian town centre at Wroxeter in Shropshire, for example, is probably an instance of Hadrian exerting the sort of pressure Tacitus was describing. On the other hand, in London, to which the hub of government had moved since the reconstruction of the province after Boudicca, the building of an enormous public hall (*basilica*) and accompanying forum (*piazza*) probably did originate with an emperor himself, paid for from central funds and possibly in the first place intended for his own use. It is easy, but wrong, to concentrate on general economic, social or military causes and to underestimate the effect on a province of an imperial visit or imperial wishes. Indeed, as we shall see, the effects of these were to grow stronger.

From early to late Empire

The snapshot of Britain in the middle of the second century presented above is convenient, but it does only represent a moment in a continuous process of change. By the later years of that century an enormously complex series of movements were under way that were radically to alter the pattern of life. In Britain an outbreak of apparently unanticipated and serious frontier warfare, though for the time being satisfactorily concluded, seems to have inflicted a severe shock on the confidence of the province. Henceforth there was a perceived need to spend the local councillors' money on defences of increasingly elaborate sorts in a province most of whose cities and towns had until now been unwalled and open (see illustration of Verulamium gate on p. 69). It may well be that this halted the full flowering of classical urban development in Britain just as it was gaining sufficient momentum to be carried through by the energies and resources of the local notables alone.

The phenomenon appears peculiar to the island. Across the English Channel, the vast majority of towns were not fortified at this time. Their citizens had not yet, in the later second century and the early part of the third, experienced anything to change traditional priorities. That was to come in the later third century, with renewed civil war and terrible barbarian incursions across the Rhine. In Britain, one has the strong impression that already the days had returned when it needed specific imperial interest to spur renewal in the amenities of the major towns. This certainly seems true in London, where it is reasonable to associate a burst of major public works and a general air of revival, in a city that had been going downhill for some time, with the arrival of the Emperor Septimius Severus (193–211) and the whole Imperial Family to conduct spectacular frontier campaigns from the province that had for a while been the base of his most persistent rival for the throne.

In another way, too, the Severan dynasty, by nakedly basing itself on the cultivation of the army, marked the beginning of major change in the empire at large, in the course of which the fairly wide dispersal of wealth and choice in society, on which the classical culture of the Early Empire had been founded, was reversed. A whole series of near-catastrophes in the middle of the century fed and were fed by continuous struggles for the throne. They included massive barbarian pressure on the frontiers, military coup after military coup, and rampant inflation threatening economic collapse.

Britain weathered the storm better than most of the ravaged neighbouring parts of the empire, being largely free from barbarian incursions, but by the end of the third century changes were already apparent, corresponding to those occurring elsewhere, from which Late Roman (or 'Late Antique') culture emerged. The Roman world was at last coming out of its period of near disintegration, and entering the age of renewal for which the names of the emperors Diocletian (AD 284–305) and Constantine the Great (AD 306–337) justifiably provide labelling. It is characteristic of the Romans throughout their history that this revival was marked by a combination of intense conservatism and revolutionary innovation.

In broad terms of society, the effect was a much more rigid structure, with far less social mobility. A sharp decline in the fortunes of the middling orders in society was matched by the growth in wealth of a smaller number of very large landowners. The influence of the latter was balanced by a vast increase in the numbers in the imperial service, as central government expanded to take over civil functions previously performed by local institutions and as the size of the armed forces was massively enlarged.

The enormous direct patronage of the emperors made the court a rival centre of prestige and social influence to that of the older aristocracy, a process which Constantine in particular encouraged, deliberately aiming to create a new nobility of office. Art played an important part in the conscious distancing of the emperor and his family from ordinary life, by deliberately enhancing their majesty. The Byzantine public image of the emperor at the centre of this court was being created. The old families of the senatorial aristocracy tended to see themselves in the fourth century as the guardians of tradition, and most but not all continued to profess the old religions. The court and army, however, largely followed Constantine's lead. The official end of the persecution of Christians with the Edict of Milan in AD 313 ('The Peace of the Church') was, within little more than a decade, followed by the decisive replacement of the Imperial Cult and the Roman pantheon by Christianity as the state religion. A new element was thus added to the alienation of the old aristocracy from the emperors that had become serious since their virtual exclusion from prestigious military commands in the middle of the previous century.

The men surrounding the fourth-century emperor included a new group of the utmost historical importance, army officers of barbarian origin, largely Germanic, who in the course of the century rose to the highest military commands, becoming largely assimilated to their adopted culture. They were not isolated adventurers, though it is clear that single barbarians often sought their fortunes in the Roman service and sometimes returned home subsequently. From the end of the third century certain barbarians were deliberately settled inside the empire in return for regular military service. The precise details and extent of the cultural effect of these immigrants on the arts is a matter for scholarly debate: that they had important influences on the society of the Late Roman Empire is not in dispute.

Centralisation was accelerated by measures taken to tackle the economic crisis, but it was paradoxically accompanied in certain respects by a fragmentation of production and trade. Interruption of long-distance trade in the economic and military chaos of the third century had broken the pattern by which specialist centres of production had served markets dispersed widely over the empire. One curious effect was that previously 'underdeveloped' provinces tended to become much more self-sufficient in industry and agriculture. On the other hand, though fiscal and monetary reform from Diocletian onwards did much to restore stability to the currency, benefits in kind were now a much more important part of remuneration. This applied at every level of employment, from the common soldier to the highest office-holder. Ordinary soldiers, for example, had formerly bought most of their own equipment and uniform out of pay from small craftsmen and dealers. Now, the State found itself setting up a huge system of imperial factories to manufacture and supply weapons and clothing free of charge to the troops. Higher up the scale, privileges and perquisites became increasingly prized. Even the cash donations that were used to reward loyalty now tended to be in the form of ingots rather than money, and for higher ranks periodic gifts of plate served the same purpose. This perfectly suited a society that was more and more obsessed with the outward marks of an increasingly elaborate system of grades and ranks.

Church, state and the arts

Intellectually, the period is marked by the religious revolution by which the
ancient cults were at first neglected and then officially displaced by a series of
competing philosophies and mystery religions, culminating in the triumph
and transformation of Christianity under Constantine the Great. This
resulted artistically in a new range of subjects and new reasons for creating
works of art, though the Church absorbed so much of traditional classical
culture that there was an enormous interchange of motifs between works of
pagan and Christian inspiration. By the middle of the fourth century the
State had taken on the task of enforcing unity and conformity in the Church.
Not only were official attempts made at first to discourage and then to forbid
pagan observances, but heresy became for the chilling first time a political
issue closely bound up with loyalty. Nevertheless, pagan imagery as such did
not fall out of favour, but passed into the merged culture where it is often
impossible to distinguish one from the other.

In this new world, to be a member of the municipal gentry was no
longer the enviable thing it once had been. By the end of the third century
membership of the councils had ceased to be striven for and had become a
compulsory burden. The tradition of local munificence, which had been the
main source of the public adornment of the cities and countryside, including
religious institutions and monuments, had, by Constantine's day, for some
time been dead more or less everywhere. He effectively made sure it would
not revive when he transferred the funds of the municipalities to the State
and confiscated those of the pagan temples. The beneficiaries were the
recipients of imperial bounty, which became of increasing importance and
helped to bind elements in society to the emperor. Most of all, it converted
the Church into a great property-owning institution. Subsequently, following
the example of the emperors, a new practice began to emerge among the rich
of benefactions to the Church. Similarly, the funding of works of Christian
charity, specifically for the benefit of the very poor, started in a small way to
take the place of the old tradition of private patronage of public amenities,
which had aimed at profiting and impressing the citizenry at large.

In the new society personal adornment and the beautification of the private
residence replaced public munificence as the most favoured form of
ostentation. This greatly stimulated such arts and crafts as mosaic (see pp. 85,
88) and the making of gold and silver plate and other objects in precious
metals. The adoption of more colourful fashions in clothes – and the
assumption for formal purposes by civil officers of uniforms and
distingushing marks of rank based on military equivalents – gave new
opportunities to textiles, jewellery and other accessories to dress. In Britain,
the late third century saw the beginning of a process of enlarging, rebuilding
or replacing villas that transformed the picture of the countryside.

In the first half of the fourth century lowland Britain had become a land of
grand country houses and estates. We do not in fact know who the
inhabitants of these late villas were. Had the indigenous gentry been less
effected by disaster than elsewhere? Or did great landowners with estates in
many provinces now decide that peaceful Britain offered greater security than

elsewhere? It is certainly true that Britain as a land of milk and honey becomes a literary cliché in this period. But, whoever these well-heeled citizens were, it is interesting to note that a distinct conservatism in the island is suggested by a relatively high level of continuation, even revival, of the old religious cults.

The smaller towns that served the villas show increased activity at this time. The large towns and cities, however, seem to be less populous. There was probably rather less commercial activity in these larger centres, and changes in their physical appearance may reflect a switch in principal administrative function from being centres of local government to providing locations for branches of central government. The latter were certainly more numerous. At the provincial level, for example, Britain had been divided into two in the early third century, and in the fourth was reorganised into four (and eventually five) provinces, with a new upper tier of government having its seat in London. It can confidently be assumed that other levels of administration similarly proliferated.

Major alterations in the organisation and composition of the Roman armed forces may also have been reflected in changes in the urban settlements. Military technology had certainly developed new forms, and there is reason to suppose that the fortified cities and towns now played an important part in the revised structure of defence. The new thinking is certainly marked architecturally by a much less clear division between forts and fortresses on the one hand and civil towns on the other, by the refortification in the course of the fourth century of many of the towns, following the precepts of Late Roman military architecture, and by the creation of a series of new, mostly coastal, forts in the same Late Roman style.

The legacy of Constantine

It is impossible to avoid the feeling that the remarkable prosperity of Britain in the first half of the fourth century owed more than a little to Constantine the Great himself. His unconstitutional elevation to the throne by his late father's troops occurred at York, and he returned at least once to Britain thereafter. He was a man given to grand gestures in the Hadrianic style. His early capital – Trier – was adorned with great buildings, and his last, Constantinople, was his own creation. He courted popularity, and enriched those who were in his favour. On the basis of the renewed strength of the empire established by his immediate predecessors he gave a new direction to society. Henceforth we have to remember that Roman Britain was part of a world in which society moved round more than one centre. In many respects the north-western quarter of the empire had already come to hang together as a unit, and the new institutions of central government reflected this, centered usually at Trier, on the Moselle. The highest prestige still lay with the senatorial society that revolved round Rome itself, but the City rarely saw the emperor. By the end of Roman rule in Britain the western court had habitually been at Milan. The East, and for long periods the empire as a whole, was governed from Constantinople.

What Constantine most notably failed to achieve was a solution to the problem of political strife at the highest level. His own route to the throne provided the worst possible example. The brilliance of early fourth century Britain survived the power struggles among the sons of Constantine, but collapsed following the failure in AD 353 of an outsider to make good a bid for the throne. A vicious purge of alleged supporters by the surviving son, Constantius II, seems to have done massive damage to society in Britain (and elsewhere). Henceforth Britain, though remaining an important reservoir of resources for the imperial government, seems to have lived at a lower level, subject to increasingly powerful attacks by sea-borne barbarian raiders. To a large extent, periodic recovery from disasters now depended on intermittent imperial intervention by means of task forces sent from Gaul, the most notable being large-scale physical and administrative reconstruction by the Emperor Valentinian I's (AD 364–375) general, the elder Theodosius, following a combined barbarian assault which had occurred in AD 367. From this date, there is a distinct revival detectable archaeologically in the fortunes of the island. By the beginning of the fifth century, despite renewed civil wars and barbarian invasions, there was no particular reason to suspect that the western Roman empire, recently reunited with Constantinople and restored to the control of a single emperor, Theodosius the Great (AD 379–395), was in serious danger of disintegration.

Within ten years, in-fighting in the imperial government, civil war, and incredible mishandling of the much more powerful barbarian nations with whom the empire now had to deal, found Britain isolated. Several factors seem to have been critical in changing the state of Britain. It is not clear just how much Britain was affected by troop withdrawals in this period. Probably most decisive was a cessation in central payments of wages. A final attempt at the imperial throne launched from Britain went sour. In AD 409 the provincials rose and expelled the officials whom the latest claimant had appointed. Neither he nor the central government, now retreated to Ravenna on the Adriatic, was subsequently in a position to regain control.

Post-Imperial Britain

What happened in the next half-century is tantalisingly obscure, all the more so as it must contain the origins both of Anglo-Saxon England and of its Celtic neighbours. The literary sources are meagre and difficult to interpret, and the archaeology bedevilled by the fact that what material there is becomes exceedingly difficult to date. The end of the circulation of new coinage, and the apparent closure of the factories producing pottery on a large scale, leave us without the principal sources of close archaeological dating that serve so well up to this point. At the same time, the dating and significance of the items of metalwork that by some have been thought to prove the presence of Germanic mercenaries are disputed.

What is reasonably certain is that no one can have suspected in AD 409 that this was the end of Roman rule in Britain, least of all the Britons. There is no reason to think that this was a proletarian revolution and even less that it was a national revolt. The people who had most to gain from the expulsion of officials were the landowning class, tired of taxation and conscription of labour from their estates to support an army that now seemed likely to do little to protect them. With luck, they could consolidate their position, for the moment free from burdens, and hope that the eventual reassertion of imperial control would bring better emperors. It is difficult to imagine they would have done anything to hasten that day, or, on the other hand, taken measures to set up anything permanent to take the place of the centralised system in abeyance. The literature does make it clear that a number of 'usurpers' arose. The archaeology of the towns strongly suggests widely differing circumstances in different places, and it is highly probable that the country quite quickly fragmented into a number of embryo kingdoms or city states.

Two important changes were occurring inside the empire at the time the revolt happened in Britain. One was that the Roman aristocracy was largely becoming reconciled to Christianity. The other was a very much greater military reliance on barbarian forces under their own commanders, sometimes paid in cash, sometimes allowed to settle in national groups within the frontiers. In what very little we can dimly detect about society in Britain after the revolt, both these factors seem to be playing a part. In fourth-century Britain, Christianity is present but unspectacular. In the first half of the fifth century, it suddenly seems at the centre of affairs. Individual Britons unexpectedly start to make major impacts on the life of the Church, and the Church in Britain itself becomes so turbulent as to require repeated visits by senior ecclesiastics to deal with internal disputes and heresy. It is the Romano-British landowning class that is at the heart of these movements. It even had a central part in the evangelising of Ireland, for St Patrick was the son of a Romano-British landowner, from whose estate he was kidnapped by Irish pirates while still a youth. This happened early in the fifth century: arguments as to whether it was before or just after the end of Roman rule do not affect the fact that his background was that of an upper-class Roman provincial. On the other side, the theological writings of Pelagius, living in Rome from the end of the fourth century, are not only the earliest known literature produced by a Briton but were responsible for one of the greatest heresies of the early fifth. How strong Pelagianism became in Britain is uncertain, but it is thanks to the fact that the Church felt it necessary to send St Germanus, the statesman-bishop of Auxerre, to tackle it, that we have one clear glimpse of Britain a decade after the break with Roman rule. Germanus is described as engaging in public debate (apparently at Verulamium) with men of influence, 'conspicuous for their riches, brilliant in dress, and surrounded by a fawning multitude'.

It is not difficult to visualise such an aristocratic society surviving in substantial parts of Britain for some considerable time after AD 409, with dependants and workers on their estates – not to mention craftsmen and other providers of goods and services – even more reliant upon them now that the vast patronage of the Roman state had gone. For the arts, the immediate consequences of the break with Rome are likely to have been a complete halt in anything relying on the initiative of central government or on its continuing employment in Britain of a large number of people, civil as well as military. Fairly soon, too, the breakdown of what survived of the money economy must have had direct effects. The middling ranks of society are likely to have been worst affected. We might, in contrast, expect to find archaeologically some continuing work on the country houses of the rich, where they felt themselves secure, or signs of movement to houses in new locations, such as within towns' walls or other defences. We may, too, expect some signs of construction or repair of buildings by usurpers for their own use, within the materials and skills available in the immediate neighbourhood. The latter is probably what is represented by the large timber buildings of the latest period at Wroxeter.

Much the most likely universal development among the surviving men of influence, however, is an even greater interest in moveable works of art, particularly those containing precious metals or jewels. In this new situation, those are likely to have been the most useful assets to possess, and their owners those able to reward barbarian soldiers of fortune with the gifts of portable wealth – and possibly land – which they most valued. It is very likely that some of the finds of Late Roman plate and other valuables in neighbouring barbarian lands (including, it has been suggested, some of the hoards usually attributed to pirates) represent such payments. Moreover, such soldiers themselves formed a market for items of adornment, which is where we find ourselves entering into the territory of early Anglo-Saxon (in Continental terms, 'Migration Period') archaeology. Such employment of individual barbarians or bands of barbarians by Romano-British leaders to replace the regular troops who had been withdrawn – or had deserted *en masse* when no longer paid – is, indeed, not out of line with the fifth century elsewhere.

There are major difficulties of detail in the traditional account of the 'arrival of the Saxons', but it is hard not to feel convinced that somewhere in the middle of the fifth century something happened that hit the way of life of the former provincials so hard that it never revived in a recognisable form. Gildas in the sixth century and Bede in the eighth believed there was a catastrophic mutiny of barbarians recruited to assist in the defence of one of the principal Romano-British regimes. That there were other factors in the collapse of this society seems very likely, but that a mutiny of this dimension proved the turning point is easy to accept.

Part II
Studies in the Individual Arts

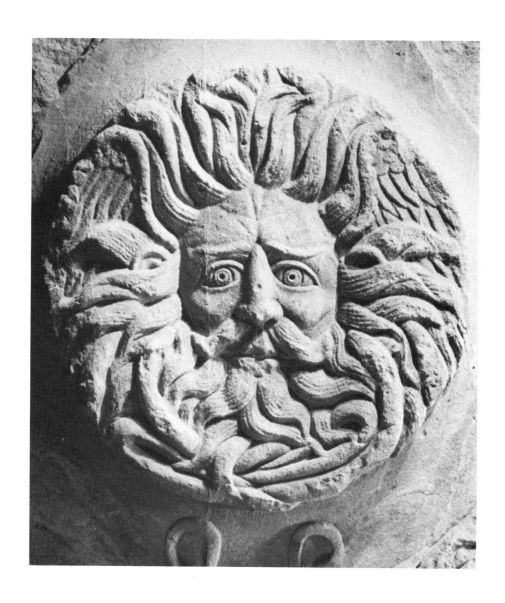

Stone relief of Gorgon's head on the pediment of the temple of Sulis Minerva at Bath (first century).

1 Architecture

BARRY CUNLIFFE

Introduction

The century and a half before the Roman invasion of AD 43 saw the tribes of
south-eastern Britain coming under greater and greater Roman influence
largely as the result of the activities of traders. Italian wine, Spanish oil and
fish sauce and loads of luxury tableware were being imported, while local
rulers were putting Latin legends on their coins, but for all this, building
remained essentially in the native idiom. In the upland areas, where good
stone was easily accessible, circular dry-stone houses were built: in the
lowlands where timber prevailed as the principal building material,
traditional carpentry continued to be practised, but circular house plans
began to be replaced by rectangular, at least in the more civilised parts of the
south east. Mortar and concrete were unknown and sculpture was
rudimentary. This was the land which Rome was to conquer.

In the four decades or so following the invasion of AD 43 the army
provided the greatest influence on architectural development in the new
province. The Roman army was a highly skilled institution containing within
its ranks engineers and surveyors accustomed to large-scale landscape
reorganisation, the layout of roads, the planning of forts, and building in
timber and turf, and in masonry. What they could contribute, above all, was
a sense of order, regularity and rectangularity. In all probability military
engineers were employed in a range of civil projects such as the laying out of
early towns, and quite possibly in the construction of public buildings. In
Verulamium, the precursor of St Albans, the earliest of the timber-built shops
to be recognised in the centre of the town have a distinct regularity about
them reminiscent of military barrack buildings; and at Silchester, beneath the
masonry forum and basilica, excavation has brought to light a timber
courtyard building which was replaced c. AD 80–85 by a massive timber-built
basilica modelled on the *principia* (headquarters building) of a typical fort. It
is difficult to resist the view that a military engineer was seconded to the local
community to help with the layout of their urban centre and the design of its
principal buildings. The classical historian Tacitus provides a possible

context when, writing of the activities of Agricola, who was governor of Britain AD 78–84, he says that he made a deliberate attempt to

give private encouragement and official assistance to the building of temples, public squares and private mansions,

adding that the population was gradually led into the demoralizing temptations of arcades, baths and sumptuous banquets. The unsuspecting Britons spoke of such novelties as 'civilization', when in fact, they were only a feature of their enslavement.

Very early on in the development of the province, the engineers would have prospected for good building stone. The fine oolitic limestone of the Bath region was soon discovered and exploited, and on the 'Island' of Purbeck in Dorset, in the vicinity of Corfe Castle, several local stones were located which could be used for decorative purposes. These included Purbeck marble, a blue fossiliferous limestone which would take a high polish, together with fine-grained white and grey stones which could easily be sawn into elements for *opus sectile* pavements (floors made of geometric shapes of stone) or into strips from which the tesserae for mosaics could be cut. The province could provide adequate supplies of building stone but for high quality decorative veneers, designers had to rely largely on imports.

Although the army could supply planning and engineering advice, and local labour could quickly be taught the skills of mortar and concrete manufacture and basic building, the skilled craftsmen – the mosaicists, stucco workers, wall painters and stone carvers – were immigrant specialists coming mostly from the long-established towns of Gaul, no doubt attracted to Britain by the anticipated demand for their services.

Standing back from the detail, the archaeological evidence, as it is at present available, shows that in the thirty years or so after the invasion, Britain was being introduced to the glories of Roman architecture. Towns were erecting public buildings in masonry (though not on as large a scale as had previously been thought), at least one of the major shrines was being monumentalised in an unprecedented manner, and a number of private patrons in the south east were having country villas built for themselves in the Roman mode. How much of this was pure private enterprise and how much was politically inspired, and paid for by the central government, it is impossible to say. The volume of work, particularly in the sixties, seventies and eighties was sufficiently great to imply the continuous presence of skilled craftsmen from abroad. Many came from the towns of northern Gaul, but the Fishbourne capitals suggest that a few may have come from as far afield as the Mediteranean coast of southern Gaul. Such a presence cannot have failed to have imparted knowledge and training to local workers. It was these men who would have formed the basis of the local schools of craftsmen setting up their practices to serve the increasing demands of the rapidly developing province. At first, patronage is likely to have come from central government but as the province developed, local government and wealthy individuals would have had cause to employ specialists to aggrandise their towns and private houses. By the early second century AD local schools of craftsmen had emerged to meet the continuing demand.

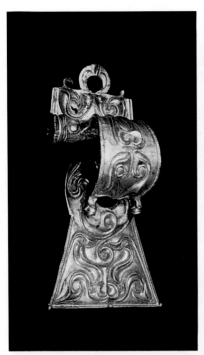

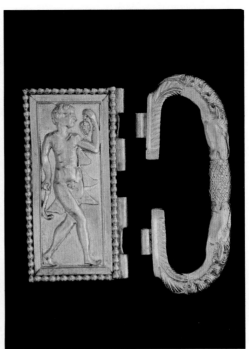

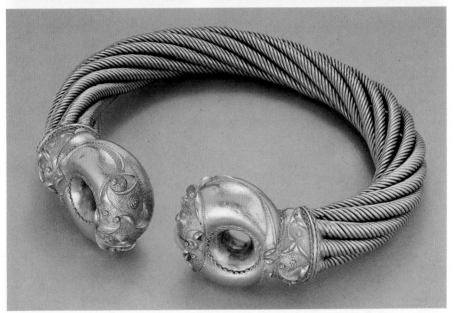

1. *Fan-tail bronze brooch, found at Great Chesters, Northumberland (late first century). (See p. 27)*

2. *Gold belt-buckle from the Thetford Treasure (buried c.390). (See p. 78)*

3. *Ornate gold torque from Snettisham, Norfolk; the late La Tène style of the eastern school. Conceivably this and other goldwork found nearby belonged to the royal house of the Iceni. (See p. 26)*

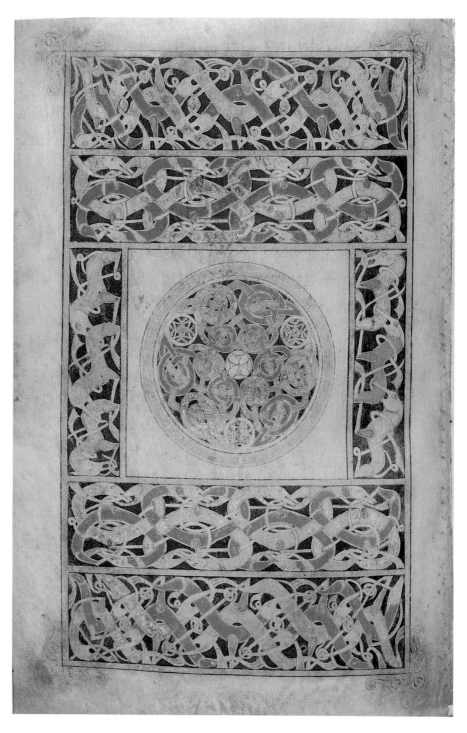

4. Ornamental 'carpet page' facing the opening of the Gospel of St John (mid-seventh century) from the Book of Durrow. (See p. 153)

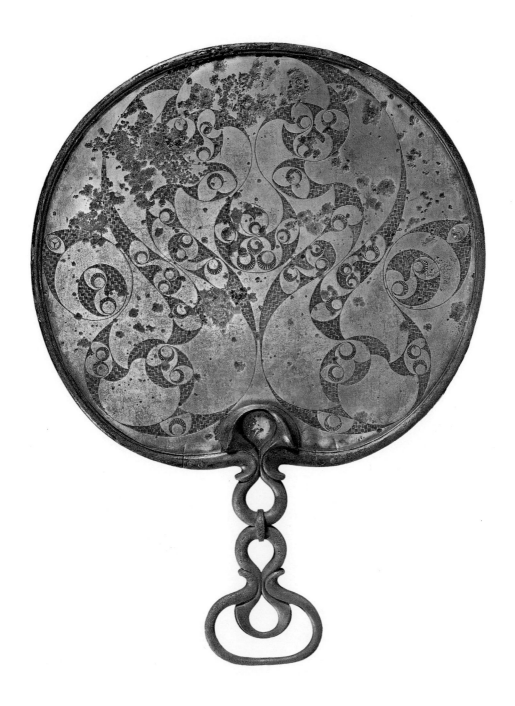

5. *An original British contribution to La Tène art lay in the decoration of hand-mirrors for great ladies. From Desborough, Northamptonshire (1st century* BC*). (See p. 26)*

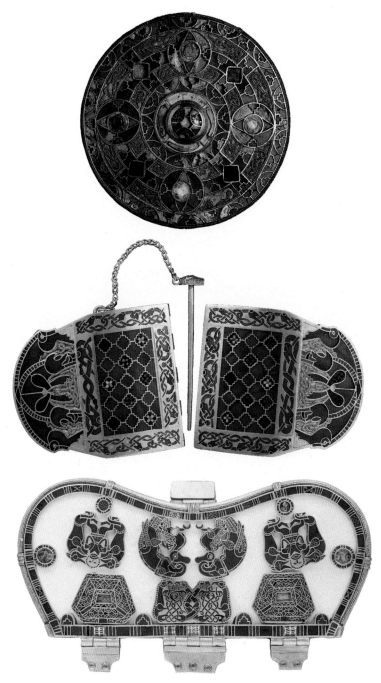

6. The Kingston Brooch, decorated with gold filigree, garnets, glass and shell (sixth century). (See p. 127)

7. Sutton Hoo shoulder-clasp, one of a matching pair, decorated with gold foil and filigree, garnets and millefiori glass (first quarter of the seventh century). (See p. 137)

8. Sutton Hoo purse-lid, part of the magnificent treasure deposited in the burial of an East Anglian king (first quarter of the seventh century). (See p. 137)

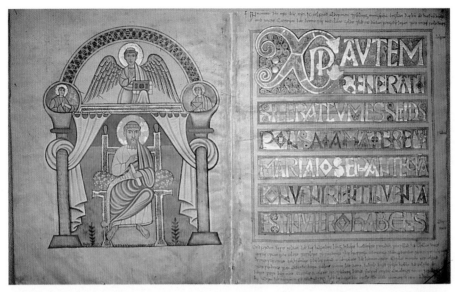

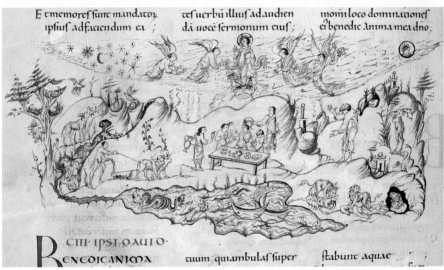

9. *St Matthew accompanied by his symbol the angel, facing the decorated initial page of Matthew I: 18,* Christi autem generatio *(mid-eighth century), from the* Codex Aureus. *(See p. 162)*

10. *Literal illustration of Psalm 103 (c.1000), from the* Harley Psalter. *(See p. 167)*

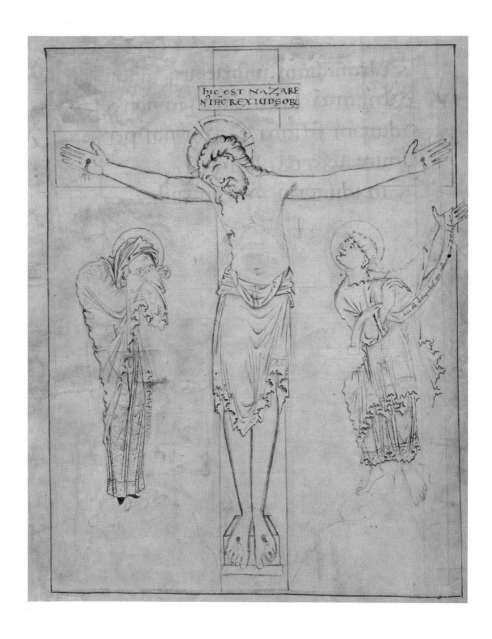

11. Frontispiece illustration of the Crucifixion, with the Virgin Mary and St John the Evangelist attendant (late tenth century), from the Ramsay Psalter. *(See p. 167)*

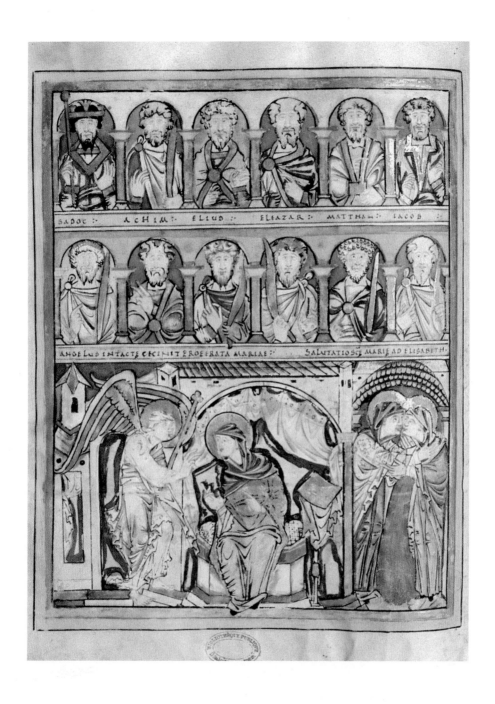

12. *Frontispiece illustration to the Gospel of St Matthew, with the Ancestors of Christ, the Annunciation and the Visitation (late tenth century), from the* Boulogne Gospels. *(See p. 167)*

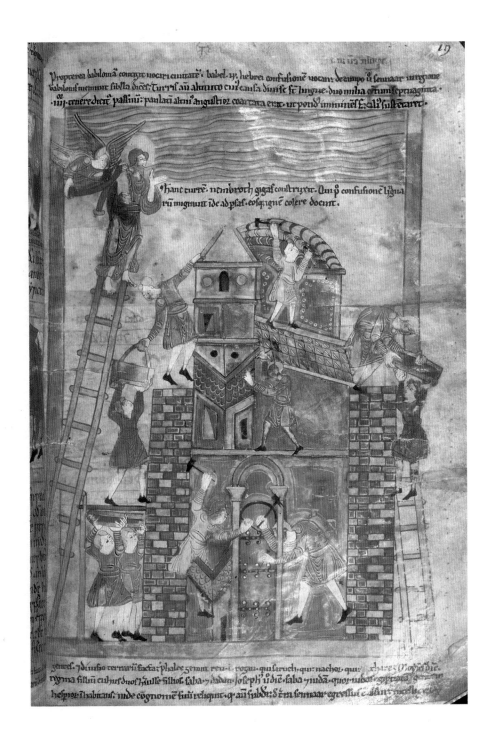

13. Construction of the Tower of Babel, in Anglo-Saxon fashion (second quarter of the eleventh century), from the Old English Hexateuch. *(See p. 174)*

Official and urban monuments of the first century

The earliest of the official building projects to be undertaken in the raw, new province was the construction of a temple to the deified Emperor Claudius, put up in the centre of the colonia at *Camulodunum* (Colchester). Very little is known of the building but its sub-structure (around which Colchester Castle was later to be built) survives in sufficient detail to show that the temple was a massive octostyle (eight-columned) building of classical plan. In front lay an altar surrounded by a screen wall ornamented with marble veneer. This complex, put up in the fifties, was a blatant symbol of Rome's dominance over Britain and an ill-conceived attempt to focus the religious fervour of the indigenous population on Rome. Politically it was a failure and became the focus for the rebellion led by Queen Boudicca in AD 60, but architecturally it must have been a source of wonder to a people totally unused to masonry building – a frightening symbol of power yet at the same time an example for the more forward-looking to follow.

A rather different expression of official architecture, used to symbolise authority, is provided by the 'Monument' at Richborough in Kent. Richborough was almost certainly one of the landing places of the invading force in AD 43 and very soon became the principal supply base for the army. With the completion of Agricola's campaigns in the north, in the mid-eighties, the conquest of Britain was over. It was appropriate, therefore, that the act of conquest should be commemorated, and the decision taken seems to have been to erect a quadrifrons (a two-way monumental arch) at Richborough at what was essentially the gateway to Britain and the beginning of the first military road to the heart of the province. An almost exact parallel, in concept, is the Arch of Trajan at Ancona which stood on the harbour mole. Its inscription records the *accessus Italiae*, the point of access from the sea to the road system leading to all parts of Italy.

Apart from the massive masonry foundation little is known of the actual form of the quadrifrons. It was built of blocks of white oolitic limestone and brown lower greensand carefully cut and clamped together and was faced with white marble from the Luna (Carrara) quarries in Italy. The design seems to have been austere, with half columns and pilasters framing plain areas enlivened only by simple panelled treatment, but in its harsh white severity must have lain a stark grandeur. On top of the monument stood a greater-than-life-size group of bronze statuary, very probably an equestrian group dominated by the emperor, in this case Domitian. The Richborough quadrifrons was no second-rate provincial piece. In size, style and execution it could hold its own among the monumental arches of the empire. It is all the more sad, therefore, that it is reduced now to nothing more than a heavily-weathered concrete foundation.

The Colchester temple and the Richborough quadrifrons were official monuments put up to symbolise different aspects of the Roman control over the peoples of Britannia. There would have been other monuments of this kind, not least in the provincial capital of London, but little is yet known of them.

The official monuments were a constant reminder to the aspiring provincials of what it meant to be a Roman. Hardly surprising, then, that some of the more wealthy, in their desire to embrace Roman style and manners, began to commission elaborate masonry buildings. It was probably in this way that the forum and basilica came to be built in Verulamium during the governorship of Agricola. Verulamium had been raised in status to a *municipium*, giving its residents certain legal rights in Roman law (see chapter 2). Growing affluence and pride, combined with official encouragement, led to the commissioning of an impressive town centre, designed in Gallic manner, with the main forum area dominated by three temples, perhaps dedicated to the Capitoline triad, Neptune, Minerva and Juno. It is the only example of the kind yet known in Britannia and must have been designed by a civilian expert brought in for the purpose, probably from Gaul.

Fishbourne Palace and the south coast villas

In the south east of Britain, particularly in Sussex and Kent, there is growing evidence for the erection of a number of elaborate masonry buildings within the first half century after the invasion. One of the best known of these is the villa, or palace, at Fishbourne, near Chichester, in Sussex, the early development of which has been tentatively linked to the career of the local client king, Tiberius Claudius Cogidubnus.

The earliest masonry building at Fishbourne dates to the sixties and is

Model of a late first century Roman villa at Fishbourne, near Chichester, Sussex.

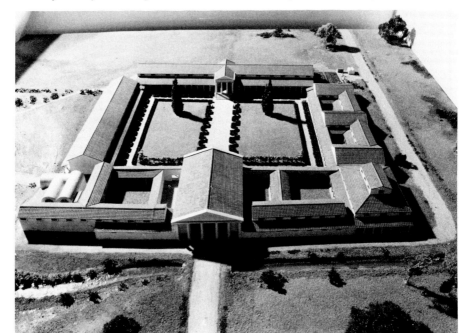

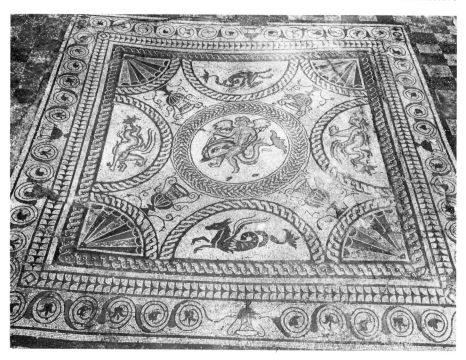

Mosaic floor at Fishbourne Palace (c.160 AD).

referred to as the 'protopalace'. Although the plan is by no means completely known, it can be seen to consist of a bath suite attached to a colonnaded courtyard, both being flanked by a range of rooms. The plan itself would be unremarkable were it not for its very early date in the British context. What is surprising is the elaboration of the decoration. Although little survives *in situ* it is possible to show that the floors were decorated with mosaics and with *opus sectile* – patterns made up from geometric shapes of coloured stone. The walls were plastered and painted in firm, near-primary, colours providing a simple 'architectural' framing to small figurative paintings, one of which was a harbour scene, executed with very considerable skill.

Of the actual architecture of the building there is little that can be said except that somewhere within it was a set of Corinthian columns, incorporating grotesque human masks in leafy frames in place of the usual rosettes on the abacus (uppermost flat element of the capital). The workmanship is not of the highest quality but for a southern British site in the sixties the columns would have been a sight of stunning novelty. Certain stylistic considerations suggest that they were carved by southern Gaulish craftsmen familiar with Mediterranean styles, who must have joined the small army of craftsmen – stucco workers, painters, mosaicists – brought in specifically for the contract. It is tempting to see here the hand of a single organising architect able to create a team suitable to provide for his customer's demands.

The protopalace remained in use for a comparatively short time before, in the mid-late seventies, it was incorporated into a vast new palatial building more than 150 m square. The building is without parallel and was clearly created for a person of considerable wealth and status. It was planned in the form of four wings arranged around a large central garden, planted with a formal arrangement of hedges and other vegetation emphasising the wide path across the centre which served as the main east–west axis. The building was evidently designed to perform two discrete, but interlocked, functions, one public the other private. The public domain consisted of a massive entrance hall, enlivened internally by a small centrally placed pool and fountain, which opened out on to the central path. In front, on the west side of the garden, lay a long range of rooms raised a metre and a half above the garden and the rest of the building and unified by a continuous colonnade 100 m long broken only by a grand portico fronting the central room. All the rooms of the west range opened from a colonnaded verandah, and the corridors around it were designed as wide *ambulatories*. The central room, with bench-lined apsidal recess and polychrome mosaic of exquisite quality, is most likely to have been an audience chamber.

The other public space was a massive aisled hall built into the north-east corner of the palace complex and opening outwards on to a fronting verandah. Apart from the impressive volume of the room it appears to have been of little elaboration. It may have been an assembly space of some kind but was clearly not part of the more formal life of the palace.

The private accommodation divides into two. The north and east ranges were composed of suites of rooms opening on to colonnaded courtyards, while the southern range was unified by a long southern verandah looking over a large 'wilderness' garden to the sea beyond. It is tempting to interpret the north and east ranges as accommodation for visitors. If so then the north range, with its more spacious rooms, was for those of higher rank: the east range accommodation consisted of simpler suites fronting larger communal courtyards.

The south wing, with its back turned on the main complex, its secluded southern garden and the proximity of the bath suite, is most likely to have been the residential range.

The entire building was decorated throughout with mosaic floors, mainly black and white, and with painted walls and ceilings, but the most impressive aspect of the complex was the skill with which the spaces were arranged to provide visual cohesion and yet variety. The architect had a keen eye for creating vistas, especially half-seen vistas, and for changing the mood by providing dramatic spacial contrasts. In this, and the sheer scale of the enterprise, lie the significance of the Fishbourne palace to Romano-British architecture.

Three of the structural elements are notable: the two massive halls in the east wing and the audience chamber in the west wing. The halls were huge structures involving spans of 21 and 25 m: the technical skills required, and the knowledge of the load-bearing potentials of the materials and the bedrock, would have been available only to an expert thoroughly conversant with the construction of monumental buildings. The audience chamber, though smaller, was a carefully contrived piece of design. It was roofed with a stuccoed vault and, to cope with the considerable lateral thrust which such a structure would have created, the foundation widths of the side walls were increased while the two flanking corridors were vaulted to create buttressing masses. A hall of this kind, with its high vaulted roof, painted in bright blue and purple, and its apsidal recess covered with a semi-dome, was very similar in concept to the audience chamber of Domitian's palace in Rome – it was designed to show the occupant sitting in majesty, as it were, like a god in heaven.

Whoever was responsible for the erection of the Fishbourne palace in the seventies, whether the local client king Cogidubnus or another high-ranking Roman official, it was clearly a person of enormous wealth able to command a team of Mediterranean specialists thoroughly conversant with current fashion. A project of this magnitude, which must have taken years to complete, cannot have failed to have had an impact on local susceptibilities. It is hardly surprising, therefore, that other broadly contemporary buildings should be erected in the south east, adopting elements of planning and design represented in a more cohesive form at Fishbourne. It may well be that surveyors and craftsmen employed on the Fishbourne project found employment under other patrons. Certainly there seems to have been a rash of fine villas erected at this time in Sussex and Kent at Pulborough, Angmering, Southwick, Eastbourne and Eccles and there may well have been others.

Bath: the sanctuary of Sulis Minerva in the first and second centuries

Individual patronage must have created a considerable demand for skilled architects and craftsmen in the second half of the first century, not only for the rural building projects but also in the newly-emerging urban centres and at well-endowed sanctuaries. Of the latter, the sanctuary of Sulis Minerva at Bath provides an informative example.

At Bath, three hot springs emerge from the depths of the earth. So dramatic a phenomenon cannot have failed to have impressed on the primitive mind a feeling of awe and reverence and there can be little doubt that the springs were regarded as sacred in the pre-Roman period – the preserve of the goddess Sulis. Immediately after the invasion of AD 43 a Roman military road was driven through the centre of the shrine, quite possibly as a deliberate act of desecration. For twenty years or so nothing more seems to have been done until the late sixties when the road was removed and the entire complex fitted out with a remarkable architectural ensemble in purely classical form. Why this change of attitude should have been adopted it is impossible to say. One possibility is that local patronage was instrumental in the renovation but another, more plausible, explanation is that the monumentalising of the shrine was an officially inspired act – an attempt by the government, in the aftermath of the disastrous Boudiccan rebellion, to establish a rapprochement with the indigenous population by aggrandising one of the prime native shrines. Significantly the presiding goddess was now known as Sulis Minerva – a conflation of native and classical – symbolising the unity of the two traditions. If this explanation is correct then Bath provides another example of the use of architecture for political ends.

The first-century building programme at Bath was ambitious. With a temple, a bathing establishment and probably also a theatre, the shrine of Sulis Minerva took on the appearance of a grand sanctuary in the Gaulish manner. It was designed for the service of pilgrims coming to seek a cure. They could attend sacrifices in the temple precinct, immerse themselves in the curative waters in the baths or attend a religious performance in the theatre. What is most remarkable is that, in spite of being in the centre of a now-thriving city, so much of the Roman structures survive and, apart from the theatre, the exact location of which is still uncertain, virtually the entire plan of the temple complex and the baths has been recovered, together with significant parts of the superstructure.

The first-century temple was a purely classical structure set on a high podium. The facade was tetrastyle (four columned) Corinthian and supported an elaborately sculptured pediment. Stylistic consideration of the capitals and the cornice mouldings of the pediment suggests that northern Gaulish craftsmen were brought in for the job and they, too, presumably carved the famous 'Gorgon's' head pediment. The iconography is as complex as it is fascinating. In the centre is a fearsome male head, with facial characteristics so commonly seen in Celtic art, surrounded by a mat of hair and beard, rather in the style of a classical Gorgon, but here aggressively male and not unlike representations of Oceanus or a river god. The head is held aloft on a shield by two winged Victories. Beneath are attributes of Minerva: two helmets, one Corinthian representing her martial aspect, the other with an owl perched on top reflecting her wisdom. The lower angles are filled with tritons. The pediment defies detailed analysis but is clearly meant to communicate the power of the conflated deity, held victorious above the world. The overall design, and most of the iconography, are purely Roman, but the central head is so blatantly Celtic in style that the pediment is best seen as a deliberate and highly successful mixing of the two traditions.

The temple building was fronted by an open area carefully paved with lias limestone flags upon which was set the sacrificial altar elaborately carved with depictions of the gods of whom Jupiter, Mercury, Hercules and Bacchus have been positively identified together with less certain renderings of Mars and Juno. The entire complex, including the sacred spring, was enclosed within a colonnaded precinct.

The containment of the spring was a masterpiece of engineering. First, all the mud and sand choking the top of the fissure was removed and then a wall of massive limestone blocks was built around the main outlets, to a height of two metres. When complete the inner face of the wall was lined with thick sheets of lead and the base angle sealed with concrete to prevent leakage. An added refinement was an outfall drain, leading from the bottom of the reservoir, closed by a bronze sluice. All the time that the sluice was shut the reservoir would remain full, the excess water being channelled off from the top to fill the Great Bath. In this way the reservoir provided the necessary head of water to serve the bathing establishment. But there was also an added

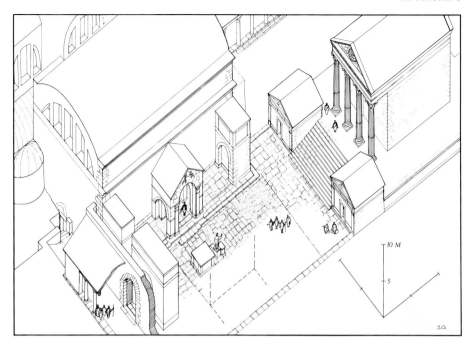

Reconstruction of the Roman temple of Sulis Minerva at Bath (first century).

subtlety: the depth of water ensured that the sand, brought up by the force of the spring, would not flow off into the baths but would settle in the reservoir. The purpose of the sluice and outfall drain was to allow the system to be scoured out from time to time as the sediment built up.

The bathing establishment, in its first-century form, was simply designed and executed in plain, massive masonry. It was arranged in two units separated by an impressive hall, which served as part of the *frigidarium* (cold room) and provided a carefully contrived view northwards, across the sacred spring, to the altar beyond. To the west lay the suite of artificially heated rooms, while to the east was the huge hall containing the thermal swimming bath with two smaller baths beyond.

The architecture of the Great Bath was comparatively simple. Two sets of aisle piers took the main weight of the roof. At ground floor level they formed an arcade framed with plain pilasters supporting an entablature. Above, it seems that the framing was contrived with engaged half-columns, instead of pilasters, and between were lunettes providing clerestory light. The aisles on either side were enlivened with rectangular and semicircular *exedrae* (recesses), for the bathers to sit in, and were probably roofed at first floor level. The structural principles involved were not dissimilar to those of the broadly-contemporary Fishbourne entrance hall though the Great Bath hall was a little larger.

There is sufficient structural evidence to show that the baths, spring and temple were laid out together as part of a single scheme. They were also carefully designed around two visual axes, crossing at the altar, an east–west axis through the temple, altar and the monumental entrance to the precinct, and a north–south axis across the hall of the *tepidarium* (warm room) and through the spring to the altar. Such a contrived scheme suggests a high level of planning. This, together with the engineering skills involved in the construction of the baths, both hydraulic and structural, and the decorative craftsmanship lavished on the temple, leave little doubt that an army of Continental specialists were at work in Bath in the sixties and seventies.

The Emperor Hadrian's itinerary when he visited Britain in AD 122 is unknown but it is quite likely that a man of such intellectual curiosity would have visited the great sanctuary at Bath. If so he may have been responsible for making a dedication or inspiring others to do so. Such may be the context of a remarkable circular temple (or *tholos*), known only from fragments found in the nineteenth century. Sufficient survives to suggest a circular building of diameter exactly equivalent to the width of the temple. Its columns were unfluted but with Corinthian capitals, which supported a highly decorated entablature carved on both the outer and inner faces. The frieze depicted a series of panels in some of which were figures, probably of the gods. The inner face bore a continuous flowing vine scroll. The decoration of the architrave incorporated a Greek-key motif. Stylistically the carving is of the first half of the second century and can be closely paralleled at Sens, in northern Gaul. The decoration of the Bath tholos is so unlike the known local schools of sculpture that an immigrant craftsman was probably involved.

Circular temples in classical mode are most unusual in north-western Europe. They developed in the Greek world and were adopted in Italy in the first century BC, at the time when Roman culture was experiencing a high degree of Hellenisation. Hadrian was well known for his love of things Greek. Had he wished to make a dedication at the sanctuary of Sulis Minerva, at Bath, an elegant tholos would have been both appropriate to the setting and in keeping with his susceptibilities. The suggestion is persuasive but unless an inscription is discovered, we will never know.

Where the tholos stood in relation to the known buildings is unproven, but the most likely possibility is that it occupied a separate precinct in front (that is, to the east) of the temple of Sulis Minerva. The corner of a precinct has been identified, and the fragments of the monument were found quite close, but much of the crucial area is now obscured by the abbey. Such an arrangement with two temples, one of which was circular, set in adjacent precincts aligned on the same axis, is known at the Gallo-Roman shrine at Sanxay in the Loire valley. Thus, in spite of the novelty of its classical tholos, the shrine at Bath can be seen to be within a north-west European tradition.

The next phase of development at Bath dates to the late second century and is of particular interest both from an architectural point of view and in terms of changing religious practices. This was a time of extensive rebuilding. The temple itself was now surrounded by a raised platform creating an ambulatory, and a new low-level frontage was added, incorporating a flight of steps between two flanking rooms, or side chapels. The arrangement was such that it no way obscured or detracted from the view of the original temple, which remained visually dominant, but the overall effect was to create a structure closely similar to the traditional form of Romano-Celtic temple, with a *cella* (main chamber) set within an ambulatory. The most reasonable explanation is that modifications were required by a change in ritual, away from the purely classical to a more indigenous style of practice.

At about the same time dramatic changes were happening at the spring and the baths. The spring, which had hitherto been completely open, was enclosed within a large hall roofed with a masonry vault. Access was now restricted to a small door in the north wall and three large openings in the south wall, through which the spring could be seen from the frigidarium of the baths. The restricted north door probably served for purely ritual purposes whereas the larger southern openings were used by the public, so that they could approach the water to commune with the deity and to deposit their offerings.

The motive for enclosing the spring can only have been dictated by changes in ritual. What had been open to all was now restricted and mysterious. Visitors had now to approach the sacred waters along a darkened corridor and the only light penetrating the chamber would have come in through lunettes set high up in the ends of the vault. The changes, therefore, introduced a new mystery to the proceedings.

The vaulting of the spring was an effective piece of engineering. Sufficient remains to show that it was constructed on a skeleton of brick ribs and a 'backbone' of stone wedge-shaped voussoirs, with the intervening spaces filled with hollow box tiles to reduce the weight. The vault sprang from the wall tops but its base was embedded in a haunching of rubble and concrete disguised as an attic storey.

At the same time as the spring was being enclosed the entire bathing establishment was reroofed with similar masonry vaults. It was a colossal undertaking which involved strengthening all the walls and piers to take the greatly increased lateral thrust. The calculations involved and the construction of the complex of timber centring upon which the new vaults were to be constructed, would have required engineering skill of a high order. The construction of concrete vaults and domes was now normal practice for Romano-British architects used to building bath suites, but the sheer scale of the problem posed by the baths at Bath would have taxed the most competent. That it was largely successful is a comment on the building expertise that was now on call in Britain.

Forum–basilica complexes in the second century

The second century saw the consolidation of the established urban centres. Although most of the domestic buildings – the shops and the private houses – continued to be erected in insubstantial materials, usually with timber framing infilled with wattle and daub, public buildings were now built, or replaced, in masonry. So it was in the cantonal capital of *Calleva* (Silchester in Hampshire) where excavations have shown that the timber forum and basilica complex of c. AD 80–85 was swept away in the second quarter of the second century to make way for a masonry structure of comparable size and plan. The new basilica was adorned with Corinthian columns supporting capitals carved from oolitic limestone. Stylistically the carving is reminiscent of north-eastern Gaulish work, though whether they were carved by a local school or immigrants is unknown. Most likely they were the work of local craftsmen trained in techniques and styles introduced half a century or so earlier.

The Silchester capitals are closely comparable in style to examples from Cirencester, Gloucester and Caerwent – a distribution which hints at the sphere of influence of a single school based in the Cotswolds where good quality oolitic limestone was close at hand. Indeed a working yard belonging to one sculptor, Sulinus, has been identified at Cirencester.

The early second century was the time when a number of forum-basilica complexes were built: Silchester has already been mentioned; Wroxeter is dated by an inscription to AD 129–130; the capitals from the Cirencester and Caerwent basilicas hint at an early second century date; and the London basilica was rebuilt in grand style in c. AD 100–130. The buildings at Leicester and Caistor-by-Norwich are more broadly dated to the Late Hadrianic or Antonine period (c. AD 125–175). This great upsurge in building activity may well have resulted from the Emperor Hadrian's visit to Britain in AD 122 when he set in train the building of the northern frontier defences which bear his name. The Imperial presence in the province may have given the southern cities confidence in their future and provided the spur needed to revive civil building programmes.

London: the monumental arch of the third century

Bath has been considered in some detail because it provides by far the best range of evidence available for major buildings and their superstructues, but comparable enterprises must have existed in some of the other major towns. A hint of such a complex comes from London where the excavation of the fourth-century riverside wall yielded a number of sculptured blocks reused in the wall foundation. The majority of them belonged to two monuments, a screen wall and a monumental arch.

The screen wall was highly decorated: it was divided into three zones by plain pilasters and within each zone were a pair of niches each supporting a smaller than life-size deity, Vulcan and Minerva, Mercury and Diana, and an unknown deity paired with Mars. The original location of the screen is unknown but it probably came from a temple precinct.

The arch was altogether more impressive. The parts of the upper storey which survived showed it to have been decorated with full length representations of classical deities including Minerva and Hercules, with busts of the seasons in roundels set in the spandrels. Above, in the attic frieze were busts of other classical deities, representing the days of the week. The style of the carving and the general arrangement of the individual elements show a broad similarity with comparable monuments in northern Gaul and

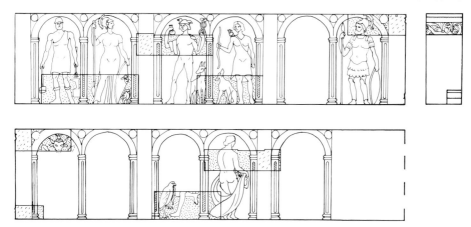

The Screen of Gods at the Roman riverside wall, London
(restored elevation; early third century).

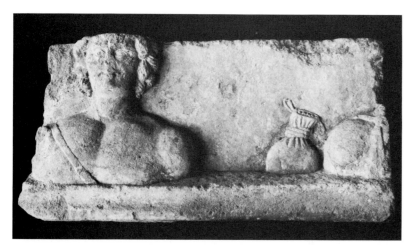

Block from the frieze of the Roman monumental arch in London, showing Mars and purse
(early third century).

the Rhineland but there is nothing about the London arch, or the screen, which demands the hand of an immigrant craftsman. The design and execution are assured but within the competence and repertoire of native British workshops.

Stylistic considerations suggest a date in the early third century for the arch and probably also the screen, and this raises the intriguing possibility that they may have been inspired by the visit to Britain of the Emperor Septimius Severus and his wife Julia Domna in AD 208. Severus remained in Britain from AD 208 until AD 211 and his son Geta was based in London as governor of Britannia Superior. Imperial patronage or civic pride could well have led to the building programme of which the arch and screen are the only surviving fragments. Nothing is known of the building complex to which they belonged (always assuming they come from the same building) but,

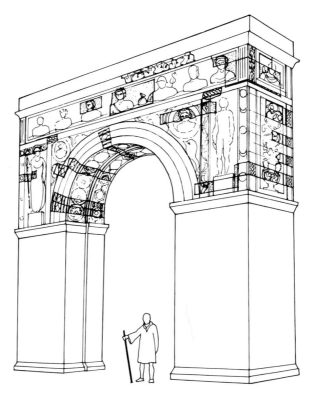

Reconstruction of the Roman monumental arch in London (early third century).

given the predominantly religious iconography, it is most likely to have been a temple. The monumental arch would have been appropriate as the precinct entrance while the screen wall may have enclosed, or partly enclosed, the altar. Other arrangements are possible, but unless the actual site is discovered and excavated, we can only speculate. Wherever it lay the building had only a short life: erected in the early third century, it was demolished for reuse in the foundations of the riverside wall in the late fourth.

Bath: the temple precinct in the third and fourth centuries

For some indication of the architecture of the late third and fourth centuries we must return, finally, to Bath. In spite of the care taken to ensure the stability of the reroofing programme, it seems that the north wall of the reservoir enclosure was inadequately founded and after a while the thrust of the vault began to force it forwards. The only solution to the problem was to add massive buttresses but this meant encroaching upon the precinct immediately in front of the temple. The solution adopted was to build three buttresses along the wall but to disguise them as architectural embellishments. The two end masses, close to the corners, were recessed and arched while the centre buttress was designed as a quadrifrons (a two-way arch) providing a grandiose approach to the doorway leading to the reservoir. More surprising is the form which its main facade took: it appears to have incorporated an arch set within a pediment – an arrangement known as a Syrian arch because of its popularity in the eastern provinces. Sufficient survives of the pediment to give some idea of its decorative scheme. In the centre, above the arch, is a rock from which water flows, and above is a roundel depicting Sol held aloft by two nymphs. The symbolism is clear enough; Sol, the sun god, is the protector of the sacred spring.

To balance the facade incorporating the buttress, a new screen wall (or front of a building otherwise unknown) was erected to the north of the altar facing the quadrifrons. The screen consists of a series of fluted pilasters between which were shell-canopied niches depicting gods, with smaller recesses above containing cupids playing the parts of seasons. In the attic above the screen was a pediment containing, in a central roundel, Luna, goddess of the moon.

The balance in the iconography is deliberate: Luna faces Sol, both controlling a hemisphere, Luna the dark north, Sol the light south. Beyond them, to the west and rising high above, is the pediment of the temple of Sulis Minerva, the god-head held aloft by the Victories, commanding all. Clearly the sculptural decoration was carefully contrived to inform the initiated about the gods and their relationships, and about the powers presiding in the sacred place.

Conclusion

The London arch and screen and the late third- or early fourth-century modifications to the temple precinct at Bath, though provincial work, reflect what was happening generally to art and architecture in the late Roman world. Innovatory ideas were no longer coming from Italy but instead we find major developments occurring in north Africa, particularly in the third century, and in the eastern provinces. The London arch, in its decorative style, is a distant echo of Severan work in Africa, while the Syrian arch at Bath, and the appearance of the sun god Sol in a dominant position on the Bath quadrifrons, are reflections of what was happening in the east. Together these examples show that, even in the fourth century, Britain was still sharing in empire-wide developments.

With so few examples to build on, and so much more to be found, it is unwise to generalise. Yet the overriding impression one gets is that the energetic investment in architecture of high quality in the late first century, bringing to Britain the most up-to-date styles, soon gave way to a provincialism in the early second century. Even so the native craftsmen and builders remained aware of Continental developments and were prepared to modify their repertoire while serving the undemanding needs of their patrons.

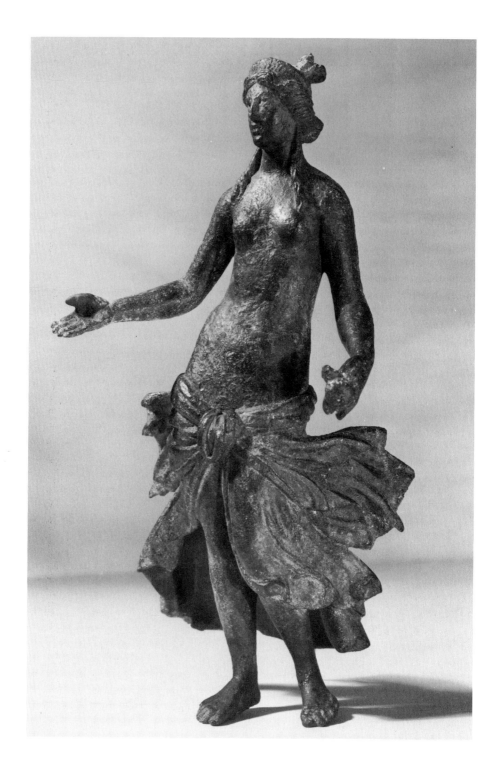

Bronze statuette of Venus, found at Verulamium and probably made in Gaul (height 20 cm; early second century).

2 Verulamium: Social and Artistic Development

SHEPPARD FRERE

The towns of Roman Britain were usually so well sited in relation to communications and the geography of settlement that they are still centres of population, and the remains are consequently damaged and largely inaccessible. Occasionally, however, some special factor caused abandonment at the end of the Roman period or a shift of position: today these open sites are of great value because of what they can reveal to aerial survey and to excavation. Verulamium is one such open site, for in the early middle ages the focus of population shifted eastwards across the river to the vicinity of St Albans Abbey on the opposite hillside.

Excavation in 1930–34 and in 1955–61, although confined to a fraction of the whole, threw a good deal of light on the town-planning, public and private buildings and history of the place. Coins of the pre-Roman king Tasciovanus carrying the mint-mark VERLAMIO, together with remains of contemporary settlement, show that the place was not a new creation of the Romans in a hitherto vacant area, but one which began as a native capital in the late first century BC; it was already a centre of population. Soon after the invasion of AD 43 a fort was established at the intersection of the new Roman Watling Street with another road from Colchester to Silchester. But military occupation was shortlived, for c. AD 50 a new city was established, probably with the charter of a municipium, and defences were erected around it. However, these did not save the place from sack during the uprising of Queen Boudicca in AD 60, and for a while there was setback. But by the end of Vespasian's reign in AD 79 a new beginning had been made, possibly with official aid and thereafter progress was slow but steady, leading to expansion of the inhabited area and to larger and more permanent forms of housing.

Until recently our picture of Romano-British cities was much influenced by the early excavations at Silchester (1890–1908) and by the results of aerial photography at other open sites. Both approaches emphasised the large masonry houses which show best from the air and which were the main discoveries yielded by the limited skills of early excavators. It is only in the post-war period that we have come to realise that these masonry buildings were mainly a phenomenon of the second and later centuries and that, apart from a few public buildings, the early cities of Roman Britain were built in half-timber. A whole new dimension has been added to our understanding which can still best be illustrated at Verulamium.

The Roman government, unlike modern ones, had no huge army of civil servants to run its affairs; but experience showed that if they supported the richer classes, the richer classes in turn would look after the rest. At first the richer classes were identical with the old native nobility; but one of the advantages of the Roman social system was the ease by which, if a man made money, he could change his class, or at any rate the class of his children. The introduction of Roman rule thus spelt social change, for the way lay open for new energetic businessmen to supplant or at least to supplement the old ruling nobility. In the early days of the occupation there was naturally military government; but the troops were urgently needed elsewhere, and it was important to press ahead with the establishment of reliable local authorities; this meant the establishment of cities, for in the ancient world the city was the natural centre of civilised life and administration.

Urban centres in Roman Britain accordingly fell into two types. Those intended to be the administrative centres of regions received the imprint of formal Roman town-planning, whereas the lesser centres, serving only as local markets, were left to develop piecemeal. Regular street grids and public buildings such as a town hall (forum with basilica), theatre or amphitheatre, monumental arches or large public baths were provided to serve the purpose, and to mark the prestige, of the administrative centres (civitas capitals),

Verulamium: plan of central area.

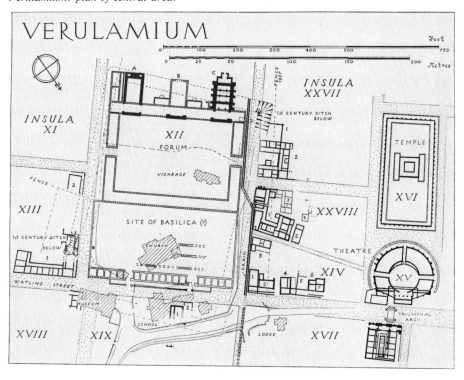

which were also intended to be the homes of the governing classes, where their children could be educated in Roman ways.

At Verulamium these developments took time to reach fruition. The huge forum covering almost two hectares is dated by an inscription of AD 79; the cost of construction must have been enormous, involving as it did transport of immense quantities of building-stone from a distance and the employment of architects and masons from Italy or Gaul: we may believe that a government subsidy was made, as a remark of Tacitus implies. At Silchester, a smaller city, the contemporary forum and basilica were only built of wood.

Other early buildings at Verulamium are almost all of half-timber, constructed in a technique certainly introduced by the army. Indeed, granted the urgent need of the government to have the cities built, it seems likely that army technicians were seconded to oversee the work. One of the earliest structures known is a row of shops along the main street, which closely resembles a military barrack. As there were over nine shops under a single roof, the block probably had a single landlord who let out the premises to his retainers or freedmen specialising in metalworking, bakeries and other services. It is interesting to observe that, in later rebuildings of these shops during the first half of the second century, some expanded at the expense of others and some even became free-standing, as if individual proprietors with increased prosperity were able to buy their premises and set up on their own. Thus some social advancement may be deduced.

Until the second century, however, there is little sign of large private

Reconstruction of the south-east gate, originally built for the second-century earthwork defences and later incorporated in the city wall.

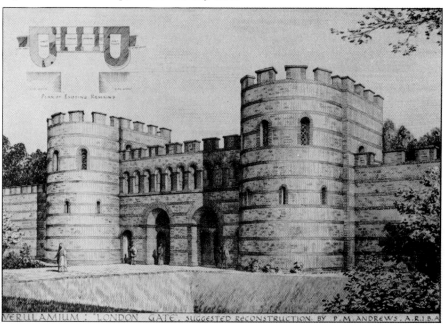

houses suitable for the landowners themselves, and it may be that it took time to convince them of the advantages of taking up urban residence.

By the reign of Hadrian (AD 117–138) some houses were already furnished with tessellated and even mosaic floors in the full Roman manner – mosaic pavements were patterned, whereas 'tessellated' is used of floors with plain (usually large) red, grey or brown *tesserae* with no pattern (a room might have a mosaic in the middle and tessellation round the edges). The walls were increasingly decorated with colourful painting reminiscent of Pompeii. These were status symbols of growing wealth and sophistication; in some of them the large dining room can be identified, another hallmark of the Romanised way of life.

It seems likely from their designs that the mosaicists working in mid-second-century Verulamium were a branch of a Colchester firm; their repertoire for the most part consisted of geometric or floral designs. Figured mosaics are rare in towns, but Verulamium can show a pair of dolphins playing in the jets of a fountain, and a lion bearing off the head of a stag. Both are of purely classical inspiration. The wall paintings were certainly at first the work of immigrant craftsmen, for example the mid-first-century still-life of a lyre, and a bow with its quiver. But again it was not long before local schools of painters came into being. The most common designs show panels, often in red or green, divided by alternated candelabra. A house of c. AD 180 has yielded a ceiling decorated with doves and a wall carrying a scroll of

Head of Neptune; central panel of mosaic found at Verulamium (late second century).

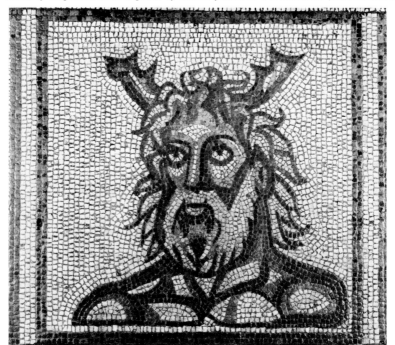

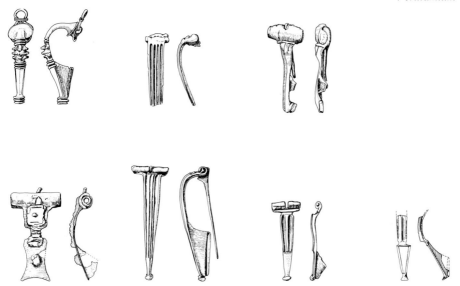

Bronze brooches found at Verulamium (first century).

acanthus leaves peopled by alternating panther heads and pheasants. All
these features show the strong attractions offered by the Roman way of life.

Already by the end of the first century a market precinct had been built
containing nine shops either side of a courtyard. At least two temples also
existed though neither was of classical type. Half a century later a theatre was
provided. Like all ancient theatres this was of course open-air, and the
seating was carried on an earthen ramp. Its relationship with the nearby
temple recalls similar relationships in Gaul and suggests that the Verulamium
theatre had primarily a religious function, designed to accommodate large
congregations during sacred rites. Before the middle of the second century we
have evidence for a piped water supply and for plank-lined sewers along the
streets; the aqueduct which brought water to the city has, however, not yet
been located. All this shows that the amenities proper to a city were gradually
being provided. They also illustrate the enormous influence of Roman
civilisation upon the populace.

There was obvious prosperity in mid-second-century Verulamium, with a
great deal of mercantile and petty manufacturing activity in the shops and
workshops lining the main streets: this included the lathe-turning of bronze
vessels for the table or kitchen, blacksmithing and the sale of foodstuffs, and
even a goldsmith's workshop. The city was one of the main outlets for the
products of the very important local pottery industry, which in its heyday
exported vessels as far afield as central Scotland; it was also, of course, the
market centre for a wide region round, where the agricultural surplus of the
villas was exchanged for manufactured or imported goods. Tablewares of
Gaulish red-gloss samian and vessels of Rhenish glass could be purchased in
the shops together with wine and olive oil from Spain and Gaul; no doubt,
too, locally-woven cloth was on sale.

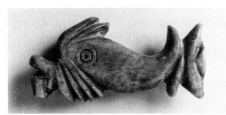

*Dolphin ornament of polished bone
(4.8 cm; third or fourth century).*

Verulamium was also a religious centre. Here the local rites of the cult of
the emperor and his deified predecessors and the cult of the city's patron
goddess would be observed in addition to the worship of other deities, native
in origin but soon assimilated with their Roman equivalents. Who these gods
were is unfortunately unknown because no inscriptions survive to inform us;
but there were at least three temples of the local Romano-Celtic type as well
as another which has been attributed to Cybele – a suggestion strengthened
by the mention of *dendrofori Verulamenses* on a vessel from a burial at
Dunstable, for *dendrophori* were attendants closely associated with her cult
and the commemoration of Attis. One building contained a domestic shrine,
reminding us of the worship of the household gods which most families
observed in ancient times. Elsewhere a very fine bronze statuette of Venus
was unearthed, which could well have adorned a similar shrine.

The steady development of ancient cities was not infrequently interrupted
by disastrous fires, especially where many of the buildings were of
inflammable materials. Verulamium had once been destroyed by Boudicca; a
century later a second conflagration swept through the city centre, destroying
at least twenty hectares. By this time the town had already overspread its
earlier defences and a new bank and ditch, designed to enclose 93.6 ha (about
twice the original area), had been put in hand when the fire called a halt. It
was a serious setback, and there were long delays before rebuilding was
accomplished. When it came, the result suggests a profound change in the
social and economic character of the place. Gone were the numerous small
half-timbered shops and workshops. During the century following the fire of
AD 155 their place was taken by very large town-houses of masonry,
obviously the dwellings of wealthy people, sprawling long distances along the
street frontages, but often surrounded by their own grounds on the other
sides. The governing classes had clearly moved in to town, and the new
structures show in their tiled roofs and walls of clay or stone a reaction to the
danger of fire. They sometimes cover over eight times the area of earlier
small houses and contain three times as many rooms. Unfortunately it is
almost always impossible to define the uses to which any individual room was
put; but analogy suggests that some of those along the frontages would have
been let out as shops. If so the apparent change from commercial to
residential may not have been as striking as at first appears. But there
certainly seems to be less evidence for petty manufacturing than there was in
earlier times. It may be that this sort of industry had grown more centralised
and that the city now become a more purely retail outlet.

The lack of inscriptions, particularly those on tombstones, is a serious
drawback to any attempt to describe the character of the population. Even its
size is hard to reckon; a total of 15,000 in the late first century rising to

20,000 during the second has been estimated. The character of local government, with its council (the *ordo*) electing two annual chief magistrates (*duoviri*) and two *aediles* (magistrates responsible for superintending public works and shows) and sometimes other officials as well, is known from continental evidence; in a municipium the chief magistrates were regularly promoted to Roman citizenship. Unfortunately none of them is known at Verulamium. All we have are the names of some nineteen inhabitants scratched on various metal or pottery vessels; only one is certainly a Roman citizen, but almost all the rest do have Latin names. As far as it goes, this is evidence for the spread of the Latin language and is matched by another graffito on a coarse-ware bowl setting out most of a Latin pentameter. More extensive evidence for the use of Latin by artisans come from Silchester and Leicester.

The spread of Latin among all classes in the city should not surprise us. Latin was the language of civilisation, law and the administration; its use was a part of the wider impact of a superior culture, marked by the arrival of new architecture, fresh art-forms and by new fashions in food and its service, as well as by mass-produced trappings of everyday living, which transformed the native population within a single generation.

At Verulamium it was the third century which saw its transformation to the city best known to us today, for it was then that many of the large town-houses were built and the city wall was constructed. By this date the majority of towns in Roman Britain were being walled – a programme which suggests a growth of insecurity occasioned by the menace of sea-raiders who were such a feature of the period. Once the walls were built, they tended to fossilise the form and size of the settlement, for many were repaired and maintained to the end of the middle ages. At Verulamium, as at Silchester and Wroxeter, their life was shorter, for these cities did not continue as inhabited centres. Why was this?

Throughout the fourth century Verulamium had continued prosperous. Although the upper levels have been much disturbed by agriculture and by the removal of building-material in later centuries, evidence does survive for maintainance and rebuilding throughout the period. Indeed, on two sites it could be shown that civilised habitation continued far into the fifth century.

The date and causes of the end of towns in Roman Britain are still shrouded in obscurity. At very few, if any, was there a straight continuity of occupation through the Saxon period. Urban life depended upon an intricate substructure of communications, trade, industry and the availability of a food supply. In the disturbed conditions of the fifth and sixth centuries this substructure broke down. For a long time the inhabitants of Verulamium and its surrounding region were able to resist the encroachments of Saxon settlement, but it was a losing struggle. When settled conditions returned, some Roman cities were re-occupied because of their excellent siting and surviving walls. At Verulamium the post-Roman settlement centred on the Abbey of St Albans, founded or re-established by King Offa at a spot on the opposite hill where, according to Bede, Christian traditions had been – if only tenuously – maintained. The ruined Roman city was thereafter used only as a quarry for building material and as the haunt of robbers.

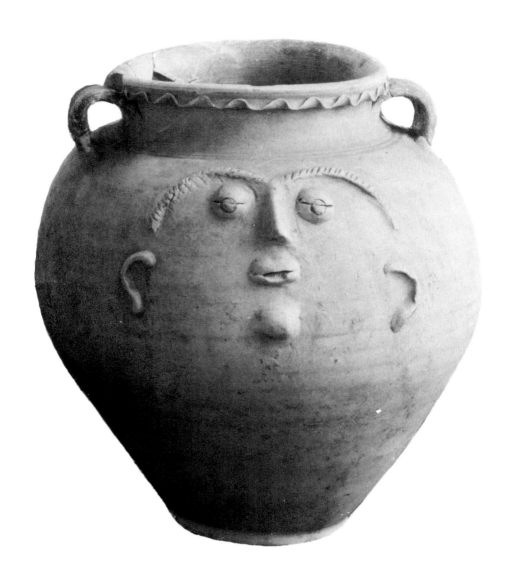

Face pot (second century).

3 The Visual Arts and Crafts

JANET HUSKINSON

Introduction

The architecture of Roman Britain is justly famous: Bath, Fishbourne, and
Hadrian's Wall are impressive by any standards. The visual arts and crafts of
Roman Britain may be less striking in aesthetic terms, but they still provide a
richly varied source of interest, both as works of art and in other positive
ways too.

The first interesting aspect is their diversity: as we shall see, the different
artistic traditions and social backgrounds of the craftsmen and patrons create
a wide variety of styles and subject-matter. For this reason the very term
'Romano-British art' begs a number of questions about what was made for
whom and why. Secondly, Britain has yielded several works of outstanding
historical interest. In the specific field of early Christian art, for example,
there are the Lullingstone frescoes (see p. 94), the Hinton St Mary, Dorset,
mosaic with its juxtaposing of pagan and Christian figures, and the church
plate from Water Newton, Cambridgeshire (see p. 76). These same examples
illustrate a third area of interest since they were all found relatively recently;
for through systematic excavation and sometimes through amazing chance,
archaeology continues to make finds which enlighten and surprise. Such
recent discoveries have greatly added to our knowledge of mosaic and wall
painting, for example.

That Romano-British art is most fruitfully seen in its historical and social
context is clear from the way that major phases in the province's history (as
outlined in Part I) each brought scope for new development in the arts and
crafts – pre-Conquest contacts with the Roman world, the arrival of the
army, urbanisation in the second century, and the prosperity of rural villas in
the fourth. Most crucial in this respect were the years immediately after the
Conquest in AD 43. Prior to then native art had concentrated chiefly on the
decoration of metalware, with abstract curvilinear patterns or stylised animal
forms; while contact with classical art – whether via Gaul or further afield –
was limited to objects (usually small bronzes and red-gloss pottery) imported
by the nobility or perhaps received by them as diplomatic gifts (as the silver

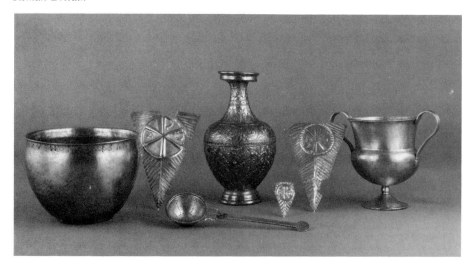

Gold and silver plaques: church plate from Water Newton, Cambridgeshire (fourth century).

cups from Hockwold, Norfolk may have been), and is also reflected in the classically inspired coin-types used by certain British mints. The Conquest changed this by confronting the native artistic tradition with new media (like large-scale stone sculpture, mosaic, and wall painting), new purposes (such as the expression of religious or political themes), and, above all, with the essentially different stylistic approach inherent in the naturalism of classical art.

The diversity of Romano-British art results from the interaction of these two artistic traditions. The sections which follow this Introduction will concentrate on monuments selected to illustrate different aspects of this; but it might be useful first – at the risk of overgeneralisation – to outline the recognisable traits of the styles which are commonly labelled 'Celtic' and 'classical'.

The main characteristic of Celtic decorated metal-work was a strong sense of pattern, whether in abstract linear designs or in the stylised treatment of natural forms. The continuation of this style well after the Conquest is visible in the decoration of various types of brooch; the famous fan-tail brooch of late first century date found at Great Chesters, Northumberland (Aesica) bears an intricate scroll design, while the 'dragonesque' brooches, popular slightly later, show an effortless translation of an animal form into a highly stylised two-dimensional pattern. This same sense of form and line comes to be seen in stone sculpture, as a sign of local craftsmanship. Most striking are representations of the human head, like the young man from Gloucester and the funerary (?) head from Towcester, Northants now in the British Museum: both of these derive their power from the patterning of the facial features rather than from a conscious pursuit of naturalism. Typical of the 'local' style are the large, rather bulging eyes, the delineation of the hair, and an individuality that is undeniable but hard to pinpoint. The linear style is even more at home in relief work where it serves to differentiate planes and to enhance contrasts of light and shade. A good example of this appears on the tombstone of a mother and child from Murrell Hill in Carlisle. Pattern can also be achieved in the grouping of figures, as may be seen in reliefs depicting a trinity of gods like the *Genii Cucullati* (from Housesteads, Northumberland), the Mother Goddesses (from Cirencester, Gloucestershire), and Water-Nymphs (from Carrawburgh, Northumberland).

By contrast, the salient feature of the 'classical' Graeco-Roman style is naturalism, with an emphasis on harmonious proportion and three-dimensional form. In painting and mosaic this last point is illustrated by the use of highlights and shading to indicate volume (in contrast to the two-dimensional effects of outline and flat colour to be seen in the Europa mosaic at Lullingstone, and in relief, by the use of several intermediate planes and the higher working of figures. The composition of scenes and poses of figures is usually based on long-established types familiar throughout the Empire; innumerable bronze figurines of Graeco-Roman gods exemplify this. 'Classical' figures tend towards the ideal and generalised, except for some portrait heads which may be lifelike after the particularly Roman fashion.

Immediately after the Conquest few British craftsmen could have been capable of working, in any style, in the media new to them. Imported wares filled this initial need, whether for private possessions or for official purposes like the display of imperial portraits; and even when local artists could produce acceptable work, high-quality artefacts continued to be brought into Britain. Marble sculpture, for instance, was imported to decorate villas (as at Woodchester, Gloucestershire) or temples (like the Walbrook Mithraeum; City of London; see pp. 63–4); or in the case of the two second century portrait busts at Lullingstone (see p. 90), perhaps to form part of the 'family gallery' of some visiting Roman official. Other wares were imported which were not usually made in Britain, like decorative glass and silverware, and Samian ware (a red-gloss pottery) from Gaul and the Rhineland, until British kilns took over in the third century.

Craftsmen practised in classical art also came to work in Britain. Presumably many of the original influx came from Gaul (and the names inscribed on objects like the Prickwillow skillet from Cambridgeshire are probably Gaulish rather than British); more unexpected is the Palmyrene sculptor who worked in the South Shields area in the third century. The later part of the period saw further immigration from Gaul and the Rhineland in the face of barbarian threat; and this may be reflected, for example, in features shared by some British and continental floor-mosaics of that time. Certainly in terms of the transmission of themes and subjects fourth-century pavements in Britain raise interesting questions about the circulation of craftsmen and motifs across the Empire, since certain features find their closest parallels in far-distant provinces. This is also true for some British lead coffins which share motifs with examples from the Middle East.

Fundamental to Romano-British art, therefore, is the heterogeneous background of the patrons and artists, and the meeting of two styles essentially dissimilar. The interest lies in how the outcome of this may vary, either within an individual piece, or comprehensively in terms of media (wall painting, for instance, was scarcely affected by 'local' tendencies, while

British pottery was a 'late starter' in terms of an individual decorative style), the treatment of local stone, shale and jet, time, place, and clientele. The individual examples which follow have been chosen to illustrate different aspects of this artistic encounter, and many of them are important works of art in their own right.

Yet this is not to undervalue the contribution of a different sort made by innumerable examples of what are so misleadingly described as the 'minor arts': skilled craftsmanship and a context in everyday life give them an immediacy which some larger pieces lack, so that they are sometimes more successful in giving us a feeling for what the inhabitants of Roman Britain enjoyed in their art. Animals, for instance, clearly gave a lot of pleasure as subjects, whether represented naturalistically, as in figurines of bronze or jet, or in stylised form, as in brooches or buckles like the spectacular gold belt-buckle from the 'Thetford Treasure' (colour pl. 2, now in the British Museum). Lively hunting scenes were popular decoration on pottery as wares made in the Nene Valley region attest, whereas similar pieces depict scenes of gladiators or charioteers. Other representations of the human figure seem robustly humorous: terracotta figurines found in a child's grave of the mid first century AD at Colchester depict, with a touch of the grotesque, participants in a banquet. These were imported into Britain; but examples of even funnier faces, made in this country, can be found on a double-headed jet hair-pin discovered in York (possibly a German import?) and, most enjoyable perhaps, on the series of face- and head-pots. Artefacts like these certainly give a vivid sense of popular tastes and interests, but they too can be seen in the context of the meeting of two different artistic traditions.

Representations of Mercury

Comparing different versions of a single subject is a vivid way of seeing the range of artistic traditions to be found in Roman Britain. Our subject is Mercury, as represented in certain pieces of sculpture.

Mercury, the messenger of the gods and protector of cattle, merchants, and travellers (both in this world and the next) is commonly characterised in classical art by his distinctive attributes of *caduceus* (herald's staff), purse, and wings on his head (or hat) and ankles. Of the classical gods he was a popular subject and was depicted in works of art of all kinds.

Some sculptural representations of Mercury were clearly imported into Britain from other parts of the Western Empire, and show all the naturalistic modelling and usual iconography of the classical style. An attractive example is the statuette (25 cm high) in the Museum of London which shows Mercury resting on a rock. It was found on the site of the Walbrook Mithraeum where it was apparently hidden for safekeeping sometime in the early fourth century, along with other imported statuary. Quite apart from any religious significance which it may have had, this piece must have been prized for its quality; and it is interesting that it seems to have been repaired in antiquity before its burial caused further damage. Skilled craftsmanship is obvious in the careful all-round treatment of the group, in the modelling of the figure, and in the textural contrasts between the highly polished surfaces of the flesh, the curly hair, and heavy folds of drapery; this, and the fact that the marble is Italian, suggests that the sculpture was made in Italy and subsequently brought to Britain. Although it is probably second century in date, the sculpture reproduces a figure-type which was evolved in Greece during the fourth century BC, showing the god in an informal rather than hieratic pose. Weary young man though he seems, his identity is revealed through the usual attributes – wings on his head, purse in his left hand, traces of a caduceus in his right, and two animals, ram and tortoise, which allude, respectively, to his custody of flocks and to his invention of the lyre (the lyre is made from tortoise-shell).

Another import – this time probably from Gaul – is a larger (53 cm) figure of the god, hollow cast in bronze, found at a temple-site at Gosbecks Farm outside Colchester. Like the Walbrook piece it may have had some votive or devotional function; and it may have been part of a larger group since the god is shown as if alighting and turning slightly to his left. He is completely nude, revealing a strong, well-modelled torso, and he has distinctive facial features with a slightly worried look. The large wings, which sprout from his thick head of hair, are the only identifying features to survive, since both arms are lost below the shoulders. This piece too is probably of second century date.

Bronze statue of Mercury, found at a temple-site outside Colchester, Essex (c.200).

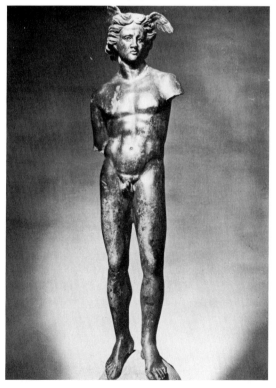

A fusion of classical iconography and classical traditions of naturalistic rendering with a Celtic sense of form characterises the work of many of the more skilled Romano-British craftsmen: it could be said that general form and subject-matter are 'imported' from Graeco-Roman art, whereas the individual treatment results from a local approach. Two heads from Gloucestershire – both worked in local limestone – illustrate this. The first, found at Cirencester, is 15 cm high and shows Mercury wearing a winged hat. His face looks stolid, with heavy jaw, eyes set quite close together under a prominent brow, and a broad but badly damaged nose. It is this sense of individuality, albeit within the prescript of a classical form, and the stylisation of the hair which make this piece 'Romano-British' work in the fullest sense. The second head also probably dates to the second century, but is much larger, belonging as it did to the over lifesize cult statue of Mercury from the temple at Uley, Gloucestershire. (It is now in the British Museum.) It is, arguably, more classical than the Cirencester head since its slight inclination, the tilted set of the eyes, straight brow, and gently parted lips, all hark back to Greek types of the fifth and fourth centuries BC. Yet here again, the stylised curls, large eyes, and delineated lids exemplify a local treatment of the classical forms.

This treatment is at the fore in a small bronze figure (11 cm high) in the British Museum; it was found at Southbroom, near Devizes, together with seven other statuettes which may also represent Graeco-Roman deities. So strong, however, is the local interpretation in terms of style and iconography that Mercury is the most recognisable character, and this by his winged hat and purse (?). He is shown, bearded and half-draped standing with both hands outstretched, the purse in his right and a small dish (?) in his left. Like others in the group, the small figure has a dignity and quiet strength which is enhanced by the regular diagonal patterning of the drapery folds. Although the head is disproportionately large and the attributes oversimplified, there is nothing hesitant or incompetent about the figure to identify it as the work of an unskilled craftsman, ignorant of his classical model. On the contrary, it asserts a set of formal values that differ from the classical and owes little, apart from its subject, to Graeco-Roman art.

Small bronze statuettes of Mercury and other Graeco-Roman deities, found at Southbroom, near Devizes, Wiltshire (third century).

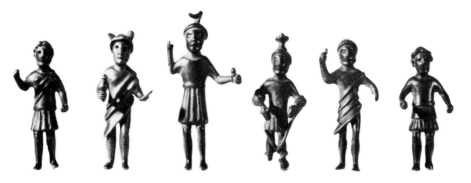

Distance slabs from the Antonine Wall

Interaction of local workmanship with well-established Roman themes is also illustrated by army art, with its emphasis on the official and functional, and, in particular, by a self-contained series of reliefs from the Antonine Wall. This frontier-line was constructed in AD 142–143 between the Clyde and the Forth, and the reliefs were attached at relevant points to demarcate the sections built by specific detachments of legions. Those which survive form a group which is unusual in the Roman world.

In size, composition and quality the reliefs vary considerably, but share as their principal feature the inscription recording the unit of troops and the distance completed. The plainest carry only this, framed by a beaded moulding; but most add some decoration, of abstract motifs or figured scenes, or include within the inscription panel itself figures of the animals which symbolise particular legions. Of abstract motifs the *pelta* (a stylised crescent-shaped shield) is the most common, forming, as it were, elaborate terminals to the panel; yet even among these the depth and delicacy of the relief work varies. On other reliefs the inscription panel has two wedge-shaped 'handles', within which prance the elongated and rather flatly-modelled figures of cupids.

Most interesting are the more developed scenes which decorate four of the slabs. From the western end of the Wall comes perhaps the most sophisticated of the reliefs, in the shape of a small pedimented shrine housing the figure of a winged Victory; she reclines in a dignified but languid pose, extending a large wreath in her right hand. The inscription is divided between the pediment, the wreath, and the podium where it flanks the small figure of a boar (emblem of the twentieth legion). Although the flattish

Distance slab: relief of small shrine housing a winged victory, found at the western end of Hadrian's Wall (second century).

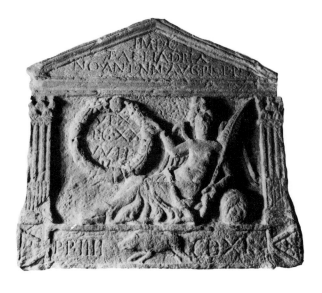

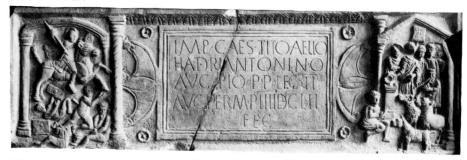

Distance slab with inscription and reliefs of the sacrifice of animals and the Roman victory, found at the east end of Hadrian's Wall (second century).

modelling of the figure, the facial features and linear treatment of the hair have a local 'look', much else is obviously classical in the iconography of Victory, the treatment of her drapery, the architectural framework, and the confident positioning of the figure in the field.

The relief erected by the second legion at the other end of the Wall at Bridgeness is also decorated, on either side of the inscription, with scenes from the repertory of Roman official art in an architectural setting. On the right is the *suovetaurilia* (the sacrifice of a sheep, pig, and ox), carried out on the legion's behalf before its campaign; on the left is shown the subsequent victory, with a Roman cavalry-man plunging his spear down into a group of hapless barbarians. Once again, subject-matter derived from the art and experience of imperial Rome contrasts strongly with a rendering which is provincial, with the strengths and weaknesses which this implies. The figures lack naturalism in terms of their grouping, proportions, and modelling of the individual features, but they have an attractive vigour, best seen in the

Distance slab with inscription and winged victories flanked by Mars and Virtus Augusti, found near Hadrian's Wall (second century).

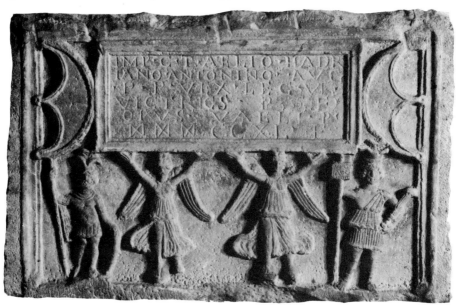

horseman panel which contrasts the strength and resolution of the victor with the limp and scattered forms of the vanquished. The sacrificial beasts are also appealing in their look of unsuspecting eagerness, and in the textural variety of their skins.

Clumsier and less imaginative is another version of the horseman scene; on this slab he is crowned by a winged Victory, and the theme carries over to the right-hand panel where a captive sits slumped below a capricorn and an eagle – creatures symbolising the legion and Rome itself.

The figures on both of these slabs, rounded in outline, but flattish in relief, contrast noticeably with those on the fourth panel. Once again, in form and subject they come straight from the repertory of classical art; the winged victories, each standing delicately on a globe, support the inscription, and are flanked by figures of Mars (left) and *Virtus Augusti* (right). Their rendering is crisp and elegant, with an emphasis on the linear treatment of wings and drapery, and in the line-up of the figures themselves.

The slabs were presumably carved close to the Wall, probably by army masons rather than local civilians, and are contemporaneous. They show how much variation was possible in the circumstances, not so much in subject-matter – many of the motifs were clearly in circulation in 'army art' elsewhere in Britain – but in presentation. Where scenes are duplicated they commemorate the same legion; but as the two cavalry-men reliefs of the second legion show, they may even so vary in artistic skill and inventiveness.

Floor mosaics from Yorkshire

Local approach to classical subjects is also illustrated in many fourth century floor mosaics, introducing questions about the interests of the private patrons and the organisation of craftsmen, since they are part of that resurgence of private art associated with the expansion of villas in the countryside. The importance of mosaic in the interior decoration of villas is confirmed by the sheer number which survive, and also by their increased sophistication as figured scenes become more popular than geometric. Very occasionally enough material remains to give a glimpse of the total decorative scheme of a room: at Kingscote (Gloucestershire) a mythological love story (Mars and Venus?) was painted on one wall, and the floor mosaic displayed a bust of Venus, and at Brantingham (North Humberside) female busts feature in the 'Tyche' mosaic and in painted plaster from the wall or ceiling. Over recent years systematic comparison of styles and motifs has led to the identification of at least five major 'schools' of mosaicists operating in the fourth century. These apparently centred on Cirencester (the 'Orpheus and Saltire' schools), Dorchester, Water Newton (Cambridgeshire), and Brough-on-Humber (Roman Petuaria), with the possibility of a Central Southern school.

It is the figured mosaics attributed to the Humberside school, together with pavements from other Yorkshire sites, which provide our examples here. They show how even in this peripheral part of the Empire there were, in the fourth century, some lively practitioners of what, after all, was originally an imported art form; but whether they operated out of a static workshop or as a mobile group of contractors and craftsmen is uncertain. The mosaics from Horkstow, Brantingham and Winterton share between them some characteristics in composition (panels radiating from a central circle or octagon), subject (Orpheus), and treatment (coloured background to some figures) which may argue for a 'Petuarian school', but other of their features also occur in mosaics found further afield, at sites like Aldborough (North Yorkshire) and Lincoln.

Given their setting in terms of time and place the Yorkshire pavements show a surprisingly wide range of classical subjects. Some are mythological topics, popular in British mosaics as elsewhere: Orpheus (at Horkstow and Winterton), the Toilet of Venus (Rudestone), Neptune (Rudestone), and the Muses (?, fragments from Aldborough). A less common subject, in mosaic, is the Roman Wolf and Twins, represented in an Aldborough pavement. Female personifications are found at Winterton (Fortuna and Providentia, perhaps) and, more spectacularly, at Brantingham. Here, set in the middle of a radial composition, is the bust of 'Tyche' (the personification of a town or community), while reclining figures of nymphs fill the semi-circular panels at the periphery. Lateral panels contain a row of four female busts set in arched frames; their identity is uncertain, but their drapery and nimbus are clearly classical in derivation. Could they and the 'Tyche' represent the Muses? Genre subjects are represented in the area by a theme popular in Roman art, namely the charioteer. In one section of the Horkstow mosaic is depicted a race of four *bigae* (two horse chariots) around a circus; and at Rudston the lone figure of a victorious charioteer, standing in a frontal four horse chariot occupies the central roundel, while those at the corners are filled (as so often in such compositions) with busts of the Seasons. Genre animal themes also appear: leopards flanking a chalice, and birds and fruit (Rudston), a sleeping lion (Aldborough), and, more unusually, in the Rudston Venus mosaic a lion and bull with huntsmen, described by inscriptions as 'the fiery lion' and 'the murderous bull'.

What do these subjects, and the style of their representation suggest about the local situation? The mosaicists obviously had some local specialities, such as the radial plan, and at Aldborough, the composition of a beast lying below a tree; but more interesting is the access which they had to scenes and motifs from the mainstream of Roman art. It is possible that the circular Orpheus composition was introduced to the area by mosaicists from the 'Corinian' school who operated out of Cirencester and made much use of this arrangement; but close parallels to the Rudston charioteer, and to the amphitheatre allusions that may be contained in the inscriptions of the lion and bull in the Rudston Venus mosaic, come from North Africa. This instantly raises questions about the circulation of designs throughout the Empire: were they conveyed by itinerant mosaicists, or perhaps via some kind of pattern books (which, as ephemera, have not survived)? In the execution of the designs the standard (as in so much Romano-British art) is variable. Even in the Rudston charioteer mosaic the bust of Spring is technically superior to the others (suggesting the work of different hands); but one need only compare this mosaic to the Venus pavement (which was laid in an adjacent building some decades later) to get the measure of the variation. Yet

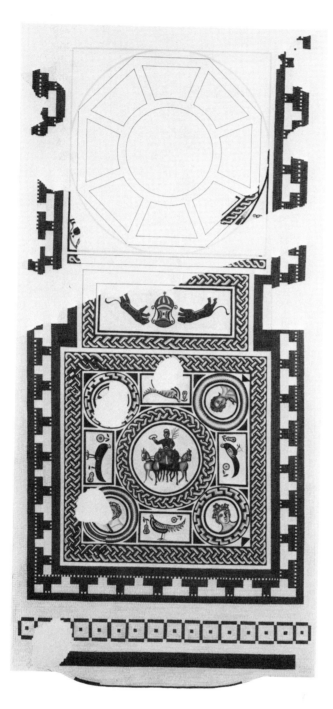

*Mosaic showing figure of a victorious charioteer, found at Rudstone, North Yorkshire
(fourth century). Drawing by David Neal.*

it would be misleading to interpret this simply as a decline. Even allowing for its coarser workmanship and for possible misunderstandings of the subject-matter, this later scene has great liveliness because of its use of bold outline and of at least a dozen colours. It represents (like the Europa mosaic from Lullingstone, pl. 000) a two-dimensional design rather than the three-dimensional approach found, for instance, in the bust of 'Spring' with its highlights and shading. The same is true of the 'stick-men' charioteers at Horkstow and of the Aldborough 'Wolf and Twins' mosaic where the unnaturalistic proportions and gauche figure-style convey a sense of tenderness and vulnerability.

As for the patrons' attitudes, these same features suggest tolerance of a wide variation in aesthetic appeal and technical competence. Some had a taste – and presumably the money – for quite elaborate designs, as at Horkstow and Brantingham, and others must have had an appreciation of classical culture. However, this is very hard to quantify; how much choice a patron had from the repertory of his local workshop, how much he understood – or even liked – the subject as finally depicted, are questions which ultimately remain open.

Silverware from late Roman Britain

For a small outlying province of the Roman Empire, Britain has made some major contributions towards our general knowledge of silverware in the fourth and fifth centuries AD; not only are some of the pieces visually magnificent but they are interesting historical documents.

From the early fourth century increased prosperity and social stability seem to have stimulated the production of silver plate (like other 'luxury goods') for wealthy private consumers, or to be used for official presentations. Although production centres have proved hard to distinguish in terms of style, cities like Rome and Constantinople are obvious candidates; most probably the silver plate so far found in Britain was made in one of these centres or in Gaul. Being so valuable it must have been collected and prized by owners, who in times of threat, which were many and various in this period, would have been anxious for the safe-keeping of their treasures and therefore in many cases resorted to hiding them. Seen against this background it is not surprising that so many hoards of this period have been found in Britain and other frontier provinces. From Traprain, in lowland Scotland and Coleraine in Northern Ireland, beyond the imperial boundaries, come hoards of silver in a different form, collected (possibly in plunder and crushed like scrap) for the melting-pot or to be used as a type of currency; here too other sites on the edge of the Empire provide parallels.

Communities might be threatened not only by barbarian invaders but by religious opponents; such reasons may have prompted the Christians of Water Newton to conceal their church plate, and the devotees of the pagan god Faunus to hide, at the end of the fourth century, the jewellery and silverware which constitute the Thetford Treasure (although in this case direct links with a cult are not so certain, and the disparate nature of the hoard may possibly be the result of separate thefts). It is relevant, perhaps, that so much of the silverware of this period, found in Britain, is decorated with figured scenes and motifs that are capable of a specifically religious interpretation whether pagan (like the shrine of Apollo on Delos illustrated on the 'Corbridge *lanx*', a rectangular dish found in Northumberland) or Christian (like the biblical scenes on a vessel from Traprain).

Even more interesting is the discovery in the same hoard of pieces relating to different religions. An excellent example is provided by the Mildenhall Treasure, deposited sometime in the mid-fourth century, in Suffolk. It is truly splendid in the richness of its ornament: virtually all of its thirty-four pieces are decorated, if only by a simple inscription. The most magnificent item is the 'Great Dish', which is 60 cm in diameter. Its decoration comprises a central mask of Oceanus surrounded by two concentric friezes, the inner of sea-nymphs and marine creatures, and the outer (and deeper) frieze of Bacchic revellers, including Bacchus himself and the drunken Hercules. The figures are all well-known classical types, but details like awkward poses and contemporary hair-styles reflect the fourth century date of manufacture. Particularly interesting in terms of the assessment of classical and Celtic influences in Romano-British art is the striking similarity between this Oceanus, appearing as it does on an imported piece, and the locally carved Gorgon head which forms the centrepiece of the Bath pediment. The Bacchic theme is depicted on two smaller dishes in the Treasure showing maenads (female devotees) with Pan and with a satyr: these are edged with heavy beading, also found on the 'Great Dish' and on other pieces in the hoard. Some of these – a bowl with a domed lid (not originally intended for each other, perhaps) and four broad-rimmed dishes are decorated with friezes of animals (centaurs on the lid) separated by human heads shown in profile; a similar head decorates the central roundel on three of the dishes. Of the spoons, three carry the Chi-Rho monogram set between Alpha and Omega (Greek letters symbolising Christ, the Beginning and the End); two more have Christian inscriptions wishing a long life to named individuals, and were perhaps christening gifts; the remaining three have a leaf pattern in the bowl. Other vessels in the hoard are decorated with abstract rather than figured designs, but are none the less attractive for that.

The sumptuousness of the plate and the presence of pagan and Christian elements in the decoration raise questions about its likely owner. One line of argument is that the treasure is pagan in origin but came into the possession of a Christian owner who added various items of Christian significance and tolerated the Bacchic dishes for their obvious aesthetic and material value; but it is also arguable that much of the pagan 'religious' decoration is really only conventional ornament which does not raise acute problems of religious affiliation. The Bacchic dishes (see p. 88) bear on the reverse the Greek inscription 'of Eutherius'. Since this is the name of one of the officials of the pagan emperor Julian, it has been suggested that Eutherius passed some plate to the Christian general Lupicinus, who was sent by Julian to Britain in AD 360. His subsequent arrest by the emperor may have led to the burial of his treasure in Britain for safety – an ingenious solution, which whether correct or not, does reflect how art objects continued to be imported into Britain by Romans of such status.

In comparison the Christian background of the Water Newton Treasure is

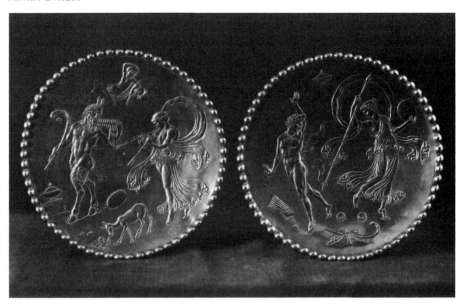

Silver Bacchic dishes: Pan, a satyr and Maenids dancing and playing, found at Mildenhall, Suffolk (fourth century).

unquestionable. Because of this it makes an important contribution to our knowledge of Christianity in Roman Britain and of early Christian silverware in general: in fact it appears to be the earliest surviving collection of church plate from anywhere in the Empire. Some of the nine vessels in the treasure may have had a liturgical function – the two-handled cups, jugs, and a large silver dish and wine-strainer which are decorated with the Chi–Rho monogram; two other bowls may have been votive gifts from church members, to judge from the inscriptions which they bear. The greater part of the Treasure comprises small triangular plaques of silver, fashioned like stylised leaves and, in many cases, having a central roundel containing a Chi–Rho with Alpha and Omega; there is also a gold disc with Chi–Rho. Analogy with pagan examples, and the wording of the inscription which survives on one, suggests these plaques too may have had some votive function, though in Christian art they are hitherto unparalleled. When – and precisely why – the treasure came to be hidden is uncertain; but evidence, including the discovery nearby of a hoard of gold coins issued between AD 330 and 350, points to a date in the mid-fourth century.

How, then, to evaluate this period in British art? Its legacy is clearer in a long-term view than in the individual features which survive into Anglo-Saxon art. Its great contribution was the wide-scale introduction into Britain, via Roman patrons, artists, and artefacts, of major new art forms, new contexts, and new means of expression; it provided contact with an artistic tradition which was long-established, and, by late antiquity, cosmopolitan and capable of adaptation. Even if Romano-British art had little impact on mainstream developments (as, for instance, the art of North Africa did), it was sufficiently evolved to share many of their general characteristics, and to make a strength out of its inevitable diversity.

Even though many of these developments were disrupted by the ending of the Roman occupation, their introduction and consolidation marks them out as an important chapter in the history of the visual arts in Britain.

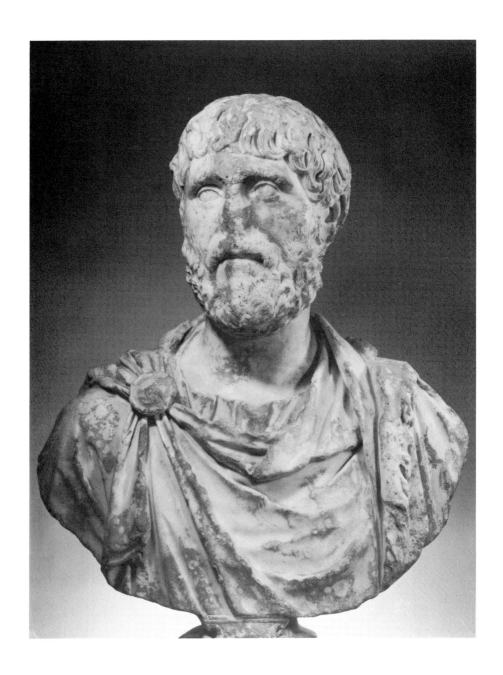

Roman portrait bust in marble (c.125–35).

4 Lullingstone Villa

ROGER LING

Lullingstone Villa in Kent is both a typical and an untypical house of the Roman period in Britain. It is typical, on the one hand, of a number of medium-sized farms in the south-east of the province. Built largely of mortared stonework, with a basically rectangular plan incorporating at its greatest extent a dozen rooms or so, it replaced a native farm or farms in the late first century AD and enjoyed phases of comparative prosperity during the late second and fourth centuries. It is untypical in the evidence which it has yielded of the cultural aspirations and religious beliefs of rural dwellers in the south-east. Not only has it produced artistic material of unusual significance, including the only marble portrait-busts from a country house in Britain and the only figured mosaics from any rural context in the south-east during the fourth century; it has also given us evidence of the practice by successive owners of pagan and Christian cults, and has revealed that at least one owner was familiar with the Latin literary classics, admitting a learned allusion to Virgil's epic poem, the *Aeneid*, in the mosaic pavement of his dining-room. In these details Lullingstone allows comparison, albeit on a smaller scale, with the wealthy fourth-century villas of the Cotswolds and Wessex.

The unusual aspects may, admittedly, be due to the accidents of survival. Most of the country residences of Roman Britain have been destroyed over the intervening centuries, especially in areas like the home counties which have seen intensive farming and pervasive building developments; and few of those which have survived are so well preserved, or have been so fully excavated, as Lullingstone. The house was examined in thirteen successive seasons of excavations, from 1949 to 1961; and the analysis of its history and of the archaeological material recovered from it has continued for a further quarter century under the general direction of the excavator, Lieutenant-Colonel Geoffrey Meates (who died in 1985). In addition, where most Roman houses survive only in their foundations or lower courses, the walls of Lullingstone are in some places preserved to more than six feet (2 m) in height. We thus have a clearer picture of life at Lullingstone than in any other comparable dwelling in the province.

The architectural history may be briefly summarised. The first villa was

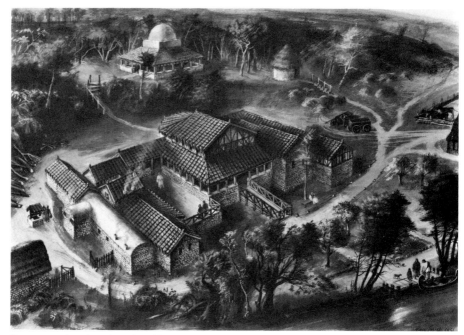

Reconstruction drawing (by Alan Sorrell) of Lullingstone Villa (c.360).

constructed about AD 80–90, on the western slope of the valley of the River
Darent, about 17 miles (27 km) south-east of Roman London. Like many
other farms in the south-east, for example those at Park Street and other
places in Hertfordshire, it succeeded a Celtic hut or huts (not actually located
but implied by archaeological finds) and was presumably built by a native
landowner who had acquired a taste for, and the financial means to support,
a Roman lifestyle. As at Park Street, the main block consisted of a sequence
of rooms laid end to end; but an unusual feature at this early date was the
addition of corridors at front and back, the one at the front being framed
(after a pattern which was widespread in northern Gaul and Germany) by
projecting rooms at either end. The social significance of the corridors is that
they introduced an element of privacy, since the rooms no longer needed to
be intercommunicating; this in turn might favour the growth of a hierarchical
family unit or even of a degree of segregation. Architecturally the corridors
imply a certain sophistication in that the central rooms must have been lit by
a clerestory system. One further feature of interest, also imported from
northern Gaul, was the semi-sunken room (the so-called Deep Room) at the
north-east corner, probably used for the storage of grain since it was
provided with a loading bay from the level of the adjacent corridor, about
1.20 m above the floor.

A major enlargement occurred about a century later, when a bath suite was
added at the south end, and further rooms were added at the north. The
baths were of the familiar Roman type, with a sequence of cold room, warm
room and hot room (the last two provided with underfloor heating from a

neighbouring furnace). The bather progressed through the successive grades of heat, being cleansed, Turkish-style, by the sweating induced by the steamy surroundings; he could rinse off the sweat in a small hot water bath in the hot room before returning to the cold room for an invigorating dip in a cold plunge. Water to service the baths was probably conducted from a nearby spring. Of the alterations at the north end of the house the most significant involved the Deep Room, which was linked with a new room immediately to the north to create a suite accessible only by a descending stairway from the west. This suite was curiously self-contained and remote from the rest of the house; while the plan of the new northern room, enclosed by a four-sided ambulatory, and entered only from a door on the far side, is unparalleled in Roman domestic architecture. Both the Deep Room and its neighbour were equipped with water receptacles in their floors, that in the Deep Room taking the form of a square well lined with chalk blocks; it is attractive therefore to think that they served some kind of religious cult in which water played a role. The new northern room with its enclosing ambulatory recalls the architecture of Celtic temples, which generally consisted of an isolated square cult-room surrounded by a low verandah.

After the early years of the third century the villa entered a period of decline, and possibly even of abandonment. Among the signs of dilapidation are the partial burial of the stairway down to the cult-rooms by collapsed mortar and the removal of the tile treads from the lowest steps. Towards the end of the century, however, it began a new lease of life, possibly in the hands of new owners. The baths were repaired, and the northern end of the building was totally altered, the entrance to the Deep Room being sealed off and the cult-chamber to the north being truncated by the construction of a new room over the former access stairs. During the course of the following century the central part of the house, too, was modified, by the insertion of the apsidal dining-room with its mythological and allegorical mosaics which forms the showpiece of the present archaeological display. Occupation of the villa continued into the fifth century, though without further additions. The main event of note was the conversion in about AD 380–385 of the northern rooms into a small house-church for the family and the neighbouring community. After that there was a steady decline, during which the baths became disused, till ultimately the building was destroyed by fire.

What do the discoveries at Lullingstone tell us about the lifestyle and artistic tastes of the successive generations of owners? First that their wealth rested at least partly on farming. This could be inferred simply from the abundance of good cultivable land in the area, but corroboration is provided by the evidence for grain collection. In addition to the probable existence of a grain store in the Deep Room before its modification in the late second century, a massive external granary was added during the rebuilding of the late third century. Secondly, working farmers or no, the owners planned their house with an eye to the amenities of its situation and outlook. Like certain rather grander villas in the south-west, notably Chedworth and Great Witcombe, the house at Lullingstone was set in a hillside. The main block was admittedly at one level, except in so far as the Deep Room exploited the fall of the ground to the east, but other structures associated with the villa (a

circular shrine or gazebo of c.AD 100, and a family mausoleum of c.AD 300)
were installed on a higher terrace to the west approached by a flight of steps,
while a steep path leading upwards from this second level implies the
existence of a still higher terrace which has not been excavated. But most
important, the main façade is oriented to take advantage of the view; it
commands a fine prospect to the south-east over the Darent valley and the
countryside beyond. Thirdly and most important the owners were able to
surround themselves with artistic objects and with the amenities of civilised
living. This is demonstrated, for example, by the interior decorations of the
house. Most of the rooms, as well as the mausoleum and the circular shrine
or gazebo, were adorned with brightly painted plaster at all periods. In the
late second century the Deep Room and its northern neighbour received
matching decorations consisting of red, yellow and green panel designs
punctuated with stylised date-palms. A niche in the Deep Room was
decorated with three water-nymphs painted in a purely Mediterranean style
and with purely classical attributes – an overturned water jug, which is a
standard symbol of water-deities in Graeco-Roman art, and (for the central
nymph) spouts of water emerging from the breasts, a feature paralleled in a

Wall-painting of water-nymphs in the Deep Room at Lullingtone Villa (late second century).

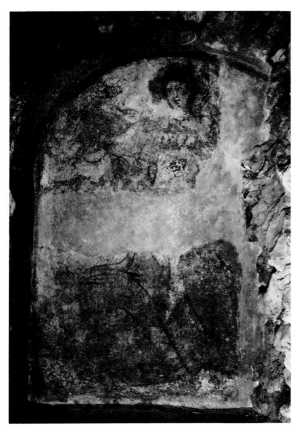

painting described by an ancient visitor to a picture-gallery in Naples. The Lullingstone nymphs may have been the patron spirits of the well in the same room, and a shelf in front of them may have carried cult-objects and offerings; but, whatever their significance, they were considered worth the expense of hiring a skilled, and no doubt well paid, figure painter. In the early fourth century further figure paintings, here almost lifesize (though too little survives for interpretation), were carried out in the mausoleum above the house. Finally, from the house-church of the late fourth century come the famous Christian paintings partially reconstructed from thousands of fragments of plaster which had collapsed into the underlying Deep Room when the villa was burnt. Among the subjects are at least three Christian monograms set in wreaths and a series of Christian worshippers, arms raised in a gesture of prayer, standing between the columns of a portico. The lurid, unrealistic colours and the hard linearity of the style are typical of the art of late antiquity.

Even more remarkable than the paintings is the mosaic pavement of the large fourth-century dining-room. This consisted of two parts: an apsidal dais carrying the couches of the diners and an approximately square ante-room, which could have been used for the service of the meal, or even for post-prandial floor-shows. In each section was a figured centrepiece framed by geometric patterns. The apse showed the rape of Europa by Jupiter in the guise of a bull; the ante-room, the duel between Bellerophon and the Chimaera, with busts personifying the four seasons at the corners. Although the execution of these scenes is at times a little uncertain, and the curious

Mosaic showing Bellerophon slaying the Chimera, in the dining room at Lullingstone Villa (fourth century).

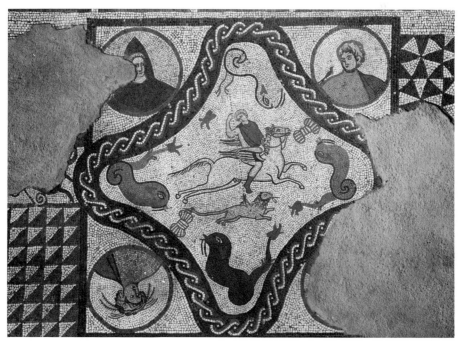

outline technique is not a normal feature of Roman mosaics, the actual figure-types show a continuing awareness of the traditional classical repertory, and the choice of subjects presupposes the presence of guests who knew and had a liking for the stories of Greek mythology. The Europa scene is also accompanied by a couple of lines of Latin verse: 'If jealous Juno had seen the swimming of the bull, more justly would she have gone to the halls of Aeolus' – a reference to the first book of the *Aeneid* where Juno hinders the plans of her consort Jupiter by rousing the winds (kept in the halls of Aeolus) to force Aeneas' ship on to the coast of Africa. Such a tag would have been meaningless to a diner who did not know his Virgil; we can therefore imagine a scenario of cultured dinner-parties for a circle of people who were not only literate but also versed in the classics.

Loose finds from the villa reinforce the picture of a relatively sophisticated lifestyle. There are large quantities of fine table pottery from all periods of occupation, as well as glassware, bronze vessels, objects of carved bone, shale and jet, brooches, finger-rings, and so forth. From the mausoleum came a complete set of thirty glass gaming pieces, fifteen white and fifteen brown, used for a game similar to our backgammon or draughts.

More specific information on the owners of the villa is lacking. We can guess, as already suggested, that the original owner was a Romanised native; and we know that one of the last owners espoused Christianity. Otherwise most of our information concerns the family of the late second century. To them must have belonged the two marble portrait-busts found in the Deep Room. Dated, respectively, to the middle and second half of the century, these show bearded men, one wearing a tunic and a military cloak, the other a toga; they are slightly over lifesize and can best be regarded as ancestral portraits venerated in accordance with a standard practice among the Roman well-to-do. Since the physiognomy of the subjects, the use of Greek marble, and the style of the carving all unmistakably indicate a Mediterranean origin, it is safe to assume that they were brought to Britain by an immigrant, perhaps a public official. This would tie up with the installation of baths, the conversion of the Deep Room from a grain store, and the commissioning of paintings which included a set of classical-style water-nymphs and a series of exotic trees, the date-palms. Carrying conjecture further, we may suggest that the dilapidation of the villa in the third century was due to the political upheavals following the rebellion of Clodius Albinus. If this chain of guesses is anywhere near the truth, we have obtained an insight into the artistic patronage of one of the more interesting phases of construction and decoration in the history of this fascinating house.

EARLY MEDIEVAL BRITAIN

Part I
The Cultural and Social Setting

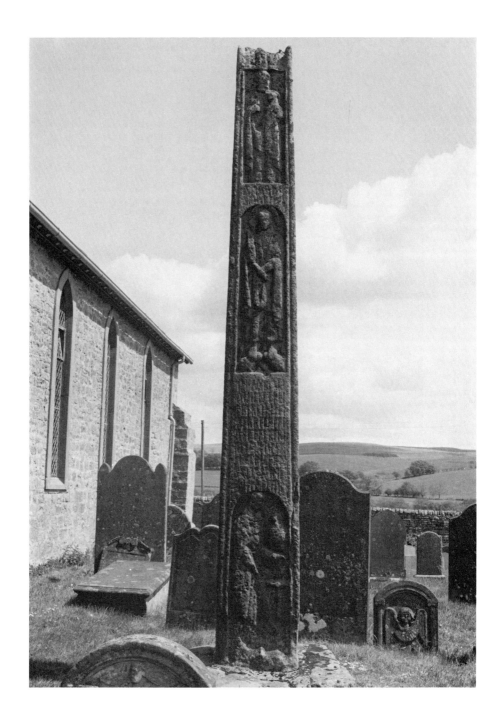

The shaft of the Bewcastle Cross, dating to the first half of the eighth century, still stands in its original socket in a churchyard which occupies part of the site of a Roman fort. The figural scenes on the west face show John the Baptist, Christ in Majesty and a (surprisingly secular) presentation of St John the Evangelist with his eagle symbol.

The Cultural and Social Setting

RICHARD N. BAILEY

Anglo-Saxon society

Two chronicle entries frame the material in this section. The first is provided
by a fifth-century Gallic writer, tracing a pattern of collapse across the
Roman Empire, who claims that, in the nineteenth year of the Emperor
Valentinian III (AD 441–442), the former provinces of Roman Britain 'long
troubled by various disasters and happenings, are brought under the
authority of the Saxons (*in dicionem Saxonum rediguntur*)'. The second comes
from a version of the *Anglo-Saxon Chronicle* copied at Peterborough where
the death of William I in 1087 provokes a moralising poem

> The rich complained and the poor lamented
> But he was too relentless to care, though all might hate him.

Historians might now argue about the accuracy of the first statement, and
contemporaries certainly had more positive views of William's reign, but
these records set the boundaries; the one marks the beginning of Anglo-
Saxon England whilst the other signals the demise of its Conqueror.

Between those two events lie six hundred years, a period of time equivalent
to that separating Chaucer from the present day. In those six centuries a
concept of Englishness first emerged, fostered by the Church and given a
precocious statement in the Venerable Bede's *Ecclesiastical History of the
English Nation* (c. 731). It was in those centuries that institutions of
government like the county shires were established in forms which were to
endure until the reorganisation of 1974. It was in this period that the
diocesan and parish network of the Church took on a pattern which persisted,
little altered, into the nineteenth century. These were the centuries also when
most of the towns and villages of England first emerged as recognisable
entities and were given the names which they still carry. And it was in those
years that the ancestral form of modern English was first spoken in Britain
and acquired a status as a literary language.

Over such a lengthy period there were, inevitably, great changes. The
various Germanic groups who settled in eastern Britain in the fifth and sixth

centuries were pagans and, in any conventional sense, illiterate; by contrast
William the Conqueror's England was wholly Christian and the scribes of its
court and monasteries could record their history, literature and law in Latin,
Anglo-Saxon and Norman French. In the early centuries after the Anglo-
Saxon settlement political power in England was divided among a myriad of
monarchs, yet the Conqueror inherited what had been a unitary kingdom for
over a century. The Germanic invaders in the fifth century had brought a
coinless economy to a coinless Britain, but the Normans took over one of the
most efficient currency systems in western Europe, operated by a complex
and highly organised administration. In the fifth century there was no such
thing as an urban society in England yet, by the time of the Norman
Conquest, York had at least 8,000 inhabitants and even a conservative
estimate gives London a population of some 12,000. To this selective
catalogue of radical change we can add one final item: in the ninth century
Scandinavian settlers took over large areas of northern England and
transformed its language, social organisation and ecclesiastical structures so
profoundly that their legacy was still visible centuries after William was dead.

Insulated by distance, there may now seem little to distinguish the fifth-
century period of Cerdic, the alleged founder of the West Saxon dynasty,
from his ninth-century successor Alfred (871–899). Alfred's England, in turn,
may now appear identical to that of Edward the Confessor (1042–66). But all
three kings moved in very different worlds and their tastes in literature, art
and architecture were no less distinct. Nor should we assume that the
patterns of patronage and production of the arts remained static throughout
the entire period. In an important sense therefore the term 'Anglo-Saxon' is
dangerously imprecise.

Alerted to the existence of change, we can now safely turn to three features
of Anglo-Saxon society which remained consistently important throughout
the pre-Norman period. The first is the surprisingly influential role played by
women. We cannot be certain of their relative status in the pagan period but
once records begin we find them taking a significant part in the foundation
and leadership of monastic houses; they own, manage and bequeath estates;
they act as patrons. Throughout the period they preserved a status which
they did not regain for centuries after the Norman Conquest.

The other two persistent features of this society are the bonds within it,
dependant on the family and on that link between lord and retainer to which
Tacitus drew attention when describing an earlier continental Germanic
peoples. This latter relationship between a leader and his 'companions'
(*comites*) depended on a reciprocal loyalty, the followers supporting their lord
in exchange for rewards of lands and treasure. These kin and *comitatus* links
were to remain basic to Anglo-Saxon society throughout the period, and were
indeed essential to its stability. Thus the legal system depended on the
protections afforded by family and lordship arrangements, and on those
groups taking responsibility for their members. They are also links which
were powerfully evoked and constantly examined in the literature of the
period. Not only, for example, do we find the *comitatus* bond ritualistically
celebrated in the poem on the *Battle of Maldon* (991), but it provided a
means by which poets could explore man's relationship with his God in terms

relevant to Anglo-Saxon experience. So Satan in *Genesis B* is depicted as illogically demanding loyalty from his followers whilst denying his own duties to God – and then further compounding his error in Anglo-Saxon eyes by failing to reward his men. In a more complex fashion the unnaturalness of the created world's destruction of its creator is expressed in the *Dream of the Rood* by the figure of the cross, whose paradoxical duty it is as a loyal servant to aid in the death of his Lord.

Family bonds and *comitatus* links both encouraged the growth and preservation of a strongly hierarchical society. As soon as the Anglo-Saxons emerge into written records in the seventh century, we find them set in a fine series of social gradings. This is clearly visible in the *wergild* system which assigned a value to each rank by which compensation to kin and lord for injury or death could be calculated. The early Kentish laws, for example, divide freemen into three groups, all at different valuations, and not only distinguish between three ranks of half-free but go on to register no less than three types of female slave. The advent of Christianity in the seventh century, far from simplifying this system, merely added further gradings and distinctions. It comes therefore as no surprise to find that one of the ordinances of Cnut (1017–35) carefully itemises the four horses (two saddled and two unsaddled), two swords, four spears, four shields, helmet, coat of mail and fifty mancuses which represent the dues of a thane *close* to the king, as against the single horse trappings and unspecified weapons due from a thane who did not enjoy that honour.

Such rankings were visibly marked in the clothing, the jewellery and the armour of both men and women and they are evident from the very earliest settlement period. Archaeologists may worry about the methodology of assuming that the appearance of the dead can easily be correlated with that of the living, but in every pagan cemetery there are some graves which are more elaborately constructed than others, that have types of jewellery which do not appear elsewhere or symbolic objects which are rare in flanking burials. Recent studies of the graves of southern England, indeed, emphasise how far such disparities increased in the course of the sixth and seventh centuries as more disposable wealth became available and was apparently concentrated in fewer hands. To compare the riches of the large royal ship-burial from Sutton Hoo (deposited in c.625) with the poverty-stricken inhumations which form the vast majority of excavated cemeteries is to recognise what variable resources were available to the different ranks within this highly stratified society. The conversion to Christianity changed nothing in this respect for it also had its rankings, its poverties and its wealth. Even St Cuthbert (c.630–687), whose retiring nature and sense of personal inadequacy were emphasised by Bede, was clothed in death in Byzantine vestments of silk with a garnet and gold pectoral cross glittering on his breast. Such contrasts of wealth and display may have provoked moralising comment; 'the superfluity of the prince is the poverty of the people' wrote Alcuin (c.735–804). But they were a fact of Anglo-Saxon life and they are inevitably reflected in the varieties of patronage available and the circulation of the art which that patronage provoked.

I have begun with certain generalisations. What now follows is not designed as a 'history'. Rather it attempts to focus on major turning points in the development of pre-Norman England which changed the patterns of patronage, the artistic expectations of those patrons, and the sources of inspiration and materials available to the artists, architects and poets of Anglo-Saxon England.

The settlement

Writing at Jarrow in c.731 the Venerable Bede devoted part of his *Ecclesiastical History* to providing his readers with a coherent narrative of the Anglo-Saxon settlement. The invaders, he claimed, came from 'three very powerful Germanic tribes – the Saxons, the Angles and the Jutes'. As he saw it, the major kingdoms which had emerged by his period could be traced back to these differing tribes. The East Angles, Middle Angles, Mercians and Northumbrians all derived from the Angles; the East, South and West Saxons descended from groups emanating from Old Saxony, whilst Kent, the Isle of Wight and neighbouring areas of Hampshire had a Jutish origin. Like the sixth-century Welsh monk Gildas, on whom he depended for much of his information, Bede believed that a significant role in the story of the settlement had been played by a revolt of mercenaries employed by the Celtic leaders of sub-Roman Britain. Unlike Gildas, however, Bede was aware that there were problems in fitting the traditional narrative into a satisfactory chronological framework. Nevertheless, by the end of his life, he (like the anonymous Gallic Chronicler) saw the middle years of the fifth century as the period of crucial change.

Many archaeologists and place-name specialists would now wish to modify Bede's account. First they would claim that the evidence of pottery and metalwork show that the settlement was a relatively lengthy process which began well before the mid-fifth century and extended into the opening decades of the sixth. This evidence also points to a degree of cultural intermingling (at least within the earliest phases of the *adventus*) which needs to be set against Bede's neat allocation of his contemporary kingdoms to Jutes, Saxons and Angles. Finally, whilst there is no doubt that it was peoples from these tribes, whose homelands stretch from the River Weser northwards into Denmark, who provided the bulk of the settlers, both archaeology and place-name evidence point to the involvement of other groups as well. Elements from Western Norway and Sweden can be traced, for example, and a significant role in the development of Kent was played by Franks from the Rhineland.

Ever since archaeologists first began to examine their material in the light of Bede's statements it is eastern Kent which has provided the greatest challenge to attempts at disentangling the various strands of settlement. Jutes, Franks and South Scandinavians all seem to have played a part in what, by the sixth century, was one of the richest areas of the country. By that time Frankish fashions current in the adjacent Rhineland were being adapted in the weaponry and jewellery of the upper ranks of Kentish society. Garnets were being imported for local jewellers and more exotic items like bronze vessels from Alexandria testify to the far-flung trading links which had developed within a century of the original settlements. Not only was glass being imported from factories in the Rhineland but it was also being manufactured within Kent itself. Gold was available in sufficient quantities to be used in jewellery and to be deposited with the dead, much of it, no doubt, drawn into Kent in the form of bullion derived from Byzantine, Merovingian and Visigothic coinage. This background of wealth, and the early emergence of an organised society capable of trading material through to the rest of the country, is presumably what lies behind the marriage alliance of King Aethelbert (c.560–616) to a Frankish princess. The presence of sixth-century graves which are almost wholly Frankish in nature suggests that this royal alliance may not have been the only cross-Channel link in this period.

With the exception of the Franks all of the settlers came from areas at some remove from the Roman world. In Roman cultural terms they were amongst the most 'barbarian' of all the new masters of the Empire. This factor needs to be taken into account as we try to assess the evidence for continuity between Roman and Saxon Britain. Any such continuity would, of course, have great significance for the arts. But, in thinking about it, we would do well to begin by recalling that England, in significant ways, was totally unlike Gaul, Italy, Spain – all of which also eventually fell under some sort of Germanic control. There are important *dis*continuities here which do not appear elsewhere. Thus in England neither Latin nor Celtic survived. By contrast the romance languages of Spain, France and Italy are in direct linear descent from Latin; Visigoths and Ostrogoths and Franks did not impose their own language on their new countries as did the Anglo-Saxons. Secondly, and connectedly, the toponymy of England is essentially Anglo-Saxon and Scandinavian and reflects little of the nomenclature of the towns, forts and villas of Roman Britain.

Thirdly there is no evidence of widespread continuity of Christianity in Britain from the Roman period. It may have survived in exceptional localities like Elmet in Yorkshire or St Albans. Churches built by the Romans were certainly still visible in Bede's day and several were refurbished by the early missionaries. But it was only in the Celtic west of Britain, away from the main areas of early pagan Anglo-Saxon settlement, and in contact with the Christian Mediterranean by the western seaways, that we can trace any continuity of organised Christianity from the later years of the fourth century. Christianity had to be *re*-introduced to lowland Britain and consequently there is no English episcopal see which can claim the kind of direct lineage back to a third/fourth-century foundation of the type readily furnished by French sites like Tours, Clermont or Lyons.

Given such massive disconnections in language and religion it is perhaps wise to view other claimed examples of continuity with a certain degree of scepticism. Apparent identities of settlement focus and land boundaries between the Roman and Saxon periods may reflect no more than enduring topographical controls on land utilisation. Similarly the fact that Winchester, York and Canterbury all emerge as secular administrative centres and diocesan sees in the seventh century (or that the main *principia* building of

Roman York remained roofed and in use until the ninth century) should not automatically be assumed to imply continuity of settlement, let alone of function. Indeed the evidence from all three of those sites suggests that what the Roman walls enclosed was not, initially, a bustling town but rather a group of royal and episcopal buildings. The population was elsewhere.

This is not to claim that Roman Britain was not still everywhere visible, obtrusive on the Anglo-Saxon landscape. Its remains were merely being put to other uses. The villa at Denton in Lincolnshire was used as a grave-site. Bede viewed the nearby Roman Wall as an ancient monument and, like a good archaeologist, saw it as a feature to be measured. St Cuthbert was shown around the remains of Carlisle in a similar spirit of antiquarianism in 684. The walls of the forts could be used to define the boundaries of monasteries like Reculver or Burgh Castle. Their ready-cut stone was a useful quarry for early churchbuilders like St Wilfrid at Hexham (674) (see p. 232) and remained available as such throughout the Anglo-Saxon period, as Matthew Paris' account of Abbot Ealdred's search for building materials for St Albans in c.1040 vividly reminds us. Similar motives inspired the monks of Ely as they searched the ruins of Roman Cambridge in the seventh century for a suitable sarcophagus in which to place Queen Aethelthryth (d.680).

But perhaps the most potent use to which these buildings were adapted was as a literary symbol of a great past, a warning in their decay of the universal ruin which Christian doctrine predicted would come at Domesday. The poets of *The Seafarer* and *The Wanderer* inherited this theme from Christian Latin poetry but it was one which would have had an immediate impact on an Anglo-Saxon audience. Centuries later Shakespeare's 'bare ruin'd choirs' was similarly relevant to the experience of post-Dissolution England.

Of course the art and architecture of Roman Britain remained constantly accessible to the Anglo-Saxons. Its gold and silver provided material for the jeweller's crucible and its coins could be made into pendants. More positively the same Roman coinage provided decorative themes for Anglo-Saxon currency as late as the Viking period; memories of legionary emblems may lie behind the standards recorded by Bede from seventh-century Northumbria, and it has been argued that the enormous wooden 'grandstand' at the Northumbrian palace site of Yeavering derives its form from a Romano-British theatre. We cannot, then, deny that the Roman past had its impact, but much of the claimed continuity of culture was a matter of chance exploitation, like the figure of Caesar added to the genealogy of the East Anglian kings, or the fourth-century sardonyx cameo showing a late Roman emperor as Jupiter, 'almost too big to hold in one hand' recorded and drawn by Matthew Paris as having been presented by Aethelraed II (979–1016) to the Abbey of St Albans – and subsequently used in an intriguing fashion as an aid to expectant mothers.

Having expressed scepticism about the extent of *romanitas* in pagan Anglo-Saxon England we must not fall into the trap of assuming that this is the only criterion available for assessing a society. It is therefore more helpful and relevant to close with some evidence to be deduced from two of its best-known monuments: the royal ship-burial from Sutton Hoo in Suffolk and the palace site at Yeavering in Northumberland.

Yeavering was one of a series of palaces which the kings of Northumbria, like their equivalents elsewhere, occupied temporarily in their progress round the kingdom. Its buildings included massive halls, several between eighty and ninety feet long. To build them, a mass of tall straight timbers, each weighing several hundredweight, had to be selected, felled, trimmed and squared before they were carted to the site and set in trenches dug to a depth of some eight feet. One structure alone required the removal of 72 cubic yards of soil before the timbers could be positioned. The logistical skills involved in these operations reflect a sophisticated society capable of deploying considerable resources into major projects. The main burial from Sutton Hoo (dated c.625) offers analagous insights into this society on the eve of its conversion to Christianity (see pp. 135–8, colour pl. 7, 8). The regalia in the burial, for example, is decorated with more than 4,000 separate garnets and a skilled gem-cutter would require at least a day to cut and polish each one. Nor should we ignore the implications of the regalia as a measurement of the scale of riches which were concentrated in royal hands, for it would be naive to assume that the material committed to Redwald's burial represented the sum total of the East Anglian treasury.

The wealth is startling; and so too is the conservatism of the burial. This accounts for the presence of those 'old treasures' which are frequently extolled in Anglo-Saxon literature, but it is most evident in the form of the funeral itself. On the eve of the conversion, a king was buried with all the traditional boat-centred rites of his Swedish ancestors. Nothing could more effectively underline that nostalgic adherence to tradition which was cultivated by a warrior society throughout the entire Anglo-Saxon period.

The conversion

Both Sutton Hoo and Yeavering are linked to the story of the conversion of England. If the main burial at Sutton Hoo is that of Redwald (d.c.625) then it honours the memory of an early, and wavering, convert; whilst it was at Yeavering that the Italian monk Paulinus baptised thousands in one of the more spectacular successes of the first mission to Northumbria.

Bede's narrative of the conversion takes us further back than either Redwald or Paulinus, however, and in so doing incidentally records one of the sources of wealth (and thus indirectly of artistic patronage) in both pagan and Christian England – the income to be derived from slaves. According to Bede it was the sight of English slaves in the market place in Rome which first inspired Pope Gregory both to a series of significant puns ('Angles' – 'angels') and to attempt the conversion of England. The mission eventually arrived in 597 in Kent, where King Aethelbert's Frankish wife had already accustomed the court to Christian practices. It was led by St Augustine 'paralysed with terror' at the prospect of dealing with a 'barbarous, fierce and unbelieving nation'. His forty-strong mission, properly and practically respectful of hierarchy (and no doubt aware of the sacral nature of Anglo-Saxon kingship), concentrated on the conversion of the royal household. Within a year Pope Gregory was able to report to the Patriarch of Alexandria that 10,000 English had been baptised. At first all seems to have proceeded apace and by 604 sees had been founded at Rochester and London, as well as at Canterbury.

But the early years of the seventh century saw setbacks as well as successes. Augustine's death at some date between 604 and 609 may have weakened the impetus of the conversion progress but certainly the bishop of London was driven from his see as the royal family turned against him, and Rochester collapsed because of lack of adequate finances. An offshoot of this Kentish mission which had begun auspiciously in Northumbria under Paulinus in c.625 also withdrew when the Deiran royal family lost power on King Edwin's death in 632. Christianity eventually did establish itself, but there were periods of uncertainty in its initial decades and there are hints that pagan practices were not so easily eradicated as Bede's narrative might suggest.

The Augustinian, Kentish-based, mission was not the only source of the conversion of Anglo-Saxon England; in areas like Northumbria, indeed, it was not even the most effective source. In the north the death of Edwin brought a rival royal family to the throne. Under Oswald it had been in exile on Iona during Edwin's reign and there had been converted to Christianity in what was effectively an Irish milieu. Oswald's victory at the Battle of Heavenfield near Hexham in 633 was followed by an invitation to the monks of Iona to send a missionary group to his new kingdom. By 635 St Aidan was established on Lindisfarne and from there began what was to prove the permanent conversion of the north.

Bede's narrative inevitably focuses upon Northumbria but it is clear that Irish missionaries were also active in other parts of the country. Men like Fursa in East Anglia and Dicuil in Sussex are less fully chronicled than Aidan, but contributed to a very complex pattern of conversion.

By the middle years of the seventh century it was apparent that the differing sources of conversion were producing awkward anomalies in organisation and in liturgical observances across the country. The problems were at their most acute in Northumbria and were only finally resolved at the so-called Synod of Whitby in 664 where the Northumbrian church resolved to bring its practices into conformity with those operating over large areas of southern England and, more importantly, on the continent. The later part of the century consequently saw a massive strengthening of links between the Northumbrian church and Mediterranean world through the travels and activities of such men as Benedict Biscop (628–690), the founder of Monkwearmouth (674) and Jarrow (681–682), and Wilfrid (634–709) archbishop of York and abbot of Ripon and Hexham.

Despite all this, the Irish links were not totally ruptured. To Bede's occasional puzzlement Englishmen still went to Ireland for training in his day and the monastery at Mayo remained an English stronghold through that century. There were also English communities in Munster and Armagh.

Equally, Irishmen were present in England: Adamnan, the great scholar-abbot of Iona paid two visits to Northumbria in the late seventh century; an Irish scribe named Ultan was working in one of the daughter houses of Lindisfarne in the early eighth century; Alcuin (c.735–804) frequently met Irishmen when at York in the later eighth century and kept up a correspondence from France with Irish scholars. The 'Irish dimension' to Northumbria's Christianity (and to that of other areas as well) did not die with the Synod of Whitby. This Irish link in fact must be seen as one of a series of strands which contributed to the remarkably cosmopolitan nature of the early church in England – a church in which leading roles were played by Archbishop Theodore of Tarsus (669–690), a North African called Hadrian and a clutch of Gallic bishops in East Anglia and Wessex.

Whatever its source, the conversion to Christianity affected every area of Anglo-Saxon experience. Within a century of the arrival of St Augustine, for example, great changes had taken place in the visible landscape. The new wooden churches on lords' estates may not have looked very different from the secular buildings which surrounded them but increasingly towards the end of the century an alien tradition of stone construction, transplanted from the Christian Mediterranean world, invaded the Anglo-Saxon horizon.

These exotic buildings involved importing foreign craftsmen. To Monkwearmouth (see p. 232) and Jarrow, Benedict Biscop, long familiar with the Christian world of Gaul and Italy through his travels, brought foreign masons and glaziers. In Bede's later life the arts of lathe-turning of stone and mortar mixing were sufficiently familiar for him to use them as images in his commentaries, but it should not be forgotten that they were alien techniques in his youth and had to be taught to the Anglo-Saxons by overseas craftsmen. The crushed brick mortar floors on which Bede walked and the painted plaster which decorated the monastic buildings he knew were equally novel to seventh-century England. So too was the art of stone carving, first used in architectural decoration before it spread to other forms like crosses and slabs. And much of the ornament of that sculpture was foreign to Anglo-Saxon experience; the ubiquitous vine-scrolls derive from eastern Mediterranean models, whilst some of Hexham's abstract circular patterns are best matched in Spain, Italy and North Africa.

Surrounded by buildings, decoration and technologies from the Mediterranean heartlands of Christianity, the focus of monastic life at places like Jarrow lay in the *Opus Dei*, the worship of God. It was a worship offered in a foreign language, Latin, which had not been heard in lowland Britain for over 200 years. Yet so familiar did it become to men like Bede that they could compose in it, and deploy all its rhetorical devices, without seeming effort.

Worship, of course, did not merely demand the reading or repetition of Latin texts. It also involved chants and singing. Again overseas instructors were required. Benedict Biscop brought the arch-cantor from St Peter's in Rome to instruct the Anglo-Saxon monks in the practice of his church, whilst in the early years of the eighth century the monks of Hexham are known to have received similar instruction. Nor was this all. The liturgy also provided types of dramatic presentations: an eighth-century manuscript from

Northumbria, now in Cambridge, has its passion narrative marked for an antiphonal reading between lector and cantor: and the ninth-century *Book of Cerne* preserves sections of a dramatic presentation of the Harrowing of Hell based on the practice of eighth-century Lindisfarne.

The liturgy celebrates the word of God as recorded in the Bible. Christianity is the religion of *a* Book and of many books. And two of the fundamental contributions of Christianity to England were literacy and the craft of book-making. There now existed, in a manner which had not hitherto been possible, the ability to record experience in a permanent non-oral form (see pp. 146–9). Initially this book-centredness of Christianity can be seen in the importation of books from the Mediterranean and Irish worlds by the early missionaries. Such is the illuminated sixth-century Italian Gospels, once in Canterbury but now in Cambridge, which could well have been the 'St Augustine Gospels' their title claims them to be. To these early imports were added, in the course of the seventh century, other books brought back by travellers like Benedict Biscop and Wilfrid to stock the libraries of their monastic houses at Jarrow and Hexham. Like their Gallic contemporaries they were plundering the libraries of Italy and southern France. Through these volumes the Anglo-Saxons became familiar with the techniques of book production, and in them they were confronted with the art of other worlds. So Eadfrith (d.721), the illuminator of the Lindisfarne Gospels, was able to use an Italian gospel book as his model, whilst the monks of Jarrow could gaze on the great picture of the temple in Jerusalem which had been prepared by the sixth-century Italian statesman, Cassiodorus, for his *Codex Grandior*, a volume which eventually found its way to Northumbria.

Foreign artistic traditions reached Christian Anglo-Saxons in other ways besides books. Benedict Biscop decorated the walls of churches at Monkwearmouth and Jarrow with paintings brought from Rome. The modelled figure carving, the iconographic arrangements and the vine-scrolls of early Anglo-Saxon sculpture clearly reflect the presence of Mediterranean ivories and metalwork in early Christian England. And the fact that St Cuthbert's body, when translated into a shrine at Lindisfarne in 698, was wrapped in vestments of Byzantine silk, reminds us of other media which could bring exotic forms of ornament to the fringes of the Christian world.

Not all of the books brought back from the continent by men like Wilfrid and Benedict Biscop were illuminated. The majority were, in fact, almost certainly working texts, designed for instruction and study in the monasteries of England. Lacking illumination most of them, along with copies made in Britain, have failed to survive but their former presence is everywhere visible in the pages of men like Bede, Aldhelm (c.640–709) and Alcuin. Bede never travelled far from Jarrow but the resources of his library, supplemented by judicious borrowings from his correspondents, gave him access to the writings of early Christian fathers like Augustine, Ambrose and Gregory, as well as his near-contemporary Isodore of Seville; Christian poets like Arator, Sedulius and Prudentius were clearly familiar to him as well as historians like Orosius and Josephus. Pliny, Ovid and Virgil also figured in his library. Nor did Jarrow stand alone. We know that Hexham had a fine set of books and, a century after Bede, Alcuin wrote a nostalgic Latin poem in which he listed the authors who had been available to him in York's great monastic collection. The stylistic impact of these writers is stamped across Anglo-Saxons' texts; so Alcuin, re-working Bede's account of the pagan priest Coefi leaving Edwin's court to destroy the pagan idols, sends him on his way in words which are a direct echo of Virgil; similarly Aldhelm's tortuous prose is a reflex of the sophisticated study of Latin works which had been available to him at Malmesbury.

These imported books opened up new vistas in time and space for the Anglo-Saxons. As Christians they recognised that they lived on the frontiers of the known world – 'almost under the north pole' claimed Bede – and that world was centred on the Mediterranean, on Rome and on Jerusalem; this was a radical change from the perceptions of their pagan ancestors. Through books, monks knew of the natural occurrence of bitumen, and of the problems involved in rendering the finer points of the Greek text of the Acts of the Apostles – both topics to be found in Bede's writings. Through books also they were familiar with the precise topography of Palestine's holy places. And in the scriptorium, the preparation of purple, ultramarine and carmine paints from exotic plants like folium, strange insects like cermes and foreign minerals like lapis lazuli, were all now part of everyday experience.

Equally significantly these books, and the art which came to Britain with them, encouraged the novel concept of patterned and abstract thought. Around the walls of Jarrow was a set of typological paintings emphasising the manner in which the events of the Old Testament shadowed the fulfilment of the New. They were the visual expression of the approach to the Old Testament adopted by the early Fathers whose works were available in the monastic library. So Isaac carrying the faggots to his sacrifice was set opposite Christ carrying his cross to Golgotha. 'Everything', as St Augustine wrote 'which happened to Abraham actually happened but it was, at the same time, a prophetic image of what was to come.' This type of thinking was forced home by the liturgy, linking the events of Christian history together, and demonstrating how the patterns are repeated in the spiritual life of each man. The Tree of Life on which Christ died was to undo the evil which sprang from that other tree in Eden – and was to appear again at the end of time as the Cross of Judgement. To refer to one event was to conjure up the others. So the poet of the *Dream of the Rood*, brought up to this type of approach, moves easily from consideration of the crucifixion to contemplation of the Last Judgement as he gazes on the vision of the cross which unites both events, just as the artist of the Durham Gospels (c.700) shows a crucifixion surrounded by a text associated with Domesday. To read Bede's works is to be reminded of the power of Christian thinking to evoke symbolism and allegory, to awaken those patterned methods of thought which led variously to the exegesis of Aldhelm, the baptismal allusions of the Anglo-Saxon poem *Exodus*, and the ambiguity of the full-page abstract ornament preceding each gospel in the *Lindisfarne Gospels* in which lurks a complex set of cruciform shapes.

It has to be admitted that much of this subtle intellectual activity and most of the technology of Christianity would be something which the average Anglo-Saxon would only glimpse from afar. Literacy was to remain a rare and a largely monastic achievement whilst the subtleties of typology can have had little impact on the average peasant or nobleman. Where both *would* be aware of a radical change triggered by Christianity would be in the impact that the church's advent had on the ownership of land, which provided the only source of substantial wealth in early medieval England.

Monasteries undoubtedly needed the resources which came from the possession of large estates. Consider, for example, the financial implications of just one Jarrow manuscript, the *Codex Amiatinus*, written by seven scribes in the period around 700 (see pp. 154–9). This enormous bible, which takes three men to carry it, uses a single calf skin for each double-spread page. There are 515 such pages in the book and we know from Bede that the same scriptorium produced two other similar volumes. The demands for just three manuscripts was therefore of the order of 1,545 calves – a substantial requirement from any estate.

It is resource needs like this which lie behind the acquisition of land by the early monasteries, and behind their careful encouragement of kings to present it to them. But buildings and books were not the only reasons. St Wilfrid, for example, had extensive holdings in Northumbria, Mercia, Sussex, Somerset and the Isle of Wight, estates which enabled him to match and stand up to kings who, as he knew from his painful experiences in Merovingian France, would take political advantage of bishops and abbots weakened by lack of income. There is then a pastoral rationale behind monastic land acquisition; land and what stemmed from it, was not only the basis for books, buildings and metalwork, but it also underpinned the organisation and preservation of the Church's spiritual function.

The Church's intervention into the pattern of land holdings was inevitably disruptive to society. Estates which passed to monasteries were not, in contrast to secular holdings, available to kings for reallocation to followers in the next generation. They were frozen into church hands. This problem was compounded by the fact that the later seventh and early eighth centuries saw the high water mark of Anglo-Saxon expansion at the expense of their neighbouring Celtic peoples; the possibility of gifting conquered territories was also being closed to Anglo-Saxon kings. Much of the political chaos of eighth-century Northumbria is attributable to the progressive impoverishment of the available supplies of land through which loyalties were cemented. And, as Bede recognised, the problem was exacerbated by the creation of monasteries which, by remaining as family institutions, allowed successive members of noble families (nominally acting as abbots) to preserve their lands from generation to generation.

Pursuit of family interest was at least one of the factors contributing to a feature of monasticism which characterised both Anglo-Saxon England and Gaul: its involvement with the aristocracy. There is, of course, no reason to believe that the spiritual energy and effectiveness of monastic houses was in any way diminished because of contacts with the social establishment of their day. But there are clear signs that the monasteries did not remain unaffected by the literary, artistic and recreational tastes of the aristocratic warrior world from which many of their leaders were drawn. And these signs are not limited solely to the 'family monasteries' which drew Bede's criticism –

Alcuin was to fulminate against the monks of Lindisfarne whom he saw as being rightly punished by God through a Viking raid because of their interest in secular myths. 'What' he wrote 'has Ingeld to do with Christ?' That Germanic hero had no place, as he saw it, in the experience of a Christian monastery. But it is quite clear that such tastes *were* widespread. Extravagant clothing, drunkenness, horse-racing, singing in the manner of secular poets are all activities mentioned by church councils and church leaders.

It is presumably this curious background of informed Christian belief, coupled with an abiding interest in the ideals and practices of a warrior aristocracy, which explains such works as the Franks Casket, a whalebone box of the eighth century whose figural art mixes Christian history with secular Germanic narrative, the adoration of the Magi being patterned against the story of Weland, the great smith of Germanic legend (see p. 175). It is presumably also to this literate monastic world that we owe important stages in the development of the *Beowulf* poem (?eighth century), in which we find an easy familiarity with biblical commentaries informing an investigation of heroic duty and of the interrelationship of wisdom and strength in a warrior society. At the heart of the literate, Christian and (in many senses) foreign world of Anglo-Saxon monasticism there lay an interest in, and concern for, the ideals and practices of the society that lay beyond the monastic vallum.

Christianity brought a new set of patrons to Anglo-Saxon England as well as bringing to it new ways of thinking, new motifs and new forms of art. The proper furnishing of the church, the preparation of an appropriate setting for the liturgy, the visible glorification of the relics of its saints all combined to make new demands on embroiderers, metalworkers, carpenters, painters and poets. Large monastic houses also provided a context in which artists in one medium could respond to those in another. So the stone grave-markers of Lindisfarne echo the cruciform carpet pages of the illuminated Gospels; and the Gospels in turn reflect contemporary metalwork.

Through the monastic network, literature and art were gifted, borrowed and copied across Anglo-Saxon England. In the course of the seventh and eighth centuries they also passed abroad, not only to Ireland and Pictish Scotland, but to the continent. Correspondence survives to show that missionaries in Germany, like St Boniface (d.754), were supplied with books and other gifts by their English contacts and supporters. By such routes English ornament had its impact on continental styles – witness the Anglo-Saxon basis to the decoration of the magnificent Tassilo chalice made for a Duke of Bavaria in 777–788. At a later date Alcuin's presence in Charlemagne's court is presumably one of the factors responsible for the English contribution to the development of Carolingian art. Just as Christianity had originally been responsible for bringing the Anglo-Saxons into contact with other artistic traditions, so it was also responsible for the transmission of English art and thought back to the continent.

Our picture of the arts between the seventh and ninth centuries is slanted by the chances of survival. Ironically, however, one of the main factors militating against survival is Christianity itself. For Christian doctrine taught that, in the words of *The Seafarer*, gold strewn with the dead would be of no

avail. The pagan practice of depositing goods in the grave has the great
advantage of ensuring their preservation for the modern archaeologist.
Christian teaching left them above ground, subject to the changing whims
and tastes of the living, and successive generations did not always see the
transmission of outdated material as one of their primary duties.

The Vikings

By the middle years of the ninth century monasticism was clearly in decline.
And that decline is inevitably reflected in the arts. There are, for example,
few illuminated books dating to the period after the opening of the century
whilst Latin literacy was certainly deteriorating, as both the manuscripts and
the recollections of King Alfred (871–899) alike testify. This steady erosion of
one of the main areas of artistic activity was suddenly accelerated by the
Viking raids and settlements.

In the year 793, according to the horrified Alcuin, Lindisfarne was
'spattered with the blood of priests, despoiled of all its ornaments'. Echoing
Amos he mourned that 'foxes have pillaged the chosen vine'. St Cuthbert's
monastery had been sacked by Vikings in the first of a series of raids which,
by the mid-century, had developed into a determined attempt to settle and
control the whole of England.

By 876 York was in Viking hands and this was followed in the next year by
seizure of the 'Five Boroughs' area of Lincoln, Nottingham, Derby, Leicester
and Stamford. The complete Scandinavian domination of the country was
only avoided by the brilliant generalship of a member of the only Anglo-
Saxon dynasty to survive the political cataclysm of the ninth century, the
West Saxon King Alfred (871–899). He evolved a strategy which finally
contained the rapidly moving forces of his enemies and, by c.886, had
established a *modus vivendi* with the Scandinavian Guthrum which left the
country politically severed between an Anglo-Saxon south and an Anglo-
Scandinavian north. It fell to Alfred's successors in the next half century to
regain political control of the north, though it was not until 954 that the last
Viking king of York, Eric Bloodaxe, was forced from his capital and killed on
Stainmoor. But even when that southern control was re-established, and
England had thus been transformed into a unitary kingdom, the north
remained socially, linguistically, legally and ecclesiastically distinct from the
south. Those moves towards a unity of English culture which can be seen
developing in the ninth century were shattered. A north/south opposition had
been established which was to last for centuries.

Historians have argued vehemently over the effects of the Scandinavian
settlement. We have rightly been brought to recognise the Vikings'
chameleon-like ability to adopt the practices of the peoples amongst whom
they found themselves. In northern England this showed itself in their rapid
conversion to Christianity and in their early alliances with the archbishops of
York in common opposition to the southern kings. But their disruptive effects
on the upper ranks of society (so crucial to artistic patronage) and on the
church cannot be ignored. The Cuthbert community, admittedly, was able to

retain most of its lands by adroit political manoeuverings but this needs to be set against the massive changes in diocesan organisation (usually the most durable of institutions) and the final extinction of the northern monasteries which followed the settlement. Wealth and estates were lost by church and secular lords alike. Monasteries *were* sacked. Alfred, in a letter to his bishops, may have been exaggerating when he spoke of 'everything' being 'ravaged and burnt', but there must have been some basis for his claims. Indeed, striking confirmation of them comes from the scribbled note on the eighth-century Gospel book, the *Codex Aureus*, recording that Ealdorman Aelfred and Werburg his wife had paid out 'true money, pure gold' to buy back the volume from the heathen. Learning and the art of monasteries had obviously suffered. Many historians now claim that there was little which was specifically anti-Christian in monastic looting, but this knowledge would only have been of purely academic interest to the monks whose chalices, shrines, book-covers, gold and silver were lost in the search for what archaeologists now disinterestedly label as 'moveable wealth'.

With the decline of monasteries a source of patronage was lost and with it that network of contacts between houses which had facilitated the easy spread of motifs, books and ideas. But in the north fresh patrons emerged, for at least some of the arts. It would appear, for example, that sculpture (hitherto an exclusively monastic medium) survived under the enthusiastic lay patronage of the emerging Anglo-Scandinavian aristocracy. Novel themes were introduced to stone carving by these new patrons: the animal art of Scandinavia and depictions of secular scenes and heroic myths which had circulated hitherto in the more perishable media of shield paintings, tapestries and wood carvings. Among these sculptures, at sites like Gosforth in Cumbria, are some startling juxtapositions of pagan Scandinavian mythology with Christian scenes, betraying the existence of some novel theological insights in the new fused culture of the Anglo-Scandinavian north.

Although monasticism in southern England had suffered less from Viking attacks than its northern counterpart we have already seen that it was weakening as an institution through the ninth century. What was also dying with it was the Latin learning which had been provided by those monasteries. Neglect of this educational essential was, in Alfred's eyes, one of the reasons for the successes of the Vikings and he devoted much of his later life to the problem. His efforts to remedy the situation were, however, not based on Latin but on a radical educational scheme which used the vernacular as a basic educational and literary medium, with knowledge of Latin limited to those who were to be pressed to higher office. In a famous letter to his bishops he enlisted their aid in providing translations of 'those books most needful for all men to know' which were demanded by this programme, and this call, accompanied by a justification of the use of English which was to be repeated centuries later by Tyndale, marks the beginning of English prose. For the translations which flowed from his initiative were as much 'sense for sense' as 'word for word' and large sections of them were original compositions.

Alfred's exploitation of the vernacular for education and literary purposes demonstrated that it had a capacity for rhetorical expression which was comparable to Latin, and encouraged its development far beyond the bounds of translations. As a result, by the time of the Norman Conquest, English was being used as a written instrument in areas such as scientific writings and biographies in a manner unparalleled anywhere else in western Europe. The irony was that the initial impetus had come from a response to a decline in ability to handle the only proper language of medieval education, Latin.

Alfred's educational reform movement depended heavily on scholars from overseas. Grimbald from Rheims (formerly of St Bertin), John the Old Saxon and the Welshman Asser were all among his helpers. In reaction to the northern orientation of the Anglo-Scandinavian areas of the country, Alfred's kingdom is characterised by links to France and the Mediterranean world and by a new intellectual content to its art. A demand for de luxe manuscripts was admittedly still not apparent but sufficient work in other media survives to show the aspirations of his period: the Alfred Jewel in which Italian and Byzantine motifs and materials are coupled to a learned iconography (see p. 127); the wall paintings from the Old Minster at Winchester with their echoes of Carolingian style; and the gilt copper-alloy purse-shaped reliquary from a Winchester cesspit which is made up from cannabalised Carolingian sheets.

These southern seeds took firmer root in the reigns of Alfred's successors as they began to re-establish political and military control over the Anglo-Scandinavian north. Edward the Elder (899–924) carried his rule to the Humber whilst Aethelstan (924–939), for a period at least, was sufficiently powerful to declare himself on his coins as *Rex Totius Brittaniae*. Aethelstan's role as patron of the arts, collector and donor matches his military achievement. There was an international flavour to his court; a Norse poet, an Irish scribe and bishop, Frankish and Italian scholars can all be traced. And the reviving monastic houses of his reign were similarly permeated with overseas scholars; witness Godescalc who was put in charge of the newly restored Abingdon, the three German names who appear in the Winchester New Minster lists or the strong German presence in London and the associated diocese of East Anglia. Aethelstan himself had a network of marriage alliances with France and Germany and was an avid book collector, owning some magnificent manuscripts prepared in continental scriptoria. And he was also a liberal donor to monastic houses. Characteristic of his generosity are his gifts to St Cuthbert's shrine at Chester-le-Street. They also give some indication of the range of art in differing media which could flow into a monastery through such donations. According to a contemporary list these included

a copy of the Gospels, two chasubles, one alb, one stole with a maniple, one girdle, three altar cloths, one chalice of silver, two patens: the one made of gold and the other of Grecian workmanship, one censer of silver, one Cross skilfully wrought of gold and ivory, one royal cap woven with gold, two (?) screens or tablets wrought in gold and silver, one missal, two copies of the Gospels ornamented in silver and gold, a life of St Cuthbert written in verse and prose, seven robes, three curtains, three pieces of tapestry, two cups (coppas) of silver with covers, three great bells, two horns (?) mounted in gold and silver, two banners, one lance and two armills of gold.

In addition to all this there were two cups filled with 'the best money' whilst his army contributed ninety-six pounds of silver. Medieval kings could be generous givers.

The Benedictine Reform movement

This renewal of monastic life in England, based upon the rules developed by Benedict of Nursia (d.c.543), derived its inspiration from reformed communities at houses like Cluny and Fleury in France and Ghent and St Omer in Flanders. It was characterised by an emphasis on the essentially liturgical character of monastic life and involved the abolition of private ownership and the strict practice of celibacy. At first the attempts at reform in England were dependent on individual initiatives; St Dunstan, for example, who had become abbot of Glastonbury in 940, was clearly sympathetic to the aims of the reformers but it was not until he was exiled in 955–956 that he came into direct contact with the continental movement (see pp. 143–6).

The key figure in the final success of the reform was the king. With the accession of Edgar (959–975) the essential impetus was given. For only the king could guarantee the donation and retention of land (and the subsequent payment of tithes) which were essential for the survival of the new and revived communities of monks. And only the king could press the reformers into influential positions within the church. This he did through three key appointments. Dunstan was given the see of Canterbury in 960. Oswald, who had studied at Fleury and reformed the house at Worcester soon after his consecration there in 961, became Archbishop of York in 971. The most energetic of the triumvirate was, however, Aethelwold, Dunstan's pupil who was Bishop of Winchester from 963–984. It was in Winchester that a Council met in c.970 to draw up the *Regularis Concordia*, a document which attempted to pull together the variant practices of the reformed houses. One of its manuscripts has a frontispiece showing Edgar flanked by Aethelwold and Dunstan; in it is encapsulated the significance of the kingship to the success of the English reform movement.

The achievements of these newly re-ordered communities are easily recognised. But the limitations of the reform ought first to be stressed. It is apparent that the reformation did not affect all monastic or quasi-monastic communities and that, even at houses like Worcester, the changes were not as thoroughgoing as later propaganda claimed. Most communities remained very small; even the New Minster at Winchester only had forty monks in 1040. What is more, the movement was also restricted geographically to southern England. Nothing could more clearly underline the division across England's cultural map consequent upon the Scandinavian settlement than the fact that Peterborough (re-founded 966) represents one of the most northerly of the reformed houses. North of the Wash the king owned little land, and the church's own holdings had been massively eroded by the Viking take-over.

These were not the conditions which encouraged new or re-newed foundations.

That said, the achievements are nevertheless quite remarkable. Significantly for architecture the Benedictine Rule's attention to elaborate liturgy (in some ways demanding more elaboration in England than was required of their continental models) demanded new kinds of building space. The *Regularis Concordia* lays stress, for example, on liturgical procession, on antiphonal singing from galleries and on the availability of chapels to the north and south of the choir. These demands find their architectural reflex in the elaborate developments at the west end of buildings and in the transept galleries constructed in the spate of church building associated with the late tenth-century reform. So too in the other arts. The *Regularis Concordia* provides evidence for the elaboration of Easter drama rituals and various manuscripts record the musical settings for a very expansive liturgy. Churches required lamps and wall hangings. Elaborate rituals needed illuminated manuscripts and liturgical vessels properly to celebrate God's word and Christ's sacrifice. The relics of saints demanded appropriate settings of gold, silver and precious stones. The art in which these needs were met and expressed, the so-called 'Winchester art', is one which draws heavily on continental motifs and concepts; strong links with the reformed monasteries in France and Germany are everywhere apparent. The *Ramsey Psalter*, for example, seems to have been prepared for Oswald yet one of its artists can also be traced working at Fleury (see p. 167, colour pl. 11).

The intellectual element of the movement left its mark in the complexities of iconography, in the scientific writings of men like Byrhtferth of Ramsey, trained by the Abbot of Fleury, and in the Latin writings of the reformers. Equally important was the fact that it was in the re-ordered setting of Winchester that Aethelwold and his school developed a form of written Old English which was to act as the national standard for over a century; whatever the local spoken variety, it was Aethelwold's written form that was accepted far beyond the bounds of Wessex, from Canterbury in the southeast, to Worcester in the west, to York in the north. These monasteries were also responsible for the manuscripts in which most of our surviving Anglo-Saxon poetry survives. For just as in the seventh and eighth, so also in the tenth and eleventh centuries, some of the monasteries and many priests retained an interest in themes more appropriate to the secular world. To that interest we owe the preservation of Anglo-Saxon poetry.

From Reform to Conquest

The reform movement survived the death of Edgar and the anti-monastic reaction which followed it. More threatening, in the sense that it involved both church and laity, was the fact that the accession of Aethelred the Unready (979–1016) coincided with a second wave of Viking invasions. The subsequent payments of Danegeld demanded vast sums of money to buy off the raiders. Inevitably the laity were badly hit, but churches and monastic institutions did not escape the taxes levied to raise these sums. The scale of

tribute was enormous. The *Anglo-Saxon Chronicle* records payments of
£10,000 in 991 and of £16,000 three years later. In 1002 and 1007 the totals
rose to £24,000 and £36,000, whilst 1018 saw a demand for £72,000. In
addition to this there were levies to meet the costs of the army and the navy.
It is indicative of the wealth of late Anglo-Saxon England that such
payments could be made and that the losses, as contemporary wills indicate,
could still be made good, but there was an inevitable effect upon the arts,
notably in the ecclesiastical sphere. At Worcester

almost all of the ornaments of the church were broken up, the altar panels furnished
with gold and silver were stripped, ornamented books and chalices were destroyed,
crosses were melted down; in the last resort even lands and villages were divested of
their wealth.

Such loss of resources affected lay and church patronage alike. In
architecture there was a resulting recession in building during the first half of
the eleventh century, though in part this might be explained by the fact that
the spate of construction for the reformed churches had met the demand.

Sustained Viking pressure eventually brought the Danish king Cnut
(1017–1035) to the English throne. Briefly, more northern tastes intruded
even into the art of the south (the St Paul's sarcophagus with its
Scandinavian-style zoomorphic art must belong to this period). But Cnut was
far from being a barbarous Scandinavian. He founded Bury St Edmunds. He
had contacts with, and made generous donations to, houses in France,
Flanders and Italy and one of the books of the period appropriately shows
him presenting an altar cross to the New Minster at Winchester alongside his
wife, Emma, who was herself also an active patron of the arts.

By the 1040s the continental links which had been such an important factor
in English life were strengthened by the return from exile of Edward the
Confessor (1042–66), who brought to his court the tastes and the personnel of
his land of exile. French language began to penetrate court English and
several of the senior posts in the church went to Frenchmen. Such elements
were bitterly resented within the country, but there is no doubt that England
was moving strongly in the direction of continental tastes even before
William made his aggressive moves to succeed. Symptomatically a
Romanesque style of sculpture was already apparent in the pre-Norman rood
at Romsey, and in architecture Westminster Abbey, which was begun in
c.1050 and in which the Confessor was to be buried, clearly exhibited that
rhythmical, ordered sense of balanced volumes which later characterises
Romanesque architecture.

To an extent, then, it is possible to argue that what followed from the
Norman takeover would have occurred without Hastings. The twelfth-
century changes within the church would have re-vitalised the monasteries,
whilst the hierarchical structure of Anglo-Saxon society already possessed all
the features which characterise the so-called feudalism of Norman England.
All of this is true, but the scale of change which followed the Conquest
should not be underestimated, particularly in that small section of society
represented by the court, the nobility and the upper ranks of the clergy.
These were the groups who set the taste of the country and in their ranks

there was much disruption. Of the twelve earls known in England in 1072 only one was English and he was executed four years later. By 1086 less than six of the 180 barons were English, whilst in 1090 only one English bishop still retained his see. The new leaders had been trained outside England and did not feel overly inhibited by respect for English traditions. Hence the radical programme of castle and church building on which they embarked. Hence also the changes in form and status of English as a literary language. Whatever the losses, however, the Conquest brought a new dynamism to English secular and spiritual life and undoubtedly gave it, thanks to the fact that the Norman kingdom straddled the Channel, a more European outlook.

Destruction and loss

The Conqueror's chaplain and biographer, William of Poitiers, breathlessly records the cartloads of treasures removed from England by William and his associates. This is just one episode in a long catalogue of destruction and loss of pre-Norman material. Viking raids, the levies associated with Danegeld, the confiscations at the Reformation, the damage inflicted in the Commonwealth era – these are all major causes of loss. And throughout the medieval period changing fashions ensured the steady destruction of pre-Norman buildings, manuscripts, metalwork, ivories and fabrics. What survives from Anglo-Saxon England is thus far from representative of what once existed. The large cathedral and monastic churches have been lost; what remains are often the buildings of impoverished communities. It is the small fragment from a shrine which is found in our museums and not work like the life-size, gem-encrusted Virgin made for Ely's Abbot Aelfsige (981–c.1019).

  In other ways also the survivors distort our understanding. Work in perishable media is not well represented. Yet the documentary sources (and occasional finds like the Glastonbury stucco, the Winchester wall painting, the nail-studded wooden saddle bow from York or the Maaseik embroideries) show that it clearly existed, often in impressive form. And finally we would do well to recall that much of what survives has come down to us through the agency of the Church, whether it be as the guardian of material or by providing the documents recording what once existed. The achievements of the secular world are thus inevitably partially screened from us.

Part II
Studies in the Individual Arts

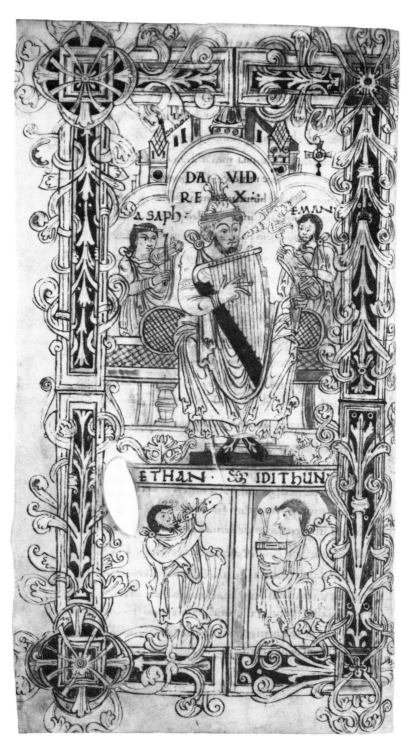

King David playing the harp, with other instrumentalists, from the Winchcomb Psalter
(eleventh century).

1 The Visual Arts and Crafts

MILDRED BUDNY

Introduction

The Anglo-Saxon period can lay fair claim to being one of the greatest and most innovative periods in the whole history of British art. Many arts and crafts flourished in a variety of media ranging from metalwork, stone sculpture and carvings in ivory, bone, wood and other materials, to manuscripts and textiles such as embroideries. The period produced such masterpieces and works of compelling beauty as the Sarre Brooch, the Kingston Brooch, the Sutton Hoo treasure, the Fuller Brooch and the Alfred Jewel (see p. 127); the Ruthwell and Bewcastle Crosses and the sculptural friezes at Breedon-on-the-Hill in stone; the coffin-reliquary of St Cuthbert in wood; the Franks Casket, the Brunswick Casket and the Alcester crosier-head in ivory and walrus-ivory; the *Book of Durrow*, the *Lindisfarne Gospels*, the *Echternach Gospels*, the *Stonyhurst Gospel*, the *Vespasian Psalter*, the *Royal Bible*, the *Benedictional of St Aethelwold*, the *Harley Psalter*, the *Boulogne Gospels*, the *Trinity Gospels* and the *Bury St Edmunds Psalter* in manuscripts; and the Durham embroideries and the Bayeux Tapestry in textiles.

The importance of this period of English art rests not just in the many masterful works which it produced, but also in the creation of significantly new, and in many ways specifically English, styles and genres. Among these are the magnificent and elaborately decorated Insular Gospel books and the coloured outline drawings of late Anglo-Saxon manuscript decoration – both fundamental contributions to the history of book design – and the splendid embroideries which laid the foundations for the development of the highly prized art of *opus anglicanum* (embroidered 'English work') of the later Middle Ages.

The Anglo-Saxon period spans more than six hundred years, from the arrival of the Angles, Saxons and other Germanic peoples in England in the sixth century, to their conquest by the Normans in the eleventh century. The Anglo-Saxon invaders and settlers established themselves in the land, overcoming the British natives and pushing them westwards to Wales and northwards to Scotland. The successive invasions of Vikings in the late

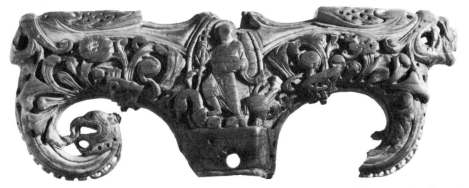

The Alcester crosier-head, with Christ standing victorious upon the Beasts (early eleventh century).

eighth and ninth centuries, and again in the late tenth and eleventh centuries, were assimilated, as were the Normans in their turn. The Anglo-Saxon period laid down the lines of many of the features of modern English life, from the basis of the very language we use to the shape and laws of our political institutions. The formation of the institutions, language, and structure of Anglo-Saxon society went hand-in-hand with the formation of the art, such that each helped to shape the other, as the intentions and aspirations of the Anglo-Saxons found appropriate expression in their arts and crafts.

In extending for so long a time the Anglo-Saxon period witnessed a complex range of changing styles, subject to many different needs and influences, both native and foreign. Along with their history, the art of the Anglo-Saxons principally divides into the pagan and Christian periods; and the Christian period has two phases, early and late. The pagan period lasted until about the seventh century, ending with the process of conversion to Christianity (which occurred in stages rather than all at once), through the efforts of Irish, Roman and other missionaries. The early part of the Christian period lasted until the ninth century and saw the consolidation of Christianity, the waxing and waning of influence of the kingdom of Mercia and the ascendence of the kingdom of Wessex, particularly under King Alfred. The Viking attacks in the late eight and ninth centuries devastated many parts of England and in a number of ways disrupted, or redirected, the activities of artistic life, producing the break or division between the early and late Christian periods. Once King Alfred had succeeded in securing his kingdom against the Vikings and established the dominance of Wessex, he and his successors turned to revitalising English learning and culture. This revival was encouraged by his successors, notably King Athelstan and King Edgar, giving rise to the widespread Benedictine monastic reform movement of the tenth and eleventh centuries. This period was marked by renewed clashes with the Vikings and the unsettled events which resulted in the Norman Conquest. The consequent formation of a new, Anglo-Norman mixture, from the last decades of the eleventh century onwards, contributed greatly to the strength, as well as to the unique quality, of the English version of the Romanesque style.

The nature and range of the evidence

When considering the visual arts and crafts of Anglo-Saxon England, it is crucial to remember that most of the evidence has been lost over the centuries, through such cumulative forces as invasion and warfare, fire and theft, decay of materials and changing fashions, and such decisive events as the Dissolution of the Monasteries in the sixteenth century and the Civil War in the seventeenth, when the property of monasteries and churches was despoiled and destroyed to a very great extent. Therefore we retain only a very small proportion of the works of art and craftsmanship produced by the Anglo-Saxons, and it is necessary to augment our knowledge and understanding of not only the survivors, but also their context within the entire range (now mostly lost), by consulting documentary and literary accounts of works of art and their makers, patrons and beholders or users.

It is also important to remember that the nature and the range of the surviving evidence in many ways helps to shape, or guide, our appreciation of Anglo-Saxon arts and crafts. In some cases the surviving objects may be representative of the original whole of Anglo-Saxon artistic achievement in one medium or another; while in other cases the objects may be individual and idiosyncratic, as the products of scribes, artists, craftsmen and craftswomen steeped in traditional forms and genres, and yet also able upon occasion – depending upon their skill, imagination and vision – to create works of exceptional and outstanding beauty, in materials ranging from the most humble to the most luxurious.

One of the most striking characteristics of Anglo-Saxon art is the way in which ornamental motifs crossed the boundaries of different media, and appeared and reappeared in different scales and forms, with dramatically different effects (as well as in different degrees of competence and invention). Ornament characteristic of pagan Anglo-Saxon metalwork, such as trumpet-spirals, interlace and highly stylised animal patterns, was transferred to the pages of decorated Christian manuscripts, such as the seventh-century *Book of Durrow*. This was as if the pagan significance of these motifs had been converted along with the Anglo-Saxon themselves, who drew upon their own native heritage while turning to new forms of art and new media required by their new religion imported from abroad. Similarly, in the eighth and ninth centuries, motifs such as hybrid, or combined, interlace, animal and foliate patterns (in which the different categories intermingled, with one running directly into the other) recurred in metalwork such as the Fuller Brooch and the Pentney Brooches, in manuscripts such as the *Royal Bible*, in stone carvings such as the Priors Barton cross-shaft, in bone and ivory carvings such as the Brunswick Casket, and in textiles such as the Maaseik embroideries. Again, in the tenth and eleventh centuries manuscript illustrations and the monumental outline drawing style owed much to the influence of softly modelled ivory carvings, while forms of ornament such as acanthus-like foliage or scrolling stems 'inhabited' with creatures of various kinds were used to decorate metalwork, carvings, manuscripts and textiles alike.

The transmigration of motifs from one medium to another makes it clear that artists and craftsmen looked over each others' shoulders and took notice of changing and developing styles. Clearly they did not inhabit only the world of their respective media, but rather their world as a whole. Sometimes they even engaged in more than one medium, as in the case of St Dunstan, renowned as artist and artisan as well as designer. Moreover, many works of art were composite objects displaying combinations of media. This was the case notably with luxurious manuscripts, with their complex blend of script and images, of calligraphy, decoration and illustration, set upon parchment or vellum leaves enclosed in bindings covered with leather and fitted with such embellishments as metal mounts, ivory plaques and gems. In their settings, the works of art were grouped in mixtures of media, for example in churches decked with wall paintings, stained glass, sculpture and hangings, and equipped with altar fittings such as a crucifix, censer (for incense), chalice and paten (cup and dish for the Eucharistic wine and bread), Gospel book and altar cloth. Thus, although we ought to consider each medium in its own terms, nevertheless, in trying to appreciate the Anglo-Saxon achievement as a whole, we need to take into account the wider context of the relations between one medium and another, and to reconstruct in our imaginations the contributions of the different media to the whole of Anglo-Saxon life.

The types of evidence concerning the visual arts and crafts in the Anglo-Saxon period differ in important respects for the pagan and Christian periods, and to a certain extent for the two parts of the Christian period as well. It is not only that for the pagan period we have little written evidence, making it a veritable 'Dark Age' in terms of what little we can glimpse of it, in contrast to the Christian period. Moreover, the reasons or forces for the survival of material objects differed significantly for the two periods, according to how and where, and for what motives, objects came to be preserved: for example as objects buried with the dead or revered as relics of saints and property of the church. The treasure of the Sutton Hoo ship-burial and the relics of St Cuthbert serve dramatically as cases in point.

Most of what we know about pagan Anglo-Saxon arts and crafts derives not so much from settlement sites but from cemeteries, from grave goods: objects buried with the dead in cemeteries or in barrows (such as Taplow in Berkshire and Sutton Hoo in East Suffolk). For the early part of the pagan period, cremation was the rule and the ashes of the dead were buried in ceramic pots or urns, frequently decorated with incised or stamped patterns of geometric designs. Some of these pots (which were shaped by hand rather than being turned on a wheel) possess considerable beauty. Gradually burial-practices changed to inhumation, whereby the bodies were not cremated but buried intact, along with the personal effects which they wore, carried, or used. These objects included garments, jewelry and ornaments (such as beaded or jewelled necklaces, pins, buckles and brooches), amulets, glass vessels and weapons (such as knives, spears, swords and shields). In accordance with changing fashions, the jewelry is very varied, like the variously saucer-shaped, cruciform, long-bowed, square-headed, equal-armed, or disc-shaped brooches, with effects as different as the delightful fifth-century parcel-gilt silver Sarre Brooch (with its double rims of frieze-like rows of speckled, crouching animals and its pair of raised, free-standing

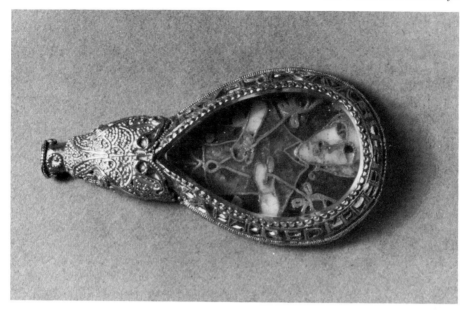

The Alfred Jewel, with gold filigree, cloisonné *enamel and rock-crystal (mid to late ninth century).*

doves which can swivel around to touch beaks) and the magnificent polychrome seventh-century Kingston Brooch (with its multiple panels of inlaid garnets, glass and gold filigree in geometric patterns and extremely stylised, ribbon-like animals on the front, and with gold filigree animal ornament on the back) (colour pl. 6).

With the conversion to Christianity, burial practices changed once again. Although inhumation continued, the dead were placed in graveyards associated with high crosses or churches, and were no longer provided with offerings to see them on their way to a next world. Therefore, although pagan Viking graves both in England and back in the Viking homelands of Scandinavia yield an important amount of grave goods acquired or plundered from Anglo-Saxon sites, our knowledge of the material culture of the Christian period depends principally upon other sources, such as settlement sites (including monastic establishments) and churches. The church became an important patron of the arts and crafts, and not only laypersons but also many ecclesiastics, from abbesses, abbots, bishops and archbishops to monks and nuns, engaged in the production of them.

Christianity introduced to Anglo-Saxon England a number of forms of art for the service and life of the church and monastic communities, including stone architecture, stone carving, stained glass and manuscripts. Stone carvings include both architectural sculpture and free-standing crosses, which were erected for such purposes as consecrating sites, marking boundaries, commemorating persons or events, or serving as the focus for preaching and instructing the laiety, as exemplified by the extraordinarily elaborate series of images and inscriptions on the Ruthwell Cross, one of the greatest works of Anglo-Saxon sculpture.

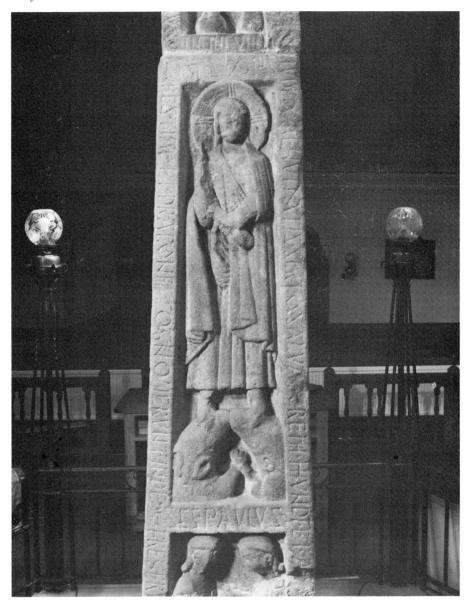

The Ruthwell Cross, central panel showing Christ in Majesty standing upon the adoring Beasts (late seventh century).

Although many of the surviving works of Anglo-Saxon sculpture are reduced to severely weathered or battered fragments, nevertheless some carvings retain sufficient traces or manifestations of both highly skilled workmanship and design, ranging from delicate to vigorous, in dramatically different styles characteristic of different regions and periods. For example, in the late Anglo-Saxon period many sculptures (particularly in northern England) display a marked taste for Viking elements, as on works as varied as the Gosforth Cross with numerous legendary scenes or the St Paul's

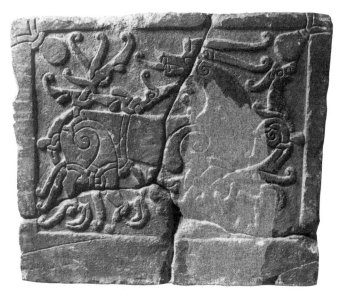

Viking-style tombstone found in St Paul's Churchyard, London (late tenth or early eleventh century).

tombstone with densely interlaced animal and tendril ornament. Other major elements of sculptural decoration of both the early and the late Christian periods include vine scrolls (often 'inhabited'), bush-like foliage, interlace and animal ornament (see p. 130). A number of carvings, such as the magnificent, classicising Ruthwell Cross and the idiosyncratic, highly stylised Sandbach Crosses, present elaborate iconographical programmes, encompassing an extensive number of scenes (primarily biblical), to highly instructive as well as highly decorative effect. The Ruthwell Cross, for example, includes such scenes as the Annunciation, the Return from Egypt, the Washing of Christ's Feet by Mary Magdelen, the Crucifixion, Paul and Anthony in the Desert and Christ standing in Majesty upon a pair of adoring Beasts with tenderly crossed paws; on one entire side of the cross there extends a scrolling, flowering and fruit-laden stem in which birds and other creatures perch and entwine, feasting upon it in much the same way as beholders of the cross were intended to derive substantial spiritual sustenance from its sculpted message.

Other stone sculptures of outstanding quality include the cross fragments of Croft, Cropthorne, Easby, East Stour, Masham and Reculver, the shrines at Jedburgh and Peterborough and the architectural decoration at Breedon-on-the-Hill, Deerhurst and Bradford-upon-Avon. With such monuments as these – despite the multiple losses of Anglo-Saxon sculpture over the centuries, and despite the damage (both deliberate and unintended) which many of the surviving examples have suffered, together with the loss or fading of the paint which originally coloured most of the sculpture, enhancing the decorative effect – it is clear that stone sculpture was one of the numerous realms in which Anglo-Saxon art and craftsmanship excelled.

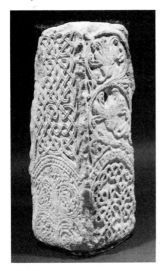

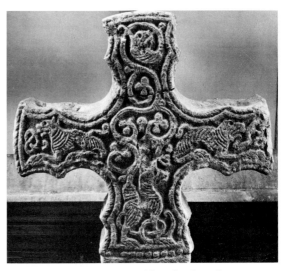

The East Stour cross-shaft, with interlace and foliate ornament (early tenth century).

The Cropthorne cross-head, with animals and inhabited foliage (early ninth century).

It was also with Christianity that the Anglo-Saxons learned to read and write books, which, in the days before the invention of paper and printing, had to be made by hand upon parchment or vellum. Thus were introduced the skills of calligraphy and illumination, which the Anglo-Saxons developed to extraordinary heights of excellence, lightening and enlightening a 'Dark Age'. Reading and writing remained principally in the hands of ecclesiastics, and most of the surviving manuscripts which carry decoration or illumination are books dedicated to the service of the church; some of them are extremely elaborately decorated, and some rank among the chief masterpieces of all time of the art of the book .

The early and late Christian periods displayed a number of differences, in keeping with the changing fortunes of different kingdoms, changing tastes (as with the influx of the Vikings) and changing preoccupations (as with the introduction of the Benedictine reform movement). The early Christian period was marked notably by the creation of the genre of highly decorated Insular Gospel books (in conjunction with Irish – and possibly also Pictish – scribes and artists), as well as by the highly classicising styles (inspired by late antique and Mediterranean models) of the manuscripts produced by the twinned monasteries of Monkwearmouth and Jarrow (home of Bede) in Northumbria and of the 'Canterbury School' in Southern England. Side-by-side with these achievements went the creation of magnificent works of art in other media such as the Ruthwell and Bewcastle Crosses and the Fuller Brooch.

For example, the Fuller Brooch, made of silver inlaid with niello (the black sulphide of silver), belongs to a style of decorated metalwork current in the late eighth and ninth centuries, which has come to be known as the 'Trewhiddle Style', after the group of objects found in a hoard at Trewhiddle in Cornwall in 1757. The perfectly preserved Fuller Brooch is decorated with

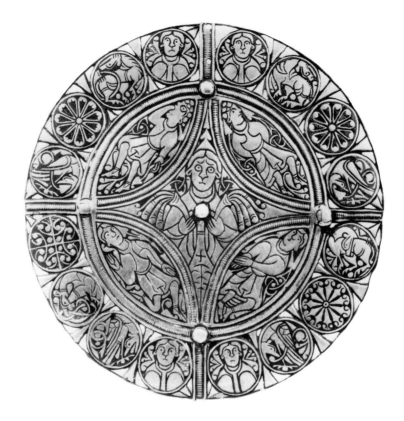

The Fuller Brooch, with personifications of the Five Senses, enclosed by roundels showing the different forms of terrestrial life (mid ninth century).

a delightful representation of the personified Five Senses enclosed within a nested series of almond-shaped and lozenge-shaped panels, forming a circular centre surrounded by a rim of roundels containing figures emblematic of the four forms of terrestrial life: human, animal, bird and vegetable. The way in which the figures and the decorative motifs on the brooch are set within the panels of various shapes, sometimes having to twist, turn, stretch out, or interlace in order to fit into them and fill them, is highly characteristic of the Anglo-Saxon approach to ornament and to art, with a lasting delight in surfaces densely and intricately covered with patterns of many kinds. Even the representations of human figures, as well as of animals and birds, frequently acquire the status of ornament, with their highly stylised features and contorted poses.

The emphasis upon ornament and pattern extends throughout the Anglo-Saxon period and characterises works as different as the great gold buckle of the seventh-century Sutton Hoo treasure, with its dense and asymmetrical network of interlacing snake-like creatures, and the tenth-century *Benedictional of St Aethelwold*, with its numerous framed pages of illustrations or elaborately decorated initials, in which the massive acanthus-like foliage emerges from, extends beyond and engulfs the trellis-like frame.

The late Christian period is marked not only by the development of earlier Anglo-Saxon trends, for example the lively decorated initials composed of interlace, foliage and creatures which abound in manuscripts, particularly textbooks, but also by the development of new genres, themes and styles. The very widespread use of acanthus-like foliate ornament, fluttering, wind-swept, or billowing folds of drapery, and the appearance of outline drawings, sometimes in multiple colours, characterises the art of this period, as represented in works as diverse as the heavily ornate *Benedictional of St Aethelwold*, the monumental frontispiece of *St Dunstan's Classbook*, and the magnificent *Harley Psalter*. The style, which has come to be known as the 'Winchester Style' (although it was not produced only there), spread throughout Southern England and established a prevailing fashion or trend. Particularly in the parts of England ruled or permeated by the Vikings, there was an increasing influence of Viking tastes and motifs in works as diverse as the Gosforth Cross, the numerous hogback tombstones, openwork metal brooches and buckles and elements of manuscript decoration. At the close of the Anglo-Saxon period, the Normans brought new tastes and approaches along with new patrons, as well as new artists and craftsmen; but at the same time the Normans were able to appreciate and to adapt many of the flourishing traditions of Anglo-Saxon arts and crafts, allowing them to continue to contribute to the achievements of subsequent periods of English art.

Some of the art of the period will seem strange to us, with the seemingly 'barbaric' stylised representations of human figures or intricately interlaced creatures. Nevertheless, the signs embedded within the surviving works allow us to observe at close hand the intentions and aspirations of the Anglo-Saxons, both pagan and Christian, lay and ecclesiastical, which found appropriate expression in their arts and crafts. For example, the Anglo-Saxon emphasis upon intricate patterns of ornament corresponds with the original sense of the word 'decoration': that which is 'decorous', 'suitable', 'fitting', in contrast to a modern sense in which it may appear merely superfluous or gratuitous. The astonishingly extensive and painstaking decoration of surfaces, covering them with ornament, for example on page after page of the *Lindisfarne Gospels* (which took its scribal artist, Bishop Eadfrith, at least two years to produce), may at first sight seem to us to arise from a simple *horror vacui* (a 'fear of the void'), as has often been observed concerning this phase of English art. Yet the densely compacted and meticulously rendered ornament illuminates and embodies a certain kind of order, a certain reverence both for the product and the process of its production, and a certain spirituality.

Many of the works of art which survive from the Anglo-Saxon period have an appeal which is immediate and direct. Even if some of them require an effort on our part to understand and appreciate their highly stylised and ornamental figural representations and their ornamental patterns, this effort can be amply rewarded, as they can readily appeal to us for their meticulous craftsmanship and for their haunting beauty.

Sources and influences

Anglo-Saxon art was shaped by a complex set of interrelationships between England, the rest of the British Isles and the European Continent; and also, at times, by a measure of isolation, which proved beneficial to the flowering of certain forms of art, as in the case of the advances which Anglo-Saxon and Irish scribal artists were able to make in the art of the book during the seventh and eighth centuries. It is this mixture of multiple sources and influences, both native and foreign, which combined to shape the special qualities of Anglo-Saxon art.

In the pagan period influences were exerted upon Anglo-Saxon art through the migrations of the Germanic peoples, in contact with both the retreating Romans and the British populations whom the Anglo-Saxons partly displaced and partly assimilated. For example, the gaudy belt-fittings from a warrior's grave at Mucking and the charming Sarre Brooch derive elements of their shape and decoration from Roman antecedants. Similarly, in the rich Sutton Hoo ship-burial, magnificent Anglo-Saxon jewelry and weapons were juxtaposed with Celtic or British objects such as hanging bowls, Scandinavian heirlooms, Byzantine silver and Merovingian coins, making the deposit emblematic of the complex interconnections between seventh-century pagan Anglo-Saxon art and its heritage and contacts.

During the Christian early period, both Irish and Mediterranean influences came very much to the fore, yielding works as varied as the *Echternach Gospels* and the *Codex Amiatinus*. These influences exerted their effect through foreign missionary-teachers, artists and craftsmen, and through imported works of art, like icons and manuscripts. Later Anglo-Saxon art was influenced greatly by the concerted revival of late antique tradition by the Carolingians and their successors, the Ottonians. The Vikings, too, brought their tastes with them and had considerable impact on Anglo-Saxon art, as did their successors the Normans.

Following the Norman Conquest, there rose a new, Anglo-Norman style. For example, there are some late eleventh-century or early twelfth-century manuscripts on which both Anglo-Saxon and Norman scribes worked together, and the Anglo-Saxon drawing style continued to flourish, as in the charming scene of King David the Psalmist and his retinue in a decorated initial 'B' in a manuscript from Christ Church, Canterbury.

The problem of discerning the sources and influences at work in the formation of Anglo-Saxon works of art is further complicated by the ways in which the different phases of Anglo-Saxon art show considerable degrees of overlap, as traditions and genres were preserved, or re-interpreted, and even rejected, in the formation of new styles. As a result it is difficult to determine where some works of art were made, whether in England, Ireland, or Pictland, or on one or another side of the Channel. A prime example of this complexity is presented by the magnificent *Book of Kells*. The elements of the decorative repertoire of the *Book of Kells* are so extraordinarily unusual in their richness and variety that it is now very difficult to point to any particular centre in the British Isles where such a mixture could have been produced. This masterpiece remains a mystery, despite all the advances in our knowledge of Anglo-Saxon and related cultures through research and discoveries.

An important example of the complexities of the interrelationships between Anglo-Saxon England and other realms as well as other periods can be seen in the impact of the *Utrecht Psalter*, a lavishly illustrated Carolingian manuscript (which is deeply imbued with late antique elements), made near Rheims in about the middle of the ninth century. Brought to Canterbury by about the year 1000, the manuscript was copied there a number of times throughout the Middle Ages. The first surviving copy, the *Harley Psalter*, upon which a number of scribes and artists collaborated over several generations, was begun in about the year 1000. The survival of both the *Utrecht Psalter* and at least some of its copies makes it possible to compare the original with its progeny, line by line, and to see in what ways the English scribes and artists both followed and deviated from, or improvised upon, the model set before them. The dynamic and lively style of the *Utrecht Psalter* exerted a very important influence upon the drawing style which is so characteristic of late Anglo-Saxon manuscripts, such as the *Bury St Edmunds Psalter*.

In the interchange between Anglo-Saxon England and elsewhere, England contributed fully as much as she received. For example, the approach to the decorated book developed within the Insular Gospel books and numerous other types of manuscripts exerted an enormous influence upon the Continent, particularly through the Irish and Anglo-Saxon missions of the seventh and eighth centuries. These influences were spread partly as a result of the books themselves being sent to the Continent, as was probably the case with the *Echternach Gospels*, and partly as a result of people imbued with Anglo-Saxon styles and traditions going to the Continent, for among the missionaries there were also scribes and artists who continued to work in Anglo-Saxon or Insular style. Such models and teachers set certain styles followed by Continental scribes and artists, leaving tangible traces of influence in such elements as the elaborate decorated initials and interlace patterns in numerous Continental manuscripts.

Thus, a number of works of art which survive on the Continent display thoroughly Anglo-Saxon characteristics. For example, the Maaseik embroideries with their multiple patterns of interlace, geometric patterns, scrolling foliate stems and stylised birds and animals, frequently caught up in interlace, and the Brunswick Casket, with its square, rectangular and triangular panels filled with animals caught in interlace or in foliate ornament, belong within the category of Anglo-Saxon exports to the Continent. Also there are a number of works made on the Continent by itinerant or immigrant Anglo-Saxons, or made by native craftsmen or scribes trained by Anglo-Saxon teachers. Anglo-Saxon elements were in some cases fully incorporated into a Continental scribe's or artist's repertoire, giving rise to a new and lively style.

The complex overlap and interchange between pagan and Christian forces in Anglo-Saxon England, can vividly be seen in two remarkable ensembles of objects in various media (including some breathtakingly beautiful works of art), which formed burial deposits accompanying two seventh-century figures:

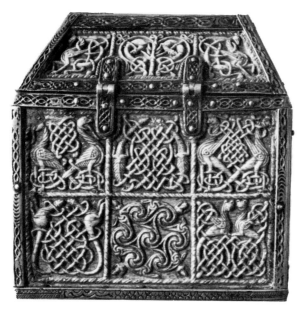

The Brunswick Casket, with interlaced creatures, foliage and trumpet-spiral patterns (late eighth century).

the Sutton Hoo ship-burial deposited all at once in about 625–35, and the relics of St Cuthbert, Bishop of Lindisfarne, who died in 687, and whose shrine kept being re-opened to receive donations of various kinds throughout the medieval period. We shall now consider in turn these two ensembles, variously pagan and Christian, one deposited all at once, and the other gathered cumulatively over some centuries, although both contain objects of considerable diversity of types, dates and places of origin.

The Sutton Hoo ship-burial

The discovery, shortly before the outbreak of World War II, of the magnificent royal ship-burial at Sutton Hoo (near Woodbridge) in Suffolk dramatically altered assessments of the quality of pagan Anglo-Saxon art. The story of the discovery of the Sutton Hoo ship-burial is almost as extraordinary as its contents. In 1938 the owner of the land, Mrs Pretty, began to investigate the contents of three of the barrows (burial mounds) on the site, under the direction of a local antiquary, Basil Brown: and when, the following year, the largest was opened the bows of a ship were discovered, on a scale which made it evident that the ship was of great size. Ultimately the shape of the ship was revealed through the shadowy, ghost-like image which its decayed timbers had imprinted upon the soil and through the iron rivets which had studded them.

A considerable amount of gold jewelry, silver plate, bowls and weapons, along with the remains of cauldrons, buckets in both bronze and iron, dishes, textiles, cups, drinking horns, a lyre (see p. 249) and other objects, were recovered from the burial chamber. Ceremonial objects, jeweled trappings and weapons lay in the after end of the ship, while kitchen utensils and other ordinary objects lay at the forward end of the chamber. Mrs Pretty generously presented the whole of the find to the nation, and it is now in the British Museum. It includes some of the most splendid, and most beautiful, works of Anglo-Saxon – or indeed English – art.

The ship itself surpasses in size any other yet found from the early medieval period, and the treasure surpasses, in terms of both sheer amount and splendour, any others known from seventh-century England. Its match is probably to be seen in the treasure found in the eighteenth century in Tournai in the tomb of the Merovingian king Childebert, whose regalia also included objects made of garnet-inlaid gold in a style similar to some of the Sutton Hoo objects. However, the Sutton Hoo find is unparalleled in British archaeology. It is the most important single 'document' for the migration period of the Germanic peoples, which lasted from the fifth to the seventh centuries, and effected the settlement of England by the various Germanic tribes, including the Anglo-Saxons, Jutes, Frisians and Franks.

The importance of the discovery resides not only in the astonishing richness of the jewelry and other objects, and in the outstanding craftsmanship which many of the Anglo-Saxon objects display, but also in the way it reflects the complex nature of the sources and influences upon which the pagan Anglo-Saxon arts and crafts drew: the native, Celtic, Germanic and Scandinavian heritage, as well as Merovingian and Byzantine contacts.

The ship – a long, open rowing boat – had been dragged up, bow first, from the River Deben, to the crest of an escarpment overlooking the estuary. There it was laid to rest in a trench. Within it, amidships, a wooden chamber was built to enclose a rich array of objects, ranging from regalia, weapons and personal ornaments to silverware and domestic equipment accompanying the dead man. Then the trench was filled in, a mound was raised above it to memorialise its place and until its excavation the burial remained – unusually, and almost miraculously – intact and unplundered. Such burials within ships are known from other Anglo-Saxon and Scandinavian contexts, although the richness of the Sutton Hoo ship-burial has no equal among those which survive. The Old English epic poem *Beowulf*, set in the Scandinavian homelands of the Anglo-Saxons, describes a ceremony in which the dead Scyld is laid out, together with a number of treasures, in a ship which is then set afire and sent out to sea (see p. 189).

No trace of a body was found at Sutton Hoo for a long time and this led to the theory that the burial of the grave-goods might represent a cenotaph, serving as a memorial of the dead man rather than as an accompaniment to his body. But recent research seems to confirm that there was a cremated body in the grave.

Among the principal objects of the Sutton Hoo deposit are an iron standard crowned by a small, finely modelled bronze stag, probably of Celtic workmanship. Alongside the standard lay a large whetstone, with a knob at either end, below which on each side is carved a sombre human face set rigidly in a pear-shaped frame. The impressive size and weight of this whetstone makes it clear that it was a ceremonial object, functioning as a sceptre. There are also the remains of a parade helmet with a formidable face-mask and a large circular shield which had a wooden core covered with leather and decorated with metal appliqué mounts, including a stylised, dragon-like bird of prey around a central iron boss.

Most of the jewelry was made in a local workshop, known as 'Sutton Hoo', by a master craftsman of exceptional skill. The jewelry is made of gold inlaid with various materials. The great gold buckle is inlaid with niello, while the other objects are inlaid with multiple cells of garnets and chequer-patterned pieces of blue, white and red *millefiori* glass, producing a brilliant, glittering, mosaic-like effect. The garnets, which were individually cut for the different cells, are usually backed with gold foil which is impressed with geometrical patterns, reflecting and refracting the light through the stones, vividly enlivening them.

The gold buckle has a concealed compartment within its front and back, perhaps suggesting its use as a reliquary of some kind. The front of the buckle has a raised roundel, filled with a pattern of interlacing snake-like creatures, at the base of the tongue. The loop contains patterns of interlace. The body of the buckle is punctuated by three raised, domed bosses around which there swarms a dense mesh of interlacing snake-like creatures; a small animal crouches at the end behind the boss and bites its own foreleg, while enlarged bird-like heads, emerging from the strands of interlace, clasp the animal between their jaws. At the other end, there is a pair of bird heads with curled beaks, resembling the bird of prey on the shield. The asymmetrical pattern of the interlacing creatures within the body of the buckle contrasts strongly with the overall symmetry of the design, and enlivens the dramatic effect of the whole.

Then there is a magnificent matching pair of gold shoulder-clasps (colour pl. 7). Each clasp has separable halves joined by a chained central hinge, with a hinge-pin embellished with an animal-headed terminal. Around the central rectangle of each half-clasp, filled with mosaic-like designs in garnet inlay and *millefiori* enamel, there are frieze-like strips of interlaced, snake-like, garnet-inlaid animals with enlarged jaws and blue-glass eyes. A pair of interlaced boars, standing sentry-like at the rounded end, with arched bodies, bared tusks and snouts pressed squarely to the ground line, are rendered mostly in garnet-inlay, with a red, white and blue checkerboard *millefiori* pattern set in their shoulders. The background between them is filled with filigree patterns, including a pair of birds in penguin-like poses tucked against the boars' lower jaws.

The coins which were contained within the purse (colour pl. 8) help to indicate the approximate date of the burial. The latest coin in the collection dates to 625, so that the collection must have been assembled at some time after that. The riches of the burial as a whole suggest that the dead man was a king of East Anglia, the most likely candidate being Redwald.

A pair of silver Byzantine christening spoons, inscribed in Greek with the names 'Paul' and 'Saul', were perhaps a gift to a baptised convert, or maybe the dead man had converted to Christianity and then relapsed, to be buried according to pagan practices. The spoons may, however, have little to do with the man's religious beliefs, and indicate little more than a wide range of contacts of trade and gift-exchange, extending to the Byzantine realm, as also represented by a large silver dish stamped with control marks of the Emperor Anastasius (491–518). The shield is of Scandinavian workmanship, as also maybe the helmet. There is a sword-pommel from the Rhineland. The three bronze hanging-bowls, with their brilliant polychrome enamelled mounts decorated with pelta, trumpet-spiral ornament or mosaic-like patterns in enamel and *millefiori* glass, are probably of Celtic workmanship.

The Sutton Hoo treasure revealed works of such splendour and beauty that it led to a complete re-evaluation of the quality of pagan Anglo-Saxon craftsmanship and design, and radically modified our views of the range of contacts which the East Anglians enjoyed. Research will continue and more discoveries will be made, yet we will remain with the mysterious and haunting quality of so large a collection of perfectly crafted gold jewelry which ranks among the greatest jewelry ever made.

The relics of St Cuthbert

The figure of St Cuthbert, seventh-century saint of Lindisfarne, served as the focal point for the production and donation of numerous outstanding Anglo-Saxon works of art of various dates and media, ranging from the seventh-century wooden coffin, the *Stonyhurst Gospel* and the *Lindisfarne Gospels*, to the tenth-century manuscripts and embroideries given by King Athelstan. Some of the objects were made for Cuthbert, or in his honour, and some were given to his shrine after having served some other use.

We know much about St Cuthbert's life from two versions of his biography written by Bede soon after the Saint's death in 687. His dedication to a hermetic life and the duties of a bishop as well as his care for animals and other living creatures made him an attractive and popular figure during his life and after his death. The body of the Saint was translated (elevated) in 698, when it was placed within a light wooden chest or coffin-reliquary. His relics had to undergo a number of migrations subsequently. The community of monks left Lindisfarne, taking the relics with them, as they fled from the Vikings in 875; they wandered for seven years before settling at Chester-le-Street, only to be evacuated to Ripon in the 990s under new Viking threat, before finally settling in Durham in 995. Moreover, Cuthbert's tomb was opened many times throughout the Middle Ages as his relics – both his body and the objects associated with it – were inspected, described and augmented. It was opened again in 1827, when the contents were examined and removed; they are now mostly on display in Durham Cathedral.

The relics include some objects which may have belonged to the Saint himself: a garnet-inlaid gold pectoral cross in the style of the Sutton Hoo jewelry; an ivory liturgical comb, with which a bishop was supposed to prepare for the seemly celebration of the Mass; and a portable altar. The pectoral cross was hung around the Saint's neck, and it was probably placed there at the time of his burial in 687. It had received some use, and two repairs, before it was deposited. It is a reliquary cross, with a shell from the

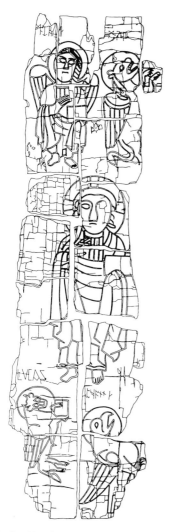

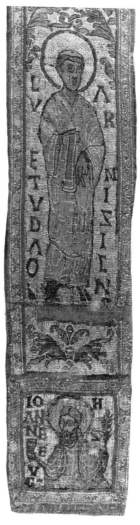

St Cuthbert's coffin-reliquary lid, with
Christ in Majesty accompanied by the four
evangelist symbols (c.698).

The Cuthbert maniple, left-hand end with
John the Evangelist and Lawrence the
Deacon (c.909–16).

Indian Ocean set behind the central stone-setting. The arms are inlaid with
garnets in cell-like cloisonné work. The gold and inlaid garnets belong in the
tradition of contemporary jewelry from southern England, but the style is
very different. It seems to have been made in a Northumbrian workshop, as a
local product, to be worn by a Northumbrian bishop.

The wooden coffin-reliquary, with its precious contents protected by
haunting stylised figures incised in outlines on all four sides and on the lid,
appears to have served as a visual litany. The lid presents the standing figure
of Christ holding a book in his veiled left hand and gesturing in blessing with
his right hand, with the full-length symbols of the evangelists accompanying
him in pairs: the angel and lion of Matthew and Mark above his head and
the bull and eagle of Luke and John below his feet. Standing for the Gospel

writers, these figures have wings and halos, and hold books which represent the Gospel texts. On the long sides of the coffin there stretch either the twelve apostles, set out in a two-tiered row of half-length figures, or a row of five archangels. The archangels Gabriel and Michael appear on one end of the coffin, while on the other end, shown in a sitting position (although no chair is visible), the Virgin Mary turns to face us and holds the Christ-child on her lap; he holds a book and gestures in blessing. The figures, identified with accompanying inscriptions, are rendered with large heads, schematic, simplified features, and their wide-opened eyes add to their solemn, otherworldly effect.

The order of the names of the apostles corresponds to the litany of the Roman Mass, while the order of the archangels corresponds to Irish prayers. Thus the figures are pictorial translations of litanies; they stand for the invocations which the monks of Lindisfarne would chant in their prayers. Here they are laid down in permanent visual form. In its iconography, the coffin of St Cuthbert fuses prayer and art in a deep, magical union, invoking the help and protection of the saints for the precious relics. By conjuring up heavenly guardians in visible form, the monks of Lindisfarne went beyond a mere recital of a prayer and sought to effect its instant, as well as perpetual, fulfilment.

Thus, this coffin differs dramatically from simple receptacles destined for burial. As a reliquary coffin it served to enshrine the remains of a popular saint and to be exhibited for popular worship.

The *Lindisfarne Gospels* was written and decorated at Lindisfarne by Bishop Eadfrith, as we know from the colophon inscription added in the tenth century by Aldred, the priest, who added the interlinear Old English gloss to it as part of his own contribution to the community. Aldred also recorded the names of others who contributed to binding the book: Bishop Ethelwald and Billfrith the anchorite were responsible, respectively, for covering the book and for adorning it with jewelled, gold and gilt-silver ornaments; this binding has been lost, unlike the *Stonyhurst Gospel*, which preserves its original binding of red leather skilfully moulded and incised with decorative designs.

Eadfrith apparently made the manuscript in honour of Cuthbert's translation in 698 (although he may have made it later, up to the time of his death in 721). Trial reconstructions of the ornament, based upon the compass marks and ruling lines left on the surface of the vellum, indicate that writing and decorating the manuscript must have taken Eadfrith at least two years, not counting time off for other duties, for illness and for cold winter days when it must have been too cold to work.

This manuscript, one of the great Insular Gospel books, contains the elaborately written and decorated Gospel texts as well as some accompanying matter, including 'carpet pages'. The term 'carpet pages' marks the resemblance of these full pages of ornamental patterns (frequently based upon cruciform shapes) to Oriental carpets. But the phenomenon probably has its origin in the late antique period when the four Gospels came to be bound together in one volume, following the tradition of binding each of the four Gospels in its own cover. The pages of ornament brilliantly imitate or equal in pigment the effect of jewelled metallic covers.

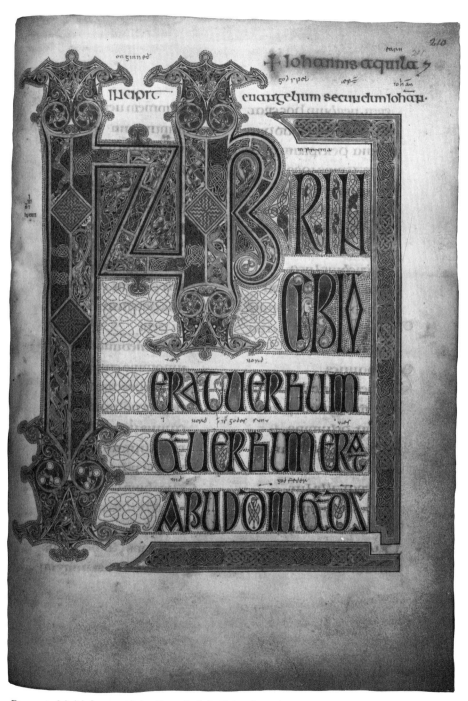

Decorated initial page of the Gospel of St John, In principio erat verbum *(late seventh century), with an Old English translation added between the lines (tenth century), from the* Lindisfarne Gospels.

In embellishing the text with decorations of such extraordinarily painstaking complexity, it is as if, in the service of holy scripture, the pains and labour taken in making, planning, drawing, painting and filling up areas with small details would make the dedication and sacrifice and value of the work – both the activity and the product – all the more worthy to serve as both a manifestation and an instrument of worship. Such work paralleled the zealous dedication to pilgrimages and voluntary exile for missionary work which characterised many Anglo-Saxons of the seventh and eighth centuries.

The remaining Anglo-Saxon works which belong to the relics are the donations which King Athelstan (who reigned from 924–939) gave the community of St Cuthbert, then at Chester-le-Street, perhaps when he visited Cuthbert's tomb in 934 during his military campaign in the north (culminating in the ravaging of Scotland). We are informed that, 'commending his expedition to the protection of the Saint', he bestowed 'many and divers gifts becoming a King', including books and luxurious textiles. Some of them survive, in whole or in part, at Durham and elsewhere. They include an elegant manuscript containing a collection of texts celebrating the life of St Cuthbert (including Bede's *Life of St Cuthbert*, in both the prose and metrical versions), preserved in Corpus Christi College, Cambridge; and embroidered vestments preserved in the Durham Cathedral Treasury.

The Cambridge manuscript is unique among the surviving books which Athelstan gave to religious foundations throughout his realm in being the only one written wholly in England during his reign, and it appears to have been commissioned especially for his presentation to Chester-le-Street. It has a frontispiece illustration showing Athelstan presenting the very book to St Cuthbert, who stands before a building (this shrine) and gestures in blessing, while the king bows his head reverentially before him. The image stands within a rectangular frame divided into panels which contain animal and foliate ornament: either scrolling stems in which appear animals and birds, or candelabra-like foliate ornament. Among the textual contents of the book there are certain signs that the manuscript must have been made between 934 and 939 (when Aethelstan died), so that it may have been promised to the community when he visited it in the summer of 934 and was delivered there when it was completed.

The embroideries were produced between 909 and 916, probably at Winchester, for Frithestan, bishop of Winchester from 909–931, at the command of Queen Aelflaed, Athelstan's stepmother (who died before 916). Executed in silk and gold-wrapped threads, the embroideries represent a variety of images (see p. 139). With identifying Latin inscriptions, the stole and maniple (vestments worn by the celebrant of the Mass), which form a matching set, carry a vertical series of single full-length or part-length human figures (prophets, popes and deacons), the Lamb of God, the Hand of God, hilly landscapes and acanthus foliate ornament. Worked on both sides, the girdle is decorated with animal ornament mixed with candelabra-type acanthus foliate ornament, resembling some of the foliage in the Cambridge manuscript. The high quality of the materials, design and craftsmanship place these embroideries in the front rank of embroideries of all ages.

St Dunstan: artist, craftsman and patron

The identity and the status of artists, craftsmen, craftswomen and patrons is sometimes known, as in the cases of Bishop Eadfrith, who wrote and decorated the *Lindisfarne Gospels*; the Biorhtelm who made the inlayed Sittingbourne scramasax (a kind of knife); the Alfred (probably King Alfred) who commissioned the Alfred Jewel; and Queen Aelfflaed, who commissioned the set of luxurious embroideries for Frithestan, Bishop of Winchester. Such people are named by inscriptions upon or within surviving works; the names of others are known through literary or documentary sources; others still have left no trace of their names, and it is their works that serve as their signatures.

The Anglo-Saxons deeply appreciated glittering materials and excellent workmanship of a quality to match the richness of the materials, as we know from many of their descriptions of works of art. They also valued the artists and craftsmen who made them. For example, Denbert, Bishop of Worcester, granted the embroideress Eanswitha at Hereford the life-lease of a farm of two hundred acres, on condition that she was to renew and augment the garments of the priests of the cathedral church. In some notable cases, such as St Dunstan, the various skills and activities came to be encompassed and embodied in a single figure.

St Dunstan (who lived from c.909 to 988) was Abbot of Glastonbury (from at least 940 to 956), Bishop of Worcester (from 957) and also of London (from 959), and finally Archbishop of Canterbury (from 960 to 988). He served as the subject of a number of biographies, starting with the *Life of St Dunstan* written soon after his death by an author who knew him, and who signed himself only by the initial 'B'. Born to a noble family near Glastonbury, Dunstan was educated partly at King Athelstan's court, partly at Canterbury (where his uncle was archbishop) and partly at Glastonbury, where he decided to enter monastic orders. During his long, colourful and distinguished career he served as adviser of kings; at one stage he had to go into exile in Flanders after having incurred the wrath of King Eadwig, although upon accession to the throne King Edgar recalled him. He was one of the principal proponents of the Benedictine Reform movement of the late Anglo-Saxon period. He was esteemed as a poet, painter, scholar, craftsman, musician and patron; associated with him there are a number of works of art in which his hand can be discerned, either directly or indirectly.

The complex story of his varied contribution to Anglo-Saxon art centres upon the renowned frontispiece drawing of Christ and a monk added to the blank first page of a ninth-century Continental grammatical manuscript which found its way to Glastonbury, and which now forms part of a composite miscellany of texts known as *St Dunstan's Classbook*. The drawing was added to it during the time of Dunstan's abbacy, and it creates a powerful, new, richly saturated iconography (see p. 178).

The unknown artist, who also wrote the inscriptions upon Christ's emblems, has been identified as the scribe of a charter written at Glastonbury under Dunstan; Dunstan added the inscription above the figure of the monk, naming himself in the first person. In the late Middle Ages an inscription was added at the top of the page, declaring that 'the image and the script seen below on this page is by St Dunstan's very own hand'. Revered as a relic of the Saint, the artefact has come more recently to be prized in modern terms as an autograph, and as a portrait – however generalised or idealised – of a well-known historical figure.

The drawing represents the upright, three-quarter-length figure of Christ, accompanied by the prostrate, full-length figure of a monk. The frontal, long-haired, bearded Christ, wearing a long tunic and mantle and arrayed with a cross-nimbus (a halo with a cross), turns his head partway towards the right and holds a long, slender rod in his right hand and a book or tablet in his left hand. He emerges above an undulating line, representing hilly ground or clouds, which cuts him off above the hem of his tunic. The much smaller figure of the monk is placed to the right of Christ's calves. Shown in profile and wearing shoes, tonsure and habit, with his cowl pulled partway back from his head, he kneels upon a hilly slope and bends forwards towards Christ. The monk stretches out his left hand, with his arm bent, and rests his head on his right hand, partly shielding his face from the awe-inspiring vision, which relates the scene closely to representations of the Ascension or Transfiguration of Christ, in which, from the late antique period onwards, the witnessing apostles frequently shield their faces from the sight of the divinity. In this case, however, by turning the traditional, 'historical' apostolic witnesses into a contemporary monk (a latter-day apostle, according to some Anglo-Saxon interpretations), the image presents a remarkable appeal to the beholder's direct participation in its many-layered message. This personal participation is augmented by the inscription above the monk, which asks Christ's mercy and protection in the name of Dunstan (thereby linking the figure with one particular monk): 'I ask you, merciful Christ, that you watch over me, Dunstan, that you not allow the Taenarian storms (at the entrance to Hell) to swallow me.'

The drawing and the inscriptions are made in brown ink; Christ's hair is blackened in with ink; and touches of orange pigment have been added to the cross-nimbus, the tip of the rod, parts of the monk and his garments and the centres of the initials of the inscription above him. By virtue of its identification with St Dunstan, the drawing (with its painted elements) is the earliest datable example of the remarkable outline drawing style which is a characteristic feature of late Anglo-Saxon manuscripts. It helped to inaugurate a new era of Anglo-Saxon illustration. At the same time, it is a notable image of considerable complexity and resonance; the artist assembled his image from several models, fusing them into a fresh, dramatic whole.

The position of the drawing at the front of a textbook adds significantly to the complexity of its meaning. Although the frontispiece does not illustrate the grammatical text which it precedes, it has a direct hortatory function in a book to be used for edification and instruction, with the ultimate aim of finding, and following, the Way of Truth. It fits well with the principles of the late Anglo-Saxon revival initiated by King Alfred, who repeatedly stressed the importance of learning and wisdom in his programme of educational and cultural revival. The drawing merits attention on a number of accounts: as a relic of St Dunstan, as a datable early representative of the

English outline drawing style, and as a work of art of considerable power.

Dunstan is known to have been diligent in his ecclesiastical work, his political work, his studies and his teachings. For example, he was the teacher of St Aethelwold, Bishop of Winchester, another leading proponent of the Benedictine Reform movement, as well as notable craftsman and patron. Dunstan enjoyed a considerable reputation in a wide range of arts and crafts. His first biographer, 'B', informs us that Dunstan cultivated the study of literature and the arts of writing, harp-playing and making some form of pictorial representation, denoted by the word *pingendi* (probably 'painting' or 'drawing'). An Anglo-Norman biographer recorded that Dunstan also learned to play various musical instruments (harp, organ, cymbals, and others) and that 'moreover he was skilled at everything by hand, being able to make pictures, shape letters, carve with a scalpel and work anything freely from gold, silver, bronze and iron'.

Of Dunstan's Anglo-Latin compositions several poems survive, and his hand has been recognised in corrections and annotations added to a number of manuscripts, including parts of the *Classbook*. These traces illustrate, and augment, the account by 'B' that Dunstan was so zealous that he began as soon as 'he could see the first light of daybreak, to correct faulty books, erasing the errors of the scribes'. It may be that his proficiency in composing verses to adorn gifts of metal objects, for example an organ, a holy-water stoup and a bell which he presented to Abingdon (these verses survive, although the objects do not), gave rise to the tradition that Dunstan was a skilled metalworker.

But, no matter how exaggerated the reports of his skill in one craft or another may have been (as might be expected in texts designed to praise a man of such distinction and to celebrate his accomplishments as well as his sanctity), there can be no doubt that Dunstan was keenly interested in the arts and crafts. Some manuscripts survive which belonged to him, which he ordered to be made for Glastonbury or elsewhere, or which after his death were copied from manuscripts which had belonged to him. Among the more luxurious examples are the *Bosworth Psalter*, which contains a number of colourful decorated initials, and the *Sherborne Pontifical* (a collection of blessings for a bishop's use), which opens with a striking series of four framed full-page drawings, showing the Crucifixion and three single monumental figures, who represent the Three Persons of the Trinity, or Christ in three guises. Dunstan probably owned the *Bosworth Psalter*, and he may have commissioned it; the *Sherborne Pontifical* was probably copied from a manuscript made for him, and he may have had something to do with designing its unusual iconography. During the course of his career, in his capacities as abbot, bishop and archbishop, and as counsellor of three kings (Edmund, Eadred and Edgar), Dunstan took care to commission, to design, and to make – or at least to have a hand in making – a wide range of works.

'B' reports an episode during Dunstan's youth, when a noblewoman named Aethelwynn asked him to make the designs for an embroidered stole (an ecclesiastical vestment) 'with divers sorts of patterns, which she would afterwards enrich with gold and gems'. Complying with her wish, he would sit with her and her workwomen and play to them on his harp, 'as was his wont'. One day, 'after a meal' (lunch or supper), he and they 'set to work once again', and his harp, hanging on the wall, suddenly started to play a hymn out of its own accord, on account of his saintliness. At this they all, 'thunderstruck', looked at one another and marvelled, 'completely forgetting all of the work in their hands' – as well they might. Although set in the context of a saint's biography, and related as a miracle story, this delightful episode helps to recapture something of the working conditions, settings and emotions involved in the production of Anglo-Saxon works of art.

The art of the book

The art of the book in Anglo-Saxon England, which flourished from the conversion of the Anglo-Saxons to Christianity in the seventh century until their conquest by the Normans in the eleventh, displayed markedly different characteristics in the early and the late periods of book production. The two periods converged in the ninth century, when, among other things, the Viking incursions throughout most of the century and King Alfred's cultural and educational programme near the end of the century by turns disrupted, extended, revived and redirected the practice of the art of the book.

It is possible to see that the art of Anglo-Saxon manuscripts is intimately related to works of art in other media, such as stone and ivory carving, decorated metalwork and embroidered textiles. Indeed, some of these media, such as ivory carvings and decorated metal plaques or clasps, decorated the covers of luxurious manuscripts, thus permitting the books to display the same kinds of motifs and styles whether they stood open or closed. In this way we might imagine, for example, that the lost luxurious covers of manuscripts such as the *Tiberius Bede* and the *Royal Bible*, with their multiple evocations of metalwork patterns, would have been fittingly embellished with Trewhiddle-style metalwork, thus presenting a uniform whole.

Unlike antique scrolls, which roll and unroll in continuous strips and series of columns, books were often displayed open in the Anglo-Saxon period; they have to be apprehended in a variety of ways, particularly when they encompass not only text but also calligraphic script, decorated initials, borders and illustrations over a series of pages. Not only did Anglo-Saxons produce books written and decorated entirely by hand upon parchment or vellum, but also they composed and enjoyed a series of scribal riddles. In these riddles, the different scribal tools and the book itself, a Gospel book, are made to speak about their former lives in the natural world and their present lives among humans. For example, the inkhorn speaks of having ridden once high upon the head of a stag alongside its brother and of digging under the snow for grass, but after it was shed in the spring a man hollowed it out and nailed it to the edge of a board, where it has to hold in its belly some foul black liquid, just as the quill pen, which formerly flew in the air along with its brothers, was removed and trimmed – but now it has to swallow up that liquid and travel back and forth between inkwell and page, and across that page, leaving dark tracks as if sowing seed. There is even a riddle about a bookworm or bookmoth who devoured words but wasn't a wit the wiser.

The book riddle is the most poignant of all. It starts out by saying that 'an enemy deprived me of worldly strength' when it was stripped from the animal. It describes the stages in the preparation of parchment and the writing of the book. When it comes to the binding process it refers to the binder not as an enemy, as before, but as a hero. In effect, in its metamorphosis from a variety of substances taken from the animal, vegetable and mineral kingdoms, being transformed into a rich, useful and glorious part of the human world, the book with its different elements comes fully and harmoniously to life.

During the Anglo-Saxon period, producing such manuscripts as Gospel books or complete bibles or procuring them from abroad called for extensive organisation and determination, and great skill. For example, the 1,030 parchment leaves of the *Codex Amiatinus* called for the skins of 515 calves or cattle. Lines were drawn on the pages, with a stylus or dry-point instrument, so as to guide the lines of writing, and then the text was copied out with a quill pen and ink made probably from bark or candle soot. Mistakes had to be scraped out with a knife and therefore many early medieval representations, including many Anglo-Saxon ones, of scribes at work show scribes holding a quill in one hand and a knife in the other. The knife also would be used for sharpening the quill's nib. Wax tablets were used for notes and sketches, which would be made with the pointed end of the stylus, while the blunted end would be used to rub them out so as to start afresh. Parts of the text were often elaborately painted with pigments of various colours, including gold and silver in the more luxurious liturgical books.

The completed book would be bound in a wooden cover, generally oak, enclosed with leather. It would be fastened with metal clasps and sometimes enriched with metal or ivory plaques and jewelled inlays. Most of these elaborate covers do not survive, but there are certain indications, both among surviving archaeological artefacts such as book mounts of one kind or another in metal or in ivory, and in representations in various manuscript illustrations of bound manuscripts shown in use. Such a case, particularly elaborately and meticulously rendered, is to be seen in the closed book held by the evangelist symbol of Matthew in the *Codex Aureus*. There, the red-covered binding closely parallels, or evokes, the red-stained leather which we know on the binding of the *Stonyhurst Gospel*; but also the book in the *Codex Aureus* shows the indications of a number of inlays, rounded and rectangular, fitted onto the leather-covered surface. Among the numerous metal mounts and ivory plaques which survive from the Anglo-Saxon period, some probably formed part of composite book bindings.

The scriptorium at Monkwearmouth-Jarrow had to cope with the heavy demand for texts from its house author and best-seller, Bede, both in England and on the Continent. Requests for copies of the texts kept coming in, for example from Anglo-Saxon missionaries on the Continent, such as St Boniface, who once received an apology from the abbot for a long delay in providing the copy on account of the dreadful winter weather.

The early period of Anglo-Saxon book production, which extended well into the ninth century, drew upon Irish, Pictish and Continental (late antique, Italo-Byzantine, Merovingian and Carolingian) as well as pagan Anglo-Saxon sources. Its products (which in some instances are difficult to distinguish from Irish ones) exerted a profound influence on the Continent through the Irish and Anglo-Saxon missions. The period is marked by the development of recognisably Northumbrian and Southumbrian styles of book decoration (with some distinct schools or centres, such as at Lindisfarne, Monkwearmouth-Jarrow and Canterbury), and of such characteristically Insular features as full-page initials, carpet pages, evangelist symbol pages (showing the symbols either singly or in groups of four), and intricate decoration which principally comprised interlace, geometric, animal and foliate ornament. During the eighth and ninth centuries these types of ornament came increasingly to be combined with one another in hybrid patterns, while certain patterns, notably trumpet-spiral ornament, passed out of fashion.

The late period of Anglo-Saxon book production, which overlapped with the rise of Anglo-Norman book production and contributed significantly to it, drew upon traditional Anglo-Saxon as well as Continental sources, both old and new (late antique, Byzantine, Carolingian, Ottonian and Scandinavian). Beginning with Alfred's 'revival', the period is characterised not only by the retention or transformation of some traditional elements from the earlier Anglo-Saxon period (such as certain forms of script and decorated initials), but also by the adoption, invention and development of many significantly new elements. There arose a dominant (but not uniform) Southern English style, known generally as the 'Winchester School' – a term to be taken in a more generic than literal (or local) sense, given the numerous interdependent centres, such as Glastonbury and Canterbury, which engaged in book production.

Manuscripts of the late period display, in various combinations, such characteristic features as acanthus-like foliate ornament, frequently occurring in conjunction with trellis-like frames beyond which it spreads; pen-drawn and sometimes also painted initials, composed of interlace, foliage and either whole animals and birds or their heads; outline drawings in one or more colours (sometimes occurring in conjunction with painted portions even in the same image); frontispiece author portraits (in addition to the traditional evangelist portraits), including the Anglo-Saxon Aldhelm; and some new, ingenious iconographic images, such as the Hell-mouth, the Tree-trunk Cross, the Anthropomorphic Trinity and the Ascending 'Disappearing Christ' seen part-length. Some of these images appear to have been Anglo-Saxon inventions, in the same way that the phenomenon of coloured outline drawings in multiple pigments constitutes a distinctively late Anglo-Saxon contribution to book design.

The emergence in Anglo-Saxon manuscripts from the tenth century onwards of frontispiece portraits of authors (besides evangelists and King David as had appeared in earlier Anglo-Saxon manuscripts) led to the development of an extraordinary type of portrait which combines the attributes of author and subject in a single emblematic figure. The portrait accorded with and served to illustrate – indeed to embody – a specific 'reading' or interpretation of the text which it accompanied, such as the *De Consolatio Philosophiae* of Boethius or the *Regula Pastoralis* of Gregory the Great, both key texts of the reform of learning and culture started under King Alfred and extended under his successors, culminating in the Benedictine Reform movement of the tenth and eleventh centuries. For example, the emblematic frontispiece portrait which prefaces the *Regula Pastoralis* in a mid-tenth-century manuscript now in St John's College, Oxford, portrays at one and the same time both the author, bearing book and cross-staff as suitable for a pope, and the subject of his text, a pastoral figure suitably equipped to go out into the world.

Detailed analysis of the author and subject portraits, along with the manuscripts in which they appear, helps to establish certain interrelations between the different illustrations and to demonstrate how a type of figure migrated from one text to another, a practice which extends far back into the classical period. By 'reading' the various illustrations line by line, it is possible to observe the processes of direct copying, adaptation, alteration, or transmutation from illustration to illustration, comparable to the ways in which the texts themselves were copied and subjected in the process to scribal or editorial emendation, alteration, or even incomprehension. Such a study embraces not only Anglo-Saxon portraits of authors but also Anglo-Saxon attitudes towards authors and their texts.

During the late period, particularly in connection with the Benedictine monastic reform movement of the tenth and eleventh centuries, book production was subjected to new contemporary Continental influences, ranging from certain types of texts to the sketch-like drawing style of the imported *Utrecht Psalter*, which, having been made in the mid-ninth century at Rheims, reached Canterbury in about the year 1000, to be copied there for the first of several times throughout the Middle Ages. As a result, different approaches to the art of the book arose and came to prevail. Book production was frequently extremely ambitious, or even over-ambitious. For example, there was considerable interest in cycles of illustrations, sometimes so extensive that they were left uncompleted; and many additions of both script and decoration (notably evangelist portraits) were made to earlier manuscripts, to a far greater extent than either the preceding or following periods of book production in England.

The Insular Gospel books

The great Insular Gospel books include notably the *Book of Durrow*, the *Durham Gospels*, the *Echternach Gospels*, the *Lindisfarne Gospels*, the *Lichfield Gospels* and the *Book of Kells*. The books contain the four Gospels, in Latin, usually in the Vulgate version translated and edited by St Jerome. The Insular Gospel books form a closely related group of manuscripts produced from the mid-seventh century to the beginning of the ninth century (depending on the date ascribed to the *Book of Kells*). This series of manuscripts presents an extraordinarily vivid and inventive creative approach to the art of the book. They stand amongst the very greatest works of art produced in the British Isles.

Their genre is Northumbrian, Irish and possibly also Pictish. But as it is somewhat difficult to distinguish precisely between the contribution of these different realms, the term 'Insular' has been adopted to refer to these books and other works in the same shared style (for example Insular metalwork found in Viking graves).

Standing at the head of the series of the great Insular Gospel books, the *Book of Durrow* points the way to a surprising, rapid development and flourishing of a particular phenomenon – Gospel books intended for display within the church and for ceremonial purposes. A number of characteristics distinguish these Gospel books and set them above many of the other manuscripts of the time in both England and elsewhere. Their elaborately decorated initials serve to point up, or point out, the beginnings of important liturgical readings and they developed over some time and throughout the series into full-page initials. This feature is one of the fundamental contributions of Anglo-Saxon and Irish scribes to book design.

Insular scribal artists treated in this way not only the openings of the four Gospels themselves but also the opening of Matthew 1:18, the Christmas reading, which begins '*Christi autem generatio sic erat*' ('and the birth of Christ was in this wise'). The opening word '*Christi*' was always abbreviated, in accordance with time-honoured tradition, as in all references to the names or Divinity; the abbreviation uses the Greek letters *Chi, Rho* and *Iota* ($\chi\rho\iota$).

Stages in the development of full-page initials can be seen in the enlarged decorated initials from the *Book of Durrow* through the *Lindisfarne Gospels* to the *Book of Kells*, where the opening word alone occupies a full page and is so densely filled and enmeshed with the background of ornament that it almost assumes the character of a carpet page. The letters become difficult to decipher, riddle-like in nature. Yet, rather than obscuring the nature of the words, which might seem the case at first glance, this meticulous, intricate embellishment encourages the beholder (for this is more than mere idle reading matter) to meditate upon the significance of these holy words.

These Gospel books frequently contained various types of ornamental frameworks enclosing the canon tables which serve as a manifestation, or an embodiment of the essential underlying harmony of the four Gospels despite their sometimes divergent accounts. In the *Lindisfarne Gospels* and the *Book of Kells* these arcades, or archways, serve as a series of entryways ushering us into the Gospel text.

Certain of the Insular Gospel books contain full-page representations of the evangelists, generally shown writing or holding their books. These scribal, or author, portraits are usually accompanied by their evangelist symbols. More often, however, the Insular Gospel books prefer full-page representations of the evangelist symbols rather than the evangelists themselves. These symbols are the attributes, or the representations, of the individual evangelists according to late antique traditions; they derived from the Apocalyptic beasts of the book of Revelations and also from particular phrases within the individual Gospels. Thus the usual symbol for Matthew is the angel or man, for Mark the lion, for Luke the bull or calf and for John the eagle.

A further important characteristic of these books is the script, which forms

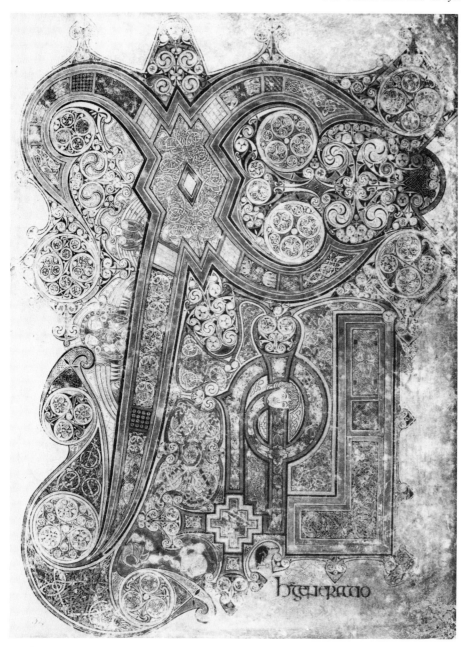

Initial page of Matthew I: 18, Christi autem generatio *(c.800), from the* Book of Kells.

an integral part of their splendour. The script carries the text, while the decoration serves to uplift it. The script belongs to a type known as Anglo-Saxon or insular majuscule: a formal and stately script which for the most part is contained within two lines presenting a bar-like appearance and yet has some ascending and descending elements which protrude from this band. (The script is a fore-runner of the minuscule handwriting which we now use for our everyday script.) The Insular Gospel books display very close interrelationships with each other in terms of their script, and it is possible that the same scribal artist was responsible for more than one of them. One of the distinguishing features of the script, frequently masterfully written within this series of luxurious books, is the way in which the script itself is elaborately embellished, with graceful and inventive pen flourishes, acquiring the status of decoration.

The major initials which open the Gospels in particular frequently display a feature known as 'diminuendo', where the following letter or letters diminish in size towards the rest of the text in standard text script. This produces a resonant transition from the elaborate beginning to the main text.

The *Book of Kells* presents an extremely elaborate version of majuscule for the main part of the text script. This version is so elaborate and painstaking to produce that it was normally reserved for a few elevated positions within a manuscript. The *Book of Kells*, however, surpassing the standard of other manuscripts by so great an extent in this, as in other respects, uses this special form of script for most of the text.

The carpet pages of the Insular Gospel books (so-called because their dense decoration makes them resemble oriental carpets) may derive from a very early stage in the history of Christianity when the four Gospels were placed in individual volumes and these pages, densely packed with ornament contained in frames, may evoke the effect of bindings. In any event, they present a block-like, or even wall-like beginning or boundary demarcating the beginning of the individual holy texts. The carpet pages very frequently incorporate cruciform patterns evoking the symbol of the cross, that symbol of the Gospel message as a whole. Sometimes these cross patterns are quite discreet within the whole page, as in some of the carpet pages in the *Book of Durrow*, where the principal ornament is interlace, trumpet-spiral or animal ornament. Sometimes the cross pattern, of one shape or another, is dominant and forms one of the structural foci of the page as a whole. Around the frames of the cross are fitted ornamental patterns which vie with the cross shape and with the frame as a reverberation between figure and ground, like a figure in a carpet.

Mechanical reconstructions of the compass marks and ruled grids used in setting out the carpet pages in the *Lindisfarne Gospels* have shown that the intricate, interlaced animal and bird ornament followed a very elaborate, and even monotonously symmetrical pattern. This contrasts quite markedly with the asymmetrical patterns in the *Echternach Gospels* or the *Book of Kells* in which the asymmetry adds greatly to the vivacity and liveliness of the image as a whole. The spirals and interlacing forms, with densely whirling movement, lead us out and yet direct us back in again in a complex interplay across the surface of the page.

A very striking feature of Insular Gospel books is the amazingly intricate patterns of ornament which decorate so many of their pages. These forms of ornament include trumpet-spiral and pelta ornament, interlace, and animal ornament, with occasional examples, particularly in the *Book of Kells*, of human ornament; with creatures frequently caught up in interlace. The menagerie in the *Book of Kells* is very extensive indeed, ranging from naturalistically rendered creatures such as fish, moths, cats and rats to strange gymnastic creatures variously human, animal, reptilian and dragonesque.

All of these features, from script and decorated initials to arcades and carpet pages, set these remarkable manuscripts apart in a class or species of their own.

The series of the great Insular Gospel books begins, as far as the evidence survives to us, with the *Book of Durrow*, produced around the middle of the seventh century, probably in Northumbria. The *Book of Durrow* appears on the scene quite unexpectedly, but the excellence of its craftsmanship and execution in terms of both script and decoration presupposes an extensive previous tradition of training and practice, experimentation and development, although few traces of that process survive. This manuscript contains not only the Gospel texts but also a series of carpet pages of various forms, a set of evangelist symbol pages set within decorated interlace frames and a series of large, decorated initials which lead into the Gospel texts in a form of diminuendo. Its decoration is very closely related indeed to the art of the Sutton Hoo treasure. The elements of correspondence include trumpet-spiral ornament of one of the carpet pages and many of the decorated initials, the types of animal ornament which closely parallel animals in the Sutton Hoo gold buckle and other pagan Anglo-Saxon jewelry, and the *cloisonné* or *millefiori* patterns. The masterful adoption of these motifs within the pages of a Gospel book attests to a fusion of pagan elements into a Christian core and it vividly reflects the ways in which Anglo-Saxon scribal artists were able to draw richly upon their native heritage while beginning to produce a basically foreign genre, the Christian book written in Latin (colour pl. 4).

The next in the series are the late seventh-century *Durham Gospels* and *Echternach Gospels*, two manuscripts perhaps written by the same master calligrapher who has been described as being 'one of the major masters of western calligraphy', just as the evangelist symbols in the *Echternach Gospels* have been described as being 'among the greatest works of western art'. The *Echternach Gospels*, which contains a series of evangelist symbol pages and also initial openings which follow the pattern of diminuendo, presents a range of breathtakingly intricate ornament such as spirals or interlace with a very limited palette of colours: yellow, red, green and purple. All but the first of its evangelist symbol pages have asymmetrical frames of coloured bands in which the different animals leap (in the case of the lion) or perch (in the case of the eagle). The feathers, or the fur, of these symbols are as meticulously and delicately rendered as the decoration within the different initials.

Then come the *Lindisfarne* and *Lichfield Gospels*, which date from the late seventh and mid eighth century respectively, and are very closely related in decoration and script. Also the extremely close resemblance of the scripts, among other things, in the *Lichfield Gospels* and the *Book of Kells* allows us to include the latter in this series, whether it was made in Anglo-Saxon England or elsewhere in the British Isles.

The *Book of Kells* is the most richly decorated Insular Gospel book of all, in terms of the density of its canon arcades, its magnificent series of carpet pages, its illustrations, decorative script and full-page initials. The *Chi-Rho* page, for example, contains in addition to intricate interlace, spiral and animal ornament, certain delightful vignettes such as the pair of moths confronting each other just underneath the upper left-hand stem of the initial, the pair of contented cats with rats perched on their backs below the tail of the stem, or, just to the right of that, an otter carrying a fish. These are vignettes of daily life which closely parallel the sorts of marginalia added by medieval scribes or readers in the course of their work, such as comments about how beautiful the sun is that day and what a pity it is that they are indoors. The *Book of Kells* also contains a series of evangelist portraits as well as a number of illustrations, including the Arrest of Christ and the Virgin Mary with Christ.

Whatever the uncertainty concerning its precise place and date of origin, the mystery and marvel of the *Book of Kells* consist in the way in which it has the power, through the sheer vitality of its creation as a whole, to transcend its own time and place and present a magnificent work of universal appeal. As we turn page after page, with each page much different from the others and yet clearly belonging to the whole, we might take comfort, despite our lack of knowledge of the names of the scribes, in the approach adopted by James Joyce in describing this great and complex work of art: 'so why, pray, sign anything, so long as every word, letter, stroke and paper space is a perfect signature of its own'.

The extraordinary profusion of ornamentation in the *Book of Kells*, extending for page after page throughout the book and not just at the beginnings of the Gospels or significant sections, sets this manuscript very much in a class of its own, making it one of the chief masterpieces of manuscript art of all time.

The Codex Amiatinus

While the *Book of Kells* and other Insular Gospel books present a richly varied mixture of Insular and Mediterranean elements, the *Codex Amiatinus* and other products of Monkwearmouth-Jarrow, home of the Venerable Bede, represent a remarkable degree of classicism in the Mediterranean tradition. By any standards the *Codex Amiatinus* is an astounding achievement.

The *Codex Amiatinus*, a complete, large-format, single-volume bible in the Latin Vulgate version of St Jerome, which is now kept in the Medici Library in Florence, comprises 1,030 folios (that is, 2,060 pages, with two pages front and back to a folio or leaf) and measures some 20 in high, 14 in wide, and 10 in thick; it weighs some 75 lb. For centuries the manuscript was venerated as a relic of Pope Gregory the Great, who was believed to have written it. It was only recently recognised to be a product not of Italian but of Anglo-Saxon scribes and artists, working at one or the other of the twin monasteries of Monkwearmouth and Jarrow on the coast of eastern Northumbria before the year 716.

The text of the book is one of the very best extant witnesses to the Vulgate, and it also contains a set of diagrams and illustrations of considerable interest and controversy. These include, among others, the framed, full-page scene showing a scribe at work in a library, with a book open on his lap, a folding table beside him, and an open bookcase behind him; a double-page illustration, seen in bird's-eye view, of the Tabernacle in Jerusalem; a framed, full-page representation of Christ in Majesty, the *Maiestas Christi*; and four full-page diagrams (one enclosing verses about the Pentateuch within sets of roundels, and three showing the divisions of the books of the bible according variously to St Jerome, to Pope Hilarius and Epiphanius of Cyprus, and to St Augustine).

As appropriate to a large-format bible, the *Codex Amiatinus* is written in two tall columns of text per page. The text is written out *per cola et commata*, that is, according to Jerome's declared principles, in sense-units (rather than run together in paragraphs) for reading out. The script is an elegant uncial (a script whose characters resemble modern capitals), with rounded letter forms, not unlike the sort of uncial produced in Italy in the sixth century. The *Codex Amiatinus* was produced in Anglo-Saxon England and sent to Rome by Ceolfrid as a gift for the pope at the time, Gregory II. It was one of the three pandects (that is, single-volume bibles) which Ceolfrid ordered to be copied at Monkwearmouth–Jarrow. We are told that in the course of his abbacy, which extended for twenty-seven years, from 689 to 716, he copiously enriched the monasteries over which he presided; 'the third [bible] he resolved to offer as a gift to Peter, Prince of the Apostles, when he was about to go to Rome,' in accordance with his wish as an old man of 74 years to go on pilgrimage and to die there. He therefore prepared a ship, drew up a list of envoys whom he intended for Rome, decided on the gifts which were to be rendered to the blessed Peter, and procured a sufficiency of the things which might be necessary for so great a journey. On his way to Rome, with a retinue of some 80 men, he died at Langres in France, where he was buried. Some of his companions returned to Northumbria and reported his death to the monastery; some chose to remain in Langres; and others 'completed the proposed journey to Rome, to deliver the presents which he had sent', among them the bible.

The manuscript was written in the distinctive script of Monkwearmouth–Jarrow which is known in a number of surviving manuscripts, such as the *Stonyhurst Gospel*, one of the relics of St Cuthbert. The *Stonyhurst Gospel* is one of the very smallest to survive from Anglo-Saxon England – as a pocket Gospel book, it fits neatly in the hand – while the *Codex Amiatinus* is one of the very largest, taking two men to carry it. These differences in scale have much to do with the differences in type of book and the functions which they were to serve.

Seven different scribes worked on the *Codex Amiatinus*, in nine separate sections, allowing several scribes to work simultaneously. The scribes allowed themselves only a few recognisably Insular elements, such as the interlace and pen-flourishes which decorate several initials. The comparative restraint in the decorated initials is all the more striking when one considers the meticulously intricate embellishment Northumbrian scribes might allow themselves, as in the opening of the Gospel of Matthew in the *Lindisfarne Gospels*, made in the late seventh century. This does not mean that Monkwearmouth–Jarrow scribes avoided Insular decoration entirely, as we know from the initials in the copy of Bede's *Historia Ecclesiastica* known as the *Leningrad Bede* (the name comes from where it is now kept), which was written at about 746.

In the *Codex Amiatinus*, the New Testament opens with a framed full-page frontispiece illustration of the *Maiestas Christi*. Within a medallion the enthroned, full-length figure of Christ, haloed, long-haired, and bearded, holds a book upright in his veiled left hand and gestures in blessing with his right. A pair of winged angels holding long staffs flank him, and the blue background with dots and concentric streaks suggest the heavens. The medallion consists of multiple rims with concentric bands bordering either a jewelled band, like the rectangular frame of the scene, or a wavy ribbon motif – features fully late-antique in nature. Above and below the medallion, set against more or less horizontal bands of colour, there stand in the four corners of the frame four haloed, full-length human figures holding books in veiled or unveiled hands. The full-length, winged evangelist symbols hover at diagonals beside them, apparently serving – in the absence of inscriptions – to identify the figures as Matthew, Mark, Luke and John.

The image of the *Maiestas Christi* is followed by the double-page illustration of the Tabernacle at Jerusalem – the largest illustration surviving among Anglo-Saxon manuscripts. It shows the court, with the names of the Twelve Tribes of Israel inscribed outside it, together with the number of their following. This accords with Numbers 2:2: 'The people of Israel shall encamp each by his own standard, with the ensigns of their fathers' houses; they shall encamp facing the tent of meeting on every side.' Within the court, we see the altar of the Holocaust before the entrance to the Tabernacle, and within its columns and drapery we see the Holy of Holies, the Ark of the Covenant guarded by two cherubs, and the instruments of the sacrifice: the seven-branched candelabrum, the table for shew bread, the blazing altar for incense. The names of the four cardinal points in Greek are inscribed within the court: *Arctos*, *Dysis*, *Anatol* and *Mesembria*, to orient the viewer. The names of Moses and Aaron stand to the east of the entrance to the Tabernacle, according to Numbers 3:38, which states that 'and those to encamp before the Tabernacle on the east, before the tent of meeting toward the sunrise, were Moses and Aaron and his sons'.

Another folio carries the portrait of the Old Testament scribe Ezra at work in a library or study. The verses above the portrait identify the figure and his activity:

> Codibus sacris hostile clade perustis
> Ezra do fervens hoc reparavit opus.

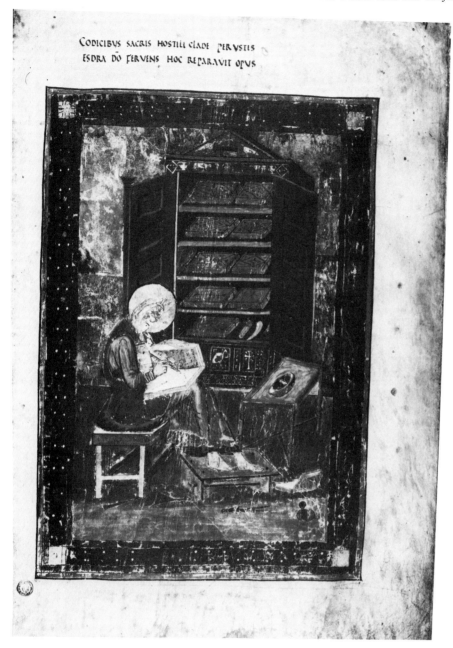

CODICIBVS SACRIS HOSTILI CLADE PERVSTIS
ESDRA DŌ FERVENS HOC REPARAVIT OPVS

The Old Testament priest Ezra copying out Holy Writ from memory, in a library setting (early eighth century), from the Codex Amiatinus.

('When the sacred books of the law were destroyed by fire, Ezra, inspired by god, made good the loss'; that is, by copying out the books of Holy Writ again from memory.) Ezra is shown unusually as an evangelist type. He wears the tallith on his head and a jewelled breastplate, the emblems of an Old Testament priest or prophet, but – even more unusually in medieval representations of him – his pose is that of a scribe, and some close parallels occur in Byzantine representations.

The illustrations and diagrams in the manuscript have frequently been taken to have been copied faithfully from the *Codex Grandior* (now lost) of Cassiodorus, the sixth-century Senator who retired to found a monastery in Squillace, in the far south of Italy near Naples. For example, the image of Ezra has been seen as embodying not only Ezra himself but also Cassiodorus, that is, Cassiodorus in his library in the guise of Ezra saving holy writ, in line with Cassiodorus' firm belief that he with his monastery was helping to save civilisation against barbarian incursions which threatened Rome and the rest of the civilised late-antique world. But for various reasons this now seems improbable.

The composite and complex Ezra image was most probably assembled at Monkwearmouth–Jarrow, like the other elements in the first quire of the *Codex Amiatinus*, as part of the conscious construction of a bible recension (or revision), which involved not only selecting the best texts available for the different books and perfecting a form of script, but also creating appropriate images to set alongside the text, as an aid for study and reflection. There are many signs in the *Codex Amiatinus* of the work of Northumbrian scribes, artists and scholars selecting, altering, and combining a number of sources so as to produce new, fresh images. The bible text, too, was copied from a variety of exemplars – a good Neapolitan text for the Gospels, a bad Irish text for Psalms, a text with local Northumbrian features for the Catholic Epistles, and good (probably Italian) manuscripts for most of the other books – as the producers of the bible selected and compared texts on the spot. The drawings in the first quire were all designed by Anglo-Saxon monks, and perhaps by Bede and Ceolfrid themselves, rather than being copied from the *Codex Grandior*. The *Codex Amiatinus* does not offer us a dim reflection of Cassiodorus' monastery Vivarium: instead, it vividly reflects the world of the Venerable Bede. As Patrick Wormald noted, 'Bede's horizons are very like those of the *Codex Amiatinus*, with its meticulous and eclectic scholarship, its ultramontane models, and its lack of contact with the tastes of the Northumbrian world outside the monastery.'

Bede in his commentary on the Book of Ezra stated that Ezra may stand for any priest or doctor of the Church. When, mindful of this, we recall that the *Codex Amiatinus* was unlikely to have been made especially for Ceolfrid's departure to Rome, but rather chosen among the available resources when he came to draw up his list of gifts for the Pope, and when we recall moreover that the two pandects placed in Monkwearmouth and Jarrow were explicitly intended for anyone there to consult them when they wished, this enables us to approach more closely the force of the Ezra image: it was intended that the user of the book identify directly with this figure as he beheld it, as one in the tradition of saving and handing on knowledge of holy scripture in the life of the Church both in Northumbria and in the world.

The scarcity of large-format bibles either extant (in whole or in part) or described from Anglo-Saxon England emphasises all the more the remarkable achievement of Ceolfrid and his monks at Monkwearmouth–Jarrow in producing not just one but three pandects, and we may reasonably suppose that the two sister pandects contained some forms of decoration and illustration, although we have no way of knowing how they would have matched or differed from the *Codex Amiatinus*. It is increasingly clear to what extent this manuscript manifests the skill in scholarship, script, and artistic invention at Monkwearmouth–Jarrow in the late seventh and early eighth century, just as the *Royal Bible* can now be seen to represent a comparable achievement, although very different in kind, at Canterbury in the first half of the ninth century. It is to the *Royal Bible* and its southern English relatives that we now turn.

The 'Canterbury School'

The art of southern English manuscripts of the eighth and ninth centuries differs in a number of respects from that of northern English and Irish manuscripts of the same period. So far as the evidence survives, southern English manuscripts, with the possible exception of the *Vespasian Psalter*, have no evangelist symbol pages or carpet pages, like those in the great Insular Gospel books. But other features, such as a remarkable degree of classicism and a predeliction for rich purple-dyed leaves, gold, silver and polychrome effects, set the southern English manuscripts apart.

Early in this century the German art historian Heinrich Zimmermann designated a group of manuscripts, including the *Vespasian Psalter*, the *Codex Aureus*, the *Royal Bible*, the *Tiberius Bede* and the *Book of Cerne*, as belonging to the 'Canterbury School', on the basis of their manifest interrelations and the signs that some of them had been made at Canterbury. Not all of the major surviving decorated southern English manuscripts were made there, but the term reflects the way in which Canterbury served as a centre of cultural and artistic production, setting the style of the day.

The *Vespasian Psalter*, which dates from about the second quarter of the eighth century, is the first in the series of lavishly decorated southern English manuscripts. Its sudden appearance, without surviving representatives of the earlier stages of development which must have led up to its assured, accomplished expertise of execution and invention, is comparable to that of the *Book of Durrow* in northern England in the seventh century. We know that the tradition of reading and writing Latin returned to southern England (after the departure of the Romans) with the mission to Kent of St Augustine, sent by Pope Gregory the Great in 597 to convert the English. Augustine's mission centred upon Canterbury, where he founded the abbey of St Peter and St Paul (later, from the tenth century onwards, known after him as St Augustine's Abbey).

The *Vespasian Psalter* launched the southern English tradition of adherence, for the most part, to the classical Mediterranean principles of figural decoration, which contrasts with much, but not all, of northern English principles (with Monkwearmouth–Jarrow comprising the principal exception). The frontispiece author portrait of the *Vespasian Psalter* shows

King David playing a six-stringed lyre-like harp (similar to the lyre found in the Sutton Hoo ship-burial) in the company of his retinue. The whole image is vividly polychrome, and both the figures and the designs are meticulously and delicately rendered (see p. 122).

In an important way, this image can be seen to stand for, and to embody, much of the essence of Anglo-Saxon art, particularly during the Christian period, in drawing together elements from many different sources of inspiration and creating new, fresh images. Not only does the image stand within a book (a genre of Mediterranean extraction), ushering us in through the arcade to the text, whose divine inspiration is made manifest in the scene, but also it places Mediterranean-derived elements – the figures of David and his retinue rendered according to classical principles – within a distinctly Insular setting: that is, within an arcade containing ornament utterly characteristic of the Hiberno-Saxon heritage. Moreover, the image evokes a variety of different activities and spheres of artistic life: architecture is implied in the arcade and its room-like or niche-like enclosure containing the figures; these carry out the activities of writing, making music and dancing; and the ornamental motifs evoke many other arts such as metalwork, for example, in the gold-leaf bearing inked designs of rosettes or interlace inset in the circular centres of the trumpet-spirals and the diamond-shaped centres of the interlace in both the arch and the pillars. The image as a whole is a testament to the varied richness of the many arts and crafts practised in Anglo-Saxon England.

It is also impressive in its own right. The king, seated upon a rectangular throne with a striped cushion, stares out towards us, as if he is meditating upon the text of his psalms. The scribes either look intently towards him or downwards towards the figures gathered below; with their wide, staring eyes, they too appear to muse upon the holy inspired words and music. Even the birds in the rounded capitals appear to gaze attentively at the king. The band-like base of the arcade not only closes off the scene, but also with its different ends adds an element of asymmetry to an otherwise mostly symmetrical design, while a few other details add to this effect of balanced asymmetry. For example, the two pairs of musicians blow differently-shaped instruments, and the scribes gaze in different directions and hold different sets of writing implements.

The *Psalter* text is enlivened with decorated initials beginning each of the Psalms, while major Psalm divisions are marked with still more elaborately decorated first lines, in which the initials are followed by a band-like line of display letters, sometimes linked together within a frame-like background figured with ornamental patterns and creatures. Two of the initials are filled with figures, illustrating the text. They show David and Jonathan making a covenant, and David rending the jaws of the lion. The figures are represented in the same manner as the frontispiece figures.

The rest of the decoration, however, is thoroughly Anglo-Saxon. Each of the major initials is accompanied by a line of elaborate display capitals, which either stand against the vellum background itself, or are enclosed within frames. Sometimes the framed lines stand against backgrounds filled with ornamental motifs or creatures, such as interlace, birds (such as a rooster),

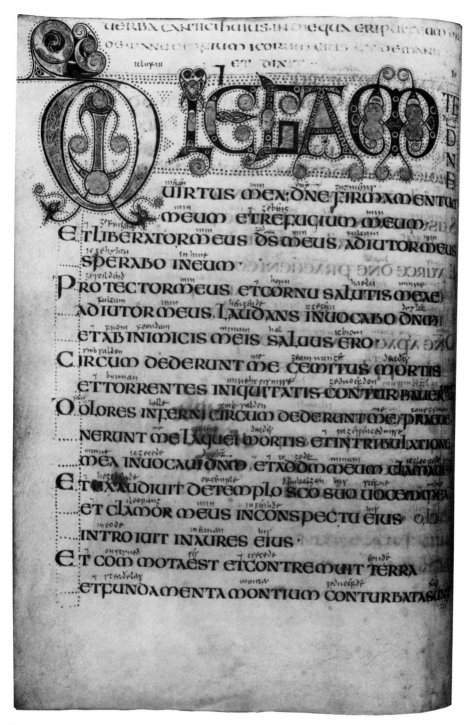

The opening of Psalm 18, with decorated opening line and uncial text script (second quarter of the eighth century), and an Old English translation added between the lines (mid ninth century), from the Vespasian Psalter.

animals (such as a rabbit, stag, or dog), or a human creature. The initials sometimes take the form of animals, or contain animals or birds within panel-like fields inserted into the body of the letter. In many cases, the initials and the display letters have scrolling tendrils which extend outwards, generally in symmetrical pairs, to end in coiled and rounded terminals. This feature has aptly been described as the 'antenna-style', due to the resemblance of the tendrils to the antennae of insects. Developed apparently by the scribal artist of this manuscript, the style enjoyed a certain vogue within Southern English manuscript decoration for some time, lingering into the ninth century.

The next major manuscript in the southern English series is the *Codex Aureus*, made somewhere in Kent in about the middle of the eighth century. In about the middle of the ninth century an inscription was added to it in Old English stating that, for the good of their souls, Ealdorman Aelfred and his wife Werburg had ransomed the manuscript back from 'the heathens' (that is, the Vikings, who must have stolen it on one of their raids in Kent, perhaps from Minster in Thanet), and had given it to Christ Church, Canterbury (colour pl. 9).

The manuscript, as its present name (meaning 'Golden Book') suggests, is very splendid indeed. It contains a set of ornamental canon arcades, executed by two different artists, one much more skilled than the other. The better artist was also responsible for the two surviving evangelist portraits, of Matthew and John. Both portraits show the holy author solemnly enthroned within an arcade and accompanied by his half-length symbol (angel or eagle, respectively) within the lunette of the arch. The evangelist gestures in blessing over his text, either a partly unrolled scroll or opened book; the triple horizontal bands of colour in the background suggest a meeting of sky and landscape, an effect enhanced by the foliage rising from the ground to either side of Matthew. With a halo and spread wings, the symbol carries a closed book, either tucked under a wing or held in a veiled hand, indicating by the covering drapery reverence to the holy text and the holy object. The detailed rendering of the cover of the book held by the Matthew symbol may allow us to glimpse something of the elaborately decorated covers, with jewelled and metal mounts upon red-stained leather, which must have decorated many luxurious Anglo-Saxon manuscripts, but which have been despoiled and lost over the centuries. Within the arcade, the curtains drawn to either side and looped around the pillars indicate, according to time-honoured tradition, that we the beholders are like initiates before a holy scene, facing a shrine in which the usual shrouding and protecting veils are drawn aside to allow us to penetrate to the holy mysteries within.

The Gospel text is richly decorated. The opening of Matthew 1:18, the *Christi autem* reading, is set out within a rectangular full-page frame of seven band-like lines of display letters, each enclosed within a rectangular frame. The enlarged first word (abbreviated, according to time-honoured tradition, by the Greek letters $\chi\rho\iota$), with the letters *rho* and *iota* nested within the right-hand side of the initial *chi*, binds together the first two lines. The lines are set out alternately in gold-leaf letters and in multicoloured letters. Both the background of the first line and the panels of the initial *chi* are filled with figured patterns: trumpet-spiral ornament, single or paired animals or birds in various poses (sometimes caught up in interlace or occupying foliage) and – demarcating the two words within the first line – a vine-like scrolling stem evocative of the source of the Eucharistic wine. In the following lines the multicoloured letters are set against a gold-leaf background, and the gold-leaf letters (sometimes containing rosettes or animal heads) are set against bare vellum background, resembling open-work metalwork. In turn, as we contemplate them, the letters and the backgrounds come to the fore and reverberate with each other, producing a most vividly dramatic and resonant image which mixes script and decoration, decorative script and scriptural ornament.

The Gospel text is set out upon leaves which alternate between undyed and purple-dyed, producing polychrome openings between pages. Enhancing the polychrome effect, the undyed pages are written with black ink and red pigment, and the purple pages are written with a mixture of gold, silver and white pigment. Moreover, the pages of text frequently present intricate geometric patterns – above all cruciform patterns – either by varying the colours of the letters themselves (producing stripes or other shapes within or across the columns of text), as the scribe would pick up quills with differently coloured pigments by turns as he wrote out the lines; or by adding outlines or dots around or behind the letters.

The purple-dyed leaves, which set off and enrich the text, are fully in keeping with the Mediterranean tradition of purple books, harking back to the late antique tradition of imperial purple, that expensive pigment of prerogative. When applied to scriptural texts, magnificent purple-dyed leaves served reverentially and richly to honour Christ the King and Holy Writ (as well as to enhance the aura and manifest the wealth of donors and owners). Extending this practice in a dramatic way, the richly decorative patterned pages in the *Codex Aureus*, with their complex interplay between coloured ground, letters and patterns, represent vivid reminders of the import of the text which they embellish, and, when cruciform, even embody.

An equally innovative approach to the use of purple-dyed leaves and to other elements of iconography occurs within the *Royal Bible*. This sumptuous manuscript, which survives as only about one-twelfth of its awesome, large-format original form (which extended to more than one thousand folio-sized leaves), was made in about the second quarter of the ninth century at St Augustine's Abbey, Canterbury. The surviving portion contains most of the gospel text and part of the Acts of the Apostles. There is a magnificent set of five canon arcades which imitate contemporary styles of metalwork decoration to an extent unparalleled in Anglo-Saxon manuscripts except for the *Book of Durrow*. In this case, the extensive repertoire of ornament matches the style current in southern English art in the late eighth and the ninth centuries, particularly in gold or silver metalwork with nielloed (or black sulphide of silver) inlay, in works like the Fuller Brooch, the Pentney Brooches, the Aethelswith Ring, the Bologna Ring and the Abingdon Sword.

As it survives, the manuscript is the work principally of one master scribal artist, who was responsible for most of the text and for all of the decoration of the book, and who created a distinctive iconography as well as a remarkable individual style. He was responsible for writing (and perhaps also

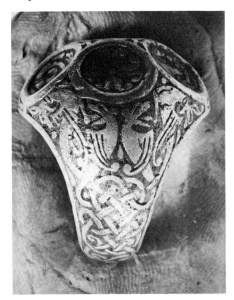

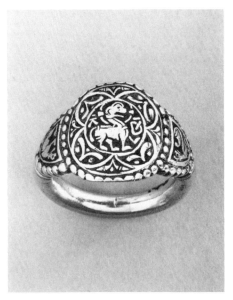

*The Bologna Ring, with foliate, animal
and interlace ornament (early ninth
century).*

*The Aethelswith Ring, with the Lamb of
God and animal and foliate ornament
(c.853–88).*

for composing) the monumental, unframed, full-page Latin inscriptions laid
out in alternate lines of gold and silver display capitals upon purple-dyed
leaves; they describe lost illustrations, such as of the Baptism of Christ or the
Annunciation to Zacharias concerning the birth of John the Baptist. This
master was also responsible for creating the extraordinary iconography of the
single surviving Gospel opening, that of Luke, similarly laid out upon a
purple-dyed leaf.

The Gospel of Luke opens most magnificently within an elaborately
decorated polychrome arcade of gold, silver and other coloured pigments.
The semi-circular arch, supported upon two pillars with enlarged bases and
circular capitals crowned by shell-like motifs, has an enlarged medallion at
the top. The lunette and the medallion at the top of the arcade contain the
haloed, half-length figures of the winged evangelist symbol of Luke (the bull)
and of Christ, subject of the Gospel text and inspirer of its author. Both
figures carry books and appear in apocalyptic guise against backgrounds of
parted clouds and sky, and perhaps also of rounded hills. The pillars,
capitals, bases, and flanks of the arch contain panels of interlace, geometric,
foliate, and animal ornament. The first two suspended words of the Gospel,
Quoniam quidem, appear to hover within the arcade.

The original arrangement, with each Gospel opening laid out similarly,
aims to make manifest the divine inspiration of the four evangelists, each in
turn, through Christ. Yet, unlike other images of inspiration, expressing the
theme directly at the moment the evangelist receives his calling or presents
his work to the world, this image expresses the theme symbolically, with the
evangelist represented only by his symbol (the bull) and by the opening

words of his text, with Christ presented as an inspiring presence in the roundel at the top, and with the opening words of the Gospel set prominently below. In effect, the image illustrates – or, rather, embodies – the evangelist author's divine inspiration as an eternal, hieratical or priestly order.

The page can be read not only horizontally across the lines of text, but also vertically down the page. The flow between the elements of the ensemble proceeds from left to right in the lines of script, as well as from top to bottom in the arcade, and back again. The arcade with its enclosed figures embodies the progression of divine inspiration from Christ at the top, triumphant in the heavens, to the evangelist, leading to, and resulting in, the words of the Gospel enshrined within the arcade. At one and the same time, the arcade functions as a portal and leads the beholder to the Gospel text within, and the Gospel text leads the contemplator to Christ in heaven.

With its very many illustrations which once adorned the text, but have been cut out and lost (leaving some traces behind), together with the extraordinarily meticulous classicism of the figural decoration which does survive, the rich purple-dyed leaves, the plentiful gold and silver pigments and the elaborate ornamentation, the *Royal Bible* was one of the very most magnificent and ambitious manuscripts the Anglo-Saxons ever made; and it rivals the illustrated ninth-century Carolingian bibles produced principally at Tours under the Anglo–Saxon Abbot Alcuin's successors. In its lavish decoration drawn masterfully from a wide variety of sources, both Continental and Anglo–Saxon, from the late antique past to the present, the *Royal Bible* represents an astounding achievement of Anglo-Saxon book production.

The 'Winchester Style'

In the tenth and eleventh centuries a new and distinctly Anglo-Saxon style emerged both in direct response to, and as an inextricable part of, the resurgence of religious, cultural and artistic life which swept through England. Its roots lay in the reign of Alfred the Great (871–899), following retrenchment against the Viking incursions and disruptions. Once he had secured his kingdom against the Vikings, Alfred launched a substantial programme of educational and cultural revival, which resulted in a fundamental redirection of earlier Anglo-Saxon artistic forms. It followed Continental models (particularly of the Benedictine Reform movement), but translated them into specifically Anglo-Saxon modes which, by the eleventh century, had achieved sufficient strength to extend not only beyond the Conquest in England, overlapping with the rise of Anglo-Norman styles, but also across the Channel to the Continent.

The far-sweeping reforms which reached into many areas of life went hand-in-hand with the production of remarkable, and often lavish, works of art, like the *Benedictional* (a collection of blessings for bishops' use) made for St Aethelwold by the scribe Godeman, and the resplendent *Trinity Gospels*, made in the early eleventh century.

The charter which Edgar granted in 966 to the newly reformed monastery of New Minster, Winchester, was presented most unusually and with great pomp in the form of a book. This was written in gold script and embellished with an elaborate frontispiece, in which the King, flanked by the Virgin Mary and St Peter (patron saints of the monastery), stands in a strangely twisted, excited pose with his back towards us and with his arms raised like an orant (in gesture of prayer), clutching the book in one hand and offering – as if brandishing – it towards Christ, who hovers above him in an almond-shaped mandorla (or enclosing frame) held up by angels. The sombre, even glum expressions of the figures reinforce the overbearingly solemn effect of the image, in which the King's act is shown to be utterly in accordance with the highest possible authority. The fluttering hems and the flying folds of the drapery, together with the heavy border densely filled with over-grown acanthus foliage, represent the earliest dated appearance in a manuscript of the so-called 'Winchester Style'. This term neglects the other important centres of artistic production (such as Canterbury), but it evokes the extent to which a given style, accorded royal assent and support, made its way throughout the land (although not without variations), in very much the same way that the West Saxon dialect of Old English rose to ascendance during the period as part of the expansion of West Saxon rule, which (to most intents and purposes) was centred upon Winchester.

In keeping with the widespread determination to provide blueprints for religious, cultural and social life (as expressed, for example, in Aelfric's homilies and Archbishop Wulfstan's abrasive, uncompromising 'Sermon to the English'), works of art, many of them highly ambitious and didactic, were employed as instruments of inculcation and propaganda. An important example of the monumental, icon-like images is the frontispiece drawing of Christ appearing to an adoring monk in the manuscript known as *St Dunstan's Classbook*, which was added to the book at Glastonbury during the time of Dunstan's abbacy (from 940 – if not earlier – to 956). It presents an intimate, highly personal image, combining elements proper to a Transfiguration or Ascension of Christ with a contemporary figure, the monk, set in the place of the traditional apostles who witnessed such events. The monk, bending prostrate before Christ, shields his face with one hand, in awe. To this drawing St Dunstan himself added two lines of verse invoking Christ's mercy on his behalf, thereby identifying himself directly with the image and turning it into a visual prayer.

In images dating from later stages in the reform movement, designed to demonstrate and to inculcate conformity with the Benedictine Rule, there is an extensive use of gold and lavish decoration in the script, decorated initials and illustrations of manuscripts, and in the body, inlays or gilding of pieces of metalwork. Magnificence seems to have been one of the primary keynotes of the period, as a specific and integral part of the public aims which governed much of the production of works of art. Yet, the drive to produce imposing works of art to serve as means of propaganda and as manifestations of authority did not overwhelm artistic invention. Among late Anglo-Saxon artists there were some who deserve to figure among the greatest English artists of any period. For example, one artist, known to have worked both in England and on the Continent during the later part of the eleventh century, left behind a number of masterful drawings and illustrations in at least four, and perhaps five, surviving manuscripts, among them the haunting Crucifixion drawn in multicoloured outline in the *Ramsey Psalter* (made apparently at Winchester), and the astonishingly extensive illustrations and embellishments of the *Boulogne Gospels* (made at St Omer). This artist was highly skilled in both the outline drawing (in single and multiple pigments) and the fully painted styles. He seems to have had a preference for hunch-backed figures, like the Virgin Mary who witnesses the Crucifixion and the evangelists who work at writing their Gospel texts. This appears to be a sort of 'signature'.

The *Boulogne Gospels* is the most extensively illustrated Gospel book to survive from the late Anglo-Saxon period. It contains not only a series of canon arcades – sometimes peopled with figures such as an archer or a harper – evangelist portraits and Gospel initials, but also a number of illustrations, among them a series of figures showing Christ's ancestors, stretching across most of three pages, to culminate in scenes of the Annunciation to Mary, the Visitation between her and Elisabeth, the Annunciation to the Shepherds and the Nativity (colour pl. 12).

One of this artist's greatest masterpieces is the hauntingly moving Crucifixion in the *Ramsay Psalter*. It shows Christ stretched on the cross, with his head turned towards the left and his eyes closed in death. At the left Mary leans towards him and raises the cloth of her garment to wipe her eyes. At the right St John, in contrast, smiles with delight and spreads his arms in ecstacy, so great that his hand bursts into the rectangular frame of the image, as he cannot contain his joy at the true import of the event, whose news he will spread in his Gospel, in bringing the possibility of redemption to mankind through the death on the Cross. Mary's garments are delicately patterned, adding a further poignant note to her dignified grief (colour pl. 11).

The distinctive style of drawings in the mid ninth-century Carolingian *Utrecht Psalter* exerted a profound impact on English manuscript art in the eleventh century; for example, in the illustrations in the *Bury St Edmunds Psalter*, in which, unlike the *Utrecht Psalter* and its copies, the drawings do not fit into spaces left between the psalms, but rather crowd into the margins around the column of text. The style of drawing favours elongated figures in twisting and turning poses, animated by dramatic gestures and swinging draperies. The scenes in this manuscript do not illustrate each and every phrase of the text, as if serving as a visual *aide-mémoire*, seen in the *Utrecht* and *Harley Psalters* (colour pl. 10) but rather they evoke or underscore striking individual passages, as the illustrations are intermingled with the text, in a vivid interplay between word and image.

During the eleventh century, styles of manuscript decoration gradually crystallised or hardened, as in the frontispiece illustration in the mid-eleventh century *Winchcombe Psalter*, showing King David accompanied by his musicians as he plucks his harp. In this image, the upswept hems of the drapery appear to be frozen, rather than billowing as in the drawings in both *St Dunstan's Classbook* and the *Bury St Edmunds Psalter*, and the acanthus foliage which engulfs the trellis-like frame is stiffly attenuated. Images such as these, produced as the Norman Conquest approached, and with it a merging with Norman styles of manuscript decoration, contributed to the emergence of the distinctive and multiform English Romanesque style, characterised by rigidity, abstraction and monumentality.

Although very different in many ways from the early Anglo–Saxon period of book production, the late Anglo–Saxon period continued its tradition of splendour, creative inventiveness and masterful design, so that the Anglo–Saxon achievement as a whole stands one of the highest points in the history of the art of the book.

The Bayeux Tapestry and the arts of warfare

One of the most famous and fascinating works of art produced by Anglo-Saxons was not made during the Anglo-Saxon period itself but shortly after the Norman Conquest. This is the so-called 'tapestry' preserved at Bayeux in Normandy; it is in fact an embroidered wall-hanging, set out in a long continuous strip of eight joined pieces of plain linen cloth worked in coloured wools, laid and couched with stem and outline stitching, leaving the background blank. It is about 50 cm tall and nearly 70 m long in its present state; the original end has been lost.

The importance of the Bayeux Tapestry as a work of art and as a monument of its period has several aspects. It serves as a major and nearly contemporary witness of the complex events which it represents – not without bias, subtlety, or wit – and at the same time it skilfully and compellingly, with many lively touches, draws us closer to the events and the people involved. It illustrates the events leading up to the Norman Conquest of England, settling the question of succession to the English throne violently and decisively. The story stretches from 1064, during the reign of Edward the Confessor, when Earl Harold Godwinson set out for Normandy, to

The Battle of Hastings, with the death of King Harold, from the Bayeux Tapestry (c.1070–80).

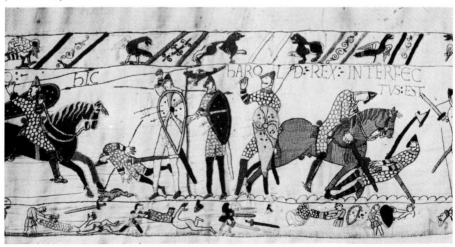

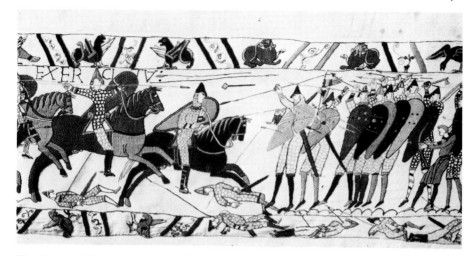

The Battle of Hastings, with the Norman cavalry confronting the Anglo-Saxon infantry and its shield-wall, from the Bayeux Tapestry (c.1070–80).

Saturday, 14 October 1066, when as king of England he was killed at the Battle of Hastings. The Bayeux Tapestry probably once went on to show the coronation of William the Conqueror as king of England on Christmas Day at Westminster Abbey, but it now breaks off at the point where the Anglo-Saxons are running away from the battlefield after being defeated, and the Normans are riding after them.

The events parade in an extended frieze-like series of scenes (usually within a single register), resembling a cartoon-strip. The scenes are shown within architectural settings (such as Westminster Abbey, in the form erected under King Edward the Confessor and consecrated in 1065, but demolished in the thirteenth century by Henry II for his own version, which still stands), townscapes (such as Dol, Mont St Michel, Rennes and Bayeux), landscapes and seascapes. The scenes are accompanied by Latin inscriptions which identify and explain them. They are enclosed within an elaborate decorative border at the top and bottom, as well as at the beginning (presumably also originally at the end).

The border contains foliage, creatures and scenes of various kinds, including representations of episodes from Aesop's Fables (such as the crow, the fox and the cheese; or the crane extracting a bone from the wolf's throat) and the appearance of Halley's Comet, taken as a frightening omen. Sometimes the principal scenes burst out into the borders, not just where buildings or ship sails rise into the upper border, but notably as the Battle of Hastings rages more fiercely and corpses and weapons fall thicker by the way. At one point, where the lower border is filled with dismembered bodies and looters, a dragonesque creature typical of the borders escapes into the main register, as if poignantly trying to get out of harm's way. Here, matters of life and death crowd out, but do not entirely displace, decoration and fantasy.

Although frequently thought to be the work of Norman embroideresses (above all William's Queen Matilda), the Bayeux Tapestry shows its English origin in many ways, including types of spellings and letter-forms (in accordance with Anglo-Saxon, not Norman, usage) and points of detailed resemblance to numerous Anglo-Saxon works of art of the period. It stands firmly within the flourishing tradition of Anglo-Saxon embroidery, which with its richness and splendour amazed the Normans when they came to England, and which laid the foundations for the development of the highly prized medieval English embroidery known as *opus anglicanum.*

The scenes, inscriptions and decoration strongly suggest that the Bayeux Tapestry was made at Canterbury within the sphere of influence or under the direct patronage of Odo, half-brother of William the Conqueror, Bishop of Bayeux from 1049–50 to 1097 and Earl of Kent from 1067 to 1082. The embroidery may have been made expressly for him, as he figures prominently within the scenes, and it probably reached the Continent through his mediation not long after it was completed. He may have intended it for the dedication of his new cathedral at Bayeux in 1077, or he may have taken it with him when he left England for good after he was released from prison, in 1087.

The story starts as King Edward the Confessor sends Harold on a mission to Normandy. After accompanying Duke William on a successful campaign against a rebellious vassal, Conan of Brittany, Harold receives arms and armour from the duke and swears an oath at Bayeux to support his claim to the English throne. Harold returns to England; King Edward dies (on 5 January 1066) and is buried in the newly completed Westminster Abbey. The English *Witan* (or council) offers Harold the crown, and he is installed by Stigand, Archbishop of Canterbury. William then orders the preparation of the Norman fleet, which sails to Pevensey. The Normans establish a camp at Hastings, followed by the decisive day-long battle there. We see messengers and scouts bringing news to the leaders of the two sides; the Norman knights setting off for the battlefield; William exhorting them; Norman knights, supported by archers on foot, attacking the English; the death of Harold's two brothers Gyrth and Leofwine; hand-to-hand fighting between the Normans and the English; Bishop Odo rallying his men; William raising his helmet in order to be recognised by his men, who had thought that he was dead and started to flee; Norman knights attacking English infantry, with the death of the English soldiers surrounding Harold, and his own death; and the English fleeing in defeat and looking back in dismay, with the Normans riding in pursuit.

Usually the scenes are shown proceeding from left to right, but there are some reversals, such as where Edward's burial is depicted before his death-scene. The architectural settings frequently show both the interior and exterior (as in the case of the church at Bosham, complete with its chancel arch which survives to this day). To some extent the stylised rendering of the figures approaches caricature, but at the same time it endows them with a hieratic, timeless, monumental quality.

The version of the events represented in the hanging shows many points of correspondence – and also of conflict – with other surviving sources, and it employs story-telling techniques similar to literary genres such as *chansons de geste* which celebrated warfare and military prowess. Yet the Bayeux Tapestry depicts its version in a highly selected and dynamically ordered way. In presenting a visual account of a recent historical event of lasting import, to complement (and even to contradict) the accounts in chronicles and other texts (many of them written a longer time after the events they recount), the Bayeux Tapestry represents a primary source of great power and complexity, and at the same time of great mystery. The ensemble mixes both naïveté and subtlety, seriousness and levity, irony and empathy, immediacy and enigma.

Despite the vivid clarity and vivacity of much of the narrative, together with the helpful accompanying inscriptions which identify certain places and figures, and despite the attention to detail and directness, certain components of the ensemble remain very puzzling and enigmatic indeed. For example, a scene involving an unnamed cleric and a woman named Aelfgyva, whom he grasps by the face, may have been well known at the time, but its meaning has mostly been lost to us. And the scene of Harold's death, apparently showing him hit in the eye by an arrow – a detail for which the Bayeux Tapestry is the only source (and this scene has been subjected to alterations in repairs) – remains as controversial as ever. Yet altogether, in combining ornamental foliate patterns and heraldic figures – birds and animals, both recognisable (such as peacocks, lions and camels) and mythical (such as a centaur and winged dragons) – with scenes of everyday life, of Aesop's Fables and of cavorting nude human figures, and with scenes of epic proportions involving the deeds (and misdeeds) of kings, invaders and defenders of England at a crucial stage in her history, the Bayeux Tapestry provides a complex mixture of contemporary fact with fiction, animal fable and bawdy human *fabliau*, in a work of great vigour and appeal.

The arts of everyday life

The Norman Conquest marked the break between the Anglo-Saxon and Anglo-Norman periods, but there was considerable overlap in many spheres of life, from political institutions to forms of language, and the Anglo-Saxon traditions of arts and crafts, from script and manuscript decoration to sculpture and embroidery, continued into the Anglo-Norman period.

Besides the evidence which the Bayeux Tapestry offers us concerning customs of everyday life and tasks such as ploughing and sowing the fields, carpentry and ship-building, a number of Anglo-Saxon manuscripts contain representations which enable us to witness at close hand the occupations of daily life. For example, sets of illustrations in calendars (which list saints' days and religious festivals) show the labours or occupations of the months in frieze-like scenes. Two manuscripts, both made at Canterbury and dating from about the first and second quarters of the eleventh century, respectively, contain such sets, beautifully rendered in both cases, but in different techniques, with dramatically different effects: one is drawn in delicate outline, and the other is fully painted. The latter forms part of a lavishly illustrated collection of works of various kinds, including computing, astronomical and geographical texts and the 'Marvels of the East' (a text, much favoured by the Anglo-Saxons, describing the fabulous, monstrous and bizarre beings found in far lands).

The cycle of the year runs according to the following pattern. January is the time for ploughing and sowing; February for pruning vines; March for digging, raking and sowing; April for feasting (while seated on a splendid bench ending in a quarter-length lion and griffin or elephantine creature); May for tending sheep (and, it would seem, whiling away the time in conversation); June for cutting wood (or reaping); July for mowing (or cutting wood); August for reaping (or mowing); September for feeding hogs; October for hunting with falcons (the prerogative of nobility); November for burning wood both to provide warmth and to smithy; and December for threshing. Cycles showing the occupations of the months have many parallels in Continental manuscripts, but these sets are the first to show predominantly rural activities.

Scenes depicting the occupations and the arts of everyday life can also be found in some other manuscripts. An especially notable case is the single surviving illustrated version of the translation, or rather paraphrase, into Old English of the *Hexateuch* (the first six books of the Old Testament). It was produced at St Augustine's Abbey, Canterbury, in about the second quarter of the eleventh century and was worked on by several artists, in different stages. It contains an extremely ambitious cycle of illustrations. In writing out the text, the scribes left room for about four hundred illustrations, but not all of the blank areas were filled in, and a number of the illustrations were left in various states of incompletion, revealing much to us about the stages of production in the scriptorium.

The illustrations derive to a great extent from a late antique cycle of biblical illustrations used at Canterbury throughout the Middle Ages, but there are numerous adaptations which bring the images up-to-date in a late Anglo-Saxon context, so that the illustrations strikingly reflect the architecture, furniture, costumes and customs of eleventh-century England. For example, in one scene Pharaoh sits in judgment with his advisers, and the chief baker is hanged. Pharoah's crown and garments closely resemble those of other kings in many late Anglo-Saxon manuscripts, and as a result the scene has sometimes been taken out of context and described as an illustration of an Anglo-Saxon king presiding over his *Witan* (council) and executing judgment, but to do this probably goes too far, as the scene was not intended, nor is it labelled, as a representation of a contemporary event, despite the contemporisations which would have helped Anglo-Saxon beholders to recognise the identity of the figures and the import of the scene, regardless of its particular context.

Even though many illustrations, in both this and other works, present us with credible renditions of day-to-day life, there is a danger in assuming that the manuscript illustrations faithfully and completely record the practices of their time. Artists in the early medieval period did not regularly have the habit of drawing directly from life, but for the most part copied, or drew inspiration from, existing images (for example as they copied texts and illustrations alike from the manuscripts before them), and so it is not always

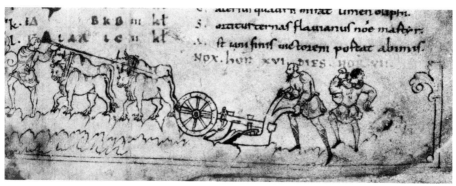

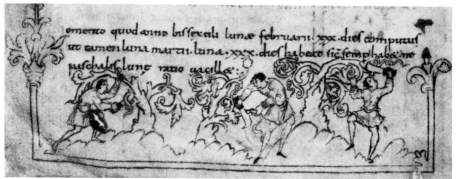

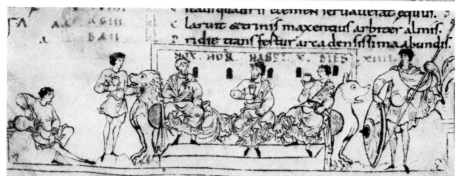

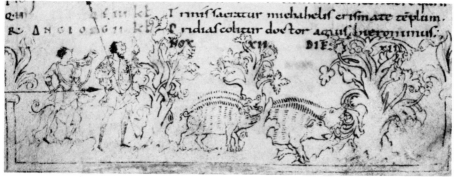

A Canterbury calendar, with the occupations of the months (early eleventh century):
   January: ploughing and sowing   *April: feasting*
   February: pruning vines   *September: feeding hogs*

certain to what extent they faithfully reproduced the appearance of the things and people which they saw around them. On the other hand, it is clear that artists introduced elements from the world about them into their copies of earlier models, thus bringing them up-to-date to a certain extent and, as it were, translating them into familiar, recognisable terms. For example, in the Old English *Hexateuch*, Noah's Ark and the Tower of Babel belong to late antique types, yet some of their elements correspond with Anglo-Saxon features. Thus the Ark has beast-headed prows in Viking style, with elaborate curling manes and curving snouts, while the decoration on the doors of both the Ark and the Tower of Babel resembles the ornamental ironwork which would have been familiar on the doors of Anglo-Saxon churches. The garments, weapons, tools and other accoutrements, including royal crowns, of many of the figures in the cycle similarly correspond with known Anglo-Saxon types (colour pl. 13).

Like the Bayeux Tapestry, the manuscript shows us scenes of occupations such as carpentry, for example when Noah is set to work building his Ark or when a number of craftsmen set about building the Tower of Babel. In preparation for this latter enterprise, there is a scene of baking bricks. As in the Bayeux Tapestry, we see scenes of death and burial, with bodies wrapped in shrouds. Abraham is shown with his flock; Tubalcain, the artificer, is shown working at a forge with hammer and anvil, in the way that many Anglo-Saxons would have done in producing many of the metal objects which survive. Noah is shown at work at his vines, as well as drunk after having imbibed their fruit. Figures are shown sleeping under bedclothes; a figure tries to shoot at a bird with bow and arrow. Armies are shown on the move and under attack, with violent scenes of warfare in which the figures have swords or other accoutrements known to be of late Anglo-Saxon types. In slinging at birds which look back in alarm and dart around, Abraham uses a sling which closely resembles the one used by a peasant in the Bayeux Tapestry. And the same is true of other scenes too, for example those involving warfare and banqueting. The Canterbury origin of both the manuscript and the embroidery may indicate a shared tradition between the artists involved, working within a generation either way of the Norman Conquest.

Such images remind us forcibly that the arts of everyday life in Anglo-Saxon England also in great measure included the art of war, which made a profound impact upon daily life, not only in wreaking havoc and imposing changes to more or less drastic extents, but also upon the arts and crafts, in both generating the need and patronage for objects ranging from swords and shields to helmets and horse-trappings, and in providing pertinant and poignant subject matter, in works as diverse as the Franks Casket and the Bayeux Tapestry. Somehow it is significant, and not just ironic, that the Norman Conquest served to spur the creation of one of the last great masterpieces of Anglo-Saxon art, the Bayeux Tapestry.

Throughout the entire Anglo–Saxon period the arts of everyday life included a wide range of media and crafts, such as pottery, leather-working (for example, decorated leather scabbards, of which a number survive, or the leather covers of book-bindings, like the *Stonyhurst Gospel* cover), wood-

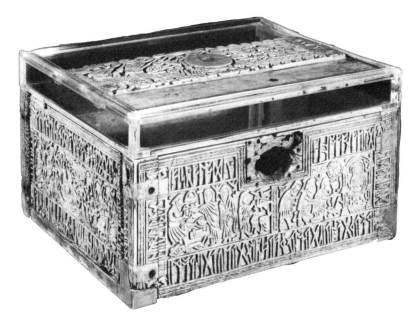

The Franks Casket, with pagan and Christian scenes and Latin and runic inscriptions (second quarter of the eighth century).

working (for example, bowls and other forms of tableware), bone- and ivory-carving (for example, boxes and spoons like some found at Winchester), and metalworking (for example, a variety of dress ornaments, ranging from elaborate jewelry or regalia like that recovered from the Sutton Hoo ship-burial, to strap-ends, buckles, hooked tags and other devices to attach garments or cloths, themselves the products of the textile crafts).

Much of the everyday life of women, of all levels of society, centred upon the textile arts, from weaving to embroidery. It was a maxim that 'a woman's place was at her tablet-weaving', that is, making narrow woven braids from a special set of tablets. There are numerous examples of these braids, some of them very beautiful, with luxurious gold brocaded designs, surviving from pagan Anglo-Saxon graves and also accompanying the Durham embroideries as decorative edging.

Embroidery was probably the most important Anglo-Saxon contribution to the textile arts, and there are many descriptions praising the splendour and skill of Anglo-Saxon embroidery, a tradition which laid the foundations for the highly prized *opus anglicanum* of the later Middle Ages. A few examples of Anglo-Saxon embroidery survive. The group of luxurious embroideries, dating from the late eighth or early ninth century, preserved at Maaseik in Belgium are worked in surface-couched gold-wrapped threads and with variously coloured silk threads; these embroideries probably were used to adorn some ecclesiastical vestments or cloths. They were made in a Southern English centre and taken soon after to the Continent, probably in support of the Anglo-Saxon missions. The early tenth-century embroideries among St Cuthbert's relics at Durham similarly served an ecclesiastical function,

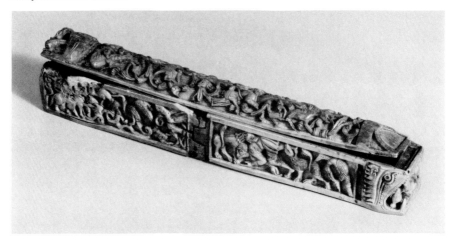

The British Museum pen-case, with scrolling foliage inhabited by creatures, hunting scenes and an animal-head terminal (early eleventh century).

having been made for Bishop Frithestan. Finally, the Bayeux Tapestry, worked in wool, contrasts with these in being principally secular in content.

The small surviving corpus of Anglo-Saxon embroideries nevertheless demonstrates a wide range of purposes and materials, humbler and richer. Documentary references inform us that many embroideries, now lost, employed pearls and jewels, which were much favoured by the Anglo-Saxons.

Of all the arts, aside from the potentially all-intrusive and all-consuming art of war, the arts of both textiles and ceramics touched each and every one of the people. Works of art of great beauty might be accessible in these media to everyone, as their quality needed not be dependent solely upon the expense or quality of the materials, and anyone with some degree of skill, application and invention could follow, or even help to direct, the styles of the day in fashioning such things as tableware or garments. However plain and humble, or intricate and luxurious, the materials and designs might have been, the products of the textile arts constituted much of the contribution by Anglo-Saxon women to the art of everyday life.

Although most Anglo-Saxon men would be able to repair their tools and make many of the household items which their families needed, and women would be expected to prepare the textiles for everyday use, some things had to be made by special craftsmen. These included the turned wooden bowls used on the table, the weapons used in battle and the jewelry worn by both men and women. Boxes or caskets were carved ingeniously in ivory, whalebone, or walrus ivory, with elaborate patterns or with legendary or Christian scenes, or both, as in the case of the Franks Casket.

The jewelry from the pagan period ranges from the simple cast-iron brooches and bead necklaces worn by almost every woman to the magnificent golden garnet-inlaid brooches or shoulder clasps, sword fittings and purse-lid from the royal burial at Sutton Hoo. Because the Anglo-Saxons, once they converted to Christianity, no longer buried objects with the dead, rather less jewelry survives from the Christian period. But the various large disc brooches, pins and finger-rings of bronze, silver or gold which do survive show that everyone still wore plenty of jewelry, sometimes outstanding works of art like the Fuller Brooch; and weapons continued to be richly decorated.

In the Christian period precious objects would also be made for the church and the clergy. These included golden altars, chalices and richly embroidered hangings and vestments. The needs of the church required new crafts and new skills: building in stone, carving stone crosses and other sculptures, making stained glass and copying, illuminating and binding books, including splendidly decorated service books like the *Lindisfarne Gospels*, one of the most resplendent books ever made. Inside, most churches were highly decorated with wall paintings, stone sculptures (often painted, and sometimes embellished with metal fittings) glass windows, rich hangings and altar fittings and objects for the service of the Mass. The overall effect, with the combined fruits of many crafts and arts, would have been very colourful, and in some cases magnificent.

The scenes of warfare in both the Bayeux Tapestry and various manuscripts enable us to recall and to appreciate the sorts of tensions and degrees of pressure which helped to produce such magnificent works of art and images of dramatic eloquence. Despite the ravages of war and unsettled times, the production of works of art and craftsmanship was able to continue throughout the period, and to thrive in many ways, and to find new and viable expressive forms. These violent centuries laid down also the foundations of much of the texture of the life and culture which we know today, ranging from the very language we use to the forms of laws and cultural institutions. Thus, both recording and reflecting, and reflecting upon the nature of the times, the arts of Anglo-Saxon England stand equal to those many periods in the history of art in which fearful and dreadful conditions of life nevertheless summoned up artists of consummate skill, and enabled (or urged) them to produce works of magnificence and universal application.

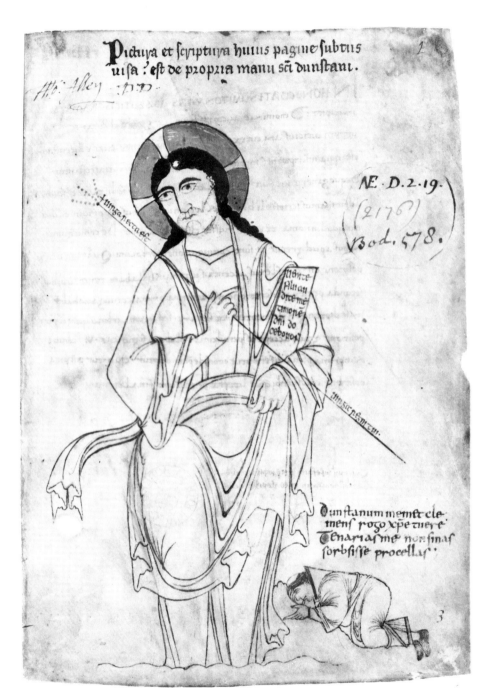

Christ and St Dunstan: the picture and writing are both from the hand of St Dunstan himself, who is kissing the hem of Christ's robe (c.950; see pp. 143–4).

2 Old English Literature

MICHAEL ALEXANDER

Introduction

> I am the scalp of myself, skinned by my foeman:
> Robbed of my strength, he steeped and soaked me,
> Dipped me in water, whipped me out again,
> Set me in the sun. I soon lost there
> The hairs I had had.

Thus begins an Old English riddle, to be imagined as spoken by an animal whose skin has been made into what we now call vellum, Old French *velin*, from *veau*, a calf.

> The hard edge
> Of a keen-ground knife cuts me now,
> Fingers fold me, and a fowl's pride
> Drives its treasure trail across me,
> Bounds again over the brown rim,
> Sucks the wood-dye, steps again on me,
> Makes his black marks.

(Exeter Book Riddle 26;
verse translations of these and other poems by MJA)

The fowl's quill is its 'pride', because birds plume themselves on their feathers; and the Anglo-Saxon riddler prides himself on his skill in innocently concealing 'quill' under the phrase 'a fowl's pride', itself a miniature riddle. Riddling is at the root of the Anglo-Saxon poetic reading and representation of the world. To write was to drive a trail of what the riddler calls 'successful drops' across the page; for what was to be learned from following the track of the quill pen was *useful*.

King Alfred, thinking of the decay of Latin in his day, used the image of a man who could see a trail but did not know how to follow it; Alfred was himself a great hunter, who could not read before he was twelve and began to learn Latin only at the age of thirty-five. His solution to the situation that confronted him after he had saved his kingdom in 878 was to translate *sumae bec, tha the niedbethearfosta sien eallum monnum to wiotonne* (those books which be most needful for all men to know) into English, and to teach the freeborn sons of the laity to read them, so that the quarry, wisdom, should again be pursued in Angelcynn. Written Old English might say, as does the Alfred Jewel itself, AELFRED MEC HEHT GEWYRCAN, Alfred ordered me to be made. Alfred thus instituted a programme for Old English prose, and for writing in the vernacular; his hopes were eventually to be fulfilled a century later in the monastic revival, which produced the manuscripts in which Old English literature now survives.

Alfred was thus the sponsor of the production of vernacular literature, finding in the decay of Anglo-Latin the ground from which Old English writing was to spring. Old English verse, which is the great prize of this production, had in fact long existed, but little of what was recorded by the monks has survived. The two earliest verse compositions extant on vellum, known as *Caedmon's Hymn* and *Bede's Death Song*, owe their multiple survival entirely to their association with the name of Bede. But the Old English translation of the Gospel of St John completed by Bede on his deathbed in May 735, which must have been a venerable book to Anglo-Saxon scribes, has not survived. What have survived abundantly are Bede's Latin works. As far as Old English verse is concerned, *In principio erat verbum* might be translated: the word was heard before it was written.

Thus emerge the three periods of Anglo-Saxon literature known to its historians, the age of Bede, the age of Alfred, and the Benedictine Revival. Bede's was the age of Anglo-Latin learning and the first written Old English verse; Alfred started Anglo-Saxon prose; and the late tenth century, a thousand years ago, saw a general development of Old English writing for a whole range of civilised and religious purposes. With these three spotlit areas, there emerge also the questions involved in defining the literary contributions made by the Anglo-Saxons to the arts in Britain. The literature of the Britons and of the Gaels in Scotland, both in Latin and in the Celtic tongues, has been masterfully neglected by the English. Anglo-Saxon literacy was Latin literacy, learned from the clerics of the universal Church, Latins and Greeks, natives of Italy, Asia Minor, and Africa, and of Ireland and Scotland. But the illiterate pagan Anglo-Saxons themselves had brought their own poetry, their own share of the Germanic oral tradition. Oral literature is a paradox as well as an awkward contradiction in terms, but the initial prevalence of an orally created poetic literature, living solely in the medium of the spoken word, is certain; indeed the Old English poetry we have is the fruit of the union of this Germanic verse with Latin literacy, a seemingly miraculous union now permanently associated with the name of Caedmon. The literacy of Anglo-Saxon England in 700 – notably of the Northumbria of the Lindisfarne Gospels and the Ruthwell Cross – was formidably conscious and verbal; but the prior genesis of Anglo-Saxon verse-making and of its habits of poetic speech, however difficult for us to reconceive, is beyond doubt. It was an emphatic, stress-based verse, balancing stresses rather than counting syllables (unlike classical verse), and employing alliteration or front-rhyme rather than final rhyme (unlike the hymns of the Church).

Bede and Anglo-Latin learning

Pope Gregory the Great remarked that the fair-haired slaves in the Roman market were not Angles but angels. On hearing that these bright folk came from the ignorant darkness of Deira (the more northerly of the two Northumbrian kingdoms), he said that they would be delivered *de ira* (from wrath) and called to the mercy of Christ. And on hearing that the king of Deira was called Aella, he made another serious jest, declaring that their homeland would rightly resound with the praise of God in the word *Alleluia*. This story told by Bede in his *Ecclesiastical History of Angelcynn* is a foundation myth of the Roman conversion. Just as Christ said (according to the Vulgate) *Tu es Petrus, et super hanc petram aedificabo ecclesiam meam*, founding his Church upon a pun, so Peter's successor (according to Bede) converted the meaning of the words and names in one language into words and names in another, and in so doing sacramentally converted their attendant realities. Theodore, Archbishop of Canterbury, the teacher of the English, was a learned Greek from Tarsus, the home of Saul whose name changed to Paul. The pair of baptismal spoons in the Sutton Hoo ship-burial are inscribed SAULOS and PAULOS, in further testimony to the power of letters in the seventh century.

A number of Theodore's Latin riddles and rhyming epistles survive, and there are collections of Latin riddles from the quills of many leading churchmen among Bede's contemporaries, including the acrostically minded St Aldhelm of Malmesbury (c.640–709). Aldhelm was, says Bede, 'a man most learned in all respects, for he had a brilliant style, and was remarkable for both sacred and liberal erudition.' Aldhelm wrote his treatise on Virginity (for the nuns at Barking) twice, once in prose and once in verse. He also wrote verse sermons, and an epistle on Metrics to King Aldfrith of Northumbria which is full of acrostics and riddles. His own collection of riddles is signed with a double acrostic on his name. A modest sample of his style is his reproach to an Englishman who had gone to Ireland:

> The fields of Ireland are rich and green with learners,
> and with numerous readers, grazing there like flocks,
> even as the pivots of the poles are brilliant with the
> starry quivering of the shining constellations. Yet,
> Britain, placed, if you like, almost at the extreme
> edge of the western clime, has also its flaming sun and
> its lucid moon . . .

(trans. M. Williams)

– it has, as he goes on to explain, Theodore and Hadrian.

Bede's own learning was a product both of the great library imported by Benedict Biscop to Monkwearmouth in 674, and of the Celtic learning of Lindisfarne. The intricacy of the initial letters in the Gospel Books made at Lindisfarne is an index of the exegetical richness of mediaeval Christian tradition; in which Omega contained Alpha, and the Greek Tau was a sign of the cross. This literacy may seem precocious so early in a literature: within a hundred years of the landing of Augustine we had produced a Bede, a learned man of European authority, the only English man to be mentioned by

Dante. But who are 'we'? Just as the Ionian colonies from the Greek mainland were more Greek than Ionian, so Bede, though an early Angle, is also a late father of the Latin church; and a channel, through Alcuin, to what has been thought a 'renaissance' at the court of Charlemagne. The Church brought to the Saxons not only literacy, the arts of reading and writing, but a lettered capacity and technique in understanding and representing the world by means of the word.

Old English oral verse

This Mediterranean tradition of observing the letter met in the darkness of Angelcynn a living and developed tradition of spoken verse composition in a barbarian society recently tribal and still warlike, whose kingdoms were ruled by aristocracies with every reason to celebrate heroic figures and warrior virtues, as at Sutton Hoo. Tacitus had said of the Germanic tribes that war-songs were the only kind of history that they possessed; he wrote of the *fractum murmur*, the dull surge of their war-songs before a battle. Old English verse is in the tradition of pre-literate Germanic verse, sharing its versification and stock of phrases. Indeed, since the specifics of verse formation and language are inextricable, no other origin for the form of Old English verse is possible. Early poems like *Widsith* and *Deor* are the fictional autobiographies of poets, showing their uses in an heroic age, which may be expressed as: No poet, no hero. At the tomb of Achilles, Alexander the Great is said to have regretted that he himself had had no Homer to proclaim his deeds and preserve his memory. Fame requires mouths and instruments. The last word of *Beowulf* is the hero's epitaph: he was *lof-geornost*, most eager for fame; not inscribed on his tomb, but spoken by the twelve riders around his funeral pyre.

Oral genesis is confirmed by analogy with other oral cultures; written evidence for it is by nature indirect, but convergent. *Beowulf* has several pictures of poets, noblemen and kings composing and reciting; so has Asser's *Life of Alfred*. Aldhelm, according to William of Malmesbury, sang to his flock in the open air. The verses in the native tongue which Aldhelm and Bede composed have perished, though some of Alfred's much later attempts survive. But the bulk of the 30,000 lines of Old English verse is anonymous: Caedmon is no longer thought to have composed the four biblical poems in the manuscript known as the Junius Book; and while 'Cynewulf' presumably composed the four poems he signed, we do not know who he was. The main poetry manuscripts (the Junius, Exeter and Vercelli Books and the *Beowulf* manuscript) contain no signed poems other than Cynewulf's. Only the Junius Book has a plan. The others are miscellaneous compilations of verses composed over several generations before the manuscripts were copied, towards the year 1000. Anonymity was the rule, perhaps the tradition. Thus the *Dream of the Rood*, the great elegies of the Exeter Book, *Beowulf* itself, even the late historical poems like *Brunanburh* and *Maldon* – all are of unknown authorship; they were not the works of *auctores*. Old English verse belongs to a tradition, like the works of Homer and the *Chanson de Roland*, oral in genesis and not essentially personal in origin.

The Dream of the Rood

The book-learning of the age of Bede seems at first hardly compatible with such oral composition, and Bede himself tells a story to describe the fusion of the two very different traditions. There was written Christian poetry by about AD 700, for the Ruthwell Cross, it is agreed, was erected about the year 700, and it has inscribed on it, as part of its original design, fifteen lines which now form part of a poem known to us as *The Dream of the Rood*. The expanded poem survives to us in the Vercelli Book of the late tenth century, but the lines on the rood at Ruthwell (which form part of the speech of the cross itself in the manuscript poem) were composed before Bede completed his *Ecclesiastical History* in 731. The poem on the Ruthwell Cross was composed in the generation after Caedmon, a farmhand at the Abbey of Whitby when Hilda was abbess there (657–680). Caedmon was a layman 'of advanced age' as Bede recounts, who

had not at any time learned anything of poems. Hence it was that sometimes when at a party, when it was decided for joyful entertainment that all in turn must recite verse to the harp's accompaniment, he when he saw the harp getting near to himself would arise from the midst of the feast and go out and walk back to his house. [Here the Alfredian version adds that it was from a feeling of shame, *for scome*, that he did this.] When on a certain occasion he had done this, and leaving the house where the party was held had gone out to the cattle-pens, as their care had been assigned to him for that night, and when there he had at the normal time given his limbs to sleep, a certain man was standing by him in a dream and, greeting him and calling him by his name, said: 'Cædmon, sing me something.' But he in answering said: 'I do not know how to sing: for it was just for this reason that I came away from the feast and departed hither, because I could not sing.' Again he who was talking with him said: 'Yet you *can* sing to me.' 'What', said Cædmon, 'must I sing?' Then the other said: 'Sing of the beginning of created things.' Now when Cædmon had received this answer, immediately he began to sing verses in praise of God the creator which he had never heard, of which this is the sense. 'Now we must praise the Author of the Kingdom of Heaven, the might of the Creator and the thoughts of His mind – the deeds of the Father of glory. [We must sing] how he who is eternal God, the Author of all marvellous things, was manifest: he who first created heaven as a roof-covering for the sons of men, and then as almighty guardian of mankind made the earth.' This is the sense but not the actual order of the words of what Cædmon had sung while sleeping. For poems, however excellently composed, cannot be translated word for word from one language into another without damage to elegance and dignity. Now when he had risen from his sleep, he retained in his memory everything which he had sung while sleeping. And to these verses he quickly added more in the same rhythm and metre in words of a poem worthy of God.

When morning had come, he went to the steward who was his chief and showed him what sort of gift he had received. He was then conducted to the Abbess and commanded to show what he had dreamed in the presence of many learned men and to recite the poem: so that by the judgment of everyone it might be tested of what kind or from whence had come what he had related. And it seemed to them all that it was a grace from heaven and granted by God. Then they expounded to him a discourse of sacred history or doctrine, and commanded him, if he could, to render this into the melody of poetry. So he, when he had finished these matters, went away: and in the morning he came back and produced it composed as had been ordered in the most excellent poetry. Wherefore the Abbess, immediately embracing the grace of

God in the man, instructed him with a proposal that he should abandon the secular habit and take that of a monk. So she added him, with his goods, after receiving him into the monastery, to the company of the brethren: and she commanded that he should be taught the whole sequence of sacred Scripture. Now he, taking all that he could learn by hearing, retaining it in his mind, and turning it over like a clean beast ruminating, converted it into the sweetest poetry. Indeed by the sweetness of its melody he made his teachers in their turn become his listeners.

(trans. C.L. Wrenn)

Caedmon evidently could neither read nor write. Although he had learned no poetry, the poem on the Creation which he composed was in Anglo-Saxon verse. Bede gives the Latin sense only, but seventeen Old English versions of Caedmon's Hymn survive, one of them in an MS of 737. In a later Old English translation of Bede, the final sentence of the extract above ends: *his song and his leoth waeron swa wynsum to gehyrenne, thaet tha sylfan his lareowas aet his muthe writon and leornodon* [his songs and his lay were so joyful to hear, that his teachers themselves wrote and learned from his mouth]. As the Word was versified and Anglified, the clerks wrote it down. Bede continues that Caedmon sang many poems relating virtually the whole of the story of the Bible and very many other religious poems besides; and that though Caedmon had followers among the Angles he had no equal as a Christian poet. It would be good to have Bede's opinion of *The Dream of the Rood*, whose author he probably knew.

A paradox of early Old English literature is that this literature conceived to be sung aloud shows reverence for writing. The word *writan* means to cut, inscribe or carve, and several of the earliest inscriptions, on swords for example, are in runic characters. Runes were straight-sided symbols often used by the Germanic peoples for secret and magical writing; *run* means 'secret'. They occur in Old English manuscripts chiefly as abbreviations, but more purposefully in the *Runic Poem*, in personal signatures such as Cynewulf's, or in semi-cryptographic contexts in riddles. The eighth-century whalebone and ivory box known as the Franks Casket is carved with scenes from Christian and pagan stories – the Visitation of Our Lady to Elizabeth, for example, is next to a scene from the life of Weland the Smith involving hamstringing, rape, murder and the eating of children. Around these two scenes a riddle-like runic inscription reads: 'This is whale bone. The sea cast up the fish on the rocky shore. The ocean was troubled where he swam aground on to the shingle.' *The Husband's Message* is a riddle poem in which a piece of wood speaks – it has been inscribed with secret tokens and now carries a message telling the wife she may now rejoin her husband; there is a runic signature. The Anglo-Saxon word for book is *boc*; the plural form is *beech*. 'The connection', as Klein explains, 'between *book* and *beech* (cp. German *Buch*, "book", *Buche*, "beech") is due to the Teutonic custom of writing runic letters on thin boards of beech.' *The Dream of the Rood* is also a riddle poem and the text found on the six-metre high standing cross at Ruthwell, Dumfriesshire, is in runic characters. Runes, though used for pagan religious purposes, were thought appropriate for a Christian inscription in Old English. All but one of the Latin texts which decorate the Ruthwell Cross are in Latin characters.

The dramatic qualities of this great poem of conversion are evident at a first reading even of a translation.

The Dream of the Rood

Hwaet!
A dream came to me
      at deep midnight
when humankind
      kept their beds
– the dream of dreams!
      I shall declare it.

It seemed I saw the Tree itself
borne on the air, light wound about it,
– a beam of brightest wood, a beacon clad
in overlapping gold, glancing gems
fair at its foot, and five stones
set in a crux flashed from the crosstree.

Around angels of God
      all gazed upon it,
since first fashioning fair.
      It was not a felon's gallows,
for holy ghosts beheld it there,
and men on mould, and the whole Making shone for it
– *signum* of victory!
             Stained and marred,
stricken with shame, I saw the glory-tree
shine out gaily, sheathed in yellow
decorous gold; and gemstones made
for their Maker's Tree a right mail-coat

Yet through the masking gold I might perceive
what terrible sufferings were once sustained thereon:
it bled from the right side.
      Ruth in the heart.

Afraid I saw that unstill brightness
change raiment and colour
      – again clad in gold
or again slicked with sweat,
      spangled with spilling blood.

Yet lying there a long while
I beheld, sorrowing, the Healer's Tree
till it seemed that I heard how it broke silence,
best of wood, and began to speak:

'Over that long remove my mind ranges
back to the holt where I was hewn down;
from my own stem I was struck away,
    dragged off by strong enemies,
wrought into a roadside scaffold.

They made me a hoist for wrongdoers.
The soldiers on their shoulder bore me,
    until on a hill-top they set me up;
many enemies made me fast there.
    Then I saw, marching toward me,
mankind's brave King;
    He came to climb upon me.

I dared not break or bend aside
against God's will, though the ground itself
shook at my feet. Fast I stood,
who falling could have felled them all.

Almighty God ungirded He,
    eager to mount the gallows,
unafraid in the sight of many:
    He would set free mankind.
I shook when His arms embraced me
    but I durst not bow to ground,
stoop to Earth's surface.
    Stand fast I must.

I was reared up, a rood.
    I raised the great King,
liege lord of the heavens,
    dared not lean from the true.
They drove me through with dark nails:
    on me are the deep wounds manifest,
wide-mouthed hate–dents.

            I durst not harm any of them.
How they mocked at us both!
            I was all moist with blood
sprung from the Man's side
            after He sent forth His soul.'

Wry wierds a-many I underwent
up on that hill-top; saw the Lord of Hosts
stretched out stark. Darkness shrouded
the King's corse. Clouds wrapped
its clear shining. A shade went out
wan under cloud-pall. All creation wept,
keened the King's death. Christ was on the Cross.

(1–56)

The poem continues for another 100 more devotional lines, showing how the victory of the Cross is the key to salvation.

Beowulf

Beowulf probably existed in nearly its present form within a century of the carving of these runes on stone at Ruthwell. After 793 when the Danes had sacked Lindisfarne, *Beowulf*'s setting in the southern Scandinavia of the sixth century, largely at the Danish court, might have seemed unwelcome. *Beowulf* is a great poem but the nature of its greatness is not commonly recognised. Both historical, legendary and mythical, it is concerned with and meditates constantly upon human destiny, on the fate of heroes, kings and empires, on human glory and human vanity, on heroic worth and its relation to 'what the unsearchable dispose of Highest Wisdom brings about'. Though unmistakably of the North, it is not a grisly folk or fairy tale in the manner of Grimm, nor is its interest antiquarian, philological or fantastic. It is what Aristotle called *philosophoteron*, more interested in wisdom, an epic poem like that of Virgil in its tragic morality, and needs to be rescued from some of its more myopic fans. W.P. Ker and Tolkien are its only first-rate critics, though modern scholars have now begun to allow the unlearned to look at their prize exhibit.

The strangeness of *Beowulf* lies in its unaccountable and early superiority. Epics are often anonymous, but their cultural matrix is usually evident enough. *Beowulf* is composed for a milieu which we cannot identify beyond saying that it seems aristocratic, Anglian, and post-conversion. Dates have been proposed between the seventh and (recently) the eleventh centuries. The unique manuscript is usually dated about the year 1000, and it contains other tales about monsters. The monsters had rather sunk *Beowulf* with serious readers until recently, when (thanks to Tolkien but also to other admirers of the pan-Germanic past) the pendulum has swung alarmingly. The pit has opened up again in our illiberal century, and one of *Beowulf*'s most telling recommendations today is its unforgiving grasp on how deeply human is the desire for vengeance. The first man born of woman was a fratricide: Cain and the Giants of Genesis are repeatedly named as the ancestors of the monster Grendel. When Beowulf has killed the man-eating Grendel, Grendel's mother takes revenge. He pursues her to her underwater lair where he kills her with the help of a providential sword. He cuts off the head of Grendel and takes it back to the civilised court of King Hrothgar. The demonic blood of Grendel melts the blade, but Beowulf presents Hrothgar with the hilt.

> Then the golden hilt was given into the hand
> Of the older warrior, the white-haired leader.
> A Giant had forged it. With the fall of the demons
> It passed into the possession of the prince of the Danes,
> This work of wonder-smiths. The world was rid
> Of that invidious enemy of God
> And his mother also, with their murders upon them;
> And the hilt now belonged to the best of the kings
> Who ruled the earth in all the North
> And distributed treasure between the seas.
> Hrothgar looked on that long-treasured hilt
> Before he spoke. The spring was cut on it
> Of the primal strife, with the destruction at last
> Of the race of Giants by the rushing Flood,
> A terrible end. Estranged was that race
> From the Lord of Eternity: the tide of water
> Was the final reward that the Ruler sent them.

On clear gold labels let into the cross-piece
It was rightly told in runic letters,
Set down and sealed, for whose sake it was
That the sword was first forged, that finest of iron,
Spiral-hilted, serpent-bladed.

(1677–98)

Here we come to the crux of the heroic world: in the North the sword is 'the accustomed remedy' for the sacred obligation of the blood feud. Beowulf when he dies boasts that he has sworn 'no unrightful oaths' and has taken on no unnecessary feuds. But 'the primal strife' is to continue after the peaceable Beowulf's death against the dragon. A messenger carries the fatal news to the people of the Geats, and in a prophecy like that which ends Shakespeare's *Richard II* ('The blood of English shall manure the ground'), foresees the reaction of the neighbouring peoples. His speech ends:

It is this feud, this fierce hostility,
This murder-lust between men, I am moved to think,
That the Swedish people will prosecute against us
When once they learn that life has fled
From the lord of the Geats, guardian for so long
Of hoard and kingdom, of keen shield-warriors
Against every foe. Since the fall of the princes
He has taken care of our welfare, and accomplished yet more
Heroic deeds.
                Haste is best now,
That we should go to look on the lord of the people,
Then bring our ring-bestower on his road,
Escort him to the pyre. More than one portion of wealth
Shall melt with the hero, for there's a hoard of treasure
And gold uncounted; a grim purchase,
For in the end it was with his own life
That he bought these rings: which the burning shall devour,
The fire enfold. No fellow shall wear
An arm-ring in his memory; no maiden's neck
Shall be enhanced in beauty by the bearing of these rings.
Bereft of gold, rather, and in wretchedness of mind
She shall tread continually the tracks of exile
Now that the leader of armies has laid aside his mirth,
His sport and glad laughter. Many spears shall therefore
Feel cold in the mornings to the clasping fingers
And the hands that raise them. Nor shall the harper's melody
Arouse them for battle; and yet the black raven,
Quick on the marked men, shall have much to speak of
When he tells the eagle of his takings at the feast
Where he and the wolf bared the bodies of the slain.

(2999–3027)

The birds and beasts of prey shall boast over their carrion in a studied parody of heroic conversation in hall. As the poet says of Heorot after Grendel's mother's revenge: 'Night's table-laughter turned to morning's / Lamentation'. In its irony and understatement and its heightening by oblique euphemism *Beowulf* displays the poetic manner at its most riddlingly sombre.

This painful poetic mastery of the truths of life is what Anglo-Saxon literature has to offer: it sees life steadily and sees it whole, but this vision is wryly encoded in settled conventions of irony, metaphor, and secrecy. A favourite theme is the limit on human knowledge. Of the ship-burial of Scyld it is said, as the boat is pushed out:

> Men ne cunnon
> secgan to sothe, sele-raedende,
> haeleth under heofenum, hwa thaem hlaeste onfeng.

(50–2)

(Men do not know how to tell truly, counsellors in hall, heroes under the skies, who received that cargo). At Beowulf's funeral the wind drops, the pyre consumes the hero's body, and the Geats mourn.

> A woman of the Geats in grief sang out
> The lament for his death. Loudly she sang,
> Her hair bound up, the burden of her fear
> That evil days were destined her
> – Troops cut down, terror of armies,
> Bondage, humiliation. Heaven swallowed the smoke.

(3150–55)

Heofon rece onswealg. Heaven gives no clues as to how it receives either Beowulf's spirit or the fears of the *Geatisc meowle* (woman). Bede's disciple Cuthbert tells us that his master at his hour of death sang

the verse of St Paul the apostle telling of the fearfulness of falling into the hands of the living God . . . and in our language also, as he was learned in our songs, speaking of the terrible departure of spirits from the body.

Then follows the text the *Death Song* in this Northumbrian version:

> Fore thaem neidfaerae   naenig uuirthit
> thoncsnotturra,   than him tharf sie
> to ymbhycggannae   aer his hiniongae
> hwaet his gastae   godaes aeththae yflaes
> aefter deothdaege   doemid uueorthae.

(Before that sudden journey no one is wiser in thought than he needs to be, in considering, before his departure, what will be adjudged to his soul, of good or evil, after his death-day.) The poem exists in twenty-nine copies, Caedmon's *Hymn* in seventeen – Bede's name thus accounting for nearly half the surviving manuscript containing Old English poetry. But Bede's *Death Song* deserves to survive as an essentially Anglo-Saxon comment on death, characteristically cooler than its Pauline prototype.

Alfred's wisdom

The necessity of wisdom, and how hard it is to get it, is a theme of Anglo-Saxon thought and life. A man must not speak before he knows from experience what is the right course of action – such is the common sentiment of the Elegies and Old English heroic poetry, Christian or otherwise, whether

the course of action is in pursuit of salvation or of vengeance. Alfred's first
act as a writer was his Preface to the *Hierdeboc* or Pastoral Care of Gregory
the Great, the first of the books he thought most needful for his bishops to
know. In it he eagerly exclaims how in the old days the men of Angelcynn *hie
lufodon wisdom*, they loved wisdom, but how their successors had allowed it
to decay. The King energetically sets about restoring learning as the way to a
Christian wisdom. The copy we have is headed θEOS BOC SCEAL TO WIGORA
CEASTRE (This book is to go to Worcester); the Preface is full of a ruler's
determination. Alfred went on to translate other books, including Boethius'
De Consolatione Philosophiae; the last of these was the *Soliloquies* of St
Augustine, a metaphysical search for wisdom in the form of a meditation on
the immortality of the soul. In a Preface the translator-king describes his own
studies in the Latin Fathers of the early Church:

Then I gathered for myself staves and posts and tie-beams, and handles for each of
the tools I knew how to use, and building timbers and beams and as much as I could
carry of the most beautiful woods for each of the structures I knew how to build. I
did not come home with a single load without wishing to bring home the whole forest
with me, if I could have carried it all away; in every tree I saw something that I
needed at home. Wherefore I advise each of those who is able, and has many
waggons, to direct himself to the same forest where I cut these posts; let him fetch
more there for himself, and load his waggons with fair branches so that he can weave
many a neat wall and construct many an excellent building, and build a fair town, and
dwell therein in joy and ease both winter and summer, as I have not done so far. But
he who taught me, to whom the forest was pleasing, may bring it about that I dwell
in greater ease both in this transitory wayside habitation while I am in this world, and
also in that eternal home which he has promised us through St Augustine and St
Gregory and St Jerome, and through many other holy fathers; so I also believe that
for the merits of them all, he will both make this road easier than it was hitherto, and
also enlighten the eyes of my mind so that I can find out the straight road to the
eternal home and to the eternal glory and to the eternal rest which is promised to us
through those holy fathers. So be it.
  It is no wonder, though, that one should labour for such material, both in the
carrying and in the building; but every man, after he has built a cottage on land
leased by his lord, with his help, likes to rest in it sometimes, and go hunting and
fowling and fishing, and from that lease to provide for himself in every way, both on
sea and on land, until the time when, through his lord's favour, he should merit
chartered land and a perpetual inheritance.

(Trans. M. Swanton)

When he wrote this, Alfred had not 'so far' had the *stillnesse* to dwell with joy
and ease in the house of wisdom he had built with his own hands out of the
forest of learning, still less to go hunting; but he was perhaps not far from
the perpetual inheritance he sought. Among the other literary achievements
of his reign was the institution of the *Anglo-Saxon Chronicle*, which
continued until the twelfth century, and the turning of Bede's *Ecclesiastical
History* into English. Alfred's achievement was to save Wessex and so keep
Anglo-Saxon England as an independent Christian country. His literary
achievement was part of that salvage and reclaiming of the vernacular
culture; his own sinewy writing has a moral integrity characteristic of the
Anglo-Saxon search for an ethical wisdom undertaken in full knowledge of

the difficult contingencies of life in this world. Among Alfred's additions to the text of Boethius are the sentences:

For every good gift and every power soon grows old and is heard of no more if wisdom be not in them. Without wisdom no faculty can be fully brought out: for whatever is done unwisely can never be accounted as skill.

Alfred's career combines military heroism of an archaic simplicity with a capacity for long-term strategic planning and an impressive personal moral and intellectual growth. It is a paradox that his crash programme of converting Christian assets from Latin into English, which had as an incidental result the authoritative establishment of a tradition of writing in English, was itself the direct result of the disastrous coincidence of the decay of monastic learning and the almost complete success of the invasions of the Danish heathen. Nowhere else in Europe was Latin literacy so thoroughly impressed on a barbarian learned elite, so nearly lost so early, and then so quickly converted for vernacular purposes.

The harvest of literacy

While for modern readers the older poetry is the most living part of Anglo-Saxon culture, and its preservation testifies to its acceptability in clerical and aristocratic circles, the chief uses of English to clerks were naturally clerical. The eventual success of Archbishop Dunstan's renewal of Anglo-Saxon monastic culture and art under King Edgar produced a flood of manuscripts in Latin and English. The vernacular work of Aelfric, Byrhtferth of Ramsay and Wulfstan is copious but principally consists of homilies. Over a hundred of Aelfric's graceful homilies survive, together with scores of Saints' Lives: these served the needs of the clergy through the liturgical year. We also have the impressive political and legal writings of Wulfstan, the computistical *Manual* of Byrhtferth, and a number of lives of Kings. The *Chronicle* began to contain some verse. There is a lively prose romance, *Apollonius of Tyre*. And there are also the four main poetry manuscripts, the Exeter Book, the Vercelli Book, the 'Caedmonian' Junius Book, and the *Beowulf* manuscript, all containing verse composed earlier.

But the net result of this new writing in English is that our prose began to perform a range of religious and civil tasks for the laity that Latin had previously done for the clergy only. Though Latin writing revived, English kept going and growing. Another way to put this is that the humane clerical culture which gradually developed in Latin in North-West Europe between the Carolingian and the twelfth century renaissances began to receive substantial expression in English by the year 1000. The Conquest put an end to this vernacular expression of high culture, part of which instead went into the new high vernacular, French in its Anglo-Norman form, robbing Old English literature of its posterity.

The most poetic flowers of this tenth century revival are *Judith*, *The Phoenix*, *Brunanburh* and *Maldon*, and they typify the range of Old English poetry. *Judith* is, in the tradition of the Caedmonian poems *Genesis*, *Exodus* and *Daniel*, a dramatic and vigorous paraphrase of an Old Testament story, in which the faithful and heroic Jewess who decapitates the drunken Holofernes must have appealed to Anglo-Saxons hard-pressed by the heathen. Aelfric's account of the martyrdom of St Edmund has a similarly embattled ring, and so does *The Battle of Maldon*, especially in the dying prayer of Ealdorman Byrhtnoth. The Christian heroism of the loyal thane went well in the Old Germanic verse forms. *Maldon* is the simplest and most accessible of Old English poems, an account of the heroic defence in 991 of a narrow place by the East Saxon militia against Vikings demanding tribute. Byrhtnoth wants a fight: he allows the heathens to cross the ford and is killed; the battle is to be lost; but the hearth-companions fight on bravely, each proclaiming his loyalty to his dead lord before advancing on the Vikings. Many of the norms of the old battle poetry are in force – the beasts of battle appear, for example.

> Then neared the fight,
> The glory-trial. The time grew on
> When there the fated men must fall;
> The war-cry was raised up. Ravens wound higher,
> The eagle, carrion-eager; on earth – the cry!
>
> (103–107)

However, the old ideals have now become more actual and historical. The second-in-command, Offa, comments on a defection:

> This Offa had told him on an earlier day
> At the council-place when he had called a meeting,
> That many gathered there who were making brave speeches
> Would not hold in the hour of need.
> And now the folk's father had fallen lifeless,
> Aethelred's Earl. All the hearthsharers
> Might see their lord lying dead.
>
> (197–204)

The place of assembly has begun to replace the joys of the mead-hall.

Brunanburh appears in the *Anglo-Saxon Chronicle* for 937. It is a more literary poem than *Maldon*, in praise of the West Saxon King Athelstan, and his famous victory at Brunanburh over the Vikings, Scots, Picts and Strathclyde Welsh. It also employs the chilling beasts of prey, and has one other panoramic periphrasis which fixes the day's action in an Olympian vision:

> The field was running
> With the blood of soldiers from the sun's rise
> At the hour of the morning when that marvellous star,
> God's bright candle, glided over the lands,
> To the time when the creature of the eternal Lord
> Sank to rest . . .
>
> (12–17)

The sun, a sign of victory, shows life and death steadily and for what they are.

The Phoenix is an allegorisation of the life, death and rebirth of the fabulous oriental bird as a type of Christ's resurrection. Its initial description of the bird is highly coloured, uniquely in Anglo-Saxon verse which is normally in plain black-and-white.

> The groves are hung with growing fruit,
> Bright to look upon; the burden of those woods
> Favoured by heaven does not fail ever.
> Nor does blossom, the beauty of trees,
> Lie waste upon the ground; wonderfully, rather,
> The branches of the trees bear always
> Perpetual plenty of fruit
> And stand out green above the grassy plain.
> It is the most glorious of groves, its gay adornment
> The work of the Holy One. The woods' canopy
> Is not to be broken, and it breathes out incense
> Through that happy land. This shall last unchanging
> For ever and ever, until the Ancient One
> Shall ordain an end to all He first created.
>
> Beautiful is the bird abiding in that wood,
> Fair and feathered strongly: Phoenix is his name.
> There he lives alone looking out upon his homeland,
> Dauntless he surveys it. Death shall not touch him
> On that lovely plain, for as long as the world shall be.

(71–89)

But this initial glamour dissipates in the lengthy academic explanation which follows. Like most Old English literature, *The Phoenix* is a domesticated import: an expansion of the exotic *De Phoenice*, formerly attributed to Lactantius, followed by a commentary based upon St Ambrose.

By the year 1000, changes in the nature of the Old English language were making it difficult to compose in the traditional measure. The circumstances which demanded oral composition had long since passed; many poems are translations and others like *Brunanburh* refer explicitly to written sources. The historical verse pieces in the *Chronicle* show a deteriorating verse technique. The great days of Old English verse were over long before the Norman Conquest. The archetypes of the old heroic poetry were not quite dead – the old cosmological conception of middle earth, lying like a gyroscope laterally in the middle of the ocean and vertically between the heavens and whatever lay under the earth, persisted on Alfred's island. But it came to an end, as the *Chronicle* records in good Anglo-Saxon terms:

The duke William sailed from Normandy into Pevensey, on the eve of Michaelmas. As soon as his men were fit for service, they constructed a castle at Hastings. When king Harold was informed of this, he gathered together a great host, and came to oppose him at the grey apple-tree, and William came upon him unexpectedly before his army was set in order. Nevertheless the king fought against him most resolutely with those men who wished to stand by him, and there was great slaughter on both sides. King Harold was slain, and Leofwine, his brother, and earl Gurth, his brother, and many good men. The French had possession of the place of slaughter, as God granted them because of the nation's sins.

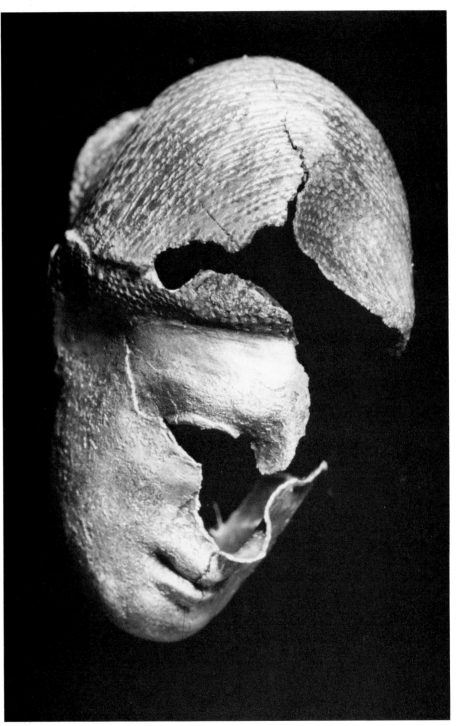

Parcel-gilt silver head from the Old Minster at Winchester; probably from a shrine or reliquary (tenth century).

3 Winchester: The Rise of an Early Capital

MARTIN BIDDLE

From the late first century AD for some three hundred years the walls of the Roman city of *Venta Belgarum* enclosed within its 58.2 hectares the usual set of public buildings, shops, and large and well-appointed town houses. These lay along the grid-planned streets, for the most part in the lower parts of the walled area, close to the River Itchen. On the higher western slopes of the valley buildings were few and there was much open space. Clearly defined, well-ordered cemeteries lay along the approach roads outside the gates, interspersed with areas of suburban settlement. As the capital of the tribal canton of the *Belgae*, and fifth-largest city of *Britannia*, *Venta* was responsible for justice, administration and finance, including tax-collection, throughout a territory stretching from the Severn to the Solent, for which it was also a principal market. The long-distance roads converging on the city from all directions demonstrated this central role. The comfortable town-houses reflected the solid prosperity which three centuries of well-ordered if not always entirely tranquil provincial administration had brought to the Iron Age farmers of the region who had accustomed themselves to quit the countryside for the pleasures of the county town.

Within a few years of 360 all this changed. The town walls were modernised by the addition of bastions capable of mounting torsion artillery and probably manned by professional troops. Many of the town-houses were demolished and replaced by open compounds. At the same time occupation spread to fill the walled area, and the cemeteries expanded in an orderly fashion beyond their former bounds. These changes suggest neither decline nor decay. Late Roman *Venta* looks more urban in many ways than it had ever been: more populous, more industrial, even perhaps more commercial. If this was the *Venta* where in the later fourth century there was a *gynaeceum*, a weaving factory producing textiles for the imperial service, as the *Notitia Dignitatum* records, we have a sufficient explanation of the changes. For such a factory would probably be located in a defended supply base dealing with the late Roman tax in kind, the *annona militaris*. County town had turned garrison.

The closing of the *gynaeceum* in 407, with the immediate cessation of money and materials, could also explain the sudden collapse of *Venta* seen so vividly in the abandonment of organised burial in its cemeteries, which simply ceased to expand for the first time in three and a half centuries.

During the next four hundred years, from the early or mid-fifth century to the mid- or late ninth, Winchester emerged from *Venta*. The frame provided by the former Roman city is as crucial to an understanding of these four centuries as it is for Alfred's refoundation in the ninth. The Roman walls, gates, and approach roads survived; the streets and buildings inside the walls did not. The exceptions to this general rule show that the place was not abandoned, but to the contrary was controlled. After a long period of decay the Roman south gate collapsed; traffic continued over the fallen stones; and the road was twice resurfaced, before the gate was blocked, first by a ditch and bank, and then by a stone wall. The process was complete by about 700.

Control of access to the walled area was thus important to some authority within, whether for defence (which seems unlikely given that the length of the perimeter was 3034 m) or for control of the through routes, perhaps for levying toll. The development of High Street, running from west to east through the city, strongly suggests that through traffic was the principal concern. High Street enters the city through what seems to be the exact site of the Roman west gate, runs downhill more or less on the line of the Roman street, and then diverges to run parallel on the north until it passes through the medieval east gate some 16 m north of the Roman gate.

Throughout the western third of its course, where it is running downhill, High Street lies in a broad hollow some 70 m wide, the north and south edges of which lie well behind the present (and medieval) frontages. This hollow, as frequent observations have shown, cuts deep into the Roman deposits and seems to have removed the Roman street itself, at least in its westernmost stretch where the slope is steepest. The medieval frontages by contrast overlap the hollow by up to 30 m on each side. At some date after the Roman period, therefore, but before the tenth century, when the present frontages were established, a large hollow formed down the hill along the line of High Street. This can be none other than a 'hollow way' of the kind which always forms where unmetalled roads negotiate a hill, and where traffic moves from side to side to secure a better footing. At Winchester, this hollow way can only have formed in the post-Roman centuries as a result of heavy traffic channelled onto this route not only by the Roman west gate, but also because the through north–south route was blocked by the closure of the south and probably also the north gate.

We still do not know when Roman *Venta* ceased to function as a town. But it seems probable, as the cemeteries suggest, that it was not a populous place for long after the beginning of the fifth century. It remained, nevertheless, a focus. From at least the sixth century a small group of pagan Anglo-Saxon cemeteries clustered around Winchester, each denoting a small settlement, and contrasting with the scattered distribution of such cemeteries elsewhere in Hampshire. This focus is seen again in the mid-seventh century in the foundation of the church later known as Old Minster within the walls. In a missionary age, such a church is not founded in a desert. By contrast, both the pagan cemeteries of the sixth century and the church in the seventh century suggest that the walled city, even if mostly deserted, remained the setting for certain regular events, perhaps markets or fairs, but particularly the conduct of the ruler's business. The hypothesis is that some of the regional administrative and judicial role of *Venta* survived its collapse and that the former city continued to be the centre from which those who had inherited at least part of its territory exercised their authority. In this sense the thread of continuity was royal power and it was in exercise of this power that in or about 648 Cenwalh, king of Wessex, founded the church of St Peter and St Paul to serve his presumably periodical residence in the former city. Strikingly, both the church and the site of the royal palace are immediately adjacent to the forum and basilica from which authority was exercised in the Roman period over the territory of the Belgae.

Very little is known of the physical state of the walled area at this time. Pottery of Pagan Saxon type, some of it datable as early as the fifth century, demonstrates the presence of a Germanic English element already within the walls. The spatial distribution of this early pottery, of the probably sixth-century types which followed it, of a few fragments of imported Frankish pottery, and of some four hundred fragments of contemporary glass vessels, also of continental origin, suggests that there was within the walls a series of discrete settlements, perhaps no more than ten in all, scattered across the ruin-field. These should probably be regarded as individual private enclosures, but they were clearly of some status, as the imports imply, and the royal residence was probably no more than a larger and more substantial version of them.

With the foundation of the church of St Peter and St Paul about 648 Winchester emerges into a slightly less opaque period. From this time on we can recognise four elements in its physical settlement as in its social hierarchy: the king, the church (from about 662 a bishop's see), a small number of private estates of relatively high social rank, and a service and possibly productive component in the low-lying part of the city within east gate. Apart from the relatively small areas occupied by these elements, the greater part of the area lay open, interrupted here and there by the ruined walls of Roman buildings but given over for the most part to cultivation.

This is the fabric of Winchester for the next two centuries and it is the base on which Alfred's restoration was founded. It was not an urban place, but rather a ceremonial centre, its role an inheritance. Fifteen miles down the Itchen valley, Hamwic, from which the shire is named, emerged as an urban place from around 700, extensive, regularly planned, densely occupied, industrial, commercial. The contrast with contemporary Winchester could hardly be greater, and in this contrast their different roles are clarified.

Nothing is yet known of the royal enclosure in Winchester at this date, although it probably lay immediately west of the cathedral church, in the area occupied by the late Saxon palace. The church itself, by contrast, is now well known, having been almost completely excavated in 1962–69. It was laid out at an angle across a Roman street south of the forum and was a large cruciform building, 27.8 m (88 Drusian, long Roman, feet) in overall length. Analysis shows that it was regularly planned with proportions of 1:1, 1:2 and 1:3, using a rod of $16\frac{1}{2}$ Drusian feet (5.50 m), and with a nave 4 rods, 66

Drusian feet (cf. one chain), in length. Although only the foundations
survived, constructed of re-used Roman material, internal features and
external details were carried out in freshly quarried Box Ground oolite
transported from near Bath. The east end and the north and south flanking
porticos were rectangular and the altar stood at the east end of the nave,
immediately in front of the opening into the east end. It is the largest church
of its date yet discovered in England. A detached tower dedicated to St
Martin was built to the west early in the eighth century, and the east end was
remodelled as an apse later in the century, but the church was not extended
or otherwise remodelled until the tenth century.

To begin with there was little or no burial around the church, but burials
began by about 700 and the surrounding cemetery became the principal
graveyard of the city until the mid-nineteenth century. The earliest burials to
break the Roman prohibition against burial within the walls of a city took
place not at the cathedral but in a small cemetery belonging to one of the
private enclosures in what is now Lower Brook Street. One of these was the
grave of a woman who wore a collar of twenty-seven silver rings and a
necklace of gold and garnet pendants and glass beads, datable to the second
half of the seventh century. By contrast the first burials at the cathedral
contained no such objects and must therefore date from a slightly later phase,
when the church had succeeded in gaining control over burials and
concentrating them in consecrated ground around the cathedral.

The Lower Brook Street necklace reveals the high social status of these
private enclosures. Over the years this one developed a complex of timber
buildings, restored the ruins of a Roman stone building, and then constructed
a square stone dwelling, probably of the kind meant by a 'bower'. Such a
stone building is a very rare element in an Anglo-Saxon domestic site. A
globule of gold and two touchstones for assaying gold were found in or near
it. The stone building itself, the earlier cemetery on the site with its rich
grave, and these traces of the working and assaying of precious metals make a
strong case for regarding this and other such enclosures as aristocratic
residences, whether occupied continuously or only used on those occasions
when the king was in Winchester, perhaps to celebrate the great feasts of the
Christian year.

In the second half of the ninth century this long-enduring pattern came to
an abrupt end. The first sign of change was the construction of a bridge over
the River Itchen outside east gate by Bishop Swithun, apparently in 859.
Presumably replacing a ford, this bridge must signal an increase of traffic on
the east–west road which had worn so great a hollow in its way downhill
through the walled area. About this time there are traces of new settlement at
the other end of this route, outside west gate, within an extra-mural enclave
defined by the still surviving ditch and bank of a pre-Roman Iron Age
enclosure. People retreating from Viking raids in 840 and 842 on the exposed
coastal town of Hamwic (Southampton) may have settled here, the first sign
of the repopulation of Winchester for over four centuries. Winchester itself
was sacked in 860 and about that time, perhaps in part through the action of
its bishop, its Roman defences were refurbished.

The restored Roman walls and gates were now the frame for the remaking

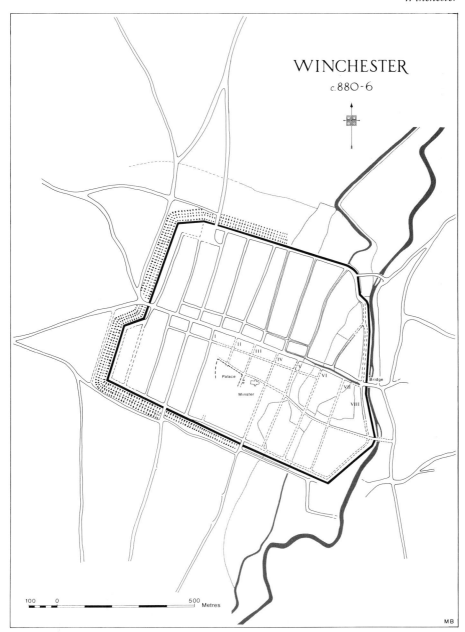

Plan of Winchester.

of the city. Some time in the later ninth century Alfred (871–899), or possibly
one of his elder brothers, laid out across the still essentially empty walled area
a complete new grid of regularly planned streets, formed on a module of 4 poles
or 66 feet (the length of a cricket pitch!), 5.6 km in total length, and surfaced
with some 8,000 tonnes of knapped flint cobbles. We still walk on the lines of
these streets today, for they gave to Winchester a pattern which has endured.
As one of the earliest of all European essays in town-planning, and one which

was to be followed in essentials not only throughout Alfred's Wessex but also in the urban foundations by which his son and grandson first held and then united the English territories which had fallen under Viking rule, the streets of Winchester are the single greatest surviving monument to the organising ability and sense of order which were to be characteristics of the late Saxon state.

The street plan has four components: the pre-existing east–west axis of High Street, the two back-streets which run parallel to High Street on either side, the regularly spaced, parallel, side-streets which run north-south from High Street, and the wall-street which runs round inside the entire circuit of the walls, linking the ends of the other streets and thus bonding the whole system to the defences.

Herein lies the purpose of the plan: it was to apportion the walled area for permanent settlement while allowing movement on interior lines for the rapid reinforcement of any threatened part of the walls. Defensive purpose and economic viability were to be interdependent. However long the repopulation of the walled area may have taken (and it was certainly well advanced already by the end of the ninth century), the plan is an index of Alfredian urban expectations. It was laid out with the clear intention of repeopling the entire walled area of 58.2 hectares and in this by the end of the next century it had been entirely successful. And by that time suburbs had long been forming outside each of the city's gates.

Remarkable as the street plan is, the use of one-quarter of the walled area for ecclesiastical and royal buildings is perhaps as striking. Here were gathered those institutions and structures which gave to late Saxon Winchester the character of an early capital.

When the new streets were first laid out, there were apparently only two major pre-existing enclosures in this south-eastern quarter to be incorporated, the cathedral and the royal palace, and the new grid was laid down around them. Within twenty years or so, two monasteries were founded here, Nunnaminster by Alfred's queen Ealhswith before 902, and New Minster in 901–903. The latter was built close alongside the cathedral (which

Reconstruction drawing of the Old and New Minsters.

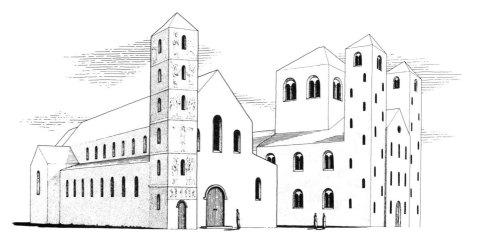

S.C.H.

was henceforth known as Old Minster), on a very cramped site which had in part to be purchased at great expense from those already living there 'by right of inheritance', a sign of the burgeoning population and pressure on land in the centre of the city only a short time after its refoundation. New Minster was established within the existing framework of the streets, but both precincts involved the blocking of some streets and their expansion in the 960s finally removed most traces of the street grid in the south-east quarter of the city.

Very little is yet known of the Anglo-Saxon buildings of Nunnaminster, but New Minster was an aisled basilica, much better adapted for large congregations than the cathedral which was still essentially in its seventh-century form. New Minster was in some way closely associated with the citizens who were able freely to choose burial in its cemetery whereas previously they would probably have had to be buried in the cathedral cemetery. The real purpose of New Minster was thus probably to serve as the principal town church of the refounded city, while Old Minster as the see church looked out to the diocese at large.

Proximity and intrusion were potent for rivalry, even conflict: 'it could be remembered that the singing of the bretheren . . . in one choir fought with the voices of those singing in the other, while the ringing of the bells made confusion worse confounded', for indeed the two churches were so close together that 'a man could scarcely walk between them'. Throughout the later tenth century the two minsters strove to out-do each other in the size and splendour of their buildings. Shortly after the dedication of New Minster in 903, the canons of Old Minster provided their church with wings which flanked the west front to give an essentially decorative façade some 30 m wide, immediately alongside New Minster.

There matters rested until both houses were reformed in 963–964 by Bishop Aethelwold. In 971 Aethelwold translated the remains of Swithun (d.862) from his original grave outside the seventh-century west front of Old Minster, and immediately began the construction around the spot of a vast double-apsed memorial building, which measured 33 m from north to south, almost exactly the diameter of Charlemagne's octagon at Aachen. Almost at once, perhaps before it was even complete, the memorial building was remodelled as a westwork of ultimately Carolingian inspiration, and was dedicated in 980. In the same moment New Minster added a tower, perhaps six storeys high, its exterior apparently embellished level by level with sculptures reflecting the dedication of each floor. Meanwhile, Aethelwold's reconstruction of Old Minster was not complete when he died in 984. It was perfected by his successor Aelfheah with the total reconstruction of the east end and the construction of a new staged bell-tower, and was dedicated in 993–994. By this date Old Minster had attained its final form and a total length of 76 m, by far the largest and most elaborate church yet known from Anglo-Saxon England, and the product of three and a half centuries of development, reflecting a complex succession of continental and insular influences.

Nothing is yet known of the appearance or components of the royal palace. Its presence is reflected, however, in the westwork of Old Minster, which

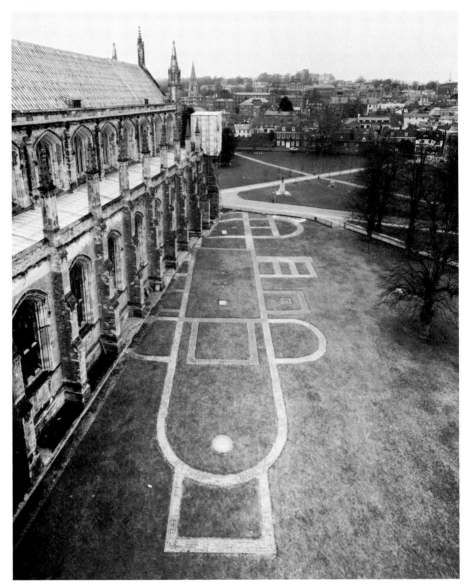

The site of the Old Minster (seventh to tenth centuries), beside Winchester Cathedral (1079–1122).

must have stood within a few yards of the palace and which, together with its liturgical and musical functions, was probably designed to provide a high seat for the king looking down the length of the church. Away in the south-east angle of the city, Bishop Aethelwold now created a second palace as a residence for himself and his successors, on the site at Wolvesey still occupied by the bishop a millenium later. By c.1000 this episcopal palace included a hall, a bed chamber, and a prison.

By the end of the Anglo-Saxon period Winchester was a prosperous city. The densely packed houses of its perhaps 8,000 inhabitants were dominated by the bulk and towers of the great buildings in the south-eastern quarter which formed perhaps the greatest group of royal and ecclesiastical buildings in any city of its time north of the Alps.

This was the city's golden age, a *Blütezeit*. The artists of the Winchester School – as art historians have described the style which reached out from the city to influence many of the greatest ateliers, themselves in monastic houses linked directly to Winchester by the closest ties of foundation, refoundation and individual monastic lives – working in paint, metal, ivory, glass, clay and stone, created works of gorgeous colour and figural and floral elegance to adorn not only the churches and their shrines but also, as a very few surviving pieces show, the individual and his home. Masons, sculptors, and carpenters built on a scale – and with an eclectic inspiration – never before attained in England. In the cloister, writers such as Wulfstan, steeped in the Latin of Virgil and other Roman poets, might yet choose to write prose or verse in a high-flown unclassical style which 'are the mark of a man with artistic tastes'. Aelfric, writing for the most part in Old English, chose simplicity: 'brevity does not always disfigure a work – often it makes it more beautiful', he wrote, as if in deliberate contrast. Music sounded throughout this quarter, whether bells, or chant, or the great sounds – to say no more – of the organ (twenty-six bellows, seventy blowers, four hundred pipes, forty slides, four hundred apertures, so we are told) 'the music of whose pipes is heard everywhere through the town'.

Yet Winchester was not the most important city of England in economic terms, lying perhaps fourth in rank, behind London, York and Lincoln, as gauged by the numbers of coins struck by its moneyers. But no city equalled it in associations with the royal house. It was in Winchester that the regalia were kept, together with the treasure, and thus it was there that the first beginnings of a permanent administration were to emerge. Duke William and his Norman followers understood well enough the city's exceptional significance.

Germanic bone comb, found beside the Roman forum (fifth century).

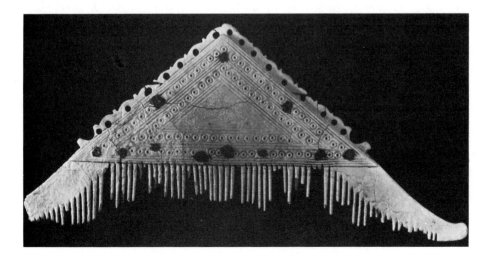

Winchester surrendered in November 1066. Within three months William fitzOsbern had begun the construction of the castle, cutting off a salient within the south-western angle of the Roman walls by a bank and ditch which destroyed the houses along two streets. Three years later, King William built a new hall and palace in the centre of the city, extending the Anglo-Saxon palace north to High Street and doubling it in size. The building of the Norman cathedral to replace Old Minster (itself barely a century old in its final form) began in 1079; the eastern arms were complete and dedicated in 1093, but the nave was not finished until perhaps 1122. In quick

Winchester Cathedral: the north transept (1079–1093).

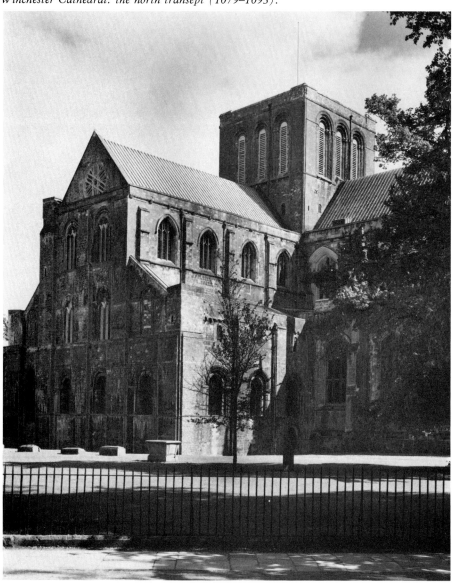

succession shortly after 1100 came the rebuilding of Nunnaminster as St Mary's Abbey, the removal of New Minster to a new site outside North Gate and its rebuilding as Hyde Abbey, and the rebuilding of the bishop's palace at Wolvesey. The size of these works – the new cathedral was then the largest church in the West save only St Hugh's new work at Cluny – and the number which were in simultaneous construction imply investment on an immense scale. They demonstrate as nothing else Norman appreciation of the city's significance and expectations for its future. Every year they were in England, William the Conqueror and his son wore their crowns each Easter at Winchester in ceremonies as significant politically as they were in religion. It was in Winchester too, at first in the palace but by 1100 in the castle, that the treasure and regalia remained, and in the castle that the treasury and the nascent exchequer first emerged as working offices. And it was thus inevitably to Winchester that the returns of the great survey were sent for reduction by royal clerks into the Domesday Book. The economic ranking of the city had also risen: with the harrying of the North, and the decline of York and Lincoln, Winchester was now second only to London, although perhaps rivalled by Norwich, and its population may have risen to perhaps 10,000 inhabitants.

But amid all these new forms, the fundamental fabric of Winchester, pattern and population, were basically unchanged. The streets and houses remained, sons succeeded English fathers in their properties; and English moneyers, the highest rank in the hierarchy of those whose interests were bounded by the city, continued to strike coins under the same system which had been evolved a century before.

Change was shortly to come. Henry I wore his crown in Winchester for almost the last time at Easter 1108. The bonds between the city and the crown weakened throughout the century and ushered in the long decline which would not be reversed until the Middle Ages were long past.

Anglo-Saxon strap-end, found in a grave at the Old Minster, Winchester (tenth century).

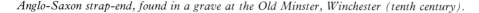

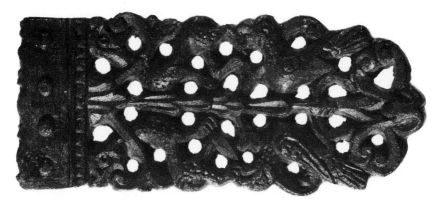

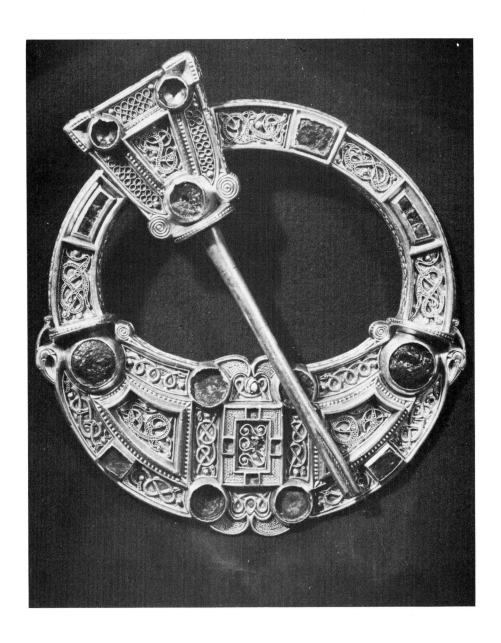

Richly ornamented Celtic silver brooch (seventh century), found at Hunterston, Ayrshire; once in Viking hands.

4 The Arts of Late Celtic Britain (AD 600–900)

ISABEL HENDERSON

By the mid-fifth century the Roman province of Britain had come to an end and Germanic peoples had settled in south-east England. By the mid-sixth century they were in the north-east. The British population in the occupied areas was not wiped out, and in the North and West powerful British kingdoms survived. From the fifth century Irish immigrants were settling along the western coasts of Britain. In western Scotland, by 600, an Irish colony known as Dalriada had been established. The cultural influence of this Irish-Celtic part of north Britain was enormous for within it St Columba (d.597) founded a monastery on the Island of Iona which was to become a spiritual and intellectual centre of international significance.

The Irish had established themselves in north-west Britain at the expense of a third Celtic people – the Picts. The Picts occupied modern Scotland north of a line drawn between the estuaries of the rivers Forth and Clyde. Some of the Picts spoke an indigenous non-Celtic language, so that strictly speaking the Picts are only partially Celtic.

In comparison with the aristocratic art of the pre-Roman Iron age the surviving art of sub-Roman Britain is unimpressive. It is not fully understood why, during the seventh century, there was a revival, indeed a renaissance, of Celtic art. What is clear is that Celtic curvilinear art – the art of the spiral, the scroll, and the curve – had survived. Sufficient continuity was maintained in workshops for the Celtic craftsman's work of the late sixth century to be a source of interest and inspiration to his equally talented Anglo-Saxon counterpart. It used to be thought that the Celtic workshops concerned had to be in Ireland but new evidence and re-assessments over the last twenty years have shown that fine metalworking could equally well have been produced in the princely strongholds of Celtic Britain. In this period no art existed without patronage and it is likely that peripatetic craftsmen took initiative in seeking out patrons who would not have been greatly concerned whether they were dealing with Irish – or Welsh – speaking Celts.

The earliest manuscript decorated with Celtic ornament is the early seventh-century psalter known as the *Cathach* of St Columba. The initial letters of the psalms are built up of spirals, curves and peltas in a style recognisably derived from the curvilinear art of the Celtic Iron Age. Innovatory, however, is the way in which the stems of the letters are split. The panels thus created are left blank in the *Cathach* but in later manuscripts they were filled with ornament to create the characteristic Insular decorated letter.

The large hanging-bowl in the Sutton Hoo ship-burial is by far the most impressive piece of Celtic metalworking which can be dated to c.600. Remains of around 150 hanging-bowls have been found, mostly in Anglo-Saxon graves where they were deposited as part of the grave-goods necessary for the pagan Anglo-Saxons' after-life. They are made of bronze and have decorated escutcheons (disks) applied at the rim, with hooks attached to hold suspension chains. Sometimes there are non-functional decorative escutcheons at the centre of the inside of the bowl, on its base, or applied at intervals on the outside surface. The large Sutton Hoo hanging-bowl is very richly ornamented indeed. It has eight escutcheons which employ three types of ornament: fine-line running scrolls reserved in bronze against red enamel, millefiori glass insets, and hatched silver bindings. Very similar spiral ornament is found on the Irish garment fasteners known as latchets and on a few Irish penannular brooches, which also have millefiori settings. One of these, the Ballinderry brooch, represents an ornamental stage very close to the escutcheons of the large Sutton Hoo bowl. Nevertheless the discovery of fine metalworking technology and materials, including millefiori glass, in the British stronghold, Dinas Powys in Glamorgan, and the more recent discoveries in North Britain of moulds for casting hanging-bowl escutcheons, support the view that initially the bowls were made by the British and acquired by the Anglo-Saxons. That the Anglo-Saxon owner of the large Sutton Hoo bowl valued it highly is clear from the silver and garnet repairs made to it in the royal workshop.

Large hanging bowl, found in the Sutton Hoo ship-burial, showing revolving fish and silver patch repair (c.600).

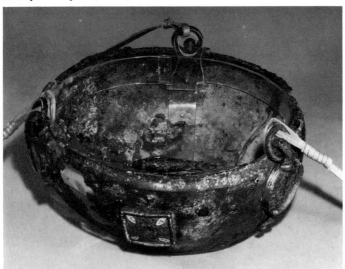

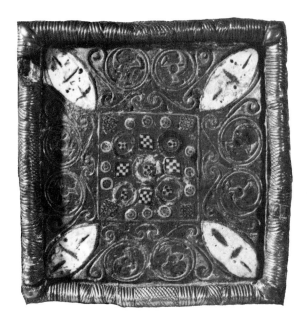

Ornamental escutcheon showing spiral-work enamel, millefiori *glass, and silver hatching on binding (early seventh century).*

An interesting connection has been noticed between the type of hatching used on the silver bindings of the escutcheons and the geometric designs found on fragments of silver in the Pictish hoard deposited in Norrie's Law in Fife. This hoard also contains pins with crescent-shaped heads decorated with fine-line spirals filled with enamel. These connections, and the moulds found in the Pictish area, show that the Picts were part of the cultural area which produced this kind of ornamental metalwork in the seventh century.

The native art of the partially Celtic Picts has survived largely on stone. The unique Pictish symbols are incised on some 250 boulder stones (early seventh century) found throughout the Pictish area. Purely as designs, the symbols have considerable interest and it is not surprising that many art-historians prefer to treat them merely as designs, shirking consideration of the more fundamental question of how they functioned in Pictish society. The geometric symbols, which are made up of rectangles, crescents, and circles, are decorated with hatching, interlocking peltas and scrolls strikingly reminiscent of the forms found on repoussé metalwork of the Celts of the British Iron Age. Professor Thomas has argued that the outlines of some of the symbols represent the impedimenta of these aristocratic, warrior Celts of the turn of the Christian era. The clearest example of this fossilisation is the Pictish mirror symbol which has the shape of the typical decorated bronze mirror of the early Celts. Part of the answer, therefore, to the question of how Celtic art was preserved in the sub-Roman period may be found in Pictish art. The symbol-bearing stones were probably erected on the analogy of Christian cross-carved grave-markers which were in use from the beginning of the seventh century but the symbolism itself, deeply entrenched, as it must have been, in Pictish society, will have existed on other media – metal. wood or even as tattoos on the skins of the Picts themselves.

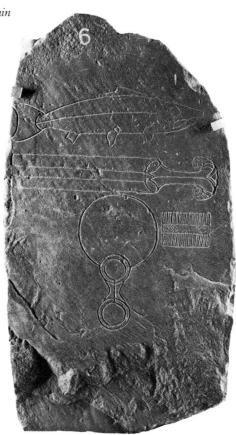

Boulder stone with incised Pictish mirror, comb, fish and tuning-fork symbols (early seventh century).

The Picts are best known for their animal art. The vigour and effectiveness of the animal symbols set a standard for animal portrayal which was maintained by the Picts into the ninth century. The animal symbols are shown in profile, pacing steadily across the surface of the stone. The naturalism of the animals is unparalleled in early medieval art. The underlying bone structure, the hang of a tail, the weight of a pad or hoof, the fins of the fish, the tines of the deer, the claws of the eagle, are all expressed so accurately that this must be the art of a people who through patient observation have managed in the lift and flow of an incised line to convey the grace and strength of indigenous wild life. Nevertheless the uniformly profile pose gives the animal designs a badge-like appearance well-suited to their use as symbols. There is also a formulaic quality about the designs which suggests underlying standardised models. Part of the animal formula is the use of stylised scrolls to emphasise the volume of haunch, shoulder and belly. The use of these body scrolls links the animal symbols stylistically with the geometric symbols. Body scrolls are found on the Lion Evangelist symbol in the *Book of Durrow*, and the Calf symbol in the slightly later *Echternach Gospels*, and on the Eagle symbol of the Corpus Christi College, Cambridge Gospel fragment.

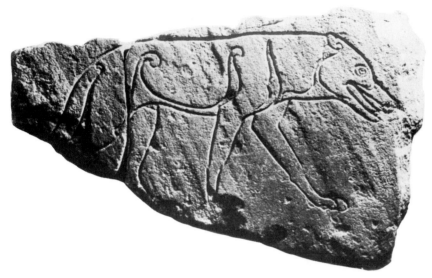

Symbol stone with wolf, from Ardross, Inverness (early seventh century).

Some writers have argued that the Pictish animal symbols were based on these designs in the Gospel Books. But it seems more probable that the artist/scribes of the earlier Gospel Books were just as dependent on native secular art for Evangelist symbol models as they were for other elements in their decorative repertoire and that they lighted on the animal art of the Picts for this purpose.

Two identical leaf-shaped silver plaques in the Norrie's Law hoard are engraved with Pictish symbols. The double-disk symbol and Beast's Head symbol are handled with a delicacy and sureness of line which comes from long experience. Traces of red enamelling have survived on one plaque. The spiral infill of the double-disks belongs, like the ornament on the pins in the same hoard, to the decorative world of the escutcheons. The Beast's Head symbol has a naturalistic dog head very similar indeed to the naturalistic dogs which are a novel feature of the decoration of the *Lindisfarne Gospels* (early eighth century). The Northumbrians occupied Southern Pictland throughout the third quarter of the seventh century so the art of the Picts would have been readily accessible.

The Norrie's Law hoard also contained two large, plain silver penannular (having a hoop with a break creating two terminals) brooches. Similar brooches were found in a hoard at Tummel Bridge in Perthshire along with hanging-bowl fragments datable to the fifth or sixth century. Some writers have argued that the plain silver penannulars belong to these centuries also and that the Norrie's Law deposit, including the symbol-bearing leaf-shaped plaques, dates to the sixth century. A seventh-century date for the symbols on the plaques would preclude a date as early as this for the Fife hoard, and the balance of opinion at present favours a seventh-century date for the plain penannular brooches also. A brooch of this type was found at Pant-y-Saer in Anglesey but the circumstances of the find do not help with absolute dating.

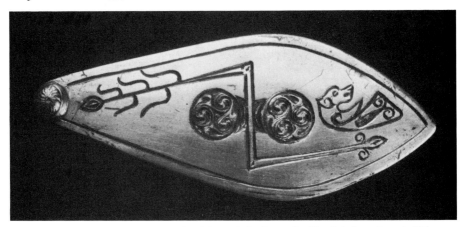

Leaf-shaped plaque engraved with Pictish symbols, from the Norrie's Law hoard, Fife (third quarter of the seventh century).

The Hunterston Brooch is the most richly ornamented complete brooch found in the Celtic north-west (see p. 206). A runic inscription scratched on the back shows that it was once in Viking hands, so that it may have been made far from its find spot in Hunterston, Ayrshire. The brooch is a good example of the interaction between Celt and Saxon in this period. The large Sutton Hoo bowl provided evidence for Anglo-Saxon craftsmen carefully repairing, with precious materials, an admired Celtic bowl, but the form and decoration of the Hunterston brooch demonstrate contemporary creative involvement. In a recent full study R.B.K. Stevenson (1974) (see Bibliography) has shown convincingly how most of the features of the brooch can be explained if it is seen as a plain Celtic brooch of the Tummel Bridge type decorated with all the techniques available to the Germanic jeweller. Stevenson points to a number of parallels between the Hunterston Brooch and the art of the *Lindisfarne Gospels* and the *Durham Gospels.* It would seem therefore that the relationship between manuscript and metalwork art was changing and that motifs developed by the scribe/artist were now influencing the repertoire of the metalworker.

Another showy piece of metalwork of uncertain provenance, but generally accepted as belonging to the Celtic North, is the miniature Monymusk Reliquary (early eighth century) now in the Royal Museum in Edinburgh. The Reliquary is decorated with escutcheon-like plaques set on a silver ground covered with flowing animal ornament drawn with lines of punched dots. This kind of ornament is used on the silver drinking bowls which are part of the St Ninian's Isle treasure (eighth century). The discovery in Shetland in 1958 of this hoard of twenty-eight silver objects, some with extremely complex ornament, added a new dimension to our understanding of the role of the Celtic North in mainstream Insular art. Once again we are reminded that the modern perception of northern Britain as provincial and isolated can be seriously misleading for this period. David Wilson's (see Bibliography) recognition that the eleven brooches in the hoard were of a specifically Pictish type at once made sense of the other scattered finds of eighth-century brooches in the north. Decorative mannerisms used in the brooches are repeated on the other fine metalwork, which includes two scabbard chapes and three heavily ornamental cone-shaped mounts, so the coherence of the treasure as Pictish is established. Some of the animal ornament on the silver bowls and cones resembles that found on the later sculpture of the Picts, to which we must now turn.

We have seen that the Picts were erecting boulders some with incised crosses and some with Pictish symbols in the seventh century. In the eighth century these two types of monument came together in the form of symbol-bearing cross-slabs carved in reliefs. The reason for this merging and development was twofold – a new coming together of the church and state in Pictland, and as a consequence, contact with the Northumbrian church.

In his *Ecclesiastical History* Bede tells of the initiative of a Pictish king, who around 710 sent messengers to Bede's abbot at the monastery of Jarrow-Monkwearmouth asking among other things for Northumbrian architects to be sent to Pictland to build a stone church. This is a unique record of a British king commissioning a building through the good offices of an abbot of an English monastery. The stone church was built and it would not have gone unfurnished. We can suppose that a whole range of other commissions and importations resulted. Northumbrian churches in this period were decorated with shallow-relief sculpture bearing Insular designs, and large inscribed slabs with undecorated full-length crosses in heavy relief were being made for memorial purposes. It is not surprising therefore that the Pictish cross-slab evolved at this period as a direct consequence of the presence of Northumbrian stone-masons in Pictland. In form it was similar to the Northumbrian memorial cross-slabs but instead of being inscribed, it bore Pictish symbols and a rich array of ornament, based not only on the shallow relief sculpture in the south, but on designs found in metalwork and manuscripts also.

Miniature Monymusk reliquary with plaques set on a silver ground (early eighth century).

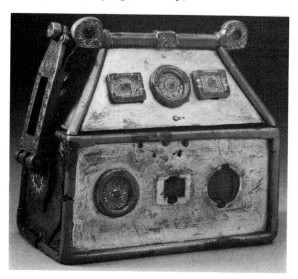

Cone-shaped metal mount with Pictish decoration (late eighth century).

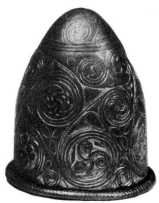

The Pictish cross-slab which illustrates this phase of Pictish sculpture best stands in the churchyard at Aberlemno in Angus (Plate IIIa). This large slab displays a cross decorated with accurately rendered circular knotwork of a complexity that suggests that the Picts may have used interlace ornament in other media before the Northumbrians taught them how to carve stone in relief. The linked animals to the left of the shaft are closely related to those found on one of the ornamental cross-pages in the *Lindisfarne Gospels* which were being written and illuminated around the time that the Pictish king approached the abbot of Jarrow-Monkwearmouth.

Pictish cross-slab at Aberlemno, Angus. The reverse depicts a naturalistic battle scene (c.700).

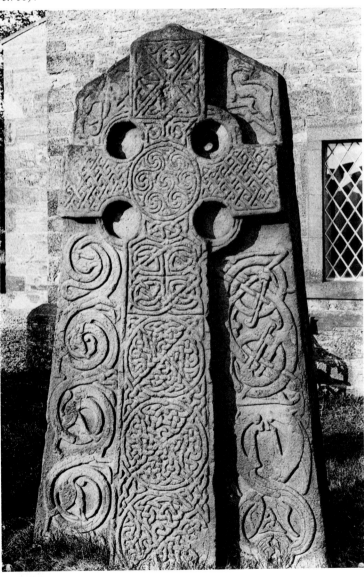

The reverse of the slab depicts, in strip-cartoon format, a battle scene in a naturalistic narrative style. The neatly executed, profile stepping horses appear on innumerable Pictish cross-slabs thereafter, usually as part of hunt scenes. The exact 'genre' of the Aberlemno battle scene has yet to be determined. From what has been written above it is evident that by a series of traceable interactions between Celtic and Saxon artists the Insular style was formed by 700. We see all its components, Celtic, Germanic and Mediterranean in position in the *Lindisfarne Gospels*. After 700 it is inappropriate to talk of Germanic or Celtic (whether Irish, British or Pictish) motifs or techniques, for the basic repertoire was by then common to all the peoples of the British Isles. After the beginning of the eighth century we find in the Celtic areas of Britain a particular interpretation of Insular art which deserves separate study because of its individual note and excellence.

After the first quarter of the eighth century art in the north and west is represented by sculpture, with the possible, massive, exception of the *Book of Kells* (second half of the eighth century) which many writers believe was at least begun on Iona. Writing of the sculpture of this period Professor Cramp (1965) has remarked 'in considering the national groups, Irish, English, Scottish, Welsh, Manx, what strikes one most is the independence of the traditions'. Some connections, iconographical, decorative and formal can be made between the later Pictish cross-slabs, the free-standing crosses of the school of Iona, and the Northumbrian crosses at Ruthwell and Bewcastle, but the differences are still very great. The very simple pillar-stone crosses of Wales and Cornwall erected at this period are different again. The eighth-century Calf of Man Crucifixion carved on a slab of local Manx slate is derived directly from manuscript and metalwork models and is the only surviving example in stone of a figure built up of shapes in a fashion directly comparable to the stylised figure style found in the early eighth-century *Durham Gospels*, the *Lichfield Gospels*, and the *Echternach Gospels*. In sculpture elsewhere this figural style never caught on, presumably because it was essentially calligraphic.

From the very beginning of the period of the production of the first cross-slabs Pictish sculptors exploited up-to-date ornament for their own purposes. The Picts, however, seem not to have been interested in the growing Insular preoccupation with New Testament iconography. They preferred to juxtapose Old Testament Salvation iconography such as Jonah and the Whale, Daniel in the den of the Lions, and David rending the jaws of the Lion, with the scene of St Paul and St Antony breaking bread in the desert. This latter episode was interpreted as a veiled reference to the Eucharist, and so stood for the Salvation of the New Testament, through the body and blood of Christ. This dualistic iconographic programme accounts for the number of representations of these desert saints in Pictish sculpture.

In addition to the Picts' symbol-bearing cross-slabs are their stone shrines of box construction, which provide the best evidence available for locating Pictish ecclesiastical sites. The most impressive box-shrine is known as the St Andrews Sarcophagus. It was found buried in the precinct of St Andrews Cathedral, Fife, where there was a Pictish monastery in the eighth century. One long panel and the two end panels have survived. The end panels have framed equal-armed crosses decorated in a way which links the shrine firmly to the art of the eighth-century cross-slabs. On the long panel there is a full-length frontal figure of David rending the jaws of the lion in a gesture of total mastery. This figure is set alongside other David imagery carved on a much smaller scale, in the manner of Early Christian sarcophagi. At the top left corner of the panel there is a thicket from which wild animals emerge. The intertwining of animals and foliage are particularly skilfully and sensitively carved.

Ambitous secular patronage for Pictish sculpture must be behind the unique recumbent monuments of the Picts, which are represented most dramatically in the Museum of Pictish Sculpture at Meigle in Perthshire. The massive, solid, grave-markers there have no overt Pictish or Christian symbolism but they are made of the same local stone used for the Meigle cross-slabs and are decorated in the same style. Monumental grave-markers of this type are not found elsewhere in the British Isles. All of them have a shallow socket on the top, presumably for holding a small cross.

Pictish sculpture at Meigle is dominated by images of force. Decoratively conceived men and beasts coil round and bite each other. Naturalistic bears eat naturalistic men. The largest Meigle cross-slab has an impressive image of Daniel surrounded by lions, centrally placed. The Daniel figure echoes the theme of animal violence but the image is a serene one implying that, as with David in the St Andrews Sarcophagus, Salvation has been achieved. An equally striking group of three horsemen riding abreast is placed above Daniel. The depiction of figures in depth is conveyed by the unsophisticated means of a triple outline but the surface modelling of the rippling muscles of the horse closest to the viewer makes this a remarkable work of art for the period. In the confined space to the left of the cross-shaft a naked figure kneels with one arm reaching down to form a human chain with two other figures who hang beneath him. These agile figures recall the men slipping between the decorated letters which begin St Luke's Gospel in the *Book of Kells*. Almost certainly, manuscripts decorated in the style of the *Book of Kells* were known to Pictish sculptors.

This relationship with the art of the *Book of Kells* is also apparent in the predominance of the snake-boss motif, a boss made up of interlacing snakes, in the other major school of Pictish sculpture centred on Easter Ross north of Inverness. The Pictish cross-slab in this group showing the greatest technical bravura is at Nigg where the versatility and ingenuity of the spiral and snake-boss ornament is matched by technical competence of a truly remarkable kind. The snake-boss is also displayed all over the principal monuments of the Iona school. In the *Book of Kells* this same decorative device appears as circles formed of interlacing snakes' bodies.

Just like the Picts, the Irish on Iona had to be taught to cut and carve stone. The double-curved shape of the free-standing Iona cross-head is taken from the Northumbrian type. The length of the span of the cross-head on St John's Cross on Iona is without precedent. It caused structural difficulties from the start which were solved by the introduction of a supporting ring. This necessity may have produced the earliest Celtic ringed cross in stone, pre-dating Irish examples. The idea of placing Biblical scenes on the reverse

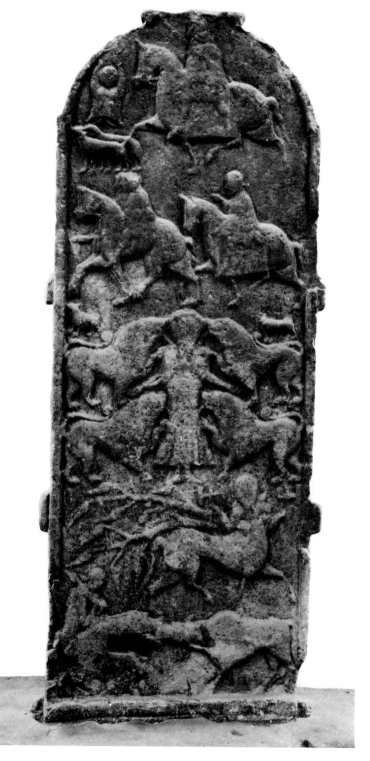

Stone cross-slab found at Meigle, Perthshire (eighth century).

of the shaft of St Martin's Cross on Iona may also have come from Northumbrian sculpture. The snake-boss ornament on the other hand, belongs to Pictish sculpture, so that the Picts may have been teachers alongside the Northumbrians. It is clear, however, from the nature of the ornament they employ that the Iona craftsmen had long experience of designing precious metalwork and of illuminating books, and that they were able to draw on this as soon as they had learned how to carve stone. The spiral ornament on the St John's Cross on Iona has frequently been compared to the art of the richly ornamented Chi Rho initial to the passage telling of the birth of Christ in the Gospel of St Matthew in the *Book of Kells*, and the image of the Virgin and Child which is used on a number of Iona crosses reflects the model used for the Virgin and Child miniature in *Kells*. In the long-standing debate on the provenance of the *Book of Kells* the evidence provided by the sculpture of the Picts and the Dalriadic Irish cannot be ignored. It supports strongly, the view that the book was part of the intellectual and artistic output of Iona in the decades before the Columban headquarters was moved to Kells in Ireland at the beginning of the ninth century. The ninth century was a time of great upheaval in the Celtic North West. Under repeated Viking attack the Columban community on Iona had no alternative to leaving the island.

For the Picts and the Irish in Dalriada (known now as the Scots) the ninth century saw an intermingling of the two peoples brought about by intermarriage of rulers and the desire of the Scots to get a foothold in the fertile Pictish heartland far removed from Viking pressure in the west. The Picto-Scottish art which resulted is generally inferior to the work of the individual schools of Iona and Easter Ross.

No illuminated manuscript can with certainty be attributed to a Pictish scriptorium, but there is one Picto-Scottish ninth-century decorated book. It is known as the *Book of Deer* because grants relating to the Celtic monastery of Deer in Aberdeenshire are written on the blank spaces of the vellum. It is often regarded as an inferior book or even a grotesquely barbarous one, but it is deftly written and is unusually heavily decorated, in spite of being a truncated version of the Gospels. The figure style is a particularly extreme example of the reduction of form which has been referred to earlier. Far from being fumbling and inept, the drawing, within this idiom, is fluent and sophisticated. The iconography does not, as some have thought, consist of curiously deviant Evangelist portraits but illustrates the text in the manner of the miniatures in the *Book of Kells*. The fifteen decorated pages of *Deer* are evidently ultimately modelled on a full-scale de luxe Gospel Book approaching the ambitious nature of *Kells* and so this sole surviving Picto-Scottish book provides evidence for the kind of manuscripts which may have been being illuminated in Pictland or Dalriada at the same time as the superlative monuments were being carved.

A great deal of high quality art was being produced in the Celtic areas of Britain during the period 600–900. The revival of early Celtic curvilinear art which made such a brilliant contribution to the Insular style of 700 was made possible by the tenacity of a style which itself had been fired by a number of continental art-styles. What is remarkable, however, is the speed with which artists in the Celtic areas assimilated and exploited the resources of Germanic and Mediterranean art so that they participated freely in the formation of the Insular style and its development. Similarly, the Germanic artists were quick to benefit from the different techniques and decorative repertoire of the Celts. The great flowering of art that took place in Anglo-Saxon England in the seventh and eighth centuries has never lacked recognition, but the fact that the flowering was taking place *throughout* Britain still needs to be emphasised.

Because so much has been lost, interpretation of the relationships between Celtic-speaking and English-speaking craftsmen and patrons can only be tentative. New finds, like the growing corpus of metalwork in North Britain have invariably called for re-appraisal. The recent recognition in the Dalriadic West of a slab decorated in exactly the manner of eighth-century cross-slabs in the Pictish east shows that peripatetic craftsmen not only travelled north and south, as was known, but east and west across political boundaries. The need for such re-assessment makes the subject endlessly interesting to the art-historian but for those less concerned about labelling and dating, and willing simply to look carefully, the inventiveness and freshness of the Insular style in the north and west will bring its own reward.

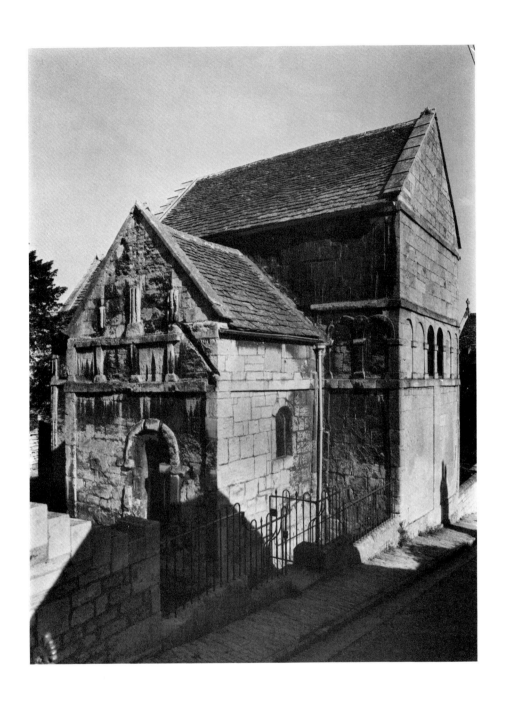

Chapel of St Laurence, Bradford-on-Avon, Wiltshire (probably eleventh century).

5 Architecture

RICHARD GEM

Anglo-Saxon settlers and Christianity (fifth century to c.750)

The Anglo-Saxon settlers of Britain came from a Continental background in which they had been accustomed to build entirely in wood, and this custom they continued to follow after their immigration. What is not certain, however, is the degree to which after their arrival they came to be influenced by traditions of timber construction already established here. For many years it was thought that the early settlers had lived in primitive wooden huts with the floors sunk into the ground, but more recently archaeological work has shown this to be an untrue picture. Sunken-floored huts were indeed used (sometimes as sheds for manufacturing processes), but they were only one aspect of a tradition that comprised a wide range of building types, many of which were of some degree of sophistication. The sites of several villages of fifth- to eighth-century date have been excavated intensively (for example, at West Stow in Suffolk, at Chalton and Cowdery's Down in Hampshire, and at Catholme in Staffordshire), and from the evidence it has been possible to reconstruct their appearance on paper – and occasionally on the ground. Besides these villages a number of other sites have been excavated or recorded which had very substantial timber buildings: these seem to have been of higher social status and were probably royal residences, as at Yeavering, Northumberland. All these sites are the expression of an essentially rural society, but the seventh century also saw the development of trading emporia such as Ipswich, Suffolk, and Southampton, Hampshire, and excavation has shown that the latter had a planned layout with a grid of streets between the timber buildings.

When Christianity was brought to the pagan Anglo-Saxons in the seventh century it came from two main directions, Ireland and the Continent, and this seems to have been reflected in church architecture. From Bede's *History* it appears that the Irish missionaries to Northumbria had a tradition of building in timber, and that the mid-seventh-century cathedral at Lindisfarne, Northumberland, was accordingly of split oak logs under a thatched roof. Likewise the earliest church at Glastonbury Abbey, Somerset, was of wattle construction – either of British or Irish inspiration. These churches must have fitted in easily with the tradition of Anglo-Saxon secular buildings.

The missionaries who came from the Continent to south-east England from around 600 onwards brought with them a revival of the tradition of masonry architecture. This tradition had never been broken in Italy and Gaul at the end of the Roman period, and stone buildings had continued to be erected, especially for the Christian Church which saw itself as the heir to Roman civilisation amidst the upheavals caused by the conquests of the Germanic peoples. It was this identification between the surviving elements of Roman culture and Christianity that was to commend the adoption of stone architecture 'in the Roman fashion' to the Anglo-Saxons as they were converted to Christianity and drawn into the Rome-centred Catholic Church. The new masonry architecture was first established in the early seventh century in Canterbury and south-east England, as at Bradwell, Essex*; but by the last third of the seventh century it had also penetrated decisively into Northumbria, where it was exemplified especially in the great monastic churches of Wilfrid at Ripon, North Yorkshire, and Hexham, Northumberland, and of Benedict Biscop at Monkwearmouth and Jarrow, Tyne and Wear*. A contemporary description of Hexham indicates the wonder which these new buildings evinced: the church was

founded deep in the earth with crypts of wonderfully dressed stonework, while above ground it was born up by various columns and many chapels, and ornamented by the marvellous length and height of the walls, and surrounded by tortuous circuits of passages leading sometimes upwards and sometimes downwards through spiral stairs.

(Aeddi, *Life of Bishop Wilfred*).

Carolingian culture and the Vikings (c.750–925)

The eighth century in England saw a consolidation of the Christian Anglo-Saxon culture that had been founded in the seventh century and which there had been no external factors to disturb. Meanwhile a comparable process of consolidation was in progress on the Continent and this saw the emergence of the Carolingian Frankish dynasty as the dominant political power in Europe, culminating in Charlemagne's restoration of the western 'Roman' Empire in 800. The Carolingian renaissance was of great importance for all the arts on the Continent, but for none more so than architecture. The new emperors aimed at a veritable revival of the architecture of the Christian Late Roman Empire, both in their own palaces and in the major churches under their patronage. But at the same time as the ambitious imperial projects, a new current also flowed through the main body of architecture bringing to it a fresh confidence and coherence. It was this architectural mainstream that

*This monument and all others asterisked are discussed in detail in the second part of this chapter, all of them illustrated.

kept Carolingian architecture going through the ninth century, after the initial imperial impulse had been lost and the dynasty had split into rival groupings. The question facing anyone seeking to understand Anglo-Saxon architecture of the period from the latter part of the eighth century to the beginning of the tenth is whether it was affected by Continental Carolingian architecture and, if so, how. That there were close links between England and the Continent in many fields during this period is well known; but the evidence for architecture is intermittent.

A building that used to be assigned to the seventh century but which is now more convincingly placed at a later date is Brixworth church, Northamptonshire*, and this shows a considerable architectural competence, even if there is only one feature that is 'Carolingian'. But a church more elaborate still than this is indicated by the contemporary description of the new cathedral built at York c.780, partly under the direction of Alcuin, who was to become one of the key figures of the Carolingian renaissance after he went abroad:

This exceedingly lofty house, born up by solid piers which are set under curved arches, is surrounded by many side chapels and has several upper chambers with various roofs; it holds thirty altars and various ornaments.
      (Alcuin, *Poem on the Bishops and Saints of the Church of York*)

– clearly this was a substantial building. Other churches of the late eighth and early ninth centuries are reported to have been founded by the great Mercian kings Offa and Coenwulf, but nothing is known of their appearance. By contrast a major aisled church has been excavated at Cirencester, Gloucestershire, but this has no documented history. The scale and form of the latter building are comparable to Carolingian buildings of the ninth-century mainstream and suggest some contact.

A few more modest buildings of the late eighth and early ninth centuries can be dated by their sculptured decoration. The most elaborate sculpture is to be seen at Breedon, Leicestershire, though the church itself does not survive; while simpler schemes remain in situ at Britford church, Wiltshire, and Edenham church, Lincolnshire. The use of sculpture in the way exemplified by these churches is English rather than Carolingian, and the same is true of the sculptures at Deerhurst church, Gloucestershire*, which seem to be of a date around the time of Alfred the Great.

For churches actually dated to the reign of Alfred we have to turn to documentary descriptions or archaeological excavations. Alfred founded a monastery at Athelney, Somerset, which was said to be modest in scale but of a new fashion of building: it had four apses (of stone?) and four wooden posts holding up the superstructure of the roof. Possibly the roof structure was one of the elaborate timber spires fashionable in Carolingian architecture at the time. At Gloucester a new church was founded by Alfred's daughter and this again, as excavation has shown, was of modest scale; but it had a western apse in Carolingian fashion. The church also had an eastern crypt added to it which was similar to the surviving four-columned crypt at Repton, Derbyshire – a building whose origins go back to the mid-ninth century and before. But the architecture of around 900 was not all on a modest scale, for Alfred's son, Edward, built a great aisled church in Winchester which can be paralleled with substantial Carolingian churches on the Continent. Perhaps also of the early tenth century is the tower of Barnack church, Cambridgeshire.

The tower arch of St John the Baptist Church at Barnack (tenth century).

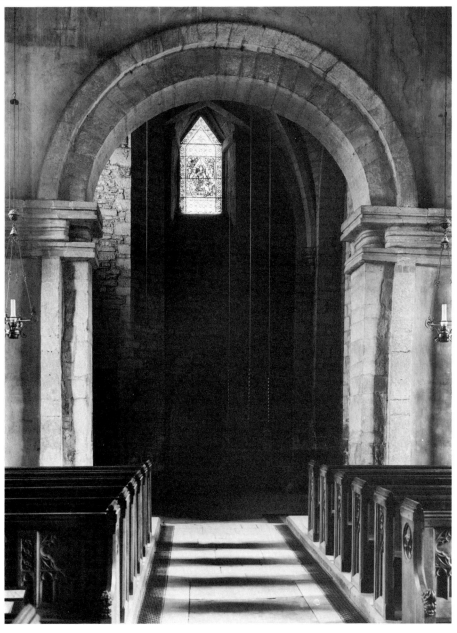

For secular architecture of the period from the eighth to the early tenth centuries the question of Carolingian influence is again of interest, but only in one instance has a stone-built palace been excavated: this was at Northampton and dated to the mid-ninth century. Elsewhere timber continued to be the major material for secular buildings, even at the top of the social scale, as indicated by excavated eighth- and ninth-century sites such as North Elmham, Norfolk, and Cheddar, Somerset. At a lower level the village of Catholme with its timber houses continued to flourish through the period into the tenth century, but elsewhere there is evidence of old villages being abandoned and new ones founded.

The trading emporia such as Ipswich and Southampton continued also to flourish during the earlier part of the period, but Southampton experienced a decline during the ninth century. On the other hand, the ninth century saw the foundation of a series of planned towns and the beginning of a process of urbanisation that developed continuously thereafter to arrive at the major cities of the later middle ages. This foundation of new towns is a phenomenon which has been attributed especially to the period of Kings Alfred and Edward, but it has also been asked whether the process does not begin earlier in the ninth century in some cases. One of the finest surviving examples of these planned towns is at Wareham, Dorset, where the grid of streets and the enclosing earthen defences (originally surmounted by a stone wall) are readily appreciated. The most impressive work of defence from the period, however, is earlier than the assumed date of these towns: the great dyke built by King Offa along his western border facing the Welsh.

Mention has been deferred so far of the Vikings, whose aggressive raids and warfare during the ninth century, culminating in the settlement of northern and eastern England, have often been supposed to have wrought a great destruction of churches and to have blighted any significant new building activity. This popular picture may have some relevance to northern and eastern England; but as far as southern and south-western England are concerned there can be little doubt that there was an essential continuity in architectural traditions through the ninth century, even though economic difficulties may have limited lavish displays of patronage.

Ottonian culture and monastic reform (c.925–1050)

The creation of the unified Kingdom of England in the first half of the tenth century was a process that once again found a Continental parallel in the consolidation of the eastern part of the former Carolingian Empire with the establishment of a new dynasty, culminating in the coronation of Otto the Great as emperor in 963. The Ottonians aimed at a restoration of the Carolingian imperial ideal and this included the field of architecture. Carolingian architectural forms were re-affirmed and developed, while attempts to rival Classical Antiquity led to the construction of some of the largest and most articulate buildings erected in Europe since the fourth century. An important consideration for this period again, therefore, is whether Anglo-Saxon architecture showed an awareness of Continental developments; but this is something that cannot be studied in isolation from the single most important factor affecting the contemporary Church (which was the biggest patron of building in stone): the monastic reform movement.

Little is known of the buildings associated with the main centres of the monastic reform on the Continent. However, in England the reform was under royal patronage and two of the major buildings connected with it suggest a deliberate emulation of Continental buildings with royal rather than monastic connotations. At Abingdon Abbey, Oxfordshire, King Eadred (c.955) personally planned the church which later descriptions seem to indicate was a rotunda in imitation of the earlier chapel in the imperial palace at Aachen. At Winchester Cathedral, Hampshire, adjacent to the royal palace, the remodelling of the west end of the church following 971 created an elaborate tower-like structure modelled closely on 'west-works' of late ninth and tenth-century date in Germany.

Outside the most immediate royal ambit, however, there is less obvious evidence of copying prestigious Continental fashions. The scale of building seems to have been more modest, and more indebted to earlier English traditions: as was perhaps suited to a strict and ascetic monastic ethos. At two of the sites connected with Archbishop Dunstan, Glastonbury Abbey and St Augustine's Abbey at Canterbury, the reform seems to have brought only modest extensions to already existing churches, and the same is the case with Bishop Aethelwold's Peterborough Abbey and Ely Abbey, Cambridgeshire. On the other hand, descriptions of Ely make it clear that the building was endowed with a great wealth of treasures in gold and silver, jewels and enamels, ivory and precious silks; and these beautiful materials may have been seen to the best effect in a modest interior space.

Of standing buildings associated with the monastic reform there are few, but the tower of Barton-upon-Humber church, South Humberside★, may have been built by Aethelwold; while the central tower of Cholsey church, Oxfordshire, may belong to Archbishop Oswald's abbey founded c.985–992. A central tower was indeed a feature of Oswald's church at Ramsey Abbey, Cambridgeshire, built 986–991, of which a contemporary description survives: it was

constructed in the fashion of a cross; with a chapel on the east, on the south and on the north; with a tower in the middle which, having been raised up, was to be supported by the chapels abutting it; finally the nave of the church was annexed to the tower on the west.

(Anon., *Life of Oswald*)

A second tower is known to have stood at the west end, while under the high altar was a crypt. The description of Ramsey suggests a comparison with such surviving churches as Dover, Kent★; Breamore, Hampshire; Wootton Wawen, Warwickshire.

The second period of Scandinavian raids on England, culminating in its conquest by King Cnut, may have inhibited the development within the early decades of the eleventh century of a more monumental architecture to compare with the latest achievements in France and Germany. The indications are in fact that traditions established in the tenth century continued into the eleventh with little variation except perhaps in ornamental detail. The search for sophisticated effects in detail is well illustrated by the tower arch of St Benet's church, Cambridge: but at the same time the craftsman's ability in handling the stone lags somewhat behind. Of the royal works associated with Cnut we have little firm evidence; but his new church of 1032 at St Edmund's Abbey, Suffolk, seems to have been a rotunda of the same type as Abingdon. Perhaps from Cnut's church came a series of glazed polychrome tiles with designs in relief, similar to examples from Winchester and other sites, which suggest a search after rich and colourful effects. In a similar vein may be seen the surviving examples of monumental sculpture on walls, as at Romsey Abbey, Hampshire; and of wall-painting, as at Nether Wallop church, Hampshire.

For secular buildings of the period the dominant material seems still to have been timber. This was true of the tenth-century developments at the royal palace of Cheddar (though the chapel was of stone), at the bishop's palace of North Elmham (where the adjacent cathedral was probably also of timber), and at the thane's hall of Goltho, Lincolnshire. But at the thane's hall at Sulgrave, Northamptonshire, the buildings were of mixed timber and stone construction; and it is difficult to believe that major secular buildings in urban centres such as Winchester were not in some cases of stone construction by now. The urban centres indeed were beginning to flourish in the tenth century and on into the eleventh, as has been shown by excavations on many sites. In the case of York some of the simple timber houses of the mid-tenth century have been partly preserved below ground and are now displayed: these are among the earliest dated substantial remains of timber buildings in England. The church of Greensted, Essex*, however, while it is undated, must stand for a much wider tradition of more sophisticated timber buildings which have disappeared except for their archaeological traces.

Romanesque architecture and the Norman Conquest (c.1050–1100)

On the Continent the eleventh century, and especially the decades from c.1020 onwards, saw the emergence in architecture of a new style, or group of regional styles, called Romanesque. The Romanesque built upon what had already been achieved in the previous half century in terms of an increased scale of construction and a clarity of relationship between the different parts within a building. But it went beyond these in at least three important respects. First, it devised a new system of articulating buildings in repeating units; secondly, it developed a new fashion in decorating arches and other architectural members with mouldings and columns that broke up visually the hard rectangular forms of the basic construction; thirdly, it attained a high degree of technological competence in handling masonry in a systematic way to exploit its inherent qualities as a building material. These changes amounted in fact to a revolution, which created a fundamentally new architecture that broke with the past (in contrast with, say, the transition from Carolingian to Ottonian architecture where there was a continuity in aims). The problem of when and how this new style arrived in England must be seen as the dominant issue in English architecture of the eleventh century.

It has already been indicated that there is no evidence of Romanesque developments in England in the early decades of the eleventh century, and it is to the middle years of the century that we must look for the first signs of change. Even then, however, the major remodelling of St Augustine's Abbey, Canterbury, with a rotunda to link together the earlier churches was essentially pre-Romanesque. At Stow church, Lincolnshire*, some decorative elements appeared that might be termed at least proto-Romanesque. But it was in the great rebuilding of Westminster Abbey, London, undertaken by King Edward the Confessor from c.1050 onwards that the new style definitively arrived. The design of this, one of the largest churches in mid-eleventh century Europe, was very closely linked to contemporary architecture in Normandy and the surviving nave of Jumièges Abbey probably gives a good idea of what Westminster looked like. The only part of the Abbey to survive today is the dormitory undercroft, which probably dates to c.1070. In theory the opening of the workshop at Westminster could have signalled the start of a wider diffusion of Romanesque architecture in England in the decade before the Conquest, but there is no concrete evidence that this happened in practice. A number of lesser churches which combine Anglo-Saxon and Romanesque features have sometimes been claimed as pre-Conquest in date, but in many cases it is more likely that they are later. One fine building that belongs in this uncertain category is Great Paxton church, Cambridgeshire*.

The Norman Conquest must be recorded here first in terms of its military architecture, which reflects most closely the substantive nature of the event. The Normans brought with them the private feudal castle which as an institution was essentially a new phenomenon; but the architectural expression of this took several forms. One of the most widespread of castle types was constructed entirely of earth and timber and comprised a lofty mound ('motte'), with a defensive work on top, and an enclosed area ('bailey') attached to it. Early examples are at Carisbrooke Castle, Isle of Wight; York; Hen Domen, Powys. Elsewhere the bailey might have a strongly defended gatehouse and sometimes might be enclosed by a stone curtain wall: for example at Richmond, North Yorkshire; Exeter, Devon; Lincoln; Bramber, Sussex. Within the bailey some castles had not a motte but a massive stone tower, known as a donjon, as at Chepstow, Gwent. The Tower of London (see chapter 7) is an elaborate version of such a donjon, providing palatial accommodation for the king – and most castles must in fact have provided domestic accommodation within their enclosure. A substantial chapel was often the accompaniment of a castle, such as those at Bramber and Durham which survive. All domestic accommodation of the new ruling class, however, was not attached to castles, and the great hall built in the Palace of Westminster by William Rufus was one of the most lavishly scaled domestic buildings ever constructed.

It was more in the field of ecclesiastical than domestic architecture that the greatest achievements were attained in the post-Conquest period. Indeed, the last three decades of the eleventh century in England were one of the most creative and fertile episodes in the whole history of European church building and it is impossible to do here more than sketch the barest outline (the period from c.1090 onwards is considered in more detail in Volume II). In the early 1070s two major new churches were started in Canterbury: the Cathedral and St Augustine's Abbey. These participated in the most recent developments of High Romanesque architecture in Normandy, and came to constitute the most important model for the creation of an indigeneous Anglo-Norman Romanesque style. They were not the only buildings to import Continental ideas, but other borrowings elsewhere were more eclectic and less influential.

The transplanting of the new style to England did not result in the subsequent mechanical copying of an atrophied formula. Quite the contrary was true in practice: the transplant took quick root and every new building that derived from it was a living growth, developing afresh the ideas inherent in the original. Thus it was that there quickly grew up regional styles in England: related to one another as sisters in the later '70s and early '80s, they had become cousins by the later '80s and '90s. By the end of the century such regional groupings were clearly established in London and the South-East, in Hampshire, in the West and South-West Midlands, in Lincolnshire, in Yorkshire, and in Northumbria.

The west front of Lincoln Cathedral.

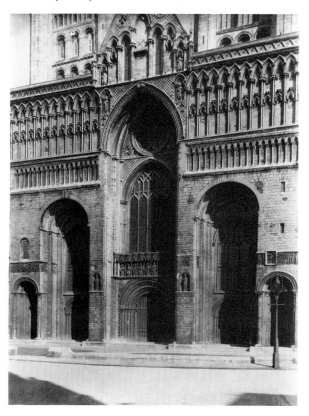

It must have been the construction of such new churches as these that led one contemporary to turn his back without regret on the old Anglo-Saxon churches that were being demolished all around, and to express delight without reserve in new buildings which were, according to his judgement 'glorious, magnificent, most lofty, most spacious, filled with light and most beautiful'. Yet if these lofty buildings and their successors have contributed most to the popular concept of medieval architecture, it is worth remembering that for nearly half a millenium previously quite different aesthetic standards were the common currency.

Some major surviving monuments

Bradwell-on-Sea, St Peter's Church, Essex

The former Roman shore fort of *Othona*, near the confluence of the River Blackwater with the North Sea, was the property of the East Saxon king Sigberht in the mid-seventh century. The king had been baptised as a Christian in Northumbria, and from there he brought the monk Cedd as a bishop to preach to his people. Sigberht gave Cedd *Othona* (later Bradwell) for founding a monastery, and by the time of the bishop's death in 664 there was a flourishing community.

The surviving church of St Peter (preserved in later years as a barn and restored only in modern times) dates from Cedd's lifetime or shortly

St Peter's Church, Bradwell-on-Sea, Essex (late seventh century); preserved as a barn, and restored only in modern times.

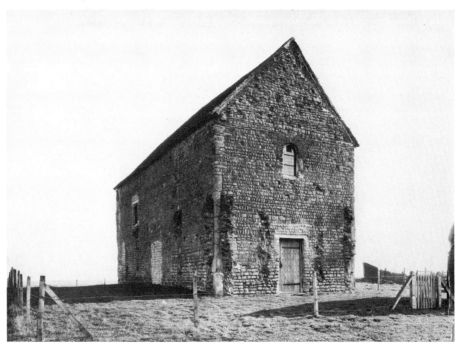

thereafter, yet its architectural inspiration comes not from Northumbria but from Kent – and it is the best surviving example of the early churches of Canterbury and south-east England. The church was set curiously within the west gate of the old fort, and was built of re-used Roman materials: stone and tile. What remains today is the rectangular nave of the church; but originally this was adjoined by an eastern apse, by north and south side chapels, and by a west porch. The surviving windows are rectangular, except for the arched one in the west gable; while in the east wall are indications of the former double chancel arch (comparable to the triple arch formerly existing at Reculver, Kent.

The moving simplicity of the architecture speaks of the missionary circumstances under which the church was built, but also of the limited economic resources of contemporary Anglo-Saxon society. Likewise the materials and design, while indicating a nostalgic look towards the Roman tradition still surviving in an attenuated form on the Continent, yet show that the skills were not available for a real revival of Roman technology.

Monkwearmouth and Jarrow, the Monastery of St Peter and St Paul, Tyne and Wear

Around 673 the Northumbrian nobleman become monk, Benedict Biscop, who had previously visited Rome to observe for himself the religious life there, was given by King Ecgfrith an estate at Monkwearmouth to found a monastery (St Peter's), and nearly ten years later was given a second estate at Jarrow to form another house (St Paul's) of the same monastery. The latter is particularly famous as the home of the Venerable Bede, but both sites retain important examples of their early buildings.

At Jarrow stands a small church (the chancel of the present building, but originally it was detached) built of coursed sandstone blocks and with small round-headed windows in the south wall. To the west of this was the larger main church, dedicated in 685: it had a long nave flanked by side chapels, and a western porch. To the south of the churches were the free-standing domestic buildings of the monastery. At Monkwearmouth the arrangement of churches may have been similar, but only the west of the main church (begun c.675), and the two-storied west porch (added before 716) remain. The latter is remarkable for its sculptured detail, still faintly surviving, and for its miniature ornamental columns or balusters.

The church at Monkwearmouth was constructed by masons and glaziers from Gaul, and the latter were presumably responsible for the coloured glass windows of which fragments have been recovered especially from Jarrow. Both churches were also decorated with icons brought from Rome, and the visual effect of the buildings must have gone a long way towards emulating contemporary churches of the Continent.

To complement this picture of late seventh century Northumbrian architecture it is necessary to look also at the crypts of Ripon Minster and Hexham Abbey, and the smaller but marvellously preserved church of Escomb. Together this group of buildings, so redolent of the age of Bede, is one of the most evocative in England.

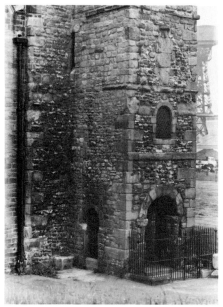

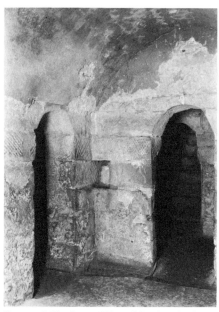

Porch of the monastery church of St Peter and St Paul, Monkwearmouth, Sunderland (c.700).

Crypt of Hexham Abbey, Northumberland (late seventh century).

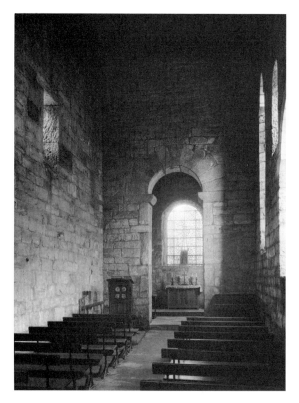

The church of St John Escomb, Durham (late seventh century).

Brixworth, All Saint's Church, Northamptonshire

Brixworth is perhaps the single most impressive Anglo-Saxon church in England, but virtually nothing is known of its historical context. Later tradition said that there was a monastery founded here from Peterborough in the late seventh century, and this may be so. But the surviving church is more likely of eighth- or ninth-century date – and is possibly to be associated with the patronage of the palace at nearby Northampton, since it must clearly have been commissioned at the highest social level.

The church, as originally designed, comprised a spacious rectangular nave, which was flanked by a series of side chapels to which access was gained by great archways. A cross wall with openings in it divided the nave proper from a square choir, while a further arch opened to an apse beyond. The apse was surrounded below ground level by a semi-circular passageway forming a ring crypt, of Carolingian type. At the west end of the nave was a two-storied porch and flanking chambers. At some later date in the Anglo-Saxon period a semi-circular stair turret was added to the west porch and the main apse was rebuilt; the nave side chapels may have been demolished at this time.

For all its elaboration in form, the church was not built with a particularly sophisticated technology. A large part of the building materials, comprising stone and tile, seems to have been brought from a demolished Roman building in the Leicester area. Roman also is the inspiration for building the nave arcades with two rings of tiles forming the heads.

Within its technological limitations Brixworth nonetheless attains a certain grandeur which cannot but move the visitor who recalls its early date. And this appreciation should help counterbalance the impression of modest scale conveyed by many of the other Anglo-Saxon churches which chance alone has selected for survival.

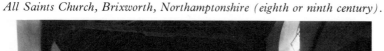

All Saints Church, Brixworth, Northamptonshire (eighth or ninth century).

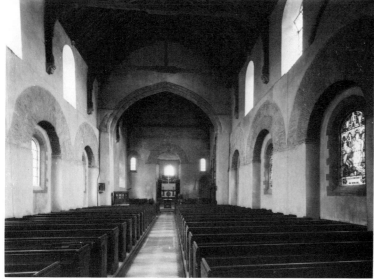

Deerhurst, St Mary's Church, Gloucestershire

Deerhurst is one of the most complex and controversial of the important Anglo-Saxon churches that have come down to us. Its foundation date is unknown, but a religious community was in existence by 804. During the period of the tenth-century Reform there was an observant monastery here; but this did not continue into the eleventh century, when Deerhurst was under the control of the powerful Earl Odda.

Church of St Mary, Deerhurst, Gloucestershire (late ninth and early tenth centuries).

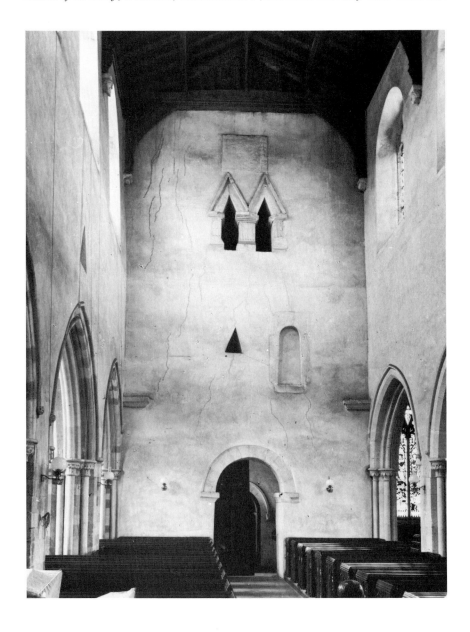

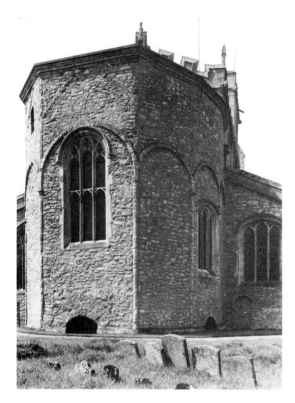

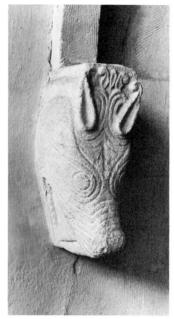

Stone horse's head from the church of St Mary, Deerhurst, Gloucestershire (late ninth and early tenth centuries).

All Saints Church, Wing, Buckinghamshire.

The present Anglo-Saxon church sits on the foundations of an earlier church. The earlier building began life with a plain rectangular nave and a west porch (perhaps rather like Monkwearmouth), to which were added subsequently a series of side chapels and an eastern apse. The later history of the church saw a phased rebuilding of the superstructure until it attained the following form: a lofty unaisled nave with the east bay forming a choir; a polygonal apse; two-storied chapels flanking the choir, with lower chapels to their east; and a three-storied west porch. The decorative detail of this rebuilt church was remarkable. The apse (now ruined, but compare that surviving at Wing, Buckinghamshire) was ornamented with a network of attenuated strips of stone devolved from the classical pilaster. The arches and doorway were enlivened with sculptured animal heads, which bear close comparison with ninth-century metalwork, such as the Alfred Jewel (see p. 127). One of the windows has classicising fluted piers carrying double triangular 'arches'. In the west porch and on the apse are set sculptures of the Virgin Mary and of an Angel. The font is the finest Anglo-Saxon example to survive.

Deerhurst church is thus especially worth visiting for its ensemble of architectural details of, broadly speaking, the latter part of the ninth century and the early tenth. At the same time, the nearby chapel built by Earl Odda in 1053–1056, to commemorate his dead brother, is one of the most complete small buildings securely dated to the mid-eleventh century.

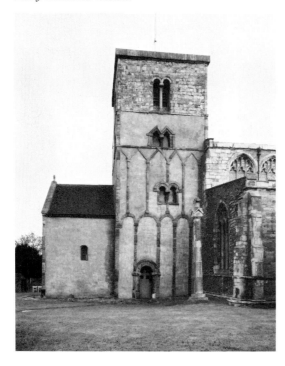

St Peter's Church, Barton-upon Humber (late tenth century).

Barton-upon-Humber, St Peter's Church, South Humberside

Bishop Aethelwold, one of the three great reformers of the tenth century, was a devoted restorer of ancient monasteries, and this may have been the reason for his acquiring in 971 the estate of Barrow-on-Humber (of which Barton formed part), since a monastery had once existed there, founded in the seventh century by Bishop Ceadda. No monastery was actually refounded at Barrow by Aethelwold, but he may have built the church at Barton as a private chapel comparable to that which he erected at Thorney Abbey – 'in the form of a tower, divided into chambers by most delicate little screens, with two floor levels, dedicated with three very small altars' (Anon., *Translation of the Saints in Thorney*).

The church at Barton seems to be dated archaeologically to the late tenth century. The main part of the building comprised a central tower, the only adjuncts of which were chapels attached to the east and west sides. The chapels had two floor levels, the upper of which was approached from a gallery in the tower, while the tower rose one stage clear of the chapels. The exterior of the tower is decorated with two orders of pilaster strips which carry semicircular and triangular arcading, and this continues the (arguably) earlier tradition of such decoration seen at Wing and Deerhurst. Barton allows the pilaster work to be seen as originally intended, with the rubble walling behind rendered smooth and only the carefully cut stonework of the pilasters exposed. Contemporary examples of pilaster work are to be seen on the Continent in the late tenth and eleventh centuries, and it may be that both these and the English examples have a common origin in the Carolingian period.

Dover, Church of St Mary in the Castle, Kent

Dover has often been regarded as providing the classic example of a Late Anglo-Saxon major church, although the building is not in fact closely dated, nor are the historical circumstances surrounding its foundation clear. A monastery had been founded at Dover, probably within the former Roman fort beside the harbour, in the late seventh century, and this community continued into the mid-ninth century. By the eleventh century Dover reappears as one of the main secular minster churches in Kent; and perhaps the clergy were then based, for security against Viking raids, at St Mary's on the eastern heights above the town (returning to the lower town around the time of the Norman Conquest).

The position of the church was related to the existing Roman lighthouse, which was incorporated into the new building as an octagonal west tower. Adjacent to this tower was constructed an unaisled nave leading eastward to a second tower, centrally placed in the building and presumably serving as the choir. East of the central tower was the rectangular chancel, and flanking it were two-storied side chapels. The church was built mainly of flint and re-used Roman tile, but delicately turned stone balusters (lost in the last war) must have been made specially for the building – probably in the same workshop as examples at Canterbury.

Churches with unaisled naves and with low side chapels (ultimately a late Roman form) were fashionable for some major Ottonian buildings; but the central tower at Dover represents a characteristic English development. Thus, set at the gateway to England, the noble silhouette of St Mary's stands for the distinctiveness of Late Anglo-Saxon architecture within a more general Continental tradition.

Church of St Mary, Dover, Kent; built mainly of flint and re-used Roman tile (eighth or ninth century).

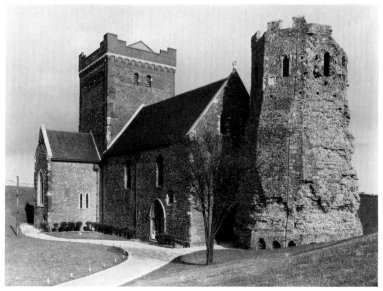

Bradford-on-Avon, Chapel of St Laurence, Wiltshire

One of the most famous of all Anglo-Saxon buildings is the chapel of St Laurence at Bradford-on-Avon, but its date has been a subject of great controversy. Around 700 a monastery was founded here by Abbot Aldhelm, but this community seems to have lapsed by the tenth century when Bradford was owned by the king. Then in 1001 the church was given to the nuns of Shaftesbury as a place of refuge from the Vikings, with a stipulation that they should found a small community there. William of Malmesbury, the first English architectural historian, wrote that in his day (c.1125) there was a small church that was said to have been built by Aldhelm in honour of St Laurence, and this is probably the surviving chapel – though this reference does not constitute dating evidence for the construction.

The chapel was not the main church of the complex, but a comparatively small building. It has a lofty nave although built on a restricted plan, and from this space low arches lead into the chancel and north and south side chapels. The building is of fine quality ashlar masonry, which externally is executed with a confident pattern of blank arcading. A sculptured Angel in flight perhaps formed part of a Crucifixion scene over the chancel arch, and if this were contemporary with the building would indicate a late tenth- or early eleventh-century date.

The extraordinary contrast between the height of the main chapel and the low archways into the ancillary spaces makes this a rather mannered building; while the polished standard of the execution suggests that the aesthetic effects were carefully thought out and not accidental. The building represents the top social levels of patronage and may point to what has been lost in more major buildings that were the work of the same craftsmen for the court and leading churchmen.

Greensted juxta Ongar, St Andrew's Church, Essex

In the late medieval period it was apparently believed that this chapel memorialised the place where the relics of St Edmund had rested when they were brought from Suffolk to London in the early eleventh century to avoid Viking raids. This, however, while it may explain the survival of the chapel, constitutes no firm evidence for dating it – whether earlier or later than the incident. Nonetheless the building is of the greatest importance as a sole survivor of what was once the most widespread of all Anglo-Saxon traditions of church construction: timber.

The church seems to have gone through two phases of construction, as indicated by excavations in the chancel. In the first phase it was built with closely spaced posts set directly into the ground: in the second a horizontal sole plate carried the vertical posts. The surviving posts of the nave are half tree-trunks, round towards the exterior and flat inside; and each post is grooved so that it can be joined to its neighbour by a separate tongue. At their tops the posts were tenoned into a wall plate, but the original plate and roof structure do not survive – there was perhaps a double plate with the tie beams trapped between.

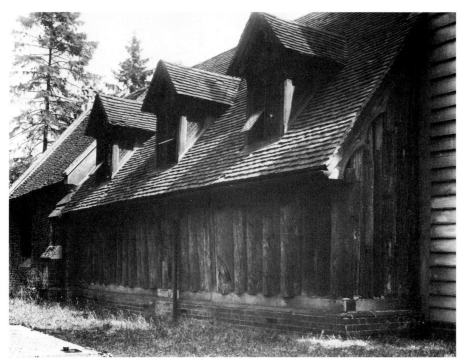

St Andrew's Church, Greensted juxta Ongar, Essex: the only surviving timber Saxon church (date uncertain).

Greensted church today has a warm and natural simplicity that is deeply appealing. But it should not be overlooked that the more sophisticated timber buildings, no longer surviving, must have been adorned with intricate carvings and paintings that would have given a much richer appearance.

Stow, St Mary's Church, Lincolnshire

How early the Minster of Stow was first founded is not known, but by the time of King Cnut it was in the hands of the bishop with pastoral responsibility for the region. A rebuilding of the church was perhaps undertaken by Earl Leofric and his wife Godgifu ('Lady Godiva') in the late 1040s, and c.1053–1055 they founded there a community of canons. This community, however, did not flourish past the Norman Conquest, and c.1091 the first bishop of Lincoln, Remi, made an abortive attempt to found a Benedictine abbey in the neglected church.

The church as it stood just before the Conquest comprised a massive central tower adjoined by four arms of equal height in a cruciform arrangement: in the angles between the main arms may have been subsidiary chapels. Of this building survive only the lower parts of the transept arms and the central tower, but the scale of these is particularly impressive. The piers of the four great arches opening from the central tower to the four arms seem likely to be of mid-eleventh-century date and are of interest on account of their decoration with pilasters and half-columns on their faces. This

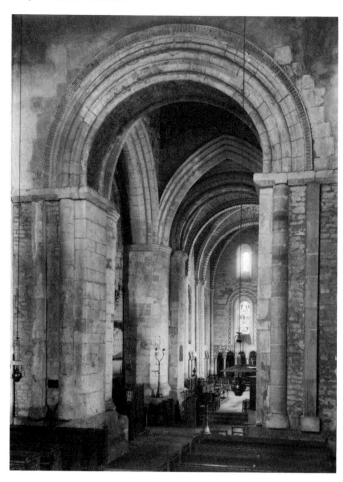

The Romanesque arches in St Mary's Church, Stow, Lincolnshire (c.1090).

decoration may relate to earlier stripwork in its positioning, but its bold re-interpretation here is parallel to Romanesque developments on the Continent. In contrast the actual arches above the piers show the direct influence of mature Romanesque design in their elaborate mouldings and must be part of the work of c.1091 for Bishop Remi. What is of interest, however, is that the later arches are more idiosyncratic than orthodox in their handling, and suggest English masons trying to copy and elaborate upon the new Norman forms.

Great Paxton, Holy Trinity Church, Cambridgeshire

Great Paxton was an important minster church probably rebuilt in the middle or latter part of the eleventh century. During this period the manor of Great Paxton, and presumably the patronage of the church with it, belonged to a succession of earls and countesses of Huntingdon who were related to all the key dynastic figures of the age: Tostig, brother of King Harold; Waltheof, cousin of Edgar the last male heir of the Anglo-Saxon royal line; Waltheof's wife Judith, niece of William the Conqueror; their daughter Mathilda, later the wife of her cousin David King of Scots. These historical connections help place in context the elaborate design of the church; but they do not help date it precisely – whether immediately before or immediately after the Conquest.

The original building was cruciform in plan, with a central crossing, an aisled nave, and transepts wider and lower than the nave. Of this, part of the nave and crossing survive and show an amazing inventiveness of detail, especially in the piers. The nave piers are composed of four grouped colonnettes, set diagonally; while the crossing piers show a rippling surface of multiple columnar shafts: the arches carried by them, however, are of plain rectangular section. The building is thoroughly Romanesque, but looks to the region of the Lower Rhine and Meuse for its inspiration, and not to Normandy. All the details are so different from the main series of post-Conquest Anglo-Norman buildings that a different context must be sought. A romantic view might suggest the involvement of Waltheof, the last great Anglo-Saxon nobleman, who was executed in 1076 – and regarded by many as a martyr. Be that as it may, Great Paxton is visually one of the most exciting Early Romanesque buildings in England.

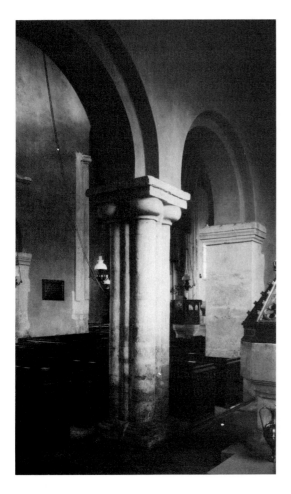

Holy Trinity Church, Great Paxton, Cambridgeshire (middle or late eleventh century).

Worcester Cathedral

Worcester Cathedral is something of an exception in that the great
Romanesque rebuilding that was undertaken in the years after the Conquest
was not the expression of a new and powerful Norman prelate taking over the
see: it was built by a saintly English bishop, Wulfstan, who survived the
Conquest in office and who wept at the necessity of destroying the old Anglo-
Saxon cathedral to make way for the new building. Work began in 1084 and
by 1089 enough of the church was completed for it to be brought into use.

By and large the design of Romanesque Worcester looked to the workshops
at Canterbury for inspiration, but it did not copy anything without modifying
it. Of the eleventh-century building there are two main survivals: one is an
archway in the south transept with beautifully sculptured capitals, the
designs of which make use of motifs found in contemporary Canterbury
manuscript paintings – motifs which, however, have an Anglo-Saxon origin.
The other and more important part of the building is the marvellous crypt
which underlay the sanctuary of the church. The crypt comprised an apsidal
central chamber and an ambulatory which ran around it to give access to a
series of radiating chapels. The crypt is covered by a vault carried on a forest
of columns, which give picturesque and ever-changing vistas as you walk
through the space. Here is an intriguing complexity that must have delighted
the Anglo-Saxon Wulfstan, but which a Norman patron might have criticised
as impractical for use.

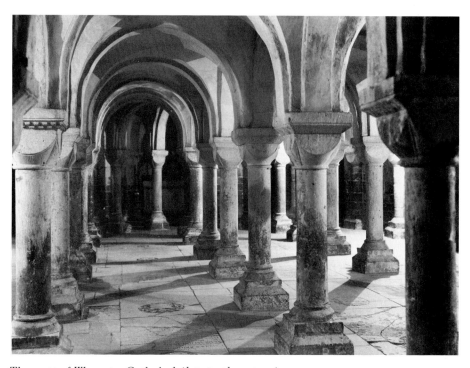

The crypt of Worcester Cathedral (late tenth century).

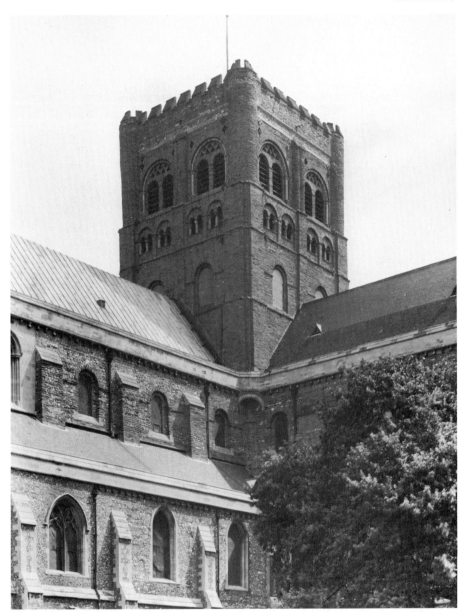

The tower of St Albans Abbey, Hertfordshire (c.1080).

St Albans Abbey, Hertfordshire

Perhaps the most complete surviving example of the church architecture of
the reign of the Conqueror is St Albans Abbey, raised up over the shrine of
the first Christian martyr in Britain outside the former Roman city of
Verulamium. The place was a focus of veneration more or less continuously
from Roman times, and the Abbey had been founded already in the Anglo-
Saxon period. A new phase in its history began, however, with the
appointment as abbot in 1077 of Paul of Caen, a relative of Archbishop

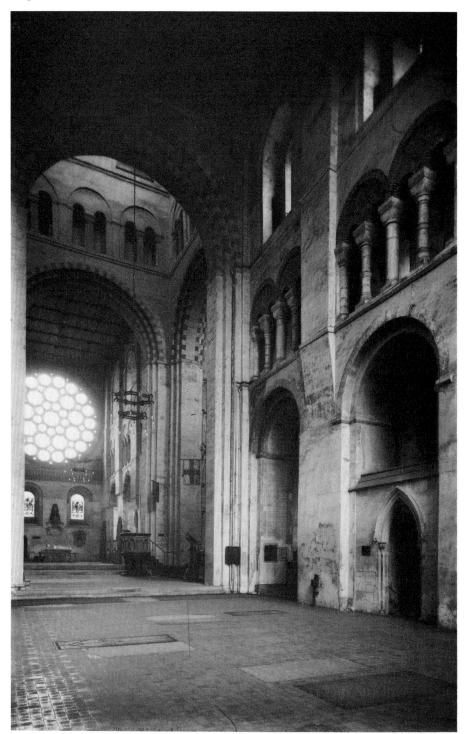

St Albans Abbey, Hertfordshire.

Lanfranc. Helped by Lanfranc, Paul energetically set about the building of a new church and monastic buildings on a grandiose scale. Within eleven years much was complete, though the finishing touches took somewhat longer: the speed of building is partly to be explained by the ready availability of materials from the Roman city. The designer was probably the mason Master Robert.

In contrast to the typical Anglo-Saxon monastery with its picturesque aggregation of churches, chapels and other buildings, everything at St Albans was planned as systematically as many a modern building complex. Dominating all was a great church built on a cruciform plan. The magnificent central tower surmounted the crossing where the monks' choir stood: east of this was the main sanctuary and a great chapel for St Alban's shrine; west of it was a hugely extended nave which was used as a processional space. The long spaces were designed in a series of repeating bays, each of three stories; and every part of the building was accessible through a network of passageways in the walls. There was little concession to architectural ornament, but the effect must have been softened somewhat by painted decoration over the rendered brickwork.

Something had been lost of humanity and sympathy in this new architecture: on the other hand, what had been gained was the opportunity for experimenting with architectural effects on a monumental scale.

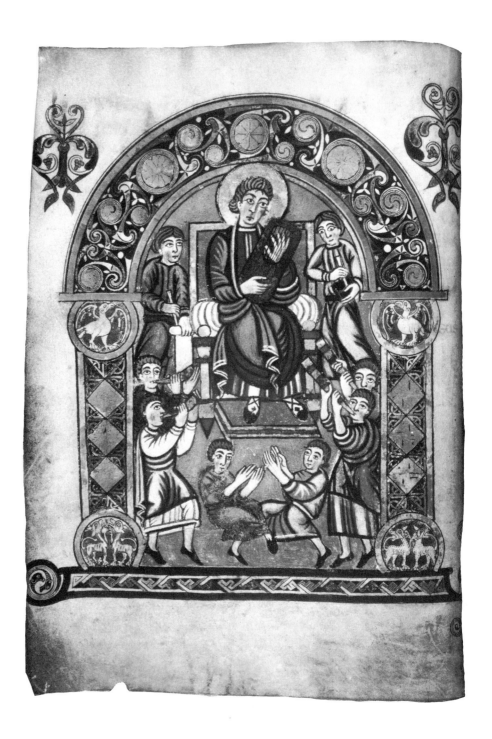

King David, singing psalms and playing the harp in the company of his scribes, musicians and dancers, within an ornamental arcade (second quarter of the eighth century), from the Vespasian Psalter.

6 Music

CHRISTOPHER PAGE

Introduction

Music, for the Anglo-Saxons, possessed a power which can be sensed by any modern reader of Old English verse. A stark contrast between indoors and outdoors colours that poetry, and to be inside is to share 'joy of the lyre' in some aristocratic hall. Outside the hall there are only battles and 'paths of exile'; often the landscape has no sky but only cruel weather, and memories of former joys, graced by music, taunt the man whose vision is darkened by death or imminent wars:[1]

> many a spear cold with the chill of morning shall be grasped in the fist and raised up in the hand; nor shall the music of the lyre awaken the fighting men; instead, the black raven, greedy for men ordained to die, will croak a good deal, telling the eagle how he had fared in his feasting . . .

This is the *Beowulf* poet, a man whose engagement with music is always humane and thoughtful. The string-players and singers he knew have left no musical traces behind them, but literary sources such as *Beowulf* help to dispel the romantic image of Anglo-Saxon England as a realm of stockades and farmsteads swathed in rural silence with only sea and wind to break the calm. There were dance-poems sung by women; convivial songs performed to the lyre; lays of the ancient heroes of the North (such as Ingeld); chants composed to celebrate the genealogies of great men such as Aethelbert of East Anglia; battle-lays, victory odes, charms and incantations.

Vernacular and Latin song

As it has come down to us, Old English poetry is mostly a sombre and learned affair. Self-consciously serious and ornate, it was designed to be declaimed or read privately, both in secular-aristocratic and monastic circumstances. Yet there may be traces of lost songs embedded within this corpus of lettered verse. Some metrical charms probably contain words that had been chanted in the countryside time out of mind, and several poems in the *Anglo-Saxon Chronicle* may be some guide to the kind of illiterate and perhaps 'improvised' poetry that must have gathered around great events like the battle of Brunanburh (937). There is even a strain of love song in *Wulf and Eadwacer*, a highly enigmatic poem in which (as so often in folk narrative verse) a woman speaks

. . . A difference exists between us.
Wulf is on an island; I am on another. That island is secure, surrounded by fen. There are deadly cruel men on the island; they want to destroy him if he comes under subjugation.
A difference exists between us.

The remains of Latin song are relatively abundant since the clerics of late Anglo-Saxon England were prepared to use musical notation (primarily a liturgical tool) to record the non-liturgical songs that impressed them. Indeed the songs they chose to record are generally more impressive than entertaining: settings of the metres from Boethius's *Consolation of Philosophy*; hymns by Prudentius and a set of verses on stars, for example. Many of these poems evoke a schoolroom atmosphere, and the same might be said for the one overtly secular piece, *O admirabile Veneris ydolum*, a love song addressed to a boy.

Boethius's Consolation of Philosophy *set to music; a folio from a collection of Latin lyrics, copied in Canterbury from the German original (mid eleventh century).*

Opposite is an example of Latin song from Anglo-Saxon England, a folio
from the celebrated 'Cambridge Songs' (a collection of Latin lyrics copied at
St Augustine's, Canterbury, towards the middle of the eleventh century, after
an original compiled in Germany, arguably at Cologne). It bears portions of
metres from Boethius's *Consolation of Philosophy*, but the melodies cannot be
deciphered since the notation indicates the direction of the melodic steps
without measuring them exactly (most Latin songs in pre-twelfth century
sources are notated in this way). It is clear, however, that some of the tunes
are florid ones, and these are surely art songs to be performed by trained
clerical singers. The texts are highly serious and learned in character – not
especially 'singable', perhaps, to modern taste:

> For twice five years did Agamemnon war,
> The ruthless son of Atreus, till at Troy
> He vengeance took for wedlock set at naught.
> The same who when he wished the Grecian fleet
> To sail, with blood did purchase favouring winds,
> Put off the father, and turned dismal priest
> To maculate a wretched daughter's throat.

These Latin songs represent an international tradition of Latin lyric, not a
distinctively Anglo-Saxon taste or musical tradition. Settings of Boethian
metres appear in many Continental manuscripts, for example, while the
melody of *O admirabile Veneris ydolum* is known from two continental sources
(and may be from Verona.)

String-playing

For signs of a distinctively English (or perhaps we should say a distinctively
'barbarian') tradition in music we must turn to one of the most famous
discoveries of twentieth century archaeology: the burial at Sutton Hoo near
Woodbridge in Suffolk. Fragments of a large lyre were among the finds
recovered from this site of the early seventh century, and pieces of similar
instruments have been lifted from seventh and eighth century graves in
Frankish territory. Taken together, these fragments suggest a coherent
tradition of lyre-design and manufacture in northern Europe that was shared
by the Anglo-Saxons. The lyres were cut from shallow planks with the yoke
(holding the tuning pegs), made separately, morticed into the arms; a
soundbox was gouged into the surface of the plank and then covered with a
soundboard fastened into place with nails. The yoke generally carried five or
six pegs tuned with a key, and to judge by the condition of the surviving pegs
the strings were of gut, or possibly of horsehair (see cover picture).

The Old English name for this kind of lyre was probably *hearpe*, and its
music – at least in the earlier centuries – is likely to have been far removed
from the Graeco-Roman musical tradition of the Mediterranean. Here, for
example, is Venantius Fortunatus (d. c.609) who had heard a *harpa* (probably
much the same instrument) amongst the Franks in Gaul:

It were as well for me to groan hoarsely as to declaim my verses amongst those who cannot distinguish the screech of a goose from the song of a swan, and where only the buzzing *harpa* strikes out outlandish songs . . .

This passage shows clearly enough that the music of Frankish *harpas* in the sixth century was not at all appealing to a man of Roman tastes, and there is nothing 'Roman' about the inclusion of a lyre amongst the regalia at Sutton Hoo. There had been a tradition of high-class and 'amateur' string-playing in Antiquity (grossly, and perhaps obliviously, parodied by Nero), but as an evocation of a Golden Age of rhapsodes it was sickly and by the time of Fortunatus or Boethius was probably dead. Indeed it is Boethius who reveals how the educated men of late-Antiquity regarded string-players with the disdain which Roman gentlemen traditionally reserved for artisans. 'Instrumentalists', he writes, 'are exiled from the true understanding of music and are of servile condition'. The situation was clearly different amongst the Anglo-Saxons; whatever associations the lyre may have possessed in the lower levels of society, amongst princes and rulers it presumably enjoyed a 'regal' mystique to warrant inclusion amongst the grave-goods at Sutton Hoo and elsewhere.

This mystique may account for the lenient view of secular music which is such a distinguishing feature of ecclesiastical life in Anglo-Saxon England. The Church fought against minstrels and entertainers with ceaseless energy throughout the Middle Ages, yet the Old English poets took a humane view of Man's need for joy. In *The Phoenix* we read that songs and instruments are 'joys which God made to gladden man in this sad world' – a view that seems to have been shared by Cuthbert, Abbot of Monkwearmouth and Jarrow, who sent this request to his fellow Englishman Lullus of Mainz in 764:

It would please me to have a string-player who can play upon that kind of stringed instrument which we call *rotta*, for I have an instrument but no player . . .

The Anglo-Saxons' esteem for string-playing shines through the biography of St Dunstan (d.988). Born of a noble family in the West country (his near kinsmen included courtiers of Aethelstan), Dunstan's early career followed a pattern found in countless lives of bishops from all over Dark Age Europe. Having been set to his schooling, Dunstan showed remarkable promise in both sacred learning and secular arts so that he eventually came to the notice of Kings Aethelstan and Edmund.

Dunstan seems to have been endowed with many artistic gifts; according to this earliest biographer, Author B (c.1000)

Between his studies of holy writings, so that he might be capable in all things he diligently cultivated the arts of writing, *cithara* playing and also painting; and if I may so put it, he shone as a judge of all useful things.

A further passage in Author B's *Life of Saint Dunstan* reveals a quiet, domestic scene of musical life in the bowers of Aethelstan's England – although it ends with a miracle. A certain noble lady named Aethelwynn asks Dunstan to design a stole for liturgical use and he sets off to her bowers 'taking with him, as was his custom, that instrument which we call *hearpe* in our native tongue so that, from time to time, he might lighten the spirits of those who attended to him'. Once there, Dunstan hangs the instrument upon a wall in the bedchamber and begins work upon the stole. The quiet is miraculously broken as the *hearpe* suddenly plays the antiphon *Gaudent in coelis animae sanctorum* of its own accord – a warning to Dunstan of coming trials.

At this date Dunstan's *hearpe* might have been the lyre discussed above, or it may have been the kind of pillar-harp which is often shown in English manuscripts from c.1000 on (see p. 246). This instrument, whose history in the West before the tenth century is obscure, comprised a soundbox, pillar and peg-arm, all of which were sometimes painted – to judge by the colours used in contemporary illustrations – and elaborated with zoomorphic details. Most Anglo-Saxon pillar-harps were fairly small instruments which rarely measured more than the distance from a standing player's shoulder to his thighs. The strings were generally of gut (and sometimes, perhaps, of horsehair); Continental literary sources suggest that there may have been as many as twenty-one strings producing a major-scale sequence (already hallowed by long usage in the 880s, according to the music-theorist Hucbald of St Amand). A good deal of Anglo-Saxon music, both vocal and instrumental, may have been built upon this scale, and there is evidence that lyres of the Sutton Hoo type were tuned in this way.

Professional musicians

Literary sources contain many references to professional entertainers and musicians, principally the gleoman and the scop. Without insisting upon a firm distinction between these two terms (which would be impossible to maintain) it may be said that the scop was primarily a maker and declaimer of poetry, and sometimes an instrumentalist also (although it is possible that the functions of lyrist and singer-declaimer were generally separated in Anglo-Saxon tradition as they appear to have been in Scandinavia). Unfortunately it is not known whether the scop generally sang, declaimed, or adopted some kind of mannered recitation bordering upon chanting.

The fortunate scop could expect to enjoy the supreme luxuries of secular life in Anglo-Saxon England: 'good standing . . . a loyal lord . . . and an entitlement to land'. So says the scop who speaks in the poem *Deor*, and a musician in favour could forge an intimate relationship with his lord. 'One man shall sit with a lyre at his lord's feet', says the poet of *The Fortunes of Men*; 'he shall receive gifts and smartly pluck the strings'. Life was often harder for the itinerant gleoman, however. As the poet of *Widsith* says:

So the people's gleomen go wandering fatedly through many lands, they declare their need and speak words of thanks. Always, whether south or north, they will meet someone discerning of songs and unniggardly of gifts . . . .

The ambivalent attitude expressed in these lines, where minstrels are described as 'fated' yet fortunate in their patrons, conveys the plight of the itinerant musician: often desparate, often optimistic. In a society founded upon gift-giving these gleomen must have known, better than any warrior in hall, the warm feelings that flooded the soul when a magnanimous man gave out gold.

The scop composed and performed commemorative poems, eulogies and other similar material, while keeping stories of ancient heroes in his repertoire. The stock-in-trade of the gleoman, however, overlapped with the jugglers, dancers and other kinds of entertainers who made a living by travelling from hall to hall. Some of these entertainers were probably dancers (there was an English manner of dancing, according to the *Gesta Herewardi*; see Volume 2 of *The Cambridge Guide to the Arts in Britain*) who would have required instrumental melodies, and perhaps songs, none of which has survived. Musicians also collaborated with jugglers of balls and knives.

In addition to such juggling-shows, gleomen were required to perform weightier material. A remarkable passage in a *Life of St Aethelbert* (preserved in a twelfth century manuscript but drawing upon sources of pre-Conquest origin) describes how Aethelbert is entertained as he sets out on a fatal journey to Offa's court. During the journey Aethelbert offers a bracelet to anyone who can perform 'royal songs' (*carmina regia*), and at once two men skilled in song began to sing (*psallere*); their songs were 'about the same king's royal ancestry' – presumably narratives or eulogies (perhaps both). It is likely that travelling gleomen were careful to keep such songs in their repertory to flatter the great men whose hospitality they sought.

Popular music

The popular music of Anglo-Saxon England has entirely vanished (although it may have left a few traces in the corpus of Old English verse, as we have seen). Bede's story of Caedmon (see p. 183–4) opens a window onto popular music-making which is all the more remarkable since nothing similar survives. It is certainly fascinating to learn that, in seventh century Northumbria, people who shared an ale-bench with the likes of Caedmon (a lay brother who worked on the monastic estates at Whitby) not only learned songs as a matter of custom, but could play a stringed instrument and perform when asked to do so. Bede does not reveal the nature of the songs which were sung at the gatherings Caedmon attended, but they may have included narratives of some kind and perhaps some fragments of heroic poetry – the context suggests that they were traditional ones of a kind known to all except Caedmon.

As for the dance, Continental evidence suggests that dancing was principally a female preserve throughout the Dark Ages and was often performed in churchyards (probably because the dances were sometimes associated with liturgical festivals, especially Saints' days). A passage from Author B's *Life of Saint Dunstan*, suggests that these dances were known in England c.1000. At one point in his narrative Author B describes how Dunstan entered a church and heard a chorus of heavenly maidens dancing in a ring and singing a hymn by Sedulius as they went 'in the manner of worldly virgins'; as a source about the poetic forms of Old English verse this is a most revealing passage (see my chapter on Music in Volume 2 of this series), but its importance here is that it seems to describe a dancing throng comprised entirely of women and centred upon a church.

Liturgical music

When St Augustine and his followers advanced upon the King of Kent in 597, 'chanting litanies and uttering prayers to the Lord' there was already a tradition of plainchant in England (perhaps an Irish one) associated with Celtic Christianity. However, Kent became the headquarters of chanting 'in the Roman manner' and the task of disseminating the repertory began. It was a tremendous labour. There was no system of musical notation available from which singers could retrieve a melody by themselves once they had been taught the rules of the system; the entire repertory of chants had to be learned by heart. Bede is full of praise for the men who had the authority and stamina to teach chanting; we hear of a certain James the Deacon in Northumbria, for example, who 'was very skilfull in church music' and who used to 'instruct many in singing, after the manner of Rome and the Kentish people', and many other teachers are named in the pages of Bede's *Ecclesiastical History*.

By the later-tenth and eleventh centuries musical notation was being systematically employed for liturgical purposes at major centres such as Exeter, Canterbury and Winchester. The music concerned is almost exclusively the monophonic plainchant of the liturgy, although Winchester in the decades around 1000 seems to have been a centre of polyphonic composition and performance. The celebrated Winchester troper contains many two-part settings in which the plainchant is accompanied by a newly-composed part. The notation of the troper has long been regarded as indecipherable but recent research suggests that all may not be lost. As they emerge from the transcriptions in Planchart's book,[2] for example, the pieces are essentially in note-against-note style (where each note of the chant sounds against one in the new part), although there are many passages where something more elaborate is attempted. The counterpoint is full of pungent dissonances, bursts of parallel fourths, momentary drone effects and a wealth of other devices. This would seem to be what the Anglo-Saxons regarded as *efenhleothrung*: a concord of voices. In many ways it is a shock and yet an inspiration to the modern ear.

Notes

1 All translations from Old English are taken from S.A.J. Bradley, *Anglo-Saxon Poetry* (London, 1982), by kind permission.
2 A.E. Planchart, *The Repertory of Tropes at Winchester*, 2 vols. (Princeton, 1977).

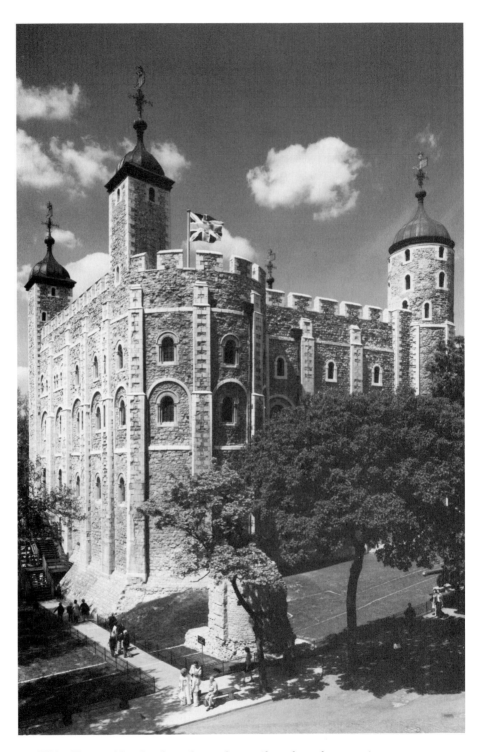

The White Tower of London from the south-east (late eleventh century).

7 The White Tower of London

ALLEN BROWN

The White Tower, so called because in the Middle Ages it was white-washed (cf. White Castle, Monmouthshire), was certainly a residence, though one of a special kind. It was the keep (a sixteenth-century word) or donjon (a contemporary word) of the royal castle in London, and so dominated it that ever since men have spoken, not of London Castle, but of the Tower of London. The keep or donjon – more prosaically 'the great tower' – of any castle was not only its ultimate military strongpoint but also contained the residential apartments of its lord. It was thus deliberately the dominant architectural feature of the castle as the particular symbol of lordship, and it is significant that the Old French word 'donjon' used to describe it is derived from the Latin word *dominium* meaning 'lordship'.

The White Tower is thus a 'strong house', a *maison forte* indeed. Further, while the great tower of stone, early established (cf. Doué-la-Fontaine and Langeais), was to become in the twelfth century the preferred type of donjon at least for those castles without mottes to be developed (the motte was another type of donjon: cf. royal Windsor and a hundred more), this one is the largest anywhere, with the single exception of Colchester which it closely resembles in plan and design. The ground measurements of the Tower are some 36 m by 32.5 m, with a height of 27.5 m to the battlements, excluding the turrets; the ground measurements of Colchester are some 46.5 m by 34 m, with its original height uncertain. Both are thus very Norman in their sheer scale and their austerity, which are the two most impressive features of Norman architecture, to which the word 'imperial' has rightly been applied. Both have also the otherwise unknown feature of a large apsidal projection from their rectangularity at the south-east angle which contains the apse of the chapel within, and both may be derived from the tenth-century great tower of the vanished ducal palace-castle at Rouen. Both were at least begun by William the Conqueror, but whereas Colchester lost its top hamper in seventeenth-century demolition, the White Tower stands complete from basement to roof, albeit restored and altered in some respects. Unique is a dangerous word in history, but there cannot be many, if any, other great fortified houses of the eleventh century surviving thus intact, and it may seem a thousand pities that its original function and proper purpose, and almost all its internal architectural details, should be hidden by its modern use as the museum of the Tower Armouries, whose exhibits themselves deserve a purpose-built display.

Nevertheless, the White Tower remains as arguably the most impressive remaining secular monument of the Norman Conquest, and of the new, because feudalised, regality of the first Norman king. Both reflections point to the motivation behind this gigantically prestigious building in London, not yet the capital but now taking the lead from Winchester as the principal royal city in the realm, already furnished with two other castles (Baynard's Castle and Montfichet), Edward the Confessor's new abbey and palace at Westminster, and in addition soon to receive one of the largest of even the Norman cathedral churches at Old St Pauls.

Though traditionally ascribed to 1078, the precise date of the White Tower is unknown. The castle in which it was later built was evidently founded at once in 1066 and begun by an advance party even before the Conqueror's own triumphal entry into the city for his coronation at Westminster at Christmas in that year. That first castle we know to have been a quite small rectangular enclosure in the south-east angle by the Thames, using the existing city wall (Roman and Anglo-Saxon) as its curtain on the south and east. Within this the great tower was in due course raised as a stronghold and to provide appropriate accommodation for the king's majesty. It was certainly under construction after 1077 because there is reference in the *Textus Roffensis* to Gundulf, bishop of Rochester, consecrated in that year, as having

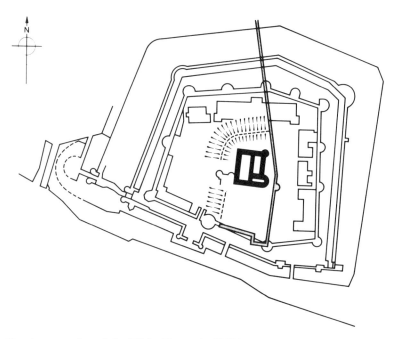

Development plan of the White Tower (c.1100).

been 'in charge of the work of the great tower of London . . . by command of king William the Great'. While it may well have been finished in the Conqueror's reign, the first reference to it as presumably complete comes in 1100 when the unpopular Ranulf Flambard, bishop of Durham and chief minister of William Rufus, was imprisoned in it by Henry I.

The White Tower externally is best seen from the south, which is the normal approach via the Bloody Tower. Here is the only original entrance, recently reopened albeit in eighteenth-century form, at first-floor level and in the westernmost bay of the south front. Here also, in the two western bays, at the top or gallery level, are the only four original or little altered windows, each of two round-headed lights under a roundheaded arch, a pair in each bay, forming a kind of arcade. All the other windows and (later) doorways owe their appearance chiefly to the early eighteenth century and are set in Portland rather than the original Caen stone. The whole exterior has, of course, been much restored, but the arrangement of the eighteenth-century windows at second-floor level, each set in a large round-headed recess between each buttress to form a much grander arcade than the one above, is doubtless an original feature to give architectural emphasis to the regality of this level containing the state apartments. The original masonry of the keep was rag-stone rubble (mostly Kentish rag), with septaria in the plinth and

Elevation drawings of the White Tower.

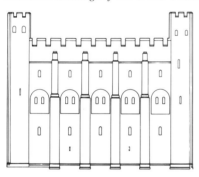 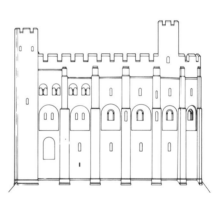

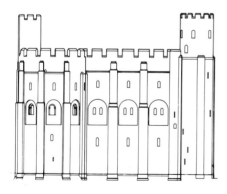 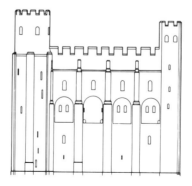

Caen stone for the ashlar dressings. The overall shape is rectangular except
for the apse-like projection at the south-east, already mentioned, and the
north-east turret which is cylindrical, containing the main vice or spiral
staircase which connects all levels internally from basement to roof. Four
turrets rise, one at each angle, including the south-east angle masked by the
apsidal projection, and each is now capped by a lead-covered cupola
surmounted by a weather-vane, inappropriate and probably dating from the
sixteenth century. Each face of the keep (and also the cylindrical turret) has
the flat pilaster buttresses characteristic of the period, stepped back and
narrowed (save for those on the turret) by two off-sets as they rise, and dying
into the main structure a little below the parapet. The walls themselves are
from 3.5 m to 4.5 m thick at the base, yet rise from a splayed or battered
plinth on three sides, east, west and south, designed to accommodate the
ground level rising from the river.

The entrance to the White Tower, placed at first-floor level for security
reasons, is now reached by a modern open timber stairway which must in
some sort reproduce the original arrangement. Nevertheless at some stage,
probably in the earlier twelfth century, a forebuilding of contemporary type
was added, that is, an annexe tower containing a stone staircase and
vestibule, and covering the entrance in the military sense. Such a
forebuilding is shown in the 1597 plan, and also in the late fifteenth-century
miniature now in the British Library where it appears to have an early two-
light window. There is now no trace of it and it is thought to have been
demolished in 1674.

The Tower of London in 1597, as surveyed by Haiward and Gascoyne.

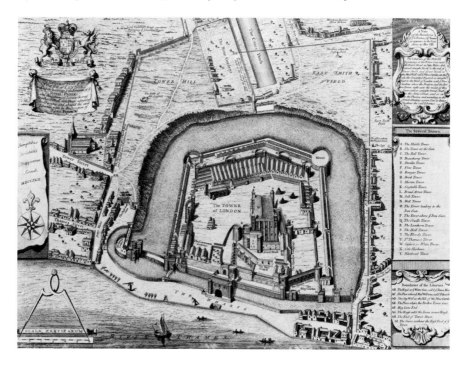

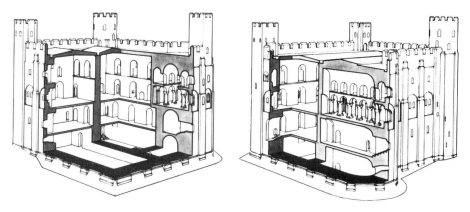

Cut-away illustrations of the White Tower, from the south-west and south-east.

Internally the great building was divided vertically into a basement and two floors, not three as now, and laterally into two not quite equal halves by a cross-wall or spine-wall running north to south. On the east side the chapel with its crypt and sub-crypt formed a further subdivision at the south end. In the north-east angle the main vice connected all levels as described above. Two other original vices, respectively in the north-west and south-west angles, commence only at second-floor level and ascend to the roof. A fourth vice contrived in the thickness of the south wall and commencing at first-floor level is evidently a fourteenth-century insertion to give access to the chapel from that level and, more particularly, direct from the forebuilding without entering the main apartments at all.

The basement is only partially below ground level to the north, and not at all to the south, because the ground itself slopes down to the river. It is, in the nature of things, not very interesting, its purpose being merely storage. It is divided into three compartments common to all levels of the keep, and the well is in the largest, that is, western, compartment. Originally it was entered only from the north-east vice, communication between the three compartments being provided by a doorway at the north end of the cross-wall and another south from the eastern compartment into the sub-crypt of the chapel. There are now several later entrances cut through from outside, and another from the western compartment into the sub-crypt. The basement was originally lit by loops set in tall and deeply splayed recesses (of which one almost survives intact in the east end of the same sub-crypt) but now obtains light from the window embrasures of the floor above via modern recessed shoots in the outside walls. One would not, of course, expect to find any residential splendours or display down here, and in fact in modern times it was used as a gunpowder store well into the nineteenth century. The two main compartments, east and west, received their ugly brick piers and vaults in the eighteenth century (c.1730), though the sub-crypt still shows its original barrel vault including the marks of centering. Nowadays the large west room is known as the 'Cannon Room' and contains various guns, while the east room is the 'Mortar Room', housing mortars and other pieces of ordnance.

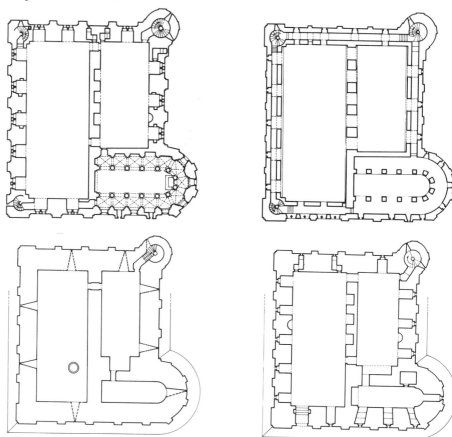

The floor-plans of the White Tower.

The first floor above the basement comprised the lower and comparatively less grand of the two residential suites which the White Tower originally contained. It has the threefold division common to all levels, the largest and western apartment, entered directly from the outside stairway and later forebuilding, serving presumably as the hall, and the smaller, eastern apartment, entered from the north-east vice, serving as the great chamber with a chapel (which is the crypt of the chapel above) opening off the south of it. The residential function is emphasised by the original, round-headed fireplaces, one in each main room (in the west wall of the hall and the east wall of the great chamber), and by the provision of two garderobes in the north wall, opening off the hall but one adjacent to the chamber. The whole was originally well lit, by six windows into the hall (five west and one south), four into the great chamber (three east and one north) and four into the chapel (one east and three south, the two outermost embrasures of the latter being skewed to avoid weakening the wall too much in this part).

Communication between hall and chamber was provided by two doorways north and south through the cross-wall which divides them, the wall space between the two doorways being decorated by three deep, tall, round-headed and no doubt useful recesses. All this has inevitably been much altered over the centuries – not least by the cutting through of the recesses just mentioned, the fitting of over-large early eighteenth-century windows into the quasi-original round-headed window recesses, and, above all, by the insertion of two rows of eighteenth-century timber posts in each of the two main apartments to support the ceiling. In addition to other alterations, in the hall the southern window embrasure has been altered to accommodate the vice inserted in the fourteenth century to give access to the chapel of St John on the floor above, while the crypt-chapel at this first-floor level has a modern barrel vault. The western room or hall is now called the 'Sporting Gallery', the eastern room or great chamber the 'Tournament Gallery', and the true function of both almost totally obscured by the exhibits of the Armouries within them.

The second floor of the White Tower suffers from the same disadvantages, including the timber posts and piercing of the three recesses in the cross-wall, and worse; for here a floor was inserted, probably early in the seventeenth century, dividing vertically into two what was built as one lofty suite rising through two stages to the roof, with a mural gallery at the upper level to bring in more light and also serve as the tribune of the chapel of St John. For this was the royal suite, the State Apartments, intended for the Conqueror himself and his Norman successors. The same arrangement of the *étage noble* rising through two stages, now lost at the Tower of London, was presumably followed at Colchester, where it is also lost, and can still be seen in the later twelfth-century keeps of Rochester, Castle Hedingham and Dover, in the last case forming the topmost floor as in London. There are other surviving signs of the particular grandeur of this floor also. It is served by the majestic chapel of St John, opening off the great chamber through an original doorway in its south wall; the lower window openings were larger and, though now fitted with early eighteenth-century windows, originally had two lights; there are two extra vices, ascending to the roof, in the north-west and south-west angles, respectively; and there is a more convenient and ample provision of garderobes (three). It is particularly interesting that, whereas the great chamber to the east has an original round-headed fireplace, the hall to the west has none – an indication that the king's hall had a central hearth, and further proof that this apartment, like the chamber and the chapel, ascended sheer to the roof. Nowadays the western apartment with its exhibits is called the 'Sixteenth-Century Gallery', and the eastern apartment the 'Medieval Gallery'.

The chapel of St John (see p. 262), mercifully restored to its proper use since the nineteenth century, still has the dignified serenity of Norman Romanesque. It is aisled with apse and ambulatory, the fourteen columns of the main arcade gathered closer together about the apse where their arches are more stilted to give a certain architectural emphasis to the east end. The varied capitals include some of the earliest cushion capitals in England and eleven have the rare embellishment of Tau crosses or T-shaped projections. Here alone in the White Tower the true purpose of the majestic building as a royal residence is immediately apparent, and here one may get closer to the Conqueror and the spirit of *Normanitas* than anywhere else in his English realm.

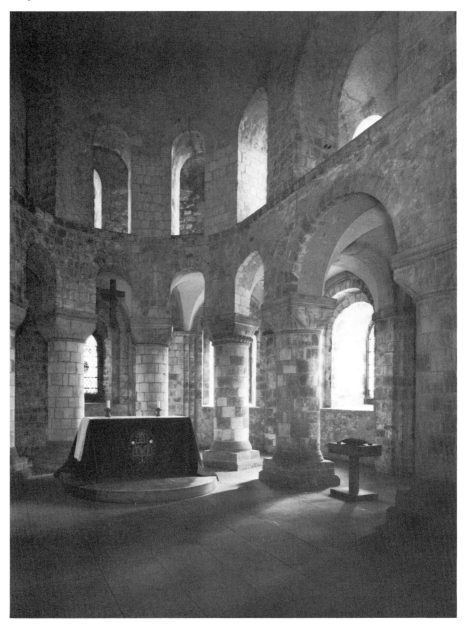

The Chapel of St John in the White Tower.

The eleventh-century internal furnishings of the White Tower must largely be informed guesswork. Architecturally the halls and chambers were austere, though that was more in conformity with contemporary Norman taste than with modern and mistaken popular notions of the necessary austerity of castle interiors. Furniture would be sparse and heavy – long tables and benches, a chair of estate. Lady Stenton once described life at court in the early Middle Ages as a grand but perpetual picnic (constantly on the move). But the grandeur included above all colour, with rich hangings and wall-paintings, warm and luxurious clothing, roaring fires, good food and wine (though we are told that the Conqueror was abstemious in his drink). Luxury may have become more sophisticated as the Middle Ages progressed, but there was sufficient *dulce vita* in the late eleventh century to be remembered when we are exposed to the maunderings of guides and guidebooks about dank and dismal castles. There is unfortunately no record of the Conqueror visiting his great tower at London, though that, of course, does not mean that he did not come (if it was finished by 1087). Spacious as its accommodation was, moreover, the biggest and most formal occasions would need to be staged in the still larger space of a great hall such as Westminster or Winchester. Nevertheless, we may imagine in the White Tower something of the splendour of regality glimpsed in the pages of William of Poitiers, the Conqueror's biographer, when he described the King's Easter court at Fécamp in Normandy in 1067:

When they [the nobles of France] saw the apparel of the king and his vassals woven and worked with gold, they thought anything they had seen before vile. They wondered also at the gold and silver cups whose number and beauty passed all belief.

Charles, Duke of Orleans in the White Tower, from a manuscript of c.1500.

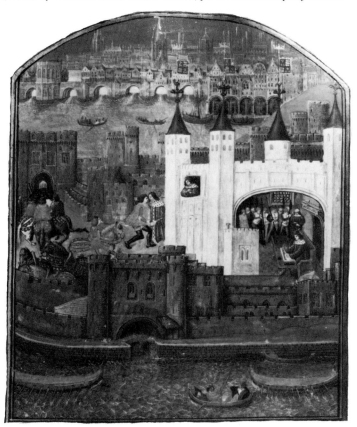

Part III
Appendix: Further Reading and Reference

CHERRY LAVELL

Contents

Abbreviations

The following abbreviations are used for
recurrent names of publishing institutions.
Place of publication is given in brackets.

BAR	British Archaeological Reports (Oxford)
CBA	Council for British Archaeology (London)
CRAAGS	Committee for Rescue Archaeology in Avon, Gloucestershire and Somerset (now defunct, its publications remain available from Alan Sutton, Publisher, Gloucester)
HBMCE	Historic Buildings and Monuments Commission (London)
LAMAS	London & Middlesex Archaeological Society (London)
OUCA	Oxford University Committee for Archaeology (Oxford)
RCHME	Royal Commission on the Historical Monuments of England (London)
SAL	Society of Antiquaries of London
VCH	Victoria County History (Oxford)

Other abbreviations used should be
reasonably clear, for example, *'Res. Rep'* for
'Research Report', *'Proc.'* for *'Proceedings'*,
'J.' for *'Journal'*, and the like.

Introduction

For the larger part of the very long span of time covered by this volume we must depend entirely on archaeological evidence for the practice of arts and crafts. It is not until shortly before the Roman conquest that we have any assistance from written materials and enter the phase that archaeologists call 'text-aided' archaeology. Moreover it is not until about the time of Bede in the eighth century that we can call on the assistance of relatively large numbers of written documents. Hence a large part of the bibliography below deals with archaeological works which, until recently, have appeared mainly in a rather bewildering variety of learned journals, whether national or local in scope. Fortunately, however, more archaeologists are coming to realise the value and enjoyment of writing books for the general public, and even while this publication is in press the list below is sure to be supplemented by new titles. (The list includes works published up to the end of December 1986.)

Wherever possible the bibliography is restricted to these more general works, but sometimes it has been necessary to list publications which are much less accessible and may require the use of interlibrary loan.

It should also be said that in recent years work on most of these topics has been proceeding at a pace which even researchers themselves have found hard to keep up with. In such a fast-moving field as archaeology, books published earlier than about 1970 can be very outdated both in detail and in theoretical framework. (There are exceptions, and these have been annotated in the list as having classic status.) The best way to keep up with new discoveries is through the serially-published bibliographies listed below. Some of these will be available only in the larger public libraries, or in specialised institutions such as the Society of Antiquaries of London or the library of the Society for the Promotion of Roman Studies.

Throughout the bibliography, comments have been added wherever they seemed helpful in pointing out particular objects or themes. 'Bib.' signifies works with good bibliographies providing still further reading. Inexpensive booklets in the *Shire Archaeology* series provide an excellent introduction to many subjects and are marked in this list as (Shire).

American editions of works originating in the United Kingdom and Ireland are not specially noted. Place of publication is given only for non-UK works or for less well-known locations.

Thanks are due to Belinda Barratt and Felicity Gilmour who helped assemble the Romano-British sections of this bibliography. In addition, several of the individual contributors to this volume offered suggestions for titles to include.

Serial Bibliographies

Annual Bibliography of British and Irish History (Royal Historical Society)

Annual Bulletin of Historical Literature (Historical Association)

Architectural Periodicals Index (Royal Institute of British Architects)

Arts and Humanities Citation Index (Institute of Scientific Information, Philadelphia, USA)

British Archaeological Abstracts (CBA)

British Humanities Index (Library Association)

Discovery and Excavation in Scotland (CBA Scotland)

International Medieval Bibliography (c/o University of Leeds)

RILA (International Repertory of the Literature of Art) (Williamstown, Mass, USA)

Répertoire d'Art et d'Archéologie (Maison des Sciences de l'Homme, Paris) (now incorporated in *RILA*)

Quarterly Checklist of Medievalia (American Bibliographic Services)

The Year's Work in English (English Association)

Magazines

Archaeology Today (formerly called *Popular Archaeology*) (24 Barton Street, Bath) is a monthly magazine with lively and well-illustrated articles drawn from all over the world, but with strong British emphasis.

Current Archaeology (9 Nassington Road, London NW3) appears about every 2–3 months and gives the latest news on excavations, books to read, etc.: it is aimed at interested amateur archaeologists. Available on subscription only.

Antiquity (Heffers, Cambridge) appears three times a year and is aimed at a much more knowledgeable audience than either of the two named above.

The London Archaeologist (quarterly from S. Broomfield, 8 Woodview Crescent, Hildenborough, Tonbridge, Kent TN11 9HD) is modestly priced and contains lively articles of interest to people living in SE England and beyond.

The Historian (quarterly) is a lively magazine available to members of the Historical Association (59a Kennington Park Road, London SE11 4JH).

History Today (monthly: 83–84 Berwick St., London W1V 3PJ) is a well-illustrated publication which contains occasional articles on art-historical or craft subjects. It is particularly useful for recent work on the social background and intellectual climate in which the arts of a specific period were carried on.

Prehistoric Britain

Most of the works discussed in this chapter can be found in three reasonably accessible works: T.G.E. Powell's *Prehistoric Art* (1966), Stanley Thomas's *Pre-Roman Britain* (1965), and I. Longworth's *Prehistoric Britain* (1985). The last of these is most attractively illustrated in colour. A number of books giving general background to help in understanding the period are listed to begin with; a selection of regional guidebooks is then given for those interested in visiting monuments. Subsequent sections are listed in the same order as the chapter text.

General

Adkins, L. and Adkins, R., *The Handbook of British Archaeology* (1983) (also available as *A Thesaurus of British Archaeology* (1982)) [the best dictionary and explanation of terms]

Brailsford, J.W., *Later Prehistoric Antiquities of the British Isles* (1953) (British Museum guide)

Clark, Grahame, *Symbols of Excellence: Precious Materials as Expressions of Status* (1986)

Coles, B. and Coles, J., *Sweet Track to Glastonbury: the Somerset Levels in Prehistory* (1986) [illustrates many artefacts including woodwork]

Coles, J.M. and Orme, B., *Prehistory of the Somerset Levels* (1980)

Coles, J.M. and Simpson, D.D.A., *Studies in Ancient Europe: Essays Presented to Stuart Piggott* (1968) [several papers on artefacts and art styles]

Cunliffe, B., *Cradle of England* (1972) (BBC booklet)

Harbison, P., *The Archaeology of Ireland* (1976) [introductory]

Langmaid, N., *Prehistoric Pottery* (1978) (Shire)

Longworth, I., *Prehistoric Britain* (1985) [good colour photos of artefacts; inexpensive British Museum paperback]

Longworth, I. and Cherry, J. (eds.), *Archaeology in Britain since 1945* (1986) [produced to accompany a major exhibition at the British Museum]

Megaw, J.V.S. and Simpson, D.D.A., *Introduction to British Pre-history* (1979) [undergraduate level text]

Muir, R., *The Stones of Britain: Landscapes and Monuments, Quarries and Cathedrals* (1986)

Piggott, S., *Ancient Europe from the Beginnings of Agriculture to Classical Antiquity* (1965) [classic work] *Scotland Before History* (rev. edn 1982 with gazetteer by G. Ritchie)

Pitts, M., *Later Stone Implements* (1980) (Shire)

Pryor, F., *Fengate* (1982) (Shire)

Renfrew, C., *Before Civilization: the Radiocarbon Revolution and Prehistoric Europe* (1976) [for understanding the revised chronologies of prehistoric Europe]

Ritchie, G. and A., *Scotland: Archaeology and Early History* (1981)

Sorrell, A., *Reconstructing the Past* (1981)

Tait, H. (ed.), *Seven Thousand Years of Jewellery* (1986) [chapters on Bronze and Iron Ages]

Taylor, M., *Wood in Archaeology* (1981) (Shire: prehistoric implements in wood)

Regional Guides to Monuments

Baldwin, J., *Exploring Scotland's Heritage: Lothian and the Borders* (1985)

Close-Brooks, J., *Exploring Scotland's Heritage: the Highlands* (1986)

Dyer, J., *Southern England: an Archaeological Guide* (1973)

Harbison, P., *Guide to the National Monuments of Ireland* (1970)

Hawkes, J. and Bahn, P., *The Shell Guide to British Archaeology* (1986)

Houlder, C.J., *Wales: an Archaeological Guide. The Prehistoric, Roman, and Early Medieval Field Monuments* (1974)

Ritchie, A., *Exploring Scotland's Heritage: Orkney and Shetland* (1985)

Ritchie, G. and Harman, M., *Exploring Scotland's Heritage: Argyll and the Western Isles* (1985)

Shepherd, I., *Exploring Scotland's Heritage: Grampian* (1986)

Stell, G., *Exploring Scotland's Heritage: Dumfries and Galloway* (1986)

Stevenson, J.B., *Exploring Scotland's Heritage: The Clyde Estuary and Central Region* (1985)

Thomas, N., *A Guide to Prehistoric England* (2nd edn 1976)

Walker, B. and Ritchie, G., *Exploring Scotland's Heritage: Fife and Tayside* (1987)

Old and Middle Stone Ages

Clark, J.G.D., *et al.*, *Excavations at Star Carr: an Early Mesolithic Site at Seamer near Scarborough, Yorks* (rev. edn 1971)

Roe, D., *The Lower and Middle Palaeolithic Periods in Britain* (1981)

Timms, P., *Flint Implements of the Old Stone Age* (2nd edn 1980) (Shire)

Waechter, J., *Man Before History* (1976) [for Hoxne handaxes and Swanscombe Man in particular]

Wymer, J.J., *Lower Palaeolithic Archaeology in Britain as Represented by the Thames Valley* (1968) (bib.)

New Stone Age; Religious Ideas; Warrior Aristocrats

Annable, F.K. and Simpson, D.D.A., *Guide Catalogue of the Neolithic and Bronze Age Collections in Devizes Museum* (1964)

Bender, B., *The Archaeology of Brittany, Normandy and the Channel Islands: an introduction and guide* (1986) [illustrates axe carvings in megalithic tombs]

Burgess, C.B., *Bronze Age Metalwork in Northern England c.1000–700 B.C.* (1968)

Childe, V.G. and Clarke, D.V., *Skara Brae* (rev. edn 1983) [official guide to the Neolithic village]

Clarke, D.V., *The Neolithic Village at Skara Brae, Orkney* (1976) (pamphlet)

Clough, T.H.McK. and Cummins, W.A., *Stone Axe Studies: Archaeological, petrological, experimental, and ethnographic* (1979) (*CBA Res. Rep. 23* [collected papers on the wide inferences about trade routes that can be made from the study of axes; includes the Lincolnshire axe with fossil.]

Eogan, G., 'Ribbon torcs in Britain and Ireland', in A. O'Connor and D.V. Clarke (eds.), *From the Stone Age to the 'Forty-Five: Studies Presented to R.B.K. Stevenson* (1983), pp. 87–126

'Sleeve fasteners of the Late Bronze Age', in F. Lynch and C. Burgess (eds.), *Prehistoric Man in Wales and the West* (1972), pp. 189–209

Gibson, A., *Neolithic and Early Bronze Age Pottery* (1986) (Shire)

Kenworthy, J. (ed.), *Early Technology in North Britain (Scottish Archaeol. Forum, 11* (1981)) [craft working of jet, stone, etc.]

Kinnes, I., 'Les Fouaillages and megalithic origins', *Antiquity* **56** (1982), 24–30

Mercer, R.J., *Hambledon Hill: a Neolithic Landscape* (1980) [excellent introduction to this period]

Norwich Castle Museum, *Bronze Age Metalwork in Norwich Castle Museum* (2nd edn, 1977)

Pearce, S.M., *Bronze Age Metalwork in Southern Britain* (1984) (Shire)

Piggott, C.M., 'The Late Bronze Age razors of the British Isles', *Proc. Prehistoric Society*, **12** (1946), 121–41

Piggott, S., *Neolithic Cultures of the British Isles* (1954) [text now out of date but good illus.]

The West Kennet Long Barrow (1962)

Savory, H.N., *Guide Catalogue of the Bronze Age Collections* (1980) (National Museum of Wales catalogue)

Shepherd, I.A.G., *Powerful Pots: Beakers in North-East Prehistory* (1986)

Smith, W.C., 'Jade axes from sites in the British Isles', *Proc. Prehistoric Soc.*, **29** (1963), 133–72

Tait, J., *Beakers from Northumberland* (1965)

Taylor, J.J., *Bronze Age Goldwork of the British Isles* (1980) [superb photographs of detail of ornaments]

Wainwright, G.J., *Durrington Walls: excavations 1966–68* (1971) (*Rep. Res. Comm. SAL*, **29**) [for possible forms of Sanctuary]

Wolters, J., 'The ancient craft of granulation: a reassessment of established concepts', *Gold Bulletin*, **14** (1981), 119–29

New Grange and the Boyne Passage Graves

Beckensall, S., *Northumberland's Prehistoric Rock Carvings: a Mystery Explained* (1983)
Rock Carvings of Northern Britain (1986) (Shire)

Brennan, M., *The Stars and the Stones: Ancient Art and Astronomy in Ireland* (1983)

Cowell, R. and Warhurst, M., *The Calderstones: a Prehistoric Tomb in Liverpool* (1984)

de Paor, M., *Early Irish Art* (1979)

Eogan, G., 'A flint macehead at Knowth, Co Meath, Ireland', *Antiquity*, **57** (1983), 45–6
Knowth and the Passage-Tombs of Ireland (1986)

Hadingham, E., *Ancient Carvings in Britain: a Mystery* (1974) (good illus.)

Herity, M., *Irish Passage Graves* (1974)

Marshall, D.N., 'Carved stone balls', *Proc. Society of Antiquaries of Scotland*, **108** (1976–77), 40–72

Morris, R.W.B., *The Prehistoric Rock Art of Galloway and the Isle of Man* (1979)
The Prehistoric Rock Art of Argyll (1977)
The Prehistoric Rock Art of Southern Scotland (except Argyll and Galloway (1981) (= *BAR* 86)

O'Kelly, C., *Illustrated Guide to Newgrange and the Other Boyne Monuments* (privately published, Blackrock, Cork, 3rd edn 1978)
'Passage-grave art in the Boyne Valley', *Proc. Prehistoric Soc.*, **39** (1973), 354–82

O'Kelly, M., *Newgrange: Archaeology, Art and Legend* (1982)

Piggott, S. and Daniel, G., *A Picture Book of Ancient British Art* (1951)

Renfrew, C. (ed.), *The Prehistory of Orkney 4000 B.C. – 1000 A.D.* (1985)

Sandars, N.K., *Prehistoric Art in Europe* (2nd edn 1985)

Twohig, E. Shee, *Megalithic Art of Western Europe* (1981) (bib.)

Late New Stone and Bronze Age Architecture: Avebury and Stonehenge

Atkinson, R.J.C., *The Prehistoric Temples of Stonehenge and Avebury* (1980) (a Pitkin Pictorial booklet)
Stonehenge and Neighbouring Monuments (1982) [official souvenir guide]
Stonehenge: Archaeology and Interpretation (rev. edn 1979)
Silbury Hill [1968] (BBC booklet)
'Silbury Hill', in R. Sutcliffe (ed.), *Chronicle: Essays from Ten Years of Television Archaeology* (1978), pp. 159–73

Bergstrom, T. and Vatcher, L., *Stonehenge* (1974) [atmospheric pictures with factual text]

Burgess, C., *The Age of Stonehenge* (1980) [life and customs through third and second millennia BC]

Burl, A., *Prehistoric Astronomy and Ritual* (1983) (Shire)
Prehistoric Stone Circles (2nd edn 1983) (Shire)
The Stone Circles of the British Isles (New Haven, 1976)
Prehistoric Avebury (New Haven, 1979)
Rings of Stone: the Prehistoric Stone Circles of Britain and Ireland (1979)

Chippindale, C., *Stonehenge Complete* (1983) [fine illus., bib.]

Clarke, D.V., Cowie, T.G. and Foxon, A., *Symbols of Power at the Time of Stonehenge* (1985) [superb illus., text has not met with universal approval; bib.]

Hadingham, E., *Circles and Standing Stones* (rev. edn 1978)

Heggie, D.C. (ed.), *Archaeoastronomy in the Old World* (1982) (a level-headed approach to Neolithic 'science')

Pitts, M., *Footprints through Avebury* (1985) [fine pictures and lively but authoritative text]

RCHME, *Stonehenge and its Environs: Monuments and Land Use* (1979)

Smith, I.F. (for A Keiller), *Windmill Hill and Avebury* (1965)

Wernick, R. *et al*, *The Monument Builders* (New York, 1973) [popular level text]

Wood, J.E., *Sun, Moon and Standing Stones* (1978)

Celtic Iron Age and La Tène Art

Aberdeen Art Gallery and Museums, *Ancient Treasures of Scotland* (exhibition catalogue, 1978)

Alcock, L., 'By South Cadbury is that
    Camelot . . .' (1972) [Iron Age hillfort
    and much else of interest]
'Celtic archaeology and art', in Elwyn
    Davies (ed.), *Celtic Studies in Wales: a
    Survey* (1963), pp. 3–46
Brailsford, J.W., *Early Celtic Masterpieces
    from Britain in the British Museum*
    (1975)
Christie, P.M., *Carn Euny Prehistoric
    Village, Cornwall* (1983) [official guide
    to the upstanding buildings]
Coles, J.M. and Simpson, D.D.A., *Studies
    in Ancient Europe: Essays Presented to
    Stuart Piggott* (1968)
Cunliffe, B., *The Celtic World* (1979)
    Iron Age Communities in Britain (2nd edn
    1978) (bib.)
    *Danebury: Anatomy of an Iron Age
    Hillfort* (1983)
Curriculum Development Unit (Dublin),
    The Celtic Way of Life (1984)
Duval, P.M. and Hawkes, C.F.C. (eds),
    *Celtic Art in Ancient Europe: Five
    Protohistoric Centuries* (1976)
Finlay, Ian, *Celtic Art: an Introduction*
    (1973)
Fox, C., *Pattern and Purpose: a Survey of
    Early Celtic Art in Britain* (1958)
Guido, M., *The Glass Beads and the
    Prehistoric and Roman Periods in
    Britain and Ireland* (1978) (*Rep. Res.
    Comm. SAL*, **35**)
Holmes, P. and Coles, J.M., 'Prehistoric
    brass instruments', *World Archaeology*,
    12 (1981), 280–86
Jackson, K.J., *The Oldest Irish Tradition: a
    Window on the Iron Age* (1964) [Irish
    epic as clue to dwellings etc.]
Jacobsthal, J., *Early Celtic Art* (2 vols.,
    1944)
Kilbride-Jones, H.E., *Celtic Craftsmanship
    in Bronze* (1980) [fine drawings]
Kruta, V., *The Celts of the West* (1985)
    [lavish illus.]
Leeds, E.T., *Celtic Ornament in the British
    Isles down to AD 700* (1933)
Lowery, P.R. *et al.*, 'Scriber, graver,
    scorper, tracer: notes on experiments in
    bronzeworking technique', *Proc.

Prehistoric Society*, **37** (1971), 167–82
    [the art and craft of Iron Age mirrors]
Macgregor, M., *Early Celtic Art in North
    Britain: a Study of Decorative
    Metalwork from the 3rd Century B.C. to
    the Third Century A.D.* (2 vols., 1976)
    [scholarly catalogue with fine
    illustrations]
Megaw, J.V.S., *Art of the European Iron
    Age: a Study of the Elusive Image*
    (1970) [scholarly catalogue with fine
    photographs]
'Problems and non-problems in palaeo-
    organology: a musical miscellany', in
    J.M. Coles and D.D.A. Simpson (eds.),
    *Studies in Ancient Europe: Essays
    Presented to Stuart Piggott* (1968), pp.
    333–58
'Penny whistles and prehistory',
    Antiquity, **34** (1960), 6–13
Megaw, R. and Megaw, V., *Early Celtic
    Art in Britain and Ireland* (1986)
    (Shire)
Morrison, I., *Landscape with Lake
    Dwellings: the Crannogs of Scotland*
    (1985)
Piggott, S., *The Druids* (rev. edn 1985) (the
    myth and the reality)
Powell, T.G.E., *The Celts* (2nd edn 1980)
Reynolds, P.J., *Iron Age Farm: the Butser
    Experiment* (1979)
Ritchie, W.F. and J.N.G., *Celtic Warriors*
    (1985) (Shire)
Rook, T. *et al.*, 'An Iron Age bronze mirror
    from Aston, Herts', *Antiq. J.*, **62**
    (1982), 18–34
Ross, A., *Everyday Life of the Pagan Celts*
    (1970)
    *Pagan Celtic Britain: Studies in
    Iconography and Tradition* (1967)
Saunders, C., 'The iron firedog from
    Welwyn, Hertfordshire, reconsidered',
    Hertfordshire Archaeology, **5** (1977),
    13–21
Stead, I.M., *Celtic Art in Britain Before the
    Roman Conquest* (1985)
    (forthcoming: publication on the
    chariot burials from Wetwang and
    Garton Slack)
    The Battersea Shield (1985)

Roman Britain

The Cultural and Social Setting

The main source for this section is Peter
Salway's *Roman Britain* (1981) which deals
in more detail with many of these topics,
and moreover has a very full and interesting
narrative bibliography, including
background material on the Roman world
at large. The works below can be consulted
for extra details or special topics. The
periodical *Britannia* contains articles by
specialists and summaries of discoveries
made during the preceding year. More
references can be found in the sections on
Roman architecture and visual arts and
crafts (respectively).

Barker, P.A., 'The latest occupation of the
    site of the baths basilica at Wroxeter',
    in P.J. Casey (ed.), *The End of Roman
    Britain* (1979), pp. 175–81 (*BAR, 71*)
Bennett, J., *Towns in Roman Britain* (rev.
    edn 1984) (Shire)
Birley, A.R., *Life in Roman Britain* (1976)
    The People of Roman Britain (1979)
    [records of named persons and what
    can be learned about them]
Bishop, M.C. (ed.), *The Production and
    Distribution of Roman Military
    Equipment: Proceedings of the Second
    Roman Military Equipment Research
    Seminar* (1985) (= *BAR Int. Ser.,
    S275*)
Blagg, T.F.C. and King, A.C. (eds.),
    *Military and Civilian in Roman Britain:
    Cultural Relationships in a Frontier
    Province* (1984) (*BAR, 136*)
Bogaers, J.E., 'King Cogidubnus in
    Chichester: another reading of RIB 91',
    Britannia, **10** (1979), 243–54 [on the
    politics of post-Caesarian Britain]

Boon, G.C., *Silchester: the Roman Town of
    Calleva* (2nd edn 1974) [somewhat
    overtaken now by recent research, but
    still useful for illustrations and many
    details of town life]
Branigan, K., *Roman Britain: Life in an
    Imperial Province* (1980)
    The Roman Villa in South-west England
    (1977)
    The Catuvellauni (1986) ['Peoples of
    Roman Britain' – Herts, Bucks, Beds,
    Oxford, Cambs approximately]
Branigan, K. and Fowler, P.J. (eds.), *The
    Roman West Country: Classical Culture
    and Celtic Society* (1976)
Braund, D., *Rome and the Friendly King:
    the Character of the Client Kingship*
    (1984)
Breeze, D., *The Northern Frontiers of
    Roman Britain* (1982)
    Roman Forts in Britain (1983) (Shire)
Breeze, D. and Dobson, B., *Hadrian's Wall*
    (1978) [standard work on the frontier]
Bulleid, A. and Horne, E., 'The Roman
    house at Keynsham, Somerset',
    Archaeologia, **75** (1926), 109–38 [for
    musical instruments on mosaic]
Burnett, A., *The Coins of Roman Britain*
    (1977) [British Museum booklet]
Casey, P.J., *Roman Coinage in Britain*
    (1980) (Shire)
Casey, P.J. (ed.), *The End of Roman Britain*
    (1979) (*BAR, 71*) [essays on various
    aspects]
Clayton, P.A. (ed.), *A Companion to Roman
    Britain* (1980) [well illustrated, with
    gazetteer of sites, museums to visit, etc.]
Collingwood, R.G. and Wright, R.P., *The
    Roman Inscriptions of Britain: 1,
    Inscriptions on Stone* (1965) [standard
    reference work, illustrated; a separate

index to it is now available,
R. Goodburn and H. Waugh, *The
Roman Inscriptions of Britain . . .
Epigraphic indexes* (1983)]

Cornell, T. and Matthews, J., *Atlas of the
Roman World* (1982) [with chapter on
Britain – art, everyday life, commerce,
etc.]

Cunliffe, B., *The Regni* (1973) ['Peoples of
Roman Britain' – Sussex area]
'Britain, the Veneti and beyond', *Oxford
J. Archaeol.*, **1** (1982), 39–68 (on the
trade patterns before the Roman
Conquest of Britain)
'Relations between Britain and Gaul in
the 1st century BC and early 1st
century AD', in Macready and
Thompson [see full ref. below under
Macready], pp. 3–23

Detsicas, A.P., *The Cantiaci* (1983)
['Peoples of Roman Britain' – Kent]

Downey, R. *et al.*, 'The Hayling Island
temple and religious connections across
the Channel', in W. Rodwell (ed.),
Temples, Churches and Religion [see full
ref. below under Rodwell], pp.
289–304

Dunnett, R., *The Trinovantes* (1975)
['Peoples of Roman Britain' – Essex,
Herts, parts of Cambs, Suff.]

Fishwick, D., 'Templum divo Claudio
constitutum', *Britannia*, **3** (1972),
164–81 [for the Colchester temple]

Fitzpatrick, A., 'The Distribution of
Dressel 1 amphorae in northwest
Europe', *Oxford J. Archaeol.*, **4** (1985),
305–40 [trade patterns shifting before
the Roman Conquest]

Frere, S.S., *Britannia: a History of Roman
Britain* (2nd edn 1978) [standard work,
a little overtaken by Salway 1981 but
still important]

Frere, S.S. and St Joseph, J.K.S., *Roman
Britain from the Air* (1983) [military
and civil installations and towns]

Galliou, P., 'Days of wine and roses? Early
Armorica and the Atlantic wine trade',
in Macready and Thompson [see full
ref. below under Macready], pp. 24–36

Grew, F. and Hobley, B. (eds), *Roman
Urban Topography in Britain and the
Western Empire* (1985) (*CBA Res. Rep.*,
59) [academic conference papers,
including mechanics of building trade,
civic pride, town planning: London,
Colchester, etc.]

Grimes, W.F., *The Excavation of Roman
and Medieval London* (1968) [includes
account of Mithras Temple, defences
of Londinium, etc.]

Hanson, W.S. and Maxwell, G.S., *Rome's
North-west Frontier: the Antonine Wall*
(1983)

Harker, S., 'Springhead: a brief
reappraisal', in W. Rodwell (ed.),
Temples, Churches and Religion [see full
ref below under Rodwell], pp. 285–88

Henig, M. and King, A. (eds), *Pagan Gods
and Shrines of the Roman Empire* (1986)
[*OUCA Monogr.*, **8** – essays on various
aspects]

Higham, N. and Jones, B., *The Carvetii*
(1985) ['Peoples of Roman Britain' –
Cumbria, part of SW Scotland]

Ireland, S., *Roman Britain: a Sourcebook*
(1986) [translations from ancient
writers, inscriptions, coin propaganda,
etc.]

Johns, C., 'The Roman silver cups from
Hockwold, Norfolk', *Archaeologia*, **108**
(1986), 1–13

Johns, C. and Potter, T., *The Thetford
Treasure: Roman Jewellery and Silver*
(1983) [for possible Boudican
residence]

Johnson, S., *Later Roman Britain* (1980,
paperback 1982)
The Roman Forts of the Saxon Shore
(1976)

Johnston, D. (ed.), *Discovering Roman
Britain* (1983) (Shire)
Roman Villas (1979) (Shire)
(ed.), *The Saxon Shore* (1977) (*CBA Res.
Rep.*, **18**) [papers from an academic
conference]

Keppie, L., *Roman Distance Slabs from the
Antonine Wall* (1979)

Macready, S. and Thompson, F.H. (eds),
*Cross-Channel Trade Between Britain
and Gaul in the Pre-Roman Iron Age
(1984) (SAL Occasional Papers, new
ser., 4)*

McWhirr, A., *Roman Gloucestershire* (1981)

Maloney, J., 'London's Past: ancient and
modern civic schemes', *Popular
Archaeology*, **6***(14)* (Dec. 1985), pp.
16–21 [for the forum-basilica]

Marsden, P., *Roman London* (1980)

Matthews, J., *Western Aristocracies and
Imperial Court, AD 364–425* (1975)
[for the place of aristocrats in
government, and their wealth]

Mattingley, H. (transl., revised S.
Handford), *Tacitus: The Agricola and
the Germania* (1970)

Merrifield, R., *London: City of the Romans*
(1983)

Milne, G., *The Port of Roman London*
(1985) [recent work on the waterfront
areas, trade, warehouses, etc.]

Morris, J., *Londinium: London in the Roman Empire* (1982) [lively speculation about what London, and indeed a much wider area, might have been like; but not approved by all authorities!]

Ogilvie, R.M. and Richmond, I.A., *Cornelii Taciti: De Vita Agricolae* (1967) [text of Tacitus' *Agricola* with extensive commentary]

Ordnance Survey, *Londinium: a Descriptive Map and Guide to Roman London* (1981)

Map of Roman Britain (4th edn, 1978) [two sheets, with accompanying text on life in Roman Britain]

The Antonine Wall (1969) [map]

Hadrian's Wall (2nd edn 1975) [map]

Partridge, C., 'Excavations at Puckeridge and Braughing 1975–79', *Hertfordshire Archaeol.*, 7 (1979), 28–132 [developing trade in Roman imported goods]

Skeleton Green: a Late Iron Age and Romano-British site (1981) (*Britannia Monogr. Series*, 2)

Percival, J., *The Roman Villa: an Historical Introduction* (1976)

Phillips, E.J., *Corpus Signorum Imperii Romani. Great Britain, vol.* 1*(1): Corbridge; Hadrian's Wall East of the North Tyne* (1977) [sculptures]

Potter, T.W., *Roman Britain* (1983) [British Museum booklet, introduction to life and society, arts and crafts, good colour illus.]

Putnam, W., *Roman Dorset* (1984)

Ramm, H., *The Parisi* (1978) ['Peoples of Roman Britain' – N Yorks and N Humberside]

Reece, R. (ed.), *Burial in the Roman World* (1977) (*CBA Res. Rep.*, 22) [papers from academic conference]

Reynolds, P.J., *Iron Age Farm: the Butser Experiment* (1979) [for farming methods of pre-Roman Britain]

Rivet, A.L.F., (ed.) *The Roman Villa in Britain* (1969) [very full bibliography]

Rodwell, W. (ed.), *Temples, Churches and Religion: Recent Research in Roman Britain* (1980) (*BAR*, 77)

Rodwell, W. and Rowley, T. (eds.), *The 'Small Towns' of Roman Britain* (1975) (*BAR*, 15) [papers from academic conference]

Salway, P., *The Origins of Roman Britain* (1982) (Open University Course A293 Unit 14, *Provincial Case Studies I: Gaul, Germany and Britain*)

The Frontier People of Roman Britain [repr. 1967; on the Romanised civil population of the northern frontier region: note that Higham and Jones (above), A.R. Birley, *The People of Roman Britain* (above), and others contain subsequent work]

'The barbarians across the Ocean: Britain through Roman eyes', *History Today*, Dec 1986, 15–20

Schofield, J., *The Building of London from the Conquest to the Great Fire* (1984) [Chapter 1, Roman and Saxon origins, is the best statement so far available on new evidence for the City and its suburbs]

Scullard, H.H., *Roman Britain: Outpost of the Empire* (1979) [accessible, well illustrated]

Sealey, P.R., *Amphoras from the 1970 Excavations at Colchester Sheepen* (1985) (*BAR*, 142) [wine, oil, and other goods traded to Britain from the Roman world before the Conquest]

Sorrell, A., *Roman Towns in Britain* (1976)

Stead, I., 'The earliest burials of the Aylesford culture', in G. Sieveking *et al.* (eds.), *Problems in Social and Economic Archaeology* (1976), pp. 401–16

Thomas, C. (ed.), *Rural Settlement in Roman Britain* (1966) (*CBA Res. Rep.*, 7) [the 'breakthrough' conference for the understanding of rural Roman Britain; somewhat out of date now but well worth reading for some lively papers]

Christianity in Roman Britain to AD 500 (2nd edn 1985) [fundamental work on this topic: includes Pelagius, Germanus, etc. as well as collecting all available evidence for RB Christianity]

Thompson, E.A., *Who was Saint Patrick?* (1985)

Todd, M. (ed.), *Studies in the Romano-British Villa* (1978) [important academic papers containing influential fresh – if sometimes controversial – thinking]

The Coritani (1973) ['Peoples of Roman Britain' – Leics, Lincs, Notts, Derbys, etc.]

Roman Britain 55 BC – AD 400: the Province Beyond Ocean (1981)

Tufi, S.R., *Corpus Signorum Imperii Romani: Great Britain, vol.* 1*(3) Yorkshire* (1983) [sculptures]

Wacher, J., *The Coming of Rome* (1979)

Roman Britain (1978)

The Towns of Roman Britain (1975)

Webster, G., *The Roman Imperial Army of the 1st and 2nd Centuries AD* (3rd edn 1985)

The Roman Invasion of Britain (1980)
The Cornovii (1975) ['Peoples of Roman Britain' – Shropshire and adjoining counties]
Wilson, R.J.A., *Guide to Roman Remains in Britain* (2nd edn 1980) [pocket-sized gazetteer of sites worth visiting]

Architecture

(References to Verulamium in this section will be found in the Verulamium section.)
Blagg, T.F.C., 'Reconstructions of Roman decorated architecture: proportions, prescriptions, and practices', in P.J. Drury (ed.), *Structural Reconstruction: Approaches to the Interpretation of the Excavated Remains of Buildings* (1982), pp. 131–51 (*BAR* **110**)
'Roman architectural ornament in Kent', *Archaeologia Cantiana*, **100** (1984), 65–80 [for Richborough Monument]
Collingwood, R.G. and Wright, R.P., *The Roman Inscriptions of Britain: 1, Inscriptions on Stone* (1965) (standard reference work, illustrated; the separate index, by R. Goodburn and H. Waugh, is *The Roman Inscriptions of Britain . . . Epigraphic Indexes* (1983))
Cunliffe, B., *Iron Age Communities in Britain* (2nd edn 1978) [for the pre-Roman background] (bib.)
The Temple of Sulis Minerva at Bath: Vol 1(i), The Site (2 vols., 1985) (*OUCA Monogr.*, **7**)
Roman Bath (1969) (*Rep. Res. Comm. SAL*, **24**)
Roman Bath Discovered (2nd edn 1984) [more accessible account than the three major reports preceding this entry; see p. 188 for Sulinus's yard]
The Roman Baths and Museum (1985) (official souvenir guide)
Excavations at Fishbourne, 1961–69 (2 vols. 1971) (*Rep. Res. Comm. SAL* **26**) (bib.)
Fishbourne: a Roman Palace and its Garden (1971) [more accessible than previous title]
Cunliffe, B. (ed.), *Excavations in Bath, 1950–75* (1979) (*CRAGGS Excavation Reports*, **1**)
Cunliffe, B. and Fulford, M.G., *Corpus Signorum Imperii Romani: Great Britain, vol. 1(2), Bath and the Rest of Wessex* (1982) [scholarly catalogue with fine photographs: p. xv for Sulinus and Cirencester workshop]
Drury, P.J., 'The Temple of Claudius at Colchester reconsidered', *Britannia*, **15** (1984), 7–50

'Form, function, and the interpretation of the excavated plans of some large secular Romano-British buildings', in P.J. Drury (ed.), *Structural Reconstruction* [full reference given under Blagg above], pp. 289–308
Fulford, M., 'Excavations on the sites of the amphitheatre and forum-basilica at Silchester, Hampshire: an interim report', *Antiq. J.*, **65** (1985), 39–81
'Silchester', *Current Archaeology*, 7*(11)* (1982), 326–31
Grew, F. and Hobley, B. (eds.), *Roman Urban Topography in Britain and the Western Empire* (1985) (*CBA Res. Rep.*, **59**)
Henig, M., *Religion in Roman Britain* (1984)
Hill, C. *et al.*, *The Roman Riverside Wall and Monumental Arch in London: Excavations at Baynard's Castle . . . 1974–6* (1980) (*London and Middlesex Archaeol. Soc. Special Papers*, **3**)
Johnston, D.E., *Roman Villas* (1979) (Shire)
Maloney, J., 'London's past: ancient and modern civic schemes', *Popular Archaeology*, **6***(14)* (Dec. 1985), 16–21 (for forum-basilica)
Mattingley, H. (transl., revised S. Handford), *Tacitus: The Agricola and the Germania* (1970)
Rivet, A.L.F. (ed.), *The Roman Villa in Britain* (1969) (bib.)
Rodwell, W. (ed.), *Temples, Churches and Religion: Recent Research in Roman Britain* (1980) (*BAR*, **77**)
Salway, P., *Roman Britain* (1981) [for forum-basilica sites at Wroxeter, Cirencester, etc.] (*Oxford History of England, vol. IA*)
Strong, D.E., 'The Monument', in B.W. Cunliffe (ed.), *Fifth Report on the Excavations of the Roman Fort at Richborough, Kent* (1968), 40–73 (*Rep. Res. Comm. SAL.* **23**)
Todd, M. (ed.), *Studies in the Romano-British Villa* (1978) [essays on various aspects of villas]

Verulamium

Frere, S.S., *Verulamium Excavations, vol. 1* (1972); *vol. 2* (1983); *vol. 3* (1984) (respectively, *Rep. Res. Comm. SAL*, **28** and **41**, and *OUCA Monogr.* **1**
Runcie, R. (ed.), *Cathedral and City: St Albans Ancient and Modern* (1977)
Wheeler, R.E.M. and Wheeler, T.V., *Verulamium: a Belgic and Two Roman Cities* (1936) (*Rep. Res. Comm. SAL*, **11**)

The Visual Arts and Crafts

The principal source for this chapter is Toynbee (1962), noted in the first section below; it should be consulted first for its fine illustrations. Other sources are noted below as appropriate.

General (including representations of Mercury)

Ellison, A. and Henig, M., 'Head of Mercury from Uley, Gloucester', *Antiquity*, **55** (1981), 43–4

Henig, M., 'Fragments of a stone cult-statue of Mercury from West Hill, Uley: an interim note', in W. Rodwell (ed.), *Temples, Churches and Religion: recent research in Roman Britain* (1980), pp. 321–25 (*BAR 77*)

Lindgren, C., *Classical Art Forms and Celtic Mutations: Figural Art in Roman Britain* (Park Ridge, N.J., 1980)

Potter, T.W., *Roman Britain* (1983) (popular account from British Museum)

Strong, D. and Brown, D. (eds.), *Roman Crafts* (1976)

Toynbee, J.M.C., *Art in Roman Britain* (1962)

Art in Britain under the Romans (1964)

The Roman Art Treasures from the Temple of Mithras (1986) (*London & Middx. Archaeol. Soc. Special Papers,* **7**)

Distance slabs from the Antonine Wall

Macdonald, G., *The Roman Wall in Scotland* (2nd edn 1934)

Keppie, L.J.F. and Arnold, B.J., *Corpus Signorum Imperii Romani: Great Britain,* vol. *1(4)*, *Scotland* (1984) [good illustrations, but text less approachable than Macdonald's]

Mosaics

Johnson, P., *Romano-British Mosaics* (1982) (Shire)

Johnston, D.E., 'The central southern group of Romano-British mosaics', in J. Munby and M. Henig (eds [see next reference], pp. 195–215

Munby, J. and Henig, M. (eds.), *Roman Life and Art in Britain: a Celebration in Honour of the 80th Birthday of Jocelyn Toynbee* (1977) (*BAR,* **41**) [essays on various aspects of mosaics and other arts, e.g. paintings, mirrors, face-pots, gemstones, and sculptures]

Neal, D.S., *Roman Mosaics in Britain: an Introduction to their Schemes and a Catalogue of Paintings* (1981) (*Britannia*

Monogr. Ser, **1**) [for Kingscote Venus, etc.]

Rainey, A., *Mosaics in Roman Britain: a Gazetteer* (1973)

Ramm, H., *The Parisii* (1978) [Yorkshire tribe]

Smith, D.J., *The Roman Mosaics from Rudston, Brantingham and Horkstow* (1976) (booklet with excellent illustrations)

'The mosaic pavements', in A.L.F. Rivet (ed.), *The Roman Villa in Britain* (1969), pp. 71–125

Stead, I.M., *Rudston Roman Villa* (1980)

Silverware of Late Roman Britain

Curle, A.O., *The Treasure of Traprain: a Scottish Hoard of Roman Silver Plate* (1923)

Kent, J.P.C. and Painter, K.S. (eds.), *Wealth of the Roman World AD 300–700* (1977)

Painter, K.S., *The Mildenhall Treasure: Roman Silver from East Anglia* (1977) [British Museum booklet]

The Water Newton Early Christian Silver (1977) [British Museum booklet]

Thomas, C., *Christianity in Roman Britain to AD 500* (1981)

Toynbee, J.M.C., 'Silver picture plates of Late Antiquity: A.D. 300 to 700', *Archaeologia,* **108** (1986), 15–65

Additional references

Allason-Jones, L. and McKay, B., *Coventina's Well: a Shrine on Hadrian's Wall* (1985) [catalogue of cult objects]

Anderson, A.C., *A Guide to Roman Fine Wares* (1980)

Anderson, A.S., *Roman Military Tombstones* (1984) (Shire)

Braithwaite, G., 'Romano-British face pots and head pots', *Britannia,* **15** (1984), 99–131

British Museum, *Guide to the Antiquities of Roman Britain* (3rd edn 1964) (for Prickwillow skillet and Southbroom Mercury, among other items)

Casey, P.J., *Roman Coinage in Britain* (1980) (Shire)

Clarke, D.V. *et al.* (eds.), *The Romans in Scotland: an Introduction to the Collections of the National Museum of Antiquities of Scotland* (1980)

Collingwood, R.G. and Richmond, I.A., *The Archaeology of Roman Britain* (1969) [partly out of date except for illustrations and factual records]

Cookson, N., *Romano-British mosaics: a reassessment and critique of some notable stylistic affinities* (1984) (*BAR,* **135**)

Crummy, P., *In Search of Colchester's Past* (1984) [for Colchester vase]

Davey, N. and Ling, R., *Wall Painting in Roman Britain* (1982) (= *Britannia Monogr. Ser.*, **3**) [includes Kingscote paintings]

Foster, J., *Bronze Boar Figurines in Iron Age and Roman Britain* (1977) (*BAR* **39**)

Green, M.J., *A Corpus of Small Cult-Objects from the Military Areas of Roman Britain* (1978) (*BAR*, **52**)

A Corpus of Religious Material from the Civilian Areas of Roman Britain (1976) (*BAR* **24**)

The Gods of Roman Britain (1983) (Shire)

Hattatt, R., *Ancient and Romano-British Brooches* (1982)

Iron Age and Roman Brooches (1985)

Henig, M., *A Corpus of Roman Engraved Gemstones from British Sites* (2 vols., 1974) (*BAR*, **8**)

Religion in Roman Britain (1984) (bib.)

'Graeco-Roman art and Romano-British imagination', *J. Brit. Archaeol. Ass.*, **138** (1984), 1–22

Vindolanda Jewellery (1975) [booklet]

Henig, M. and King, A. (eds.), *Pagan Gods and Shrines of the Roman Empire* (1986) (*OUCA Monogr.*, **8**)

Johns, C. *et al.*, 'The Wincle, Cheshire, hoard of Roman gold jewellery', *Antiq. J.*, **60** (1980), 48–58

Johns, C. and Potter, T.W., *The Thetford Treasure: Roman Jewellery and Silver* (1983)

Kilbride-Jones, H.E., *Celtic Craftsmanship in Bronze* (1980) [many drawings of artefacts]

Ling, R., *Romano-British Wall Painting* (1985) (Shire)

Liversidge, J., *Britain in the Roman Empire* (1968)

Furniture in Roman Britain (1955)

Liversidge, J. (ed.), *Roman Provincial Wall Painting of the Western Empire* (1982) (*BAR Int. Ser.*, **S140**) [includes details of many recently discovered paintings in Britain]

McWhirr, A., *Roman Crafts and Industries* (1982) (Shire)

Oswald, F. and Pryce, T.D., *An Introduction to the Study of Terra Sigillata . . .* (1920) [the standard work on 'samian' ware]

Painter, K.S., 'The design of the Roman mosaic at Hinton St Mary', *Antiq. J.*, **56** (1976), 49–54

Pitts, L.F., *Roman Bronze Figurines from the Civitates of the Catuvellauni and Trinovantes* (1979) (*BAR*, **60**)

Swan, V.G., *Pottery in Roman Britain* (3rd edn 1980) (Shire)

Toller, H., *Roman Lead Coffins and Ossuaria in Britain* (1977) (*BAR*, **38**)

Wild, J.P., *Textile Manufacture in the Northern Roman Provinces* (1970)

The Vindolanda Textiles (1975) [booklet on the finds from the Roman fort in Northumberland]

Wright, R.P. and Phillips, E.J., *Catalogue of the Roman Inscribed and Sculptured Stones in Carlisle Museum, Tullie House* (3rd edn 1975)

Lullingstone Villa

Meates, G.W., *The Roman Villa at Lullingstone, Kent: Vol. I, The Site* (1979) (*Kent Archaeol. Soc. Monogr. Series*, **1**)

See also the references to villas in 'The Cultural and Social Setting' by P. Salway, pp. 31–48.

Early Medieval Britain

The Cultural and Social Setting

The bibliography to this section is subdivided in the same way as the author's text, for ease of consultation. Further titles can be found in the sections on architecture and on visual arts and crafts for this period. A useful occasional publication is *Anglo-Saxon Studies in Archaeology and History* of which four volumes have appeared so far: it is obtainable from Oxbow Books of Oxford. *Anglo-Saxon England* (annually) contains a comprehensive bibliography of the year's publications on all aspects of AS studies. Martin Werner's *Insular Art: an Annotated Bibliography* (Boston, 1984) will be found useful for tracing further books and articles on particular subjects. Readers wishing to pursue this section into the Norman Conquest period will find the annual *Anglo-Norman Studies* indispensable.

General

Blair, J., 'The Anglo-Saxon period (c.440–1066)' in K.O. Morgan (ed.), *Oxford Illustrated History of Britain* (1984), pp. 52–103
Bonner, G., 'Bede and medieval civilization', *Anglo-Saxon Engl.*, **2** (1973), 71–90
Brooke, C. *The Saxon and Norman Kings* (rev. edn 1977)
Brooks, N.P., 'England in the 9th century: the crucible of defeat', *Trans. Royal Historical Society*, **5** ser. **29** (1979), 1–20
Brown, David, *Anglo-Saxon England* (1978) [good general introduction to archaeology of the period]

Campbell, James (ed.), *The Anglo-Saxons* (1982) [important and profusely illustrated compilation and bib. – indispensable]
Colgrave, B. and Mynors, R.A.B. (eds.), *Bede's Ecclesiastical History of the English People* (1969) [contains both Latin text and translation; is particularly important for this chapter, and contains – for instance – the reference to the Ely monks' search for a Roman sarcophagus]
Fell, C., *Women in Anglo-Saxon England* (1984)
Garmonsway, G.N. (ed. and transl.), *The Anglo-Saxon Chronicle* (2nd edn 1954)
Gelling, M., *Signposts to the Past: Place-Names and the History of England* (1978)
  Place-names in the Landscape (1984)
Higgitt, J. (ed.), *Early Medieval Sculpture in Britain and Ireland* (1984) (*BAR*, **152**) [essays on various aspects of sculpture]
Hill, D., *An Atlas of Anglo-Saxon England* (rev. edn 1984) [compendious collection of data, mostly in map form, on many aspects of the time]
Loyn, H.R., *The Governance of Anglo-Saxon England, 500–1087* (1984)
Meaney, A.L.S., *A Gazetteer of Early Anglo-Saxon Burial Sites* (1964)
Muir, R., *The National Trust Guide to Dark Age and Medieval Britain 400–1350* (1985)
Ordnance Survey, *Britain in the Dark Ages* (2nd edn 1966) [map, gazetteer, and explanatory text]
Page, R.I., *Life in Anglo-Saxon England* (1970)

Rahtz, P. *et al.* (eds.), *Anglo-Saxon Cemeteries* (1980) (*BAR*, **82**)

Reynolds, S., 'What do we mean by "Anglo-Saxon" and "Anglo-Saxons"?', *J. Brit. Stud.* **24** (1985), 395–414

Rice, D. Talbot (ed.), *The Dark Ages (The Dawn of European Civilization)* (1965)

Sawyer, P.H., *From Roman Britain to Norman England* (1978)

Smith, L.M. (ed.), *The Dark Ages* (1984) [a well-regarded London Weekend Television book – bib.]

Stenton, Sir F.M., *Anglo-Saxon England* (3rd edn 1971)

Szarmach, P.E. (ed.), *Sources of Anglo-Saxon Culture* (1986) (*Studies in Medieval Culture, XX*, Kalamazoo)

Wallace-Hadrill, J., *The Barbarian West 400–1100* (1985 edn)
  Early Medieval History (1975) [Anglo-Saxon England in the European context]

Whitelock, D. (ed. and transl.), *The Anglo-Saxon Chronicle* (1961)

Whitelock, D. (ed.), *English Historical Documents: I c.500–1042* (2nd edn 1979) [for translation of laws, Anglo-Saxon Chronicle extracts, letters, charters, etc.]
  The Beginnings of English Society (Pelican History of England, 2) (rev. edn 1974)

Whitelock, D., *et al.* (eds), *Councils and Synods, with Other Documents Relating to the Early Church: I, AD 871–1204* (2 parts, 1981) [for a mass of material on the Anglo-Saxon period and the two following centuries]

Wilson, D.M., *Anglo-Saxon Art from the Seventh Century to the Norman Conquest* (1984) [basic reference source for much of the material treated here, for example Tassilo Chalice, Viking tomb sculpture from St Paul's, etc.]
  The Anglo-Saxons (3rd edn 1981)

Wilson, D.M. (ed.), *The Archaeology of Anglo-Saxon England* (1976) [classic compilation: bib.]
  The Northern World: the History and Heritage of Northern Europe, AD 400–1100 (1980)

The settlement

[For Sutton Hoo and Yeavering see the sections on visual arts and architecture, respectively.]

Alcock, L., *Arthur's Britain: History and Archaeology AD 367–634* (2nd edn 1973)

Bell, M., 'Saxon Sussex', in P.L. Drewett (ed.), *Archaeology in Sussex to AD 1500*, (1977), pp. 64–9 (*CBA Res. Rep.*, **29**)

Bonney, D.J., 'Early boundaries and estates in Southern England', in P.H. Sawyer (ed.), *Medieval Settlement: Continuity and Change* (1976), pp. 72–82

Cameron, K. (ed.), *Place-Name Evidence for the Anglo-Saxon Invasion and Scandinavian Settlements* (1976)

Chadwick, H.M., *Studies on Anglo-Saxon Institutions* (1905)

Dixon, P.W., *Barbarian Europe* (1976)

Dumville, D.N., 'Sub-Roman Britain: history and legend', *History* **62** (1977), 173–92

Hawkes, S.C., 'Anglo-Saxon Kent c.425–725', in P.E. Leach (ed.), *Archaeology in Kent to AD 1500* (1982), pp. 64–78 (*CBA Res. Rep.*, **48**)
  'The early Saxon period', in G. Briggs *et al.* (eds.), *The Archaeology of the Oxford Region* (1986), pp. 64–108

Henderson, G., *Early Medieval (Style and Civilization)* (1972), pp. 111–12 (refers to re-use of Roman cameo)

Henig, M. and Heslop, T.A., 'The Great Cameo of St. Albans', *J. Brit. Archaeol. Ass.*, **139** (1986), 148–53

Hills, C., 'The Anglo-Saxon settlement of England', in D.M. Wilson (ed.), *The Northern World* (1980), pp. 71–94
  'The archaeology of England in the pagan period: a review', *Anglo-Saxon Engl.*, **8** (1979), 297–330

Hope-Taylor, B., *Under York Minster: Archaeological Discoveries 1966–71* (1971) [pamphlet for general public]

Jackson, K.H., *Language and History in Early Britain* (repr. 1953) [difficult text but rewarding]

Morris, R.K., *Cathedrals and Abbeys of England and Wales* (1979) [for – among other things – the Matthew Paris reference to St Albans monks re-using Roman materials]

Myres, J.N.L., *The English Settlements* (1986) (bib.)

Sisam, K., 'Anglo-Saxon royal genealogies', *Proc. Brit. Acad.*, **39** (1953), 287–348

Strang, B.M.H., *A History of English* (1970)

Thomas, A.C., *Britain and Ireland in Early Christian Times AD 400–800* (1971)
  Christianity in Roman Britain to AD 500 (2nd edn 1985) (bib.)

Todd, M., *The Northern Barbarians 100 B.C. – A.D. 300* (1975)

Winterbottom, M., *Gildas: The Ruin of Britain and other works* (1978) [Gildas text]

The conversion

The main reference for this section is Bede (see the reference under Colgrave and

Mynors in the introductory section above).
For poetry, see the references to the section
on literature; and for Lindisfarne and St
Cuthbert see the section on the visual arts
and crafts. For illuminated manuscripts the
main reference is Alexander, J.J.G., *Insular
Manuscripts, Sixth to Ninth Century* (1978)

Bailey, R.N., *The Durham Cassiodorus*
(Jarrow Lecture 1978)
Barley, M.W. and Hanson, R.P.C. (eds.),
Christianity in Britain AD 300–700
(1968)
Battiscombe, C.F. (ed.), *The relics of St
Cuthbert* (1956) [see p. 33 for reference
to Athelstan donation]
Bieler, L., *Ireland; Harbinger of the Middle
Ages* (2nd edn 1966) [beautifully
illustrated, intermediate level text]
Butler, L.A.S. and Morris, R. (eds.), *The
Anglo-Saxon Church* [for early wooden
churches and other important
statements on present knowledge; for
full reference see section on
architecture]
Campbell, A. (ed. and transl.), *Aethelwulf,
De Abbatibus* (1967)
Campbell, J., 'Bede', in T.A. Dorey (ed.),
Latin Historians (1966), pp. 159–90
Bede's Reges and Principes (Jarrow
Lecture, 1979)
Colgrave, B. (ed. and transl.), *Felix's Life of
Saint Guthlac* (1956, repr. 1985)
(ed. and transl.), *Two Lives of Saint
Cuthbert* (1940, repr. 1985)
(ed. and transl.), *The Life of Bishop
Wilfrid by Eddius Stephanus* (1927,
repr. 1985)
Cramp, R. (ed.), *Corpus of Anglo-Saxon
Stone Sculpture in England: Vol. i,
County Durham and Northumberland*
(1984)
Dodwell, C.R., *Anglo-Saxon Art: a New
Perspective* (1982) [an account of some
of the vanished items as well as those
that survived]
Dumville, D.N., 'A re-examination of the
origins and contents of the ninth-
century section of the Book of Cerne',
J. Theological Studies, n ser., **23** (1972),
374–406 [liturgical drama, and also
includes mention of the Northumbrian
manuscript now in Cambridge.]
Dunbar, J.G. and Fisher, I., *Iona* (1983)
[colour guide to the Early Christian
monuments]
Farrell, R.T. (ed.), *Bede and Anglo-Saxon
England* (1978) (*BAR*, **46**)
Fox, C., *Offa's Dyke: a Field Survey of the
Western Frontier Works of Mercia in the
7th and 8th Centuries AD* (1955) [out of
date in many details, but remains the

main source on the Dyke; see Hill
below]
Gneuss, H., 'The origin of Standard Old
English and Aethelwold's school at
Winchester', *Anglo-Saxon Engl.*, **1**
(1972), 63–83
'A preliminary list of manuscripts written
or owned in England up to 1100',
Anglo-Saxon Engl., **9** (1980), 1–60
Godman, P. (ed. and transl.), *Alcuin, the
Bishops, Kings and Saints of York*
(1982) (*Oxf. Medieval Texts*, **132**)
Haslam, J. (ed.), *Anglo-Saxon Towns in
Southern England* (1984) [individual
statements on each of the main towns]
Hassall, T.G., 'The Oxford region from the
Conversion to the Conquest', in G.
Briggs *et al.* (eds.), *The Archaeology of
the Oxford Region* (1986), pp. 109–14
Henry, F., *Irish Art in the Early Christian
Period to AD 800* (1965)
Hill, D., 'The construction of Offa's Dyke',
Antiq. J., **65** (1985), 140–42
Hines, J., The Scandinavian Character of
Anglian England in the Pre-Viking
Period (1984) (*BAR*, **124**)
Hinton, D.A., *Alfred's Kingdom: Wessex
and the South 800–1500* (1977) [bib.:
useful introduction]
Hughes, K., 'Evidence for contacts between
the churches of the Irish and English
from the Synod of Whitby to the
Viking Age', in P. Clemoes and
K. Hughes (eds.), *England Before the
Conquest: Studies in Primary Sources
Presented to Dorothy Whitelock* (1971),
pp. 49–67
Hunter Blair, P., *An Introduction to Anglo-
Saxon England* (2nd edn 1977)
Northumbria in the Days of Bede (1976)
The World of Bede (1970)
Lapidge, M. and Herren, M. (ed. and
transl.), *Aldhelm: Prose Works* (1979)
Lapidge, M. and Rosier, J.L., *The
Venerable Bede, the Rule of St Benedict
and Social Class* (Jarrow Lecture, 1976)
Lapidge, M. and Rosier, J.L. (ed. and
transl.), *Aldhelm: Poetic Works* (1984)
Mayr-Harting, H., *The Coming of
Christianity to Anglo-Saxon England*
(1972) [important reference for this
section]
Meyvaert, P., 'Bede and the church
paintings at Wearmouth-Jarrow',
Anglo-Saxon Engl., **8** (1979), 63–77
Talbot, C.H., *The Anglo-Saxon Missionaries
in Germany* (rev. edn 1981) [for
Boniface]
Thomas, A.C., *The Early Christian
Archaeology of North Britain* (1971)
(bib.)

Bede, Archaeology and the Cult of Relics
(Jarrow Lecture 1973)
Celtic Britain (1986)
Thompson, A.H. (ed.), *Bede, his Life, Times
and Writings* (1935)
Webb, J.F. and Farmer, D.H. (eds.), *The
Age of Bede. Bede: Life of Cuthbert;
Eddius Stephanus: Life of Wilfred;
Bede: Lives of the Abbots of Wearmouth
and Jarrow; with the Voyage of Brendan*
(rev. edn 1983)
Wormald, P., 'Bede, Beowulf and the
conversion of the Anglo-Saxon
aristocracy', in R.T. Farrell (ed.), *Bede
and Anglo-Saxon England* (1978), pp.
32–95 (*BAR*, **46**) [on nobility in
monasteries]
'Bede, the Bretwaldas and the origins of
the Gens Anglorum', in P. Wormald *et
al.* (eds.), *Ideal and Reality: Studies in
Frankish and Anglo-Saxon Society.
Studies Presented to J.M. Wallace-
Hadrill* (1983), pp. 99–129

The Vikings
There are very many books on the Vikings
and we give only a selection of the most
recent ones below.
Bailey, R.N., *Viking Age Sculpture in
Northern England* (1980)
Dumville, D.N., *Wessex and England from
Alfred to Edgar* (1986)
Foote, P.G. and Wilson, D.M., *The Viking
Achievement: the Society and Culture of
Early Medieval Scandinavia* (1970)
Graham-Campbell, J., *The Viking World*
(1980)
Viking Artefacts: a Select Catalogue
(1980)
Graham-Campbell, J. and Kidd, D., *The
Vikings* (1980)
Hall, R., *The Excavations at York: the
Viking Dig* (1984) [how the story of the
Anglo-Scandinavian town was
uncovered]
Hall, R. (ed.), *Viking Age York and the
North* (1978) [collection of scholarly
essays] (*CBA Res. Rep.*, **27**)
Henry, F., *Irish Art During the Viking
Invasions 800–1020 AD* (1967)
Higham, N., *The Northern Counties to AD
1000* (1986) [especially the Anglo-
Scandinavian chapter]
Ker, N.R., *Catalogue of Manuscripts
Containing Anglo-Saxon* (1957)
Keynes, S., 'King Athelstan's books', in M.
Lapidge and H. Gneuss (eds.),
*Learning and Literature in Anglo-Saxon
England* (1985), pp. 143–201

Keynes, S. and Lapidge, M. (ed. and
transl.), *Alfred the Great: Asser's Life
of King Alfred and Other Contemporary
Sources* (1983) (bib.)
Lang, J.T. (ed.), *Anglo-Saxon and Viking-
Age and Sculpture and its Context*
(1978) (*BAR*, **49**)
'The hogback: a Viking colonial
monument', *Anglo-Saxon Stud.
Archaeol. Hist*, **3** (1984), 83–176
Loyn, H., *Anglo-Saxon England and the
Norman Conquest* (1970)
The Vikings in Britain (1977)
Ordnance Survey, *Britain Before the
Norman Conquest* (1973) [map of sites
from the two centuries preceding the
Conquest]
Rice, D. Talbot, *English Art 871–1100*
(1952) (for Romsey Rood)
Roesdahl, E. *et al.*, *The Vikings in England
and in their Danish Homeland* (1981)
[catalogue of large touring exhibition]
Sawyer, P., *The Age of the Vikings* (2nd edn
1971)
*Kings and Vikings: Scandinavia and
Europe AD 700–1100* (1982)
Wheeler, R.E.M., *London and the Vikings*
(1927) (London Museum Catalogue 1)
Whitelock, D., 'The prose of Alfred's
reign', in E.G. Stanley (ed.),
Continuations and Beginnings . . .
(1966), pp. 67–103
Wilson, D.M., *The Vikings and Their
Origins* (1970)
Wilson, D.M. and Klindt Jensen, O.,
Viking Art (2nd edn 1980)
Wood, M., 'The making of King
Aethelstan's empire: an English
Charlemagne?', in P. Wormald *et al.*
(eds.), *Ideal and Reality: Studies in
Frankish and Anglo-Saxon Society.
Studies Presented to J.M. Wallace-
Hadrill* (1983), pp. 250–72
Wormald, P., 'The uses of literacy in
Anglo-Saxon England and its
neighbours', *Trans. Royal Hist. Soc.* **5**
ser. 27 (1977), 95–114
'Viking studies: whence and whither?', in
R.T. Farrell (ed.), *The Vikings* (1982),
pp. 128–53

The Benedictine reform movement
Backhouse, J. *et al.*, *The Golden Age of
Anglo-Saxon Art 966–1066* (1984) [for
Ramsey Psalter among other important
items]
Barlow, F., *Edward the Confessor* (1970)
Brooke, C.N.L. and Swaan, W., *The
Monastic World 1000–1300* (1974)

Deanesley, M., *The Pre-Conquest Church in England* (2nd edn 1962)

Knowles, D., *The Monastic Order in England . . .* (2nd edn 1963)

Parsons, D. (ed.), *Tenth Century Studies: Essays in Commemoration of the Millennium of the Council of Winchester and 'Regularis Concordia'* (1975) [important collection of essays]

Temple, E., *Anglo-Saxon Manuscripts 900–1066* (1976) [for Ramsey Psalter and other examples]

From Reform to Early Norman

Brown, R.A., *The Normans* (1984)
The Norman Conquest (1985) (*Documents of Medieval History*, **5**)
The Normans and the Norman Conquest (2nd edn 1986)
'The Norman impact', *History Today*, **36** (May, 1986), 9–16

Chibnall, M., *Anglo-Norman England 1066–1166* (1986)

Douglas, D.C. and Greenaway, G.W. (eds), *English Historical Documents 1042–1189* (2nd edn 1981) [basic source of translated contemporary texts]

English Romanesque Art 1066–1200 (1984) [Arts Council exhibition catalogue]

Kahn, D., 'The Norman world of art', *History Today*, **36** (March 1986), 34–39

Loyn, H., *The Norman Conquest* (3rd edn 1982)

Matthew, D., *The Norman Monasteries and their English Possessions* (1962)

Wilson, D.M., *Anglo-Saxon Art . . .* [see full reference in introduction to this section: for St Paul's Churchyard sculpture, among other items]

The Visual Arts and Crafts of Anglo-Saxon England

General and interdisciplinary

The works listed under 'Cultural and Social Setting' (pp. 279–83) should be consulted in addition to those given below. Many of the items treated in Dr Budney's chapter can be found mentioned in the works by Backhouse *et al.*, Campbell, and Zarnecki below, in which further references are given. Two useful reference works are Deshman, R., *Anglo-Saxon and Anglo–Scandinavian Art: an Annotated Bibliography* (Boston, Mass., 1984) and Werner, M., *Insular Art: an Annotated Bibliography* (Boston, Mass., 1984). For keeping up to date with new work, the annual bibliography in *Anglo-Saxon England* (CUP) is indispensable.

Backhouse, J. *et al.*, (eds.), *The Golden Age of Anglo-Saxon Art, 966–1066* (1984) [exhibition catalogue]

British Library, *The Benedictines in Britain* (1980) (*British Library Series*, **3**)

Brøndsted, J., *Early English Ornament: the Sources, Development and Relation to Foreign Styles of pre-Norman Ornamental Art in England* (1924) [important reference work]

Brown, G. Baldwin, *The Arts in Early England* (6 vols., 1903–37): I, *The Life of Saxon England in its Relation to the Arts* (1903); II, *Anglo-Saxon Architecture* (2nd edn, 1925); III and IV, *Saxon Art and Industry in the Pagan Period* (1915); V, *The Ruthwell and Bewcastle Crosses, the Gospels of Lindisfarne, and other Christian Monuments of Northumbria* (1921); VI, i, *Completion of the Study of the Monuments of the Great Period of the Art of Anglian Northumbria* (1930), and VI, ii, *Anglo-Saxon Sculpture* (1937). [Although superseded in certain respects by subsequent research and discoveries, this is a splendid work.

Budny, M., *St Dunstan: Poet, Artist, Craftsman and Patron* (1988).

Campbell, J. (ed.), *The Anglo-Saxons* (1982) [attractive basic work]

Carver, M.O.H., 'Contemporary artefacts illustrated in Late Saxon manuscripts', *Archaeologia*, **108** (1986), 117–45

Caviness, M., 'Images of divine order and the third mode of seeing', *Gesta*, **22(2)** (1983), 99–120

Coldstream, N. and Draper, P. (eds.), *Medieval Art and Architecture at Durham Cathedral (Trans. Brit. Archaeol. Ass. Conference*, **3** (1977, publ. 1980)

Cramp, R., *The Monastic Arts of Northumbria* (1967) [exhibition catalogue]

Cramp, R. and Lang, J., *A Century of Anglo-Saxon Sculpture* (1977) [catalogue of an exhibition]

Cramp, R. and Miket, R., *Catalogue of the Anglo-Saxon and Viking Antiquities in the Museum of Antiquities, Newcastle upon Tyne* (1982)

Deshman, R., 'Anglo-Saxon art after Alfred', *Art Bulletin*, **56** (1974), 176–200

Dodwell, C.R., 'Losses of Anglo-Saxon art in the Middle Ages', *Bull. of the John*

Rylands Library of the University of Manchester, **61** (1973), 74–92

Anglo-Saxon Art: a New Perspective (1982)

Dornier, A. (ed.), *Mercian Studies* (1977)

Evison, V.I. (ed.), *Angles, Saxons, and Jutes: Essays presented to J.N.L. Myres* (1981)

Farrell, R.T. (ed.), *Bede and Anglo-Saxon England* (1978) (*BAR*, **46**)

Fell, C., with C. Clark and E. Williams, *Women in Anglo-Saxon England and the Impact of 1066* (1984)

Henderson, G., *Losses and Lacunae in Early Insular Art* (1982) (Third Garmonsway Lecture 1975) (= *Univ. York Medieval Monogr. Series*, **3**)

Studies in English Bible Illustration, I (1985)

Henry, F., *Irish Art in the Early Christian Period (to 800 AD)* (1965)

Irish Art During the Viking Invasions, 800–1020 AD (1967)

Irish Art in the Romanesque Period (1020–1170 AD) (1970)

Hills, C., 'The archaeology of Anglo-Saxon England in the pagan period: a review', *Anglo-Saxon Engl.*, **8** (1979), 297–329 [bib.]

'The Anglo-Saxon settlement of England', in D.M. Wilson (ed), *The Northern World . . . AD 400–1100* (1980), pp. 71–94

The Blood of the British (1986)

Hubert, J. *et al.*, *Europe in the Dark Ages* (1969) (*The Arts of Mankind*. ed. A. Malraux and A. Parrot)

Kendrick, T.D., *Anglo-Saxon Art to AD 900* (1938) [general and impressionistic survey, largely outdated]

Late Saxon and Viking Art (1949)

Kirby, D.P. (ed.), *Saint Wilfrid at Hexham* (1974) [essays on sculpture and metalwork]

Leeds, E.T., *Early Anglo-Saxon Art and Archaeology* (1936, repr. 1968) [classic work, but needs to be used in conjunction with a modern one such as Campbell (above)]

Macready, S. and Thompson, F.H. (eds.), *Art and Patronage in the English Romanesque* (1986) (*SAL Occasional Papers*, **8**)

Meaney, A., *Anglo-Saxon Amulets and Curing Stones* (1981) (*BAR*, **96**)

Ogilvy, J.D.A., *The Place of Wearmouth and Jarrow in Western Cultural History* (1968, repr. 1978) (Jarrow Lecture)

Parsons, D. (ed.), *Tenth-Century Studies* (1975) [essays on illuminated manuscripts, sculpture, and metalwork]

Peers, C.R. and Radford, C.A.R., 'The Saxon monastery of Whitby', *Archaeologia*, **89** (1943), 27–88

Rice, D. Talbot, *English Art 871–1100* (1952) (Oxford Hist. of English Art, 2)

Robinson, J.A., *The Times of St Dunstan* (1923)

Saxl, F. and Wittkower, F., *British Art and the Mediterranean* (1948)

Schapiro, M., *Late Antique, Early Christian and Medieval Art* (New York, 1979) [includes essays on the Ruthwell Cross, Wearmouth-Jarrow manuscripts, and late Anglo-Saxon images of the 'Disappearing Christ'.]

Smith, R.A., *A Guide to the Anglo-Saxon and Foreign Teutonic Antiquities in the Dept of British and Medieval Antiquities* (1923)

Szarmach, P.E., (ed.), *Sources of Anglo-Saxon Culture* (1986) (*Studies in Medieval Culture*, **20**) [essays on various arts, particularly sculpture and illuminated manuscripts]

Wheeler, R.E.M., *London and the Vikings* (1927) (*London Museum Catalogues*, **1**)

London and the Saxons (1935) (*London Museum Catalogues*, **6**)

Wilson, D.M., 'An Anglo-Saxon bookbinding at Fulda (Codex Bonifatianus 1)', *Antiquaries J.*, **41**, (1961), 199–217

'Craft and industry', in D.M. Wilson (ed.), *The Archaeology of Anglo-Saxon England* (1976), pp. 253–81

Anglo-Saxon Art from the 7th Century to the Norman Conquest (1984)

Wormald, F., *Collected Writings, I: Studies in Medieval Art from the 6th to the 12th Centuries*, ed. J.J.G. Alexander *et al.*, (1984) [includes items on manuscripts and other arts]

Zarnecki, G. *et al.* (eds.), *English Romanesque Art 1066–1200* (1984) [catalogue of Arts Council exhibition]

Coins

Dolley, M. (ed.), *Anglo-Saxon Coins: Studies Presented to Sir Frank Stenton* (1961)

Anglo-Saxon Pennies (1964)

Keynes, S. and Blackburn, M., *Anglo-Saxon Coins* (1985)

Glass

Cramp, R.J., 'Decorated window glass and millefiori from Monkwearmouth', *Antiq. J.*, **50** (1970), 327–35

Harden, D.B., 'Glass vessels in Britain and Ireland, AD 400–1000', in D.B. Harden (ed.), *Dark Age Britain:*

Studies Presented to E.T. Leeds (1956), pp. 132–67

'Anglo-Saxon and later medieval glass in Britain: some recent developments', *Medieval Archaeol.*, **22** (1978), 1–24

Ivory, bone and antler

Beckwith, J., *Ivory Carvings in Early Medieval England* (1972)

Ivory Carvings in Early Medieval England 700–1200 (1974) [smaller and more accessible than his 1972 work]

Collis, J. and Kjølbye-Biddle, B., 'Early medieval bone spoons from Winchester', *Antiq. J.*, **59** (1979), 375–91

Galloway, P. and Newcomer, M., 'The craft of comb-making: an experimental enquiry', *Bull. of the Institute of Archaeology, Univ. of London*, **18** (1981), 73–90

Heslop, T.A., 'English seals from the mid-9th century to 1100', *J. Brit. Archaeol. Ass.*, **133** (1980), 1–16

Longhurst, M.H., *English Ivories* (1926) [many good black-and-white plates]

MacGregor, A., *Bone, Antler, Ivory and Horn: the Technology of Skeletal Materials Since the Roman Period* (1985)

Webster, L., 'Stylistic aspects of the Franks Casket', in R.T. Farrell (ed.), *The Vikings* (1982), pp. 20–31

Manuscript and paintings

Many important manuscripts are available in facsimile, or are reproduced in part in reasonably priced paperback editions; but the best editions are very expensive and usually found only in large or specialist libraries. The principal works of reference are Alexander (1978), Temple (1976), and Kauffmann (1975) below.

Alexander, J.J.G., *Anglo-Saxon Illumination in Oxford Libraries* (1970) [pamphlet]

'The Benedictional of St Aethelwold and Anglo-Saxon illumination of the Reform Period', in D. Parsons (ed.), *Tenth Century Studies* (1975), pp. 169–83

'Some aesthetic principles in the use of colour in Anglo-Saxon art', *Anglo-Saxon Engl.*, **4** (1975), 145–54

Insular Manuscripts, 6th to the 9th Century (1978) (*Survey of Manuscripts Illuminated in the British Isles*, **1**)

Alexander, J. and Kauffmann, C.M., *English Illuminated Manuscripts 700–1500* (1973) [catalogue of an exhibition in Brussels]

Alton, E.H. and Meyer, P. (eds.), *Evangeliorum Quattuor Codex Cennanensis: . . . The Book of Kells* (Bern, 3 vols., 1950–51) [full facsimile with commentary]

Backhouse, J., *The Lindisfarne Gospels* (1981) [many colour illustrations with commentary]

'The making of the Harley Psalter', *Brit. Library J.*, **10** (1984), 97–113 [the Anglo-Saxon copy of the Utrecht Psalter]

Bailey, R.N., *The Durham Cassiodorus* (1979) (Jarrow Lecture)

Beckwith, J., *Early Medieval Art: Carolingian, Ottonian, Romanesque* (1969, repr. 1985) (World of Art series)

Bieler, L., 'Ireland's contribution to the culture of Northumbria', in G. Bonner (ed.), *Famulus Christi: Studies in Commemoration of . . . Bede* (1976), pp. 210–28

Bishop, T.A.M., *English Caroline Minuscule* (1971) (Oxford Palaeographical Handbooks) [a highly influential type of script]

Brown, T.J., 'Northumbria and the Book of Kells', *Anglo-Saxon Engl.*, **1** (1972), 219–46

Brown, T.J. (ed.), *The Stonyhurst Gospel of St John* (1969)

The Durham Ritual, a Southern English Collector of the 10th Century . . . (Copenhagen, 1969) (*Early English MSS in Facsimile*, **16**) [facsimile of and commentary on a manuscript by Aldred]

Bruce-Mitford, R.L.S., 'The art of the Codex Amiatinus', *J. Brit. Archaeol. Ass., 3 ser*, **32** (1969), 1–25

Calkins, R.G., *Illuminated Books of the Middle Ages* (1983) [includes examination of the Book of Durrow, Lindisfarne Gospels, and Book of Kells]

de Hamel, C., *A History of Illuminated Manuscripts* (1986)

Deshman, R., 'The Leofric Missal and 10th century English art', *Anglo-Saxon Engl.*, **6** (1977), 145–73

Dodwell, C.R., *The Canterbury School of Illumination 1066–1200* (1954)

Painting in Europe, 800–1200 (1971) (Pelican History of Art)

Dodwell, C.R. and Clemoes, P. (eds.), *The Old English Illustrated Hexateuch* (Copenhagen 1974) (Early English Manuscripts in Facsimile, 18)

Gem, R. and Tudor-Craig, P., 'A "Winchester School" wall-painting at Nether Wallop, Hampshire', *Anglo-Saxon Engl.*, **9** (1981), 115–36

Grabar, A. and Nordenfalk, C. (transl. S. Gilbert), *Early Medieval Painting from the 4th to the 11th Century* (New York, 1957)

Henderson, G.D.S., *Bede and the Visual Arts* (1980) (Jarrow Lecture)
Studies in English Bible Illustration, **I** (1985) [items on manuscript illustrations and other arts]

Henry, F., 'The Lindisfarne Gospels', *Antiquity*, **37** (1963), 100–10
The Book of Kells: Reproductions from the Manuscript in Trinity College, Dublin . . . (1974) [partial, but useful, facsimile with commentary]

Higgitt, J., 'Glastonbury, Dunstan, monasticism and manuscripts', *Art History*, **2** (1979), 275–90

Hunt, R.W., *Saint Dunstan's Classbook from Glastonbury* (Amsterdam 1961) (*Umbrae Codicum Occidentalium*, **4**) [full facsimile with commentary]

Kauffman, C.M., *Romanesque Manuscripts 1066–1190* (1975) (*A Survey of Manuscripts Illuminated in the British Isles*, **3**)

Kendrick, T.D. *et al.*, *Evangeliorum Quattuor Codex Lindisfarnensis* (Olten and Lausanne, 2 vols., 1956, 1960) [full facsimile of the Lindisfarne Gospels, with extensive commentary]

Ker, N.R., *Catalogue of Manuscripts Containing Anglo-Saxon* (1957)
English Manuscripts in the Century after the Norman Conquest (1960) (Lyell Lectures 1952–53) [describes the ways in which Anglo-Saxon and Norman scripts blended in different centres]

Lawrence, A., 'Manuscripts of early Anglo-Norman Canterbury', *Trans. Brit. Archaeol. Ass. Conf.*, **5** (1979, publ. 1982), 101–11

Lowe, E., *English Uncial* (1960) [the script masterfully developed in such centres as Wearmouth-Jarrow and Canterbury]

Luce, A.A. *et al.* (eds.), *Evangeliorum Quattuor Codex Durmachensis* (Olten and Lausanne, 1960) [full facsimile of the Book of Durrow, with commentary]

McGurk, P., *et al.*, *An Eleventh-Century Anglo-Saxon Illustrated Miscellany* (Copenhagen, 1983) (*Early English Manuscripts in Facsimile*, **21** [full facsimile of manuscript which includes an illustrated calendar]

Meyvaert, P., 'Bede and the church paintings at Wearmouth-Jarrow', *Anglo-Saxon Engl.*, **8** (1979), 63–77

Mynors, R.A.B., *Durham Cathedral Manuscripts to the End of the Twelfth Century* (1939)

Nordenfalk, C., *Celtic and Anglo-Saxon Painting: Book Illumination in the British Isles 600–800* (1977)

Nordhagen, Per J., *The Codex Amiatinus and the Byzantine Element in the Northumbrian Renaissance* (1977) (Jarrow Lecture)

O'Cróinin, D., 'Rath Melsigi, Willibrord, and the earliest Echternach manuscripts', *Peritia: J. of the Medieval Academy of Ireland*, **3** (1984), 17–49

Ohlgren, T.H. (ed.), *Insular and Anglo-Saxon Illuminated Manuscripts: an Iconographic Catalogue, c.AD 625 to 1100* (with contributions by C.T. Berkhout, M.O. Budny, *et al.*, (1986) [detailed list of images in decorated manuscripts]

Pächt, O. and Alexander, J.J.G., *Illuminated Manuscripts in the Bodleian Library, Oxford: Vol. 3, British, Irish, and Icelandic Schools* (1973)

Parkes, M.B., *The Scriptorium of Wearmouth-Jarrow* (1982) (Jarrow Lecture)

Raw, B., 'The probable derivation of most of the illustrations in Junius 11 from an illustrated Old Saxon Genesis', *Anglo-Saxon Engl.*, **5** (1976), 133–48

Rickert, M., *Painting in Britain: the Middle Ages* (2nd edn, 1965) (Pelican History of Art)

Rosenthal, J., 'Three drawings in an Anglo-Saxon pontifical: anthropomorphic Trinity or threefold Christ?', *Art Bull.*, **63** (1981), 547–62 [Sherborne Pontifical]

Swarzenski, H., 'The Anhalt Morgan Gospels', *Art Bull.*, **31** (1949), 77–83

Temple, E., *Anglo-Saxon Manuscripts 900–1066* (1976) (*Survey of Manuscripts Illuminated in the British Isles*, **2**) [and see review of this by Brownrigg in *Anglo-Saxon Engl.*, **7** (1978), 239–66]

Verey, C.D. *et al.* (eds.), *The Durham Gospels* (Copenhagen 1980) (*Early English Manuscripts in Facsimile*, **20**)

Westwood, J.O., *Fac-Similes of the Miniatures and Ornaments of Anglo-Saxon and Irish Manuscripts* (1868) [important landmark in the revival of study of decorated Insular and Anglo-Saxon manuscripts]

Wheeler, H., 'Aspects of Mercian art: the Book of Cerne', in A. Dornier (ed.), *Mercian Studies* (1977), 235–44

Wormald, F., *English Drawings of the 10th and 11th Centuries* (1952)
  'The "Winchester School" before St Aethelwold', in P. Clemoes and K. Hughes (eds.), *England Before the Conquest* (1971), pp. 305–13
Wright, D.H. (ed.), *The Vespasian Psalter* (Copenhagen, 1967) (*Early English Manuscripts in Facsimile*, **14**) [full facsimile and commentary]

Metalwork and jewels

Anstee, J.W. and Biek, L., 'A study in pattern welding', *Medieval Archaeology*, **5** (1961), 71–93
Avent, R., *Anglo-Saxon Garnet Inlaid Disc and Composite Brooches* (2 vols., 1975) (*BAR*, **11**)
Bailey, R.N., 'The Anglo-Saxon metalwork from Hexham', in D.P. Kirby (ed.), *Saint Wilfrid at Hexham* (1974), pp. 141–67
Bakka, E., 'The Alfred Jewel and sight', *Antiq. J.*, **46** (1966), 277–82
Bruce-Mitford, R.L.S., 'The pectoral cross of St Cuthbert' in R.L.S. Bruce-Mitford (ed.), *Aspects of Anglo-Saxon History: Sutton Hoo and Other Discoveries* (1974), pp. 281–302
Budny, M. and Graham-Campbell, J., 'An eighth-century bronze ornament from Canterbury and related works', *Archaeologia Cantiana*, **97** (1981), 7–25 [far-ranging discussion of art styles]
Clarke, J.R. and Hinton, D.A., *The Alfred and Minster Lovell Jewels* (1979)
Davidson, H.R.E., *The Sword in Anglo-Saxon England* (1962) [literary and social setting for swords]
Dickinson, T.M., 'On the origin and chronology of the early Anglo-Saxon disc brooch', *Anglo-Saxon Studies in Archaeology and History*, **1** (1979), 39–80 (*BAR*, **72**)
Harbert, B., 'King Alfred's aestel', *Anglo-Saxon Engl.*, **3** (1974), 103–10
Hawkes, S.C., 'The Jutish Style A. A study of Germanic art in southern England in the 5th century AD', *Archaeologia*, **98** (1961), 29–74
Hinton, D.A., *A Catalogue of the Anglo-Saxon Ornamental Metalwork 700–1100 in the . . . Ashmolean Museum* (1974)
  'Late Anglo-Saxon metalwork: an assessment', *Anglo-Saxon Engl.*, **4** (1975), 171–80
  Keene, S. and Qualmann, K., 'The Winchester Reliquary', *Medieval Archaeol.*, **25** (1981), 45–77

Howlett, D.R., 'The iconography of the Alfred Jewel', *Oxoniensia*, **39** (1974), 44–52
Jessup, R., *Anglo-Saxon Jewellery* (1974) (Shire)
Leeds, E.T., *A Corpus of Early Anglo-Saxon Square-Headed Brooches* (1949)
Maryon, H., 'Pattern-welding and damascening of sword-blades', *Studies in Conservation*, **5** (1960), 25–35, 52–60
Oman, C.C., *British Rings 800–1914* (1974)
Speake, G., *Anglo-Saxon Animal Art and its Germanic Background* (1980)
Tweddle, D., *The Coppergate Helmet* (1984)
Wilson, D.M., *Anglo-Saxon Ornamental Metalwork 700–1100 in the British Museum* (1964)
  'Some neglected late Anglo-Saxon swords', *Medieval Archaeol.*, **9** (1965), 32–54
  'Tenth-century metalwork', in D. Parsons (ed.), *Tenth-Century Studies* (1975), pp. 200–7
Wilson, D.M. and Blunt, C., 'The Trewhiddle hoard', *Archaeologia*, **98** (1961), 75–122

Pottery

The following small selection of the more accessible works on pottery introduces a large, complex, and sometimes forbidding subject.
Haslam J., *Medieval Pottery* (1978) (Shire)
Hodges, R., *The Hamwic Pottery: the Local and Imported Wares from 30 Years' Excavations at Middle Saxon Southampton . . .* (1981) (*CBA Res. Rep.*, **37**)
Hurst, J., 'The pottery', in D.M. Wilson (ed.), *The Archaeology of Anglo-Saxon England* (1976), pp. 283–348
Kennett, D.H., *Anglo-Saxon Pottery* (1978) (Shire)
Myres, J.N.L., *A Corpus of Anglo-Saxon Pottery of the Pagan Period* (2 vols, 1977)

St Cuthbert

Battiscombe, C.F. (ed.), *The Relics of St Cuthbert* (1956) [The classic work on St Cuthbert's coffin and accoutrements]
Cramp, R., *The Background to St Cuthbert's Life* (1980) (Durham Cathedral Lecture)
Cronyn, J.M. and Horie, C.V., *St Cuthbert's Coffin: the History, Technology and Conservation* (Durham, 1985) [the most up to date study of the coffin itself]
Kitzinger, E., *The Coffin of St Cuthbert* (1950)

Sculpture and crosses

Bailey, R.N., *Viking Age Sculpture in Northern England* (1980)

Bond, F., *Fonts and Font Covers* (1908)

Clemoes, P., 'Cynewulf's image of the Ascension', in P. Clemoes and K. Hughes (eds.), *England Before the Conquest: Studies . . . presented to Dorothy Whitelock* (1971), 293–304 [sets stone images in the context of Old English poetry]

Collingwood, W.G., *Northumbrian Crosses of the Pre-Norman Age* (1927) [classic work with many interpretative drawings]

Cottrill, F., 'Some pre-Conquest stone carvings in Wessex', *Antiquaries J.*, **15** (1935), 144–51

Cramp, R.J., *The Bede Monastery Museum* (1980) [guide to museum at Jarrow]
'The Anglian sculptures from Jedburgh', in A. O'Connor and D.V. Clarke (eds.), *From the Stone Age to the Forty-Five: Studies . . . presented to R.B.K. Stevenson* (1983), 259–84

Cramp, R.J. et al., *Corpus of Anglo-Saxon Stone Sculpture in England: General Introduction to the Series and Vol. 1, County Durham and Northumberland* (2 vols., 1984) [bib.]

Cramp, R.J. and Miket, R., *Catalogue of the Anglo-Saxon and Viking Antiquities in the Museum of Antiquities, Newcastle upon Tyne* (1982)

Haverfield, F.J. and Greenwell, W., *A Catalogue of the Sculptured and Inscribed Stones in the Cathedral Library, Durham* (1899)

Higgit, J., 'The dedication inscription at Jarrow and its context', *Antiquaries J.*, **59** (1979), 343–74

Howlett, D., 'Two panels on the Ruthwell cross', *J. Warburg and Courtauld Institutes*, **37** (1974), 333–36

Jewell, R.H.I., 'The Anglo-Saxon friezes at Breedon-on-the-Hill, Leics.', *Archaeologia*, **108** (1986), 95–115

Lang, J.T. (ed.), *Anglo-Saxon and Viking Age Sculpture and its Context (1978)* (*BAR*, **49**)

Mercer, E., 'The Ruthwell and Bewcastle Crosses', *Antiquity*, **38** (1964), 268–76

Peers, C.R., 'Reculver: its Saxon church and cross', *Archaeologia*, **77** (1927), 241–56

Rix, M., 'The Wolverhampton cross-shaft', *Archaeol. J.*, **117** (1960), 71–81

Saxl, F., 'The Ruthwell Cross', *J. Warburg and Courtauld Institutes*, **6** (1943), 1–19

Schmitt, M., '"Random" reliefs and "primitive" friezes: reused sources of Romanesque sculpture?', *Viator*, **11** (1980), 123–45

Stoll, R., *Architecture and Sculpture in Early Britain: Celtic, Saxon, Norman* (1966) [fine photographs]

Stone, L., *Sculpture in Britain: the Middle Ages* (1955)

Swanton, M., 'The "dancer" on the Codford Cross', *Anglo-Saxon Studies in Archaeology and History*, **1** (1979), 139–48 (*BAR*, **72**)

Taylor, J. and Taylor, H.M., 'Architectural sculpture in pre-Norman England', *J. Brit. Archaeol. Ass., 3 ser*, **29** (1966), 3–51

Thompson, F.H. (ed.), *Studies in Medieval Sculpture* (1983) (*SAL Occasional Papers, n ser.* **3**) [several articles relevant to this section]

Williamson, P., *Catalogue of Romanesque Sculpture* (1983) [in the Victoria and Albert Museum]

Zarnecki, G., *English Romanesque Sculpture 1066–1140* (1951)

Sutton Hoo

Bruce-Mitford, R.L.S., *Aspects of Anglo-Saxon Archaeology: Sutton Hoo and Other Discoveries* (1974)
The Sutton Hoo Ship burial (2 vols., 1975, 1978) [the full, official publication of the most spectacular find ever made in Britain: bib. See also Evans below]

Enright, M.J., 'The Sutton Hoo whetstone sceptre: a study in iconography and cultural milieu', *Anglo-Saxon Engl.*, **11** (1983), 119–34

Evans, A.C. (ed.), *The Sutton Hoo Ship Burial . . . Vol. 3* (1983) [continuation of the full publication noted under Bruce-Mitford above]
The Sutton Hoo Ship Burial (1986) [guide for the general reader, from the British Museum]

Hicks, C., 'The birds on the Sutton Hoo purse', *Anglo-Saxon Engl.*, **15** (1986), 171–80

Textiles and embroidery

Bernstein, D.J., *The Mystery of the Bayeux Tapestry* (1986)

Brooks, N.P. and Walker, H.E., 'The authority and interpretation of the Bayeux Tapestry', *Proc. Battle Conference*, **1** (1978), 1–34

Budny, M. and Tweddle, D., 'The Maaseik embroideries', *Anglo-Saxon Engl.*, **13** (1984), 65–96

'The earliest English embroideries', *Illus. London News* (July 1984), 65

'The early medieval textiles at Maaseik, Belgium', *Antiq. J.*, **65** (1985), 353–89 [bib.]

Crowfoot, E. and Hawkes, S.C., 'Early Anglo-Saxon gold braids', *Medieval Archaeol.*, **11** (1967), 42–86

Gibbs-Smith, C.H., *The Bayeux Tapestry* (1973)

Owen, G.R., 'Wynflaed's wardrobe', *Anglo-Saxon Engl.*, **8** (1979), 195–222

Owen-Crocker, G., *Dress in Anglo-Saxon England* (1986)

Stenton, F. and others, *The Bayeux Tapestry: a comprehensive survey* (2nd edn, 1975)

Wilson, D.M., *The Bayeux Tapestry* (1985)

(See also articles on textiles in Battiscombe (ed.), noted in St Cuthbert section above)

Old English Literature

Note: regular bibliographies will be found in *Old English Newsletter* published by Center for Medieval and Early Renaissance Studies, State University of New York, Binghamton, NY, USA.

Alexander, M.J., *Old English Literature* (2nd edn 1986)

Old English Riddles from the Exeter Book (1980)

The Earliest English Poems (2nd edn 1977)

Alexander, M.J. (ed.), *Beowulf* (1973)

Allen, M.J.B. and Calder, D.G. (transl.), *Sources and Analogues of Old English Poetry* (1976)

Blake, N.F. (ed.), *The Phoenix* (1964)

Bradley, S.A.J., (transl.), *Anglo-Saxon Poetry: an Anthology of Old English Poems* (1982)

Calder, D.G., 'Histories and surveys of Old English literature: a chronological review', *Anglo-Saxon Engl.*, **10** (1982), 201–44

Campbell, J. (ed.), *The Anglo-Saxons* (1982)

Cramp, R., '*Beowulf* and archaeology', *Medieval Archaeol.*, **1** (1957), 57–77

Garmonsway, G.N., *et al.*, *Beowulf and its Analogues* (1968)

Greenfield, S.B., *A Critical History of Old English Literature* (1966)

Greenfield, S.B. and Robinson, F.C., *A Bibliography of Publications on Old English Literature to the End of 1972* (Toronto, 1980)

Henderson, G., *Early Medieval* (1972) (Pelican, Style and Civilisation series)

Jackson, K.H., *A Celtic Miscellany: Translations from the Celtic Literatures* (1971)

Kennedy, C.W., *The Earliest English Poetry: a Critical Survey of the Poetry Written Before the Norman Conquest* (1943, repr. 1971)

Early English Christian Poetry (New York, 1952: repr. 1965)

Klaeber, F. (ed.), *Beowulf and the Fight at Finnsburg* (Boston, Mass, 3rd edn 1950)

Shippey, T.A., *Old English Verse* (1972)

Beowulf (1978)

Stanley, E.G. (ed.), *Continuations and Beginnings: Studies in Old English Literature* (1966)

Swanton, M.J. (transl. and ed.), *Anglo-Saxon Prose* (1975)

(ed.), *The Dream of the Rood* (1970)

Tolkien, J.R.R., 'Beowulf, the monsters and the critics', *Proc. Brit. Academy*, **22** (1936), 245–95

Whitelock, D., *The Audience of Beowulf* (1951)

Wrenn, C.L., *A Study of Old English Literature* (1967)

Wrenn, C.L. (ed.), *Beowulf: with the Finnsburg Fragment* (3rd edn, rev. W.F. Bolton, 1973)

Winchester

The basic reference for this section is Martin Biddle's 'The study of Winchester: archaeology and history in a British town', *Proc. Brit. Academy*, **69** (1983), 93–135 (with good bibliography, and available as an inexpensive reprint), but the books and articles listed below may also be found useful. Note particularly that the series *Winchester Studies*, edited by Martin Biddle and planned to take up eleven volumes, provides the deepest analysis ever performed on a British town; it is abbreviated below as '*WS*'.

Biddle, M. 'Felix urbs Winthoniae: Winchester in the age of monastic reform', in D. Parsons (ed.), *Tenth Century Studies* (1975), pp. 123–40

'Hampshire and the origins of Wessex', in G. de G. Skeveking *et al.* (eds.), *Problems in Economic and Social Archaeology: Papers Presented to Grahame Clark* (1976), pp. 323–42

'Archaeology, architecture, and the cult of saints in Anglo-Saxon England', in L.A.S. Butler and R.K. Morris (eds.), *The Anglo-Saxon Church: papers . . . in honour of Dr H.M. Taylor* (1986), pp. 1–31 (*CBA Res. Rep.*, **60**)

*Pre-Roman and Roman Winchester: i,
Venta Belgarum* (in preparation) (*WS
3(i)*)

*The Crafts, Industries, and Daily Life of
Early Winchester* (forthcoming
c.1988–89, *WS 7(ii)*)

*Wolvesey. The Old Bishop's Palace,
Winchester* (1986) [English Heritage
guidebook]

Biddle, M. (ed.), *Winchester in the Early
Middle Ages: an edition and discussion of
the Winton Domesday* (1976) (= *WS 1*)

Biddle, M. and Barclay, K., 'Winchester
Ware', in V.I. Evison *et al.* (eds.),
*Medieval Pottery from Excavations:
Studies Presented to Gerald Clough
Dunning* (1974), pp. 137–65

Biddle, M. and Hill, D., 'Late Saxon
planned towns', *Antiq. J.*, **51** (1971),
70–85

Biddle, M. and Kjølbye-Biddle, B., *The
Anglo-Saxon Minsters of Winchester* (in
preparation) (= *WS 4 (i)*)

Collis, J.R., *Winchester Excavations
1949–60, vol. ii. Excavations in the
suburbs and the western part of the town*
(1978)

Cunliffe, B., *Winchester Excavations
1949–60, vol. i.* (1964)

Gem, R.D.H., 'The Romanesque cathedral
of Winchester: patron and design in the
11th century', *Trans. Brit. Archaeol.
Ass. Conf.*, **6** (1980, publ. 1983), pp.
1–12

Hinton, D.A. *et al.*, 'The Winchester
Reliquary', *Medieval Archaeol.*, **25**
(1981), 45–77

Kjølbye-Biddle, B., 'The seventh-century
minster at Winchester interpreted', in
L.A.S. Butler and R.K. Morris (eds.),
*The Anglo-Saxon Church: papers . . . in
honour of Dr. H.M. Taylor* (1986), pp.
196–209 (*CBA Res. Rep.*, **60**)

Lapidge, M. (ed.), *The cult of St Swithin*
(in preparation, *WS 4 (ii)*)

McKinnon, J.W., 'The tenth-century organ
at Winchester', *The Organ Yearbook*, **5**
(1974), 4–19

Winchester Cathedral Treasury, *Winchester
Saxon and Norman Art. The Artistic
Achievement of an Early Medieval
Capital, AD 900–1150 – a Revised
Exhibition* (1973)

Wormald, F., 'The "Winchester School"
before St Aethelwold', in P. Clemoes
and K. Hughes (eds.), *England Before
the Conquest . . .* (1971), pp. 305–13

The Arts of Late Celtic Britain (AD 600–900)

Alcock, J., *Dinas Powys* (1963)
*Arthur's Britain: History and Archaeology
A.D. 367–634* (2nd edn 1973) (bib.)

Alexander, J.J.G., *Insular Manuscripts,
Sixth to Ninth Century* (1978)

Allen, J.R. and Anderson, J., *The Early
Christian Monuments of Scotland* (1903)

Bruce-Mitford, R.L.S., *The Sutton Hoo
Ship Burial* (3rd edn, 1979) [but see
also 4th edn under Evans below]

Close-Brooks, J. and Stevenson, R.B.K.,
*Dark Age Sculpture. A Selection from
the Collections of the National Museum
of Antiquities of Scotland* (1982)

Cramp, R.J., *Early Northumbrian Sculpture*
(1965) (Jarrow Lecture)

Cruden, S., *The Early Christian and Pictish
Monuments of Scotland. An illustrated
introduction . . .* (1964)

Cubbon, A.M., *The Art of the Manx
Crosses* (2nd edn 1977)

Evans, A.C. (ed.), *The Sutton Hoo Ship
Burial, vol. III* (1983) [part of the full
scholarly record]
The Sutton Hoo Ship Burial (4th edn,
1986) [British Museum handbook]

Henderson, I., *The Picts* (1967)
'Pictish art and the Book of Kells', in
D. Whitelock *et al.* (eds.), *Ireland in
Early Medieval Europe* (1982), pp. 79–105
'The "David Cycle" in Pictish art', in
John Higgitt (ed.), *Early Medieval
Sculpture in Britain and Ireland* (1986),
pp. 87–123 (*BAR*, **152**)
(forthcoming), 'The snake-boss motif', in
M. Ryan (ed.), *Proceedings of a
Conference on Insular Art held in the
University of Cork, 1985* (Dublin:
Royal Irish Academy)

Henry, F., *Irish Art in the Early Christian
Period (to 800 A.D.)* (1965) (bib.)
*Irish Art During the Viking Invasions
800–1020 A.D.* (1967) (bib.)

Hicks, C., 'A note on the provenance of the
Sutton Hoo stag', in R.L.S. Bruce-
Mitford (ed.), *The Sutton Hoo Ship
Burial, vol. II* (1978), pp. 378–82

Hughes, K., *Celtic Britain in the Early
Middle Ages* (1980)

Jackson, A., *The Symbol Stones of Scotland*
(1984)

Jackson, K.H., 'The Pictish language', in
F.T. Wainwright (ed.), *The Problem of
the Picts* (1955), pp. 129–66

Lang, J.T., 'Hogback monuments in
Scotland', *Proc. Society of Antiquaries
of Scotland*, **105** (1975, for 1972–74),
206–35

Mitchell, F. *et al.*, *Treasures of Irish Art 1500 B.C. – 1500 A.D.* (1977)

Mowbray, C. (Mrs. Cecil Curle), 'Eastern influence on carvings at St Andrews and Nigg, Scotland', *Antiquity*, **10** (1936), 428–40

Nash-Williams, V.E., *The Early Christian Monuments of Wales* (1950)

Nordenfalk, C., *Celtic and Anglo-Saxon Painting* (1977)

RCAMS, *Argyll: an Inventory of the Monuments, vol. 4, Iona* (1982)

Ritchie, G. and Ritchie, A., *Scotland: Archaeology and Early History* (1981)

Stevenson, R.B.K., 'Pictish art', in F.T. Wainwright (ed.), *The Problem of the Picts* (1955), pp. 97–128

'Sculpture in Scotland in the sixth–ninth centuries A.D.', in V. Milojčič (ed.), *Kolloquium über spätantike und frühmittelalterliche Skulptur, Heidelberg 1970* (Mainz 1971), pp. 65–74

'The Hunterston Brooch and its significance', *Medieval Archaeol.*, **18** (1974), 16–42

'The earlier metalwork of Pictland', in J.V.S. Megaw (ed.), *To Illustrate the Monuments* (1976), pp. 246–51

Thomas, C., 'The interpretation of the Pictish symbols', *Archaeol. J.*, **120** (1963), 31–97

The Early Christian Archaeology of North Britain (1971)

'Ninth-century sculpture in Cornwall: a note', in J. Lang (ed.), *Anglo-Saxon and Viking Age Sculpture* (1978), pp. 75–83 (= *BAR*, **49**)

Wilson, D.M., 'The treasure', in A. Small, C. Thomas, and D.M. Wilson, *St Ninian's Isle and its Treasure, vol. 1* (1973), pp. 45–148

Anglo-Saxon Art from the Seventh Century to the Norman Conquest (1984) (bib.)

Architecture

Note: There are two sections below: the first treats the general works for the pre-Conquest and Norman/Romanesque periods, respectively, and the second picks up the more specialised works for particular buildings mentioned in the text.

General

(A) PRE-CONQUEST

Addyman, P.V., 'The Anglo-Saxon House: a new review', in *Anglo-Saxon Engl.*, **1** (1972), 273–307 (bib.)

Bede, *History of the English Church and People* see under Colgrave below

Biddle, M., 'Towns', in D.M. Wilson (ed.), *The Archaeology of Anglo-Saxon England* (1976), pp. 99–150 (bib.)

Biddle, M. and Hill, D., 'Late Saxon planned towns', *Antiq. J.*, **51** (1971), 70–85

Biddle, M. *et al.*, 'Anglo-Saxon Architecture and Anglo-Saxon studies: a review [of H.M. and J. Taylor's volumes of 1965, etc.]', *Anglo-Saxon Engl.*, **14** (1985), 293–317

Brown, G. Baldwin, *Anglo-Saxon Architecture* (2nd edn, 1925) [vol. ii of *The Arts in Early England*, 6-vol. set: classic work still much used, but see Taylor and Taylor below]

Butler, L.A.S. and Morris, R. (eds.), *The Anglo-Saxon Church: Papers in Honour of Dr. H.M. Taylor* (1986) (*CBA Res. Rep.*, **60**) [important essays marking a great advance in understanding]

Cherry, B., 'Ecclesiastical architecture', in D.M. Wilson (ed.), *The Archaeology of Anglo-Saxon England* (1976), pp. 151–200

Clapham, A.W., *English Romanesque Architecture Before the Conquest* (1930)

Colgrave, B. and Mynors, R.A.B. (eds.), *Bede's Ecclesiastical History of the English People* (1969)

Cramp, R., 'Monastic sites', in D.M. Wilson (ed.), *The Archaeology of Anglo-Saxon England* (1976), pp. 201–52

Dixon, P.W., 'How Saxon is the Saxon house?', in P.J. Drury (ed.), *Structural Reconstruction* (1982), pp. 275–87 (*BAR*, **110**)

Fernie, E., *The Architecture of the Anglo-Saxons* (1983)

Gem, R.D.H., 'Towards an iconography of Anglo-Saxon architecture', *J. Warburg and Courtauld Institutes*, **46** (1983), 1–18 [includes Ramsey Abbey and others]

Haslam, J. (ed.), *Anglo-Saxon Towns in Southern England* (1984) [important statements on each of the main towns: bib.]

Early medieval towns in Britain c.700 to 1140 (1985) (Shire)

James, S. *et al.* (eds.), 'An early medieval building tradition', *Archaeol. J.*, **141** (1984), 182–215 [6th–8th century secular timber building: bib.]

Kerr, M. and N., *Anglo-Saxon Architecture* (1983) (Shire)

Kerr, N. and M., *A Guide to Anglo-Saxon Sites* (1982)

Morris, R., *The Church in British Archaeology* (1983) (*CBA Res. Rep.*, **47**; bib.)

Radford, C.A.R., 'Pre-Conquest minster churches', *Archaeol. J.*, **130** (1973), 120–40

'The later pre-Conquest boroughs and their defences', *Medieval Archaeol.*, **14** (1970), 83–103

'The pre-Conquest boroughs of England, 9th–11th centuries', *Proc. Brit. Academy*, **64** (1978 publ. 1980), 131–53 (available as offprint)

Rahtz, P., 'Buildings and rural settlement', in D.M. Wilson (ed.), *The Archaeology of Anglo-Saxon England* (1976), pp. 49–98

Rodwell, W., *The Archaeology of the English Church: the Study of Historic Churches and Churchyards* (1981) [concerned mainly with how to examine a church]

Taylor, H.M. and Taylor, J., *Anglo-Saxon Architecture* (3 vols., 1965, 1965, 1978) [essential work, referred to below as 'Taylor and Taylor']

(B) NORMAN (ROMANESQUE)

Blair, J. (ed.), *The English Parish Church in the 11th and 12th Century* (provisional title: in preparation, Oxford Univ. Dept. for External Stud.)

Brown, R.A., *English Castles* (3rd edn 1976)

Cherry, B., 'Romanesque architecture in eastern England', *J. Brit. Archaeol. Ass.*, **131** (1978), 1–29

Clapham, A., *English Romanesque Architecture, II: After the Conquest* (1934)

Gem, R.D.H., 'A recession in English architecture during the early 11th century, and its effect on the development of the Romanesque style', *J. Brit. Archaeol. Ass., 3 ser.*, **38** (1975), 28–49

'English Romanesque architecture', in *English Romanesque Art 1066–1200* (1984), pp. 27–40 (Arts Council exhibition catalogue)

Kidson, P. *et al.*, *A History of English Architecture* (1965)

Little, B., *Architecture in Norman Britain* (1985)

Morris, R.K., *Churches and Cathedrals: the Building Church 600–1540* (1979)

Pevsner, N. (and successors), *The Buildings of England* [46 volumes, 1951 to date, for individual counties]

Stoll, R., *Architecture and Sculpture in Early Britain – Celtic, Saxon, Norman* (1967) [fine photographs]

Tatton-Brown, T., 'The use of Quarr stone in London and east Kent', *Medieval Archaeol.*, **24** (1980), 213–15

Webb, G., *Architecture in Britain: the Middle Ages* (2nd edn 1965) [= Pelican History of Art]

Wood, M., 'Norman domestic architecture', *Archaeol. J.*, **92** (1935), 167–242

Zarnecki, G., '1066 and architectural sculpture', *Proc. brit. Academy*, **52** (1966), 87–104

Individual buildings [*a selection of major surviving monuments, together with lesser references in text*]

(For the following monuments, see Taylor and Taylor, vols. i–iii: Bradwell, i; Britford, i; Cambridge St. Bene't, i; Edenham, i; Escomb, i; Hexham, i and iii; Peterborough, ii; Ripon, ii; Romsey Abbey (Hants), ii.)

Abingdon Abbey: Biddle, M. *et al.* 'The early history of Abingdon, Berkshire, and its abbey', *Medieval Archaeol.*, **12** (1968) 26–69

Barnack: Taylor and Taylor, i, 43–47

Cramp, R., 'Anglo-Saxon sculpture of the reform period', in D. Parsons (ed.), *Tenth Century Studies* (1975), pp. 184–99

Barton-upon-Humber: Rodwell, W., *St. Peter's Church, Barton-upon-Humber* (1983) [official HBMCE guide]

Rodwell, W. and K., 'St Peter's Church, Barton on Humber', *Antiq. J.*, **62** (1982), 283–315

Bradford-on-Avon: Taylor, H.M., 'The Anglo-Saxon chapel at Bradford-on-Avon', *Archaeol. J.*, **130** (1973), 141–71

Bramber Castle: Barton, K.J. and Holden, E.W., 'Excavations at Bramber Castle, Sussex, 1966–7', *Archaeol. J.*, **134** (1977), 11–79

VCH Sussex, vi(i) (1980), pp. 212–14 [for the collegiate chapel of St Nicholas, Bramber]

Breamore: Taylor and Taylor, vol. i, pp. 94–96

Rodwell, W. and Rouse, E.C., 'The Anglo-Saxon rood and other features in the south porch of St Mary's Church, Breamore, Hampshire', *Antiq. J.*, **64** (1984), 298–325

Breedon: Taylor and Taylor, vol. i, pp. 97–98

Taylor, H.M., 'Architectural sculpture in pre-Norman England', *J. Brit. Archaeol. Ass., 3 ser.*, **29** (1966), 3–51

Jewell, R.H.I., 'The Anglo-Saxon friezes at Breedon-on-the-Hill, Leics', *Archaeologia*, **108** (1986), 95–115

Brixworth: Audouy, M. *et al.* 'Excavations at the church of All Saints, Brixworth, Northants, 1981–2', *J. Brit. Archaeol. Ass.*, **137** (1984), 1–44

Sutherland, D. and Parsons, D., 'The petrological contribution to the survey of . . . Brixworth. . .', *J. Brit. Archaeol. Ass.*, **137** (1984), 45–64

Bury St Edmunds: Gem, R. and Keen, L., 'Late Anglo-Saxon finds from the site of St. Edmund's Abbey', *Proc. Suffolk Institute of Archaeology and History*, **35** (1984), 1–30

Canterbury: Taylor and Taylor, vol. i., pp. 134–48; vol. iii, 1079

Taylor, H.M., 'St. Augustine's Abbey', *Archaeol. J.*, **126** (1969), 228–33

'The Anglo-Saxon cathedral church at Canterbury', *Archaeol. J.*, **126** (1969), 101–30

Gem, R., 'The significance of the 11th century rebuilding of Christ Church and St Augustine's, Canterbury, in the development of Romanesque architecture', *Trans. Brit. Archaeol. Ass.*, **5** (for 1979, publ. 1982), 1–19

Carisbrooke Castle: Rigold, S.E., 'Recent investigations into the earliest defences of Carisbrooke Castle, Isle of Wight', *Château Gaillard*, **3** (1969), 128–38

Catholme: see James, S. *et al.* in 'General: pre-Conquest' section above

Chalton: Addyman, P.V. and Leigh, D., 'The Anglo-Saxon village at Chalton, Hants: 2nd interim report', *Medieval Archaeol.*, **17** (1973), 1–25

[Selkirk, A.], 'Chalton: the excavation of an Anglo-Saxon village', *Current Archaeol.*, *4(2)* (1973), 55–61

Cheddar: Rahtz, P., *The Saxon and Medieval Palaces at Cheddar: Excavations 1960–62* (1979) (*BAR*, **65**)

Chepstow: Knight, J.K., *Chepstow Castle* (1986) [official guide]

Cholsey: Gem, R.D.H., 'Church architecture in the reign of King Aethelred', in D. Hill (ed.), *Ethelred the Unready: Papers from the Millenary Conference* (1978), pp. 105–14 (*BAR*, **59**) [also treats Bradford-on-Avon and Dover St Mary in Castro]

Cirencester: Brown, David, 'Archaeological evidence for the Anglo-Saxon period', in A.D. McWhirr (ed.), *Studies in the Archaeology and History of Cirencester* (1976), pp. 19–45 (*BAR*, **30**)

Cowdery's Down: Millett, M., 'Excavations at Cowdery's Down, Basingstoke, Hampshire, 1978–81', *Archaeol. J.*, **140** (1983), 151–279

Deerhurst: Butler, L.A.S. *et al.*, 'Deerhurst 1971–4', *Antiq. J.*, **55** (1975), 346–65

Odda's Chapel: Taylor and Taylor, i, pp. 209–11

Currie, C.R.J., 'A Romanesque roof at Odda's Chapel, Deerhurst, Gloucestershire?', *Antiq. J.*, **63** (1983), 58–63

Dover, St Mary in Castro: Taylor and Taylor, vol. i, pp. 214–17 [see also under Cholsey above]

Durham Castle Chapel: *VCH Durham, iii* (1928), pp. 86–8

Ely: Fernie, E., 'Observations on the Norman plan of Ely Cathedral', *Trans. Brit. Archaeol. Ass. Conf.*, **2** (1976, publ. 1979), 1–7; *VCH Cambridge, vol. ii* (1948), pp. 199–203

Exeter Castle: Blaylock, S.R., 'Exeter Castle gatehouse', in *Exeter Archaeology 1984–85* (1985), pp. 18–24 (Exeter Museum Archaeol. Field Unit report)

Glastonbury: Rahtz, P.A., 'Excavations on Glastonbury Tor, Somerset, 1964–66', *Archaeol. J.*, **127** (1970), 1–81

Gloucester: Heighway, C., *Gloucester: a History and Guide* (1985), pp. 18–38 [for St Oswald's Priory, etc.]

Taylor, vol. iii, 1073

West, J.K., 'A carved slab fragment from St Oswald's Priory, Gloucester', in F.H. Thompson (ed.), *Studies in Medieval Sculpture* (1983), pp. 41–53 (*SAL Occas. Paper, new ser. 3*)

Wilson, C., 'Abbot Serlo's Church at Gloucester 1089–1100: its place in Romanesque architecture', *Trans Brit. Archaeol. Ass. Conf.*, **7** (1981, publ. 1985), pp. 52–83

Goltho: Beresford, G., 'The reconstruction of some Saxon buildings at Goltho, Lincolnshire', in P.J. Drury (ed.), *Structural Reconstruction* (1982), pp. 113–23 (*BAR*, **110**)

Beresford, G., 'Goltho Manor, Lincolnshire: the buildings and their surrounding defences c.850–1150', in *Proc. Battle Conf.*, **4** (1981), 13–36

Great Paxton: Fernie, E., *The Architecture of the Anglo-Saxons* (1983), pp. 129–34

Greensted: Christie, H. *et al.*, 'The wooden church of St. Andrew at Greensted, Essex', *Antiq. J.*, **59** (1979), 92–112

Hen Domen: Barker, P. and Higham, R., *Hen Domen, Montgomery: a Timber Castle on the Welsh Border* (1982) (*Roy. Archaeol. Institute Monogr.*)

Lincoln: see *Archaeol. J.*, **103** (1946), 102–3 and 105–18

Gem, R., 'Lincoln Minster: *Ecclesia pulchra, ecclesia fortis*', *Trans. Brit. Archaeol. Ass. Conf.*; (due 1986)

Monkwearmouth and Jarrow: Cramp, R., 'Jarrow Church', and 'Monkwearmouth

Church', *Archaeol. J.*, **133** (1976), 220–8 and 230–7

Taylor, vol. iii, pp. 1081–2

Nether Wallop: Gem, R. and Tudor-Craig, P., 'A "Winchester School" wall-painting at Nether Wallop, Hampshire', *Anglo-Saxon Engl.*, **9** (1981), 115–36

Northampton: Williams, J.H. *et al. Middle Saxon Palaces at Northampton* (1985) (*Northampton Development Corp. Archaeol. Monogr.*, **4**)

Williams, J.H. and Shaw, M., 'Middle Saxon "palaces" at Northampton', *Current Archaeol.*, **8(2)** (1982), 38–41

North Elmham: Wade-Martins, P., *Excavations in North Elmham Park, 1967–72* (1980) (*East Anglian Archaeol.*, **9**)

Taylor and Taylor, vol. i, pp. 228–31

Offa's Dyke: Selkirk, A., 'Offa's Dyke and Wat's Dyke', *Current Archaeol.*, **6(1)** (1978), 21–23

Hill, D., 'The construction of Offa's Dyke', *Antiq. J.*, **65** (1985), 140–2

Noble, F. (ed. M. Gelling), *Offa's Dyke Reviewed* (1983) (= *BAR*, **114**)

Ramsey Abbey (Cambs.): Fernie, E., *The Architecture of the Anglo-Saxons* (1983), p. 114

Gem, R.D.H., see 1983 work cited in section (a) above

Repton: Taylor and Taylor, vol. ii, pp. 510–16

Biddle, M. and Kjølbye-Biddle, B., 'The Repton Stone', *Anglo-Saxon Engl.*, **14** (1985), 233–92

St Albans Abbey: RCHME, *An Inventory of the Historical Monuments in Hertfordshire* (1910), pp. 177–87

RCHME, *A Guide to Saint Albans Cathedral* (1982)

Biddle, M., *Saint Albans Abbey: Chapter-House Excavations 1978* (1979) (*Fraternity of Friends of Saint Albans Abbey Occasional Papers*, **1**)

Biddle, M. and Kjølbye-Biddle, B., *The Origins of Saint Albans Abbey: Excavations in the Cloister 1982–3* (1984) (*Fraternity of Friends of Saint Albans Abbey Occasional Papers*, **2**)

Southampton (Hamwic): Holdsworth, P., 'Saxon Southampton: a new review', *Medieval Archaeol.*, **20** (1976), 26–61

Stow: Taylor, vol. iii, pp. 1084

Field, N. (forthcoming publication)

Sulgrave: Davison, B.K., 'Excavations at Sulgrave, Northants, 1960–76: an interim report', *Archaeol. J.*, **134** (1977), 105–14

Davison, B.K., 'Excavations at Sulgrave, Northants, 1968', *Archaeol. J.*, **125** (1968), 305–7

Wareham: Keen, L., 'Wareham Town Walls' and 'St Martin's Church', *Archaeol. J.*, **140** (1983), 52–5

Westminster Abbey: Gem, R.D.H., 'The Romanesque rebuilding of Westminster Abbey', *Proc. Battle Conf. (Anglo-Norman Studies)*, **3** (1980), 33–60

West Stow: West, S., *West Stow: the Anglo-Saxon Village* (1985) (= *East Anglian Archaeol.*, **24**)

Winchester: see main Winchester section, also Taylor, vol. iii, p. 1077

Gem, R., 'The Romanesque cathedral of Winchester: patron and design in the 11th century', *Trans. Brit. Archaeol. Ass. Conf.*, **6** (1980, publ. 1983), pp. 1–12

Wing: Taylor and Taylor, vol. ii, pp. 665–72; vol. iii, 1085

Taylor, H.M., 'The Anglo-Saxon church at Wing in Buckinghamshire', *Archaeol. J.*, **136** (1979), 43–52

Wootton Wawen: Taylor and Taylor, vol. ii, pp. 685–88

Gem, R.D.H., 'Wootton Wawen church', *Archaeol. J.*, **128** (1971), 225–7

Radford, C.A.R., 'The church of St Peter, Wootton Wawen', *Archaeol. J.*, **136** (1979), 76–89

Worcester: Gem, R.D.H., 'Bishop Wulfstan II and the Romanesque cathedral church of Worcester', *Trans. British Archaeol. Ass. Conf.*, **1** (1975, publ. 1978), pp. 15–37

Zarnecki, G., 'The Romanesque capitals in the south transept of Worcester Cathedral', *ibid.*, pp. 38–42

Yeavering: Hope-Taylor, B., *Yeavering, an Anglo-British Centre of Early Northumbria* (1977) (*Dept. of the Environment Archaeol. Rep.*, **7**)

York: Phillips, D., *Excavations at York Minster, vol. 2: The Cathedral of Archbishop Thomas of Bayeux* (1985)

Hall, R., *The Excavations at York: the Viking Dig* (1984)

Addyman, P.V. and Priestley, J., 'Baile Hill, York . . .', *Archaeol. J.*, **134** (1977), 115–56

Music

Anderson, L.F., *The Anglo-Saxon Scop* (Toronto, 1903)

Cable, T., *The Meter and Melody of Beowulf* (Urbana, 1974)

Crane, F., *Extant Medieval Musical Instruments: a Provisional Catalogue by Types* (Iowa City, 1972)

Galpin, F., *Old English Instruments of Music: their History and Character* (4th edn, rev. T. Dart, 1965)

Lawson, G., 'An Anglo-Saxon harp and lyre of the ninth century', in D.R. Widdess and R.F. Wolpert (eds.), *Music and Tradition: Essays on Asian and Other Musics Presented to Laurence Picken* (1981), pp. 229–44

McKinnon, J.W., 'The tenth century organ at Winchester', *The Organ Yearbook*, 5 (1974), 4–19

Opland, J., *Anglo-Saxon Oral Poetry: a Study of the Traditions* (New Haven, 1980)

Padelford, F.M., *Old English Musical Terms* (Bonn, 1899)

Page, C., 'The Boethian metrum "Bella bis quinis": a new song from Canterbury', in M. Gibson (ed.), *Boethius: his Life, Thought and Influence* (1981), pp. 306–11

Panum, H., (Engl. edn. rev. and ed. J. Pulver), *The Stringed Instruments of the Middle Ages: their Evolution and Development* (1940)

Planchart, A.E., *The Repertory of Tropes at Winchester* (2 vols., Princeton, 1977)

Remnant, M., *English bowed instruments from Anglo-Saxon to Tudor Times* (1986)

Stevens, J., *Words and Music in the Middle Ages: Song, Narrative, Dance and Drama, 1050–1350* (1986)

The White Tower of London

Armitage, E.S., *The Early Norman Castles of the British Isles* (1912)

Bayley, John, *The History and Antiquities of the Tower of London* (2 vols., London, 1821, 1825)

Brown, R.A., 'An historian's approach to the origins of the castle in England', *Archaeol. J.*, **126** (1969), 131–48

'Some observations on the Tower of London', *Archaeol. J.*, **136** (1979), 99–108

Brown, R.A. and Curnow, P.E., *Tower of London* (1984) (esp. pp. 5–13 and 59–68)

Brown, R.A. *English Castles* (3rd edn 1976)

Charlton, J. (ed.), *The Tower of London: its Buildings and Institutions* (1978)

Clark, G.T., *Medieval Military Architecture in England*, (2 vols., London, 1884), ii, pp. 203–72

Colvin, H.M. (ed.), *The Middle Ages (History of the King's Works)*, Vol. 1 (1963), pp. 19–32 for White Tower

Hammond, P., 'Royal Fortress': the Tower of London through Nine Centuries (1978)

Pevsner, N. (rev. B. Cherry), *The Buildings of England: Cities of London and Westminster* (rev. edn 1973), pp. 205–8

Renn, D.F., *Norman Castles in Britain* (1973)

Sturdy, D., 'Nine hundred years of the Tower', *London Archaeol.*, **3** (1979), 270–73

Wood, M., *Norman Domestic Architecture* (1974)

Sources of Illustrations

The publishers gratefully acknowledge the help of the many individuals and organizations who cannot be named in collecting the illustrations for this volume. In particular they would like to thank Carol Varley and Erica Schwarz for their help with picture research. Every effort has been made to obtain permission to use copyright materials; the publishers apologise for any errors and omissions and would welcome these being brought to their attention.

2 Matthew Ford; *9* Commissioners of Public Works, Ireland; *10* Michael J. O'Kelly; *13* Courtesy of the Trustees of the British Museum; *14* Cambridge University Museum of Archaeology and Anthropology; *15, 16* Wiltshire Archaeological and Natural History Society; *17, 25* National Museums of Scotland; *27* J.V.S. Megaw/Courtesy of the Trustees of the British Museum; *30* Otto Fein/The Warburg Institute; *50* B.W. Cunliffe; *54, 55* Sussex Archaeological Society; *59* B.W. Cunliffe; *63a, b, 64* Courtesy of the Museum of London; *66, 68, 69, 70* Courtesy of the Verulameum Museum; *71* Courtesy of the Society of Antiquaries, London; *72* Courtesy of the Verulameum Museum; *74* Colchester and Essex Museum; *76* Courtesy of the Trustees of the British Museum; *79* Colchester and Essex Museum; *80* Courtesy of the Trustees of the British Museum; *81* Reproduced by permission of the Hunterian Museum, University of Glasgow; *82a* National Museums of Scotland; *82b* Reproduced by permission of the Hunterian Museum, University of Glasgow; *85* English Heritage; *88* Courtesy of the Trustees of the British Museum; *90* The Warburg Institute; *92, 94, 95* English Heritage; *100* University of Durham, Department of Archaeology; *122, 124* Courtesy of the Trustees of the British Museum; *127* Ashmolean Museum, Oxford; *128* University of Durham; *129* Museum of London; *130a* Courtesy of the Trustees of the British Museum; *130b* Courtesy of the Rector of Mildenhall Parish Church/Photo: Mick Sharp; *131* Courtesy of the Trustees of the British Museum; *135* David M. Wilson; *139a, b* The Dean and Chapter of Durham; *141* Courtesy of the Trustees of the British Library, London (Cotton Nero DIV. f.211);

151 Trinity College Library, Dublin; *157* Biblioteca Medicea Laurenziana, Firenze (Amiat. 1,c.v); *161* Courtesy of the Trustees of the British Library, London (611 Vesp. AI. f.21v); *164a* Bologna Museo Civico Medievale; *164b* Courtesy of the Trustees of the British Museum; *168, 169* By special permission of the town of Bayeux; *173* By Courtesy of the Trustees of the British Library, London (Cotton Julius. AVI. f.3, 3v, 4v, 7); *175, 176* Courtesy of the Trustees of the British Museum; *178* Bodleian Library, Oxford (MS. Auct. f.4.32); *194, 199, 200, 202, 203, 204, 205* Winchester Excavations Committee; *206* National Museums of Scotland; *208, 209* Courtesy of the Trustees of the British Museum; *210* Royal Commission on Ancient Monuments, Scotland; *211* Isabel Henderson; *212, 213a, b* National Museums of Scotland; *214* Royal Commission on Ancient Monuments, Scotland; *217* Scottish Development Department; *220, 224, 229, 230, 232a, b, c, 233, 234, 235a, b, 236, 237, 239, 240, 241, 242, 243, 244* Royal Commission on the Historical Monuments of England; *246* By permission of the Syndics of Cambridge University Library (C.U.L. MS. Ff.1.23); *248* Bodleian Library, Oxford (MS. Auct. F.1.15); *254, 256, 257, 258, 259, 260, 262, 263* Department of the Environment (Crown Copyright); *263* Courtesy of the Trustees of the British Library, London (Royal 16. F.2. f.73)

Plates

1 Museum of Antiquities, University and Society of Antiquaries, Newcastle upon Tyne; *2, 3* Courtesy of the Trustees of the British Museum; *4* Trinity College, Dublin; *5* Courtesy of the Trustees of the British Museum; *6* Liverpool Museum; *7, 8* Courtesy of the Trustees of the British Museum; *9* Mildred Budny; *10* Courtesy of the Trustees of the British Library, London (Harley MS.603. Ill. to Psalm 103. f.51b, detail); *11* Courtesy of the Trustees of the British Library, London (Harley MS.2904. f.3v); *12* Sudy Lowry; *13* Courtesy of the Trustees of the British Library, London (Cotton Claudius B.IV. f.19).

Index